Also by Arthur S. Lefkowitz

The Long Retreat: The Calamitous American Defenseof New Jersey 1776

George Washington's Indispensable Men: The 32 Aides-de-Camp Who Helped Win American Independence

Bushnell's Submarine: The Best Kept Secret of the American Revolution

Benedict Arnold's Army

The 1775 American Invasion
of Canada During the Revolutionary War

Arthur S. Lefkowitz

SB

Savas Beatie

New York and California

Benedict Arnold's Army: The 1775 American Invasion of Canada During the Revolutionary War

Cataloging-in-Publication Data is available from the Library of Congress.

ISBN 13: 978-1-932714-03-6

10 9 8 7 6 5 4 3 2 1
First edition, first printing

SB

Published by
Savas Beatie LLC
521 Fifth Avenue, Suite 3400
New York, NY 10175
Phone: 610-853-9131

Editorial Offices:

Savas Beatie LLC
P.O. Box 4527
El Dorado Hills, CA 95762
Phone: 916-941-6896
(E-mail) editorial@savasbeatie.com

Savas Beatie titles are available at special discounts for bulk purchases in the United States by corporations, institutions, and other organizations. For more details, please contact Special Sales, P.O. Box 4527, El Dorado Hills, CA 95762. You may also e-mail us at sales@savasbeatie.com, or click over for a visit to our website at www.savasbeatie.com for additional information.

This book is dedicated to my friend
George C. Woodbridge (1930-2004)

Best known as an illustrator for MAD Magazine, George Woodbridge was also an expert on American military history. He combined his talent as an artist with his knowledge of history to create marvelous pictures of American soldiers that were unrivaled for their accuracy. George completed the illustrations for this book shortly before he died. They are a better testimonial to his gift for depicting history than any words can express.

Portrait of Benedict Arnold by Pierre-Eugene Du Simitiere.
Executed in Philadelphia in 1779, it is the only known
portrait of Arnold believed to be drawn from life.

Author's Collection

Contents

Contents (continued)

Contents (continued)

Illustrations

A selection of photos and illustrations have been distributed throughout this book for the convenience of the reader.

Maps

Preface

The courage of the men and women who participated in the 1775 Arnold Expedition makes it one of the most inspiring episodes in American history. The event has interested me since childhood and I am thrilled to have had the chance to research the campaign and traverse its route across Maine and Canada. I believe that many diaries were kept during the campaign, with unusual diligence, because the people on the expedition realized that they were participating in a great historical event and wanted to record their experiences.

Besides working with a fascinating story and excellent contemporary source material, I enjoyed writing this book because it deals with the opening months of the American Revolution. This was an innocent period in our War for Independence, uncomplicated by the problems that would later plague the patriots. At the start of the Revolution, for example, the colonists were able to raise a large army of volunteers while printing presses cranked out millions of dollars in paper money to pay for the war.

During my research, I discovered a long out of print book about the campaign called *Arnold's Expedition to Quebec* by John Codman, II. This obscure book, published over 100 years ago, turned-out to be the only complete history of the Arnold Expedition. I found it weak in its research but strong in its prose. Codman did such a masterful job of capturing the spirit of the event that I used relevant passages from his narrative for the chapter titles in my book.

I hope my history of the Arnold Expedition adds to our knowledge of the past, and especially of the courageous American patriots who pushed themselves to the limits of their endurance in a bid to snatch the strategic city of Quebec from the British.

Acknowledgments

I once asked my friend George Woodbridge to define the word historian for me. George said that a historian is anyone who makes their living from history. Applying this formula I am pleased to acknowledge the historians who helped me craft this book. They are economic historian John J. McCusker (Trinity College),the distinguished author Thomas Fleming; Philander D. Chase, Senior Editor of the Papers of George Washington; Arthur Spiess and Leon E. Cranmer, Historical Archaeologists with the Maine Historic Preservation Commission; Patricia Kennedy from Parks Canada; André Charbonneau, Ph.D. from the Quebec Service Center of Parks Canada who expertise is the military history of Quebec; Thomas L. Nesbitt, Park-Recreation Supervisor at Crown Point State Historic Site, New York whose special interest are bateaux; Christopher Fox, curator of the Fort Ticonderoga Museum; Eric Schnitzer, the National Parks historian at Saratoga National Historic Site, New York, economics historian Robert E. Wright, Ph.D., and Henry M. Cooke, historical costumer, researcher, and writer whose outstanding work includes the reproductions of George Washington's uniforms on display at the new Mount Vernon Visitors Center.

Among the other professionals who shared their special knowledge with me were Joseph Rubinfine, an antiques dealer and authority on early American manuscripts; Forrest R. Bonney, a Regional Fisheries Biologist with the Maine Department of Inland Fisheries and Wildlife and Lewis Flagg, Deputy Commissioner of the Maine Department of Marine Resources.

I am also pleased to also acknowledge the help of a number of my fellow enthusiasts who enjoy studying history but earn their living doing something else. Topping this impressive list is Duluth (Dude) E. Wing, a retired Maine Forest Service Ranger who is an expert on the route of the

Arnold Expedition. Dude grew up in the heart of Arnold Expedition country and it was my great privilege to have him as my guide through the Dead River, Chain of Ponds, Height of Land and Lake Magentic sections of Arnold's route. Talking to Dude about the Arnold Expedition over breakfast at the Maine Line Café in Stratton, Maine, was one of the highlights of this project.

I especially enjoyed listening to Dude's stories about the Maine wilderness. One of my favorites is how he told about going into the forest near his home with his father to hunt and fish. Dude said they would often sleep in the woods at night rather than walk back home. "In the Maine woods, there's nothing that will hurt you," Dude's father told him. "Bears usually vanish, poisonous snakes are nonexistent, and there is no poison ivy. So lay down at dark and enjoy the pine spills or fir bough bed, drink pure mountain water from the books, and feel sorry for all those people who live in the cities and have many things to fear."

The other enthusiasts who helped me were the late George C. Woodbridge, illustrator and authority on the organization, uniforms and weapons of the armies of the American Revolution; John Rees whose interest is 18th Century foods and cooking; Raymond J. Andrews, an architect and expert on the uniforms of the American Revolution; Lt. Gen. David Richard Palmer (retired), the former superintendent of West Point and the author of several military history books my favorite being *The Way of the Fox, American Strategy in the War for America*; Richard G. Bell, a lawyer and authority on the court martial of Lt. Col. Roger Enos; Dr. Richard Prouty, my eminent research companion and friend whose interest is the history of military medicine; Michael Leonard, computer analyst and U.S. Naval Reserve Commander who advised me on 18th Century nautical terms and technology and George C. Neumann, corporate executive and acknowledged as America's leading expert on Revolutionary War weapons. I am also indebted to Rusty Arsenault, a retired rural Maine truck driver and Ronald Gammage, who was the postmaster of Skowhegan, Maine for 29 years. Both are students of the Arnold Expedition and were my guides to the Great Carrying Place section of the Expedition's route.

Research was done for this book at The New York Public Library, The David Library of the American Revolution, The New York Historical Society, Princeton University Libraries Department of Rare Books and Special Collections, The Library Company of Philadelphia,

The Maine Historical Society, Rutgers University Library Special Collections and the Connecticut Historical Society.

Transforming a manuscript into a book is a arduous undertaking. I was fortunate to have a team of dedicated professionals at Savas Beatie to shepherd me through the process. Outstanding among them were my editor Terry Johnson and marketing director Sarah Keeney.

I am also grateful to my wife Susan for her patience and help during the long process of creating this book.

Arthur S. Lefkowitz
Piscataway, New Jersey, 2007

Introduction

This is the true story of a bold plan organized by General George Washington, the commander in chief of the Continental Army, to capture the fortress city of Quebec, the capital of British-held Canada and the key to controlling much of the interior of North America. Washington selected Colonel Benedict Arnold to lead the mission, which was launched in the opening months of the American Revolution.

At the time, martial exhilaration gripped the colonists, who expected a short war and an easy reconciliation with their king and his government. Arnold's secret expedition began in this mood of military exuberance. Washington's plan called for Arnold to lead a fast-moving volunteer force to Quebec through the Maine district of Massachusetts into Canada, where they would burst from the woods to surprise the city's unsuspecting garrison. This audacious mission was part of a larger American plan aimed at bringing Canada into the revolution on the side of the rebels as the fourteenth colony. The expedition, through the uncharted forests and wild rivers of Maine, by men and women who performed extraordinary, unselfish acts for the patriot cause, made them and their intrepid commander, Benedict Arnold, among the first heroes of the American Revolution.

In April 1775, at the start of the American Revolution, there were two substantial British forces in North America. The larger of the two—about 4,000 soldiers under the command of General Thomas Gage—was stationed in Boston. These men found themselves encircled by a large force of American militia, headquartered in nearby Cambridge and called the Provincial Army of Observation, whose officers reported to the Massachusetts Provincial Congress. Gage's force was too weak to break out of Boston, and although the rebels had many more troops (estimated at 17,000), they did not possess sufficient artillery to force the British out.

Guy Carleton, the royal governor of Canada, commanded the second sizable British force in America—roughly 900 troops concentrated at Quebec and Montreal, the only cities in Canada at the time.[2] Carleton had too few troops to defend his vast colony and could not expect any reinforcements until the spring of 1776. He worried over the loyalty of Canada's civilian population: Canada had been a British colony for only twelve years, and the allegiance of its predominately French-Canadian population of 100,000 was untested.[3]

The governor also grew anxious about the New England businessmen who had flocked to Canada after the French formally ceded the colony to Britain in 1763. Carleton knew that many of these estimated 2,000 recent immigrants sympathized with the rebellion. But he also had some formidable assets upon which he could draw. One resource was his colony's large Indian population, which had been well treated by the British and could be counted upon to carry out devastating raids along the frontiers of the rebellious colonies.[4]

Ample evidence of this could be found during the 150-year French occupation of Canada, when the French successfully led ruthless Indian attacks against English frontier settlements in Virginia, Pennsylvania, New York, New Hampshire, and Massachusetts. Carleton was ready to repeat their grisly success. The weather and time were another asset for Canada's British defenders; the extreme cold and deep snow of the long Canadian winters made military campaigning impractical for much of the year.

Carleton made his headquarters in a mansion in Quebec, the walled city recognized as the key to controlling Canada that competed with Montreal as the province's commercial center. Quebec, whose name literally means "the place where the river narrows," was perched on a commanding hilltop that towered above the St. Lawrence River. When the British captured Quebec in 1759, they appreciated the fortress city's strategic importance and used it as their provincial capital.

Since there were few roads in colonial America, most travel, especially the movement of bulky materials and goods, occurred by water. The extensive natural network of connecting navigable rivers and lakes made travel by water in North America relatively fast, comfortable, and safe. Commerce, settlement, and military activity followed the course of the continent's waterways. In fact, by the time of the American Revolution, there was an established water transportation network linking the Hudson, St. Lawrence, Ohio, and Mississippi Rivers to one another that made travel possible between such widely separated places as Quebec, Montreal, Albany, New York, Pittsburgh, St. Louis, and New Orleans.[5] Fortifications previously built at a number of strategic positions along these inland water routes included formidable gun batteries at Quebec to control the movement of ships on the St. Lawrence River.

The rivers and lakes that comprised the main water highway between New York City and Montreal are important to our story. Using the example of travelers starting from New York City, the first part of the journey was 150 miles up the broad Hudson River in one of the many oceangoing ships or river packets that regularly sailed between lower Manhattan Island and the river port city of Albany, New York, where goods and passengers were offloaded for the 65-mile trip north to Lake George.[6] If the water level of the upper Hudson River were high enough, passengers and freight bound for Montreal could switch to boats at Albany and follow the river an additional 45 miles north as far as Fort Edward, New York, where they continued via a crude road to the southern shore of Lake George.

Everything, including the boats, traveled along this road on carts pulled by teams of oxen and horses to Lake George, the location of Fort William Henry, built by the British during the French and Indian War. The boats were put back into the water at Lake George and reloaded for the 32-mile trip down the lake. The lake empties into a two-mile-long series of rapids called the La Chute River that connects Lake George with Lake Champlain. The La Chute is impassable for boats, and everything had to be carried around it on a road that went by Fort Ticonderoga, which guarded the strategic portage. Once past the La Chute, the journey continued north by boat on Wood Creek, then on to 100-mile-long Lake Champlain, which for more than a century served as "the great thoroughfare of war-parties."[7] Lake Champlain flows north and empties into the Richelieu River (also called the Sorel River), which in turn runs north to the St. Lawrence. There was one set of rapids on the Richelieu that had to be portaged. This portage was defended by Fort St. John on its south end and Fort Chambly on its north end. Once on the broad St. Lawrence, travelers could proceed west to Montreal and the Great Lakes or east to Quebec.

The Indians regularly traveled the Hudson River-Lake George-Lake Champlain-Richelieu River inland water route long before the arrival of Europeans, and the warring French and British armies used it for almost 100 years prior to the start of the American Revolution in their bids to gain control of North America. Immigrants flocked to the corridor, attracted by its fertile lands and access to markets via the region's rivers and lakes. However, because of the various portages, the route was not practical for large cargos such as grain, timber, and livestock, which were transported by ocean-going ships from New England coastal ports via the St. Lawrence River to Quebec and Montreal. Among the New England seamen who sailed this route was a wealthy, sharp-witted New Haven merchant named Benedict Arnold.

*   *   *

Although the following narrative is not about Benedict Arnold, the story of the American invasion of Canada cannot adequately be told without understanding him. Therefore, I have included a biography of Arnold's life prior to the assault against Quebec. Only by knowing Arnold—a controversial, contentious, and inexperienced officer—can we fully appreciate George Washington's acumen in appointing the young man to lead such an important mission.

Washington's faith in Arnold paid off, as Arnold proved to be one of American's best combat officers until his betrayal of the patriot cause in 1780. When the twice-wounded Arnold begged Washington for the command of West Point in June of that year, the general could not refuse his friend's request. Telling Washington that he needed the sedentary assignment to recover his health, Arnold's real interest in overseeing the strategic post was to use it to barter with the British for money and a senior position in the British army. Fortunately, Arnold's nefarious plot was discovered at the last moment. However, Arnold managed to escape capture and spent the rest of the war as a British general, avenging the insults he felt he had suffered at the hands of his former countrymen.

Early historians of the Revolution, many of whom lived through the emotionally charged conflict, called Arnold an unprincipled traitor "who would be received in hell riveted in chains."[8] The trend today is to treat him more compassionately, as a "troubled officer who felt deeply betrayed by the cause he had so eagerly tried to serve."[9] This assessment is correct; Arnold's truculent personality made him few friends in the army or in government.[10]

While the early historians of the Revolution portrayed Arnold as a "treacherous soul . . . a tarnished blot that nature made," they had to explain his contributions to the American patriot cause, including his command of the Arnold Expedition.[11] Historian Mercy Otis Warren (1728-1814) handled the problem neatly by characterizing Arnold as "a young soldier of fortune, who held in equal contempt both danger and principle."[12] However, many other early American chroniclers found a more plausible explanation for Arnold's behavior—his love of money. They correctly pointed out that when Arnold turned traitor in 1780 he was deep in debt, due partially to his lavish lifestyle, and they described how British agents tempted him with a large cash bounty in exchange for his complicity.

Thomas Paine was the first to voice the money theme to explain Arnold's treachery. In his pamphlet *The Crisis Extraordinary*, published in October 1780—just one month after Arnold's duplicity was uncovered—Paine called the former American general "a desperado, whose whole life has been a life of jobbs; and where either plunder or profit was the object, no danger deterred, no principle restrained him. . . . The early convulsion of the times [the first years of the American Revolution] afforded him an introduction into life, to the elegance of which he was before a stranger."[13]

Historian David Ramsay also used money to rationalize Arnold's transformation from American patriot to traitor. Writing in 1789, Ramsay said of Arnold, "His love of pleasure produced the love of money, and that extinguished all sensibility to the obligations of honor and duty. . . . In these circumstances, a change of sides afforded the only hope of replenishing his exhausted coffers."[14]

The rationale of Arnold's greed also appeared in Hannah Adams' 1799 history, in which she conveniently explained that Arnold's "taste for parade and extravagant living had deeply involved him in debt, and his necessities induced him to desert the American cause."[15]

The story of Arnold's childhood fit perfectly into the theme of someone desperate for financial gain. Thomas Paine accurately described Arnold's youth when he said, "He was born into a respected family of wealth and honor which was lost during his childhood leaving him with dishonor and poverty."

Modern-day historians recognize that the reasons for Benedict Arnold's treason are more complicated than the neat, patriotic-inspired tales of greed put forth by the early chroniclers of the American Revolution. In telling the story of the American assault on Quebec, I trace the development of Arnold's aggressive behavior, obsession with honor, lack of diplomacy, and inexperience in politics that eventually came together to consume and destroy him.

Chapter 1

Benedict Arnold Was Never a Laggard in the Path of Ambition[1]

he Arnold clan arrived in America from England in 1635 and settled in Rhode Island, where they became wealthy and active in local politics, including the governorship of the colony. Over time, the family's fortune diminished, forcing Benedict Arnold's father (Benedict senior) to be apprenticed to a cooper in order to earn a modest living as a barrel maker. But Benedict senior had bigger ideas. In 1730, after completing his apprenticeship, he went to the boom town of Norwich, Connecticut, where he met a wealthy young widow named Hannah Waterman King, whose husband Absalom had disappeared at sea while returning home from a trading voyage to Ireland. Benedict senior married Hannah on November 8, 1733, following a suitable period of mourning for her lost husband. Once married, he became the owner of Absalom King's substantial estate and was addressed as Captain Arnold. Captain Arnold and Hannah had six children, four of whom died in childhood. Only Benedict—the Revolutionary War general and traitor—and a daughter named Hannah lived to maturity.

Benedict, born on January 14, 1741, had a happy childhood in Norwich, living with his parents and sister in a handsome house. His parents had great plans for their only son, whom they sent to local schools to prepare for a college education and the family business. However, in his 1860 history of the Revolutionary War, author Benson Lossing tells a different story, depicting little Benedict as a "perfect despot." Lossing followed his tales of Arnold's truculent childhood with a little poem: "Born for a curse to virtue and mankind, Earth's broadest realm ne'er knew so black a mind."[2]

The most often repeated story the early historians loved to tell about Benedict Arnold's youth was how his father was transformed from a wealthy and respected merchant to an impoverished drunk. The story is true. The death of four of his children combined with business reverses turned the despondent Captain Arnold to drinking. This happened sometime around 1755, when young Benedict was a teenager. There still was enough money at the time in the family business to send Benedict to school, and his mother—who took over the dwindling family finances from her husband—wanted her son to attend Yale College (present-day Yale University) in nearby New Haven.

Benedict's plans to attend college ended when his parents ran out of money. With her husband sliding deeper into alcoholism, Hannah turned to help for her son from her wealthy cousins, Daniel and Joshua Lathrop, both of whom were Yale graduates and partners in a successful apothecary and general merchandise business. The Lathrops took Benedict into their firm as an apprentice. The teenage Benedict proved to have a talent for business, and sometime around 1759 the Lathrops started to send him on trading voyages, first to the West Indies and then to England.[3]

In August 1759, during Benedict's apprenticeship, his mother contracted some unknown ailment and died. Her passing only intensified Captain Arnold's depression and drinking bouts, and he died two years later. Left on his own at the age of 21, Benedict had to sell the family homestead to pay his father's debts, leaving him with nothing but a young sister to care for and his ancestor's noble name. Fortunately, the Lathrop brothers came to young Arnold's rescue with encouragement and money. Having already established one of their promising apprentices as their junior partner in a store in Hartford, they offered Arnold a similar opportunity in New Haven, and Benedict jumped at it.

New Haven was a thriving seacoast port when young Arnold arrived there in 1760. At first he opened a small shop in a rented space on Chapel Street, where he sold medicines, books, and related merchandise. Arnold's business prospered, allowing him to move to larger quarters, first on Church Street and then on Water Street along New Haven's busy waterfront. He advertised in the local newspaper, offering rum, sugar, and many other articles for cash or short credit.

Arnold maintained his ties to the Lathrop brothers, but in 1764 he formed a partnership with a promising New Haven merchant named

Adam Babcock. Arnold and Babcock purchased a small ship, the *Fortune*, which they used for trading voyages. Their business prospered and they purchased two additional vessels—the *Charming Sally* and the *Three Brothers*—the following year. Their little fleet was the means by which these two ambitious businessmen participated in the rich trade with Canada and the West Indies. They shipped horses, rum, molasses, pork, grain, and timber products, with Arnold often acting as the captain of one of their vessels. Men who knew him at the time, according to one biographer, saw a stocky, muscular form, and a bold, proud face, roughened and tanned by stormy weather and the tropic sun.[4]

On February 27, 1767, Arnold married Margaret (Peggy) Mansfield, the daughter of a wealthy New Haven merchant. The couple was happy, at least in the early years of their marriage. Peggy gave birth to three children, all boys: Benedict VI (born February 1768), Richard (August 1769), and Henry (September 1772).[5] From extant records it seems that Arnold also enjoyed a close relationship with his father-in-law, Samuel Mansfield. Benedict and Samuel became partners in profitable trading ventures in the West Indies, sailing to the islands with New England rum, dried fish, lumber, cattle, and horses, and returning with molasses. Arnold frequently commanded his own ships on these voyages, and stories filtered back to New Haven about his whoring, drinking, and dueling during these long absences from home. Much of this gossip was the result of jealousy because, by 1770, Arnold had become the most prosperous merchant in New Haven. Some of the rumors about him were true, however, including the stories of two duels that he fought in the West Indies over insults to his honor. Arnold was quick to defend his reputation, even if it meant settling the affront with dueling swords or a brace of pistols. He was an excellent marksman, and pistols were his preferred dueling weapon.

Back home, Arnold began construction in 1770 of a stately mansion that would show off his wealth and respectability. Completed the following year, the elegant Arnold mansion stood on Water Street in New Haven well into the nineteenth century. Some details of the house are worth noting, for they serve as an insight into Arnold's complicated character. The Arnold mansion was a large structure designed to impress anyone who walked by. It stood two stories tall with majestic pillars that framed its front entrance. Inside, on the first floor, detailed wood panel work and marble fireplaces attested to Arnold's wealth and good taste.

Each upstairs bedroom had its own fireplace, and there were roomy closets throughout the house. There was a special alcove built into the master bedroom to hold Arnold's many pairs of shoes, for Arnold loved shoes and clothing, and he dressed in the latest fashion. The house also had a secret stairway that led from a closet on the first floor to an upstairs room. A white picket fence with gravel walks surrounded the tall and stately house and connected it to the stables, coach house, and gardens. The estate stood on three acres of prime land, thick with beautiful fruit trees, graceful elms, and stately maples. Arnold had the house and picket fence painted white to give the property a final touch of beauty and opulence.

In the years preceding the American Revolution, Arnold lived happily in this fine mansion with his wife Peggy, their three sons, his sister Hannah, and numerous household servants. The property and home were important to him because they symbolized his financial success and dedication to his family. Looking at the view from his beautiful home, Arnold could see New Haven's harbor and watch for the arrival of his ships with their valuable cargoes. A short walk into town would take him to his store and wharves.[6]

Like most successful American businessmen at the time, Arnold led a complicated life based partially on his ability to sidestep British commercial laws and taxes. British success in the French and Indian War (1754-1763) had important consequences for colonial businessmen like Arnold. The war eliminated France as a commercial rival and opened Canada for trade. But the British government decided that the colonists should help pay for the costly war via import duties and taxes. The colonists opposed these levies, claiming that they could not be taxed without their consent. "The King has deprived us of our fundamental liberties and ensnared us in the tyrannical chains of political slavery," they argued. "[N]o taxation without representation."

Arnold was among a group of colonial merchants, along with John Hancock of Boston, who took a practical approach to the problem—they evaded the new import duties by smuggling goods into America. Other colonists were more belligerent in their opposition to British tariffs and showed their distaste for the King's "collectors, comptrollers, searchers, tide-waiters with a whole catalog of pimps sent hither" by dumping a cargo of taxed tea into Boston Harbor. The British government responded to this act of defiance by closing the port of Boston until the tea had been paid for. Outraged by this move, the radicals among the colonists organized themselves into militia companies and hired instructors to teach them how to drill and handle weapons. One observer described the scene:

> the whole country at this time was in commotion and nothing was talked of but war, liberty, or death; persons of all descriptions were embodying themselves into military companies, and every old drunken fellow they found who had been a soldier, or understood what is called the manual exercise, was employed of evenings to drill them.[7]

Sixty-five firebrands from New Haven, describing themselves as gentlemen of influence and high respectability, met on December 28, 1774, to sign articles that organized them into a militia company in preparation for a possible war with Britain. Arnold joined them and, in the middle of February 1775, received an appointment to a committee charged with procuring guns for the group. Arnold was a logical choice for such a committee since he was a merchant with numerous business contacts, especially in the Dutch- and French-owned islands in the Caribbean whose people were selling war materials to the Americans.

At the same time, the newly organized New Haven militiamen petitioned the Connecticut General Assembly to have their company appointed as the Governor's Second Company of Guards. The title was important because there was a Governor's Company of Guards in Hartford that had been granted certain rights and privileges by the colony's General Assembly, including the freedom to elect their own officers, and the New Haven men wanted the same benefits for themselves. The assembly promptly granted the New Haven men a charter naming them the Second Company of Guards.[8] On March 15, 1775, the newly created militia company elected Arnold as their captain and commanding officer. Although Arnold had no military experience at the time, he was named commander due to his high standing in the community and his skills as a leader and organizer. Membership in the Second Company of Guards was a status symbol among the radical young gentlemen of New Haven, who were required to purchase their own uniforms and weapons and contribute to the payment of a drill master—usually retired British army officers and enlisted men (or deserters)—to teach them the manual of arms. Arnold and his men soon began to drill on New Haven's village green in their smart new red and buff uniforms to the cheers of the town's insurgents, while residents loyal to Britain turned their backs on the upstart, self-important Arnold and his pretentious comrades.

The American Revolution commenced when a column of British troops marched out from Boston in the early hours of April 19, 1775, en route to destroy the military equipment that the Massachusetts militia had stockpiled in Concord, located 16 miles west of Boston. Warned of the British raid, the local militia assembled to defend the countryside. The first clash between the British army and the Massachusetts militia occurred when the British column passed through the village of Lexington. The fighting intensified during the day as additional militia companies arrived on the scene. By nightfall, the battle-scarred British column was back in Boston, surrounded by the incensed militiamen. That day's events, starting with the British march from Boston to the encirclement of Boston by the militia, became known as the Lexington alarm.

A courier arrived in New Haven a few days later with the first reports of the action. The city's conservative leaders quickly convened a town meeting and called for patience and restraint. The radicals disagreed, and the militia assembled under Captain Arnold's command, voting to march to Massachusetts to help their fellow New Englanders fight the hated British troops. Some pro-rebel students from Yale College joined them. As the town's elders watched in dismay, the Footguards mustered on the New Haven Green on April 24 before a large crowd of spectators. There were 50 of them, including Arnold, who oversaw their signing of a document that stated they were "Driven to the last necessity, and obliged to have recourse to arms in defense of our lives and liberties." The Footguards affirmed that they were not mercenaries, "whose views extend no further than pay and plunder," but rather men called to the honorable service of hazarding their lives for "the liberties and unalienable rights of mankind."[9] Following a fiery sermon, Arnold submitted a request to New Haven's officials for additional gunpowder from the town's arsenal. The conservative town elders sent an emissary to reason with Arnold, urging him to wait for instructions from the Connecticut General Assembly, to which he was said to have replied, "None but Almighty God shall prevent my marching!"[10] Fearing violence, the town's burghers gave Arnold the keys to the powder magazine. The militiamen took what they needed, reformed their ranks, and, as fifes and drums struck-up a martial tune, marched off to Boston to the cheers of their liberty-loving neighbors.

Arnold and his militiamen were on the road to Boston when they met Colonel Samuel Holden Parsons, a Connecticut militia officer who was on horseback and riding fast in the opposite direction. Parsons was on his way back to Hartford after a brief visit to the rebel camp outside Boston as a representative from the Connecticut General Assembly, which wanted reliable information on the situation. Parsons stopped briefly to talk to Arnold, explaining that the rebels had surrounded Boston but lacked sufficient artillery to do much beyond observing the Redcoats. In the course of their brief conversation, Arnold told Parsons that there were plenty of cannons at Fort Ticonderoga. Arnold had never visited the place but had been told about it by his merchant friends in Montreal, who said that it was in disrepair and that its small peacetime garrison was more interested in growing cabbages than in preparing for war.

Parsons was impressed with Arnold's second-hand information and, after reaching Hartford, organized a meeting of a handful of Connecticut's leaders and repeated what Arnold had told him.[11] Knowing that time was critical, Parsons and his friends voted to organize a force to seize the British post without waiting for Connecticut's slow-moving, conservative General Assembly to take action. Acting alone, the Connecticut radicals withdrew money from the provincial treasury and appointed Edward Mott, a captain in the militia, to command a military expedition against Ticonderoga. Anxious to recruit men for their mission, the Connecticut radicals convinced Herman Allen, the proprietor of a general store in Salisbury, Connecticut, to visit his older brother Ethan, who was the leader of a group of belligerent settlers in the nearby Hampshire Grants (present-day Vermont).[12] Calling themselves the Green Mountain Boys, Ethan Allen and his followers previously organized themselves into a quasi-military body to defend their land claims against conflicting claims from New Yorkers who called Allen and his supporters "the Bennington mob." Herman Allen's mission was to persuade his brother to mobilize his clique and join forces with Captain Mott.

Connecticut's campaign to take Fort Ticonderoga began on April 29, 1775, when Captain Mott left Hartford with a small party of volunteers and headed northwest toward Lake Champlain. Arnold arrived in

Cambridge the same day with his smart-looking Footguards Company. The American Revolution was just 10 days old when these two seemingly unrelated events occurred.

Arnold worried for the welfare of his militia company upon arriving in Cambridge, a characteristic that won him the loyalty of the men who served under him throughout his military career. Arnold worked hard to secure comfortable quarters for his company in the abandoned mansion of a local loyalist. He quickly learned that the New England troops at Cambridge were under the command of an extra-legal body called the Massachusetts Provincial Congress, whose military arm was known as the Provincial Army of Observation. Some seventeen thousand New England militiamen surrounded the city of Boston, which was defended by only 4,000 British soldiers. The logical plan was for the rebels to force the British to evacuate Boston by threatening to destroy the city with artillery. Military positions and barracks would be singled-out as targets. But as Parsons told Arnold days earlier, the rebels lacked the cannons to initiate the plan.

Arnold thought again about the cannons he heard were at Fort Ticonderoga and, with his usual assertive nature, approached Dr. Joseph Warren (1741-1775) with the idea of capturing the fort and bringing some of its cannons cross-country to Cambridge. Warren was a prominent physician and political figure in prewar Boston who had been named president of the Massachusetts Provincial Congress just prior to Arnold's arrival in Cambridge. The two men met unaware that Connecticut already had launched a campaign to capture Fort Ticonderoga. Arnold repeated his story to Warren about the cannons at Fort Ticonderoga and recommended that the rebels should seize the outpost before the British had a chance to reinforce it. Warren liked the idea and asked Arnold to put his plan in writing, which Arnold did on April 30:

> You have desired me to state the number of cannon, &c., at Ticonderoga. I have certain information that there are at Ticonderoga eighty pieces of heavy cannon, twenty brass guns, from four to eighteen pounders, and ten to twelve large mortars. . . . The place could not hold out an hour against a vigorous onset.[13]

Note that Arnold did not claim any personal knowledge of the situation at Fort Ticonderoga.

The Massachusetts Committee of Safety endorsed Arnold's plan and moved quickly to organize a Massachusetts-led attack on the fort under his command. They commissioned Arnold as a colonel in the Provincial Army of Observation on May 2, 1775, with orders to raise a body of men not exceeding 400 for the secret purpose of capturing Fort Ticonderoga. Arnold was to take possession of the cannons, mortars, stores, etc., upon the lake and return with all serviceable weaponry to Cambridge.[14] Proudly clutching his colonel's commission, Arnold bade farewell to his fellow New Haven militiamen and started west that night with a handful of junior officers to help him recruit men for his mission.[15]

One of Arnold's ablest deputies was his friend Eleazer Oswald (1750-1795), a young New Haven printer and fellow member of the Second Connecticut Foot Guards.[16] Oswald was born in Falmouth, England, the son of a sea captain. When his father disappeared (under unknown circumstances), 15-year-old Eleazer left his mother and headed to America, where he hoped to make his fortune. He arrived in New York City in 1770 and signed-on as an apprentice to printer John Holt, who also published a newspaper called *The New York Journal.* Young Oswald endeared himself to the Holt family and married their daughter Elizabeth about 1774. Holt described his son-in-law in a letter: "He has Youth, Health, Hardiness, Activity, Courage & Perseverance . . . above all his Honour & Integrity may be safely relied on."[17]

Arnold was recruiting in Massachusetts at the same time that Connecticut's Captain Mott was heading for Pittsfield, Massachusetts, the home to several influential rebels who could help him raise men for Connecticut's attack on Fort Ticonderoga. One of Pittsfield's firebrands was a young lawyer named John Brown, who had visited the fort shortly before the war. Brown stopped at the post during a secret pre-war mission to Montreal and Quebec to evaluate Canadian sentiment for the Boston Committee of Correspondence. He also contacted Ethan Allen prior to hostilities to learn where his sentiments stood should war break out between Great Britain and the 13 colonies. Allen told Brown that he would side with the rebellion and that his Green Mountain Boys were especially keen to attack Fort Ticonderoga should hostilities commence. Upon his return, Brown wrote a confidential report to the Boston Committee describing his meeting with Allen, in which he recommended that "the Fort at Tyconderogo must be seized as soon as possible should hostilities be committed by the kings Troops."[18] Mott also was interested in enlisting James Easton, a local tavern keeper and influential militia colonel, to help him raise local men for the attack on Ticonderoga. The prospect of capturing the fort excited Brown and Easton, who not only joined Mott but also recruited 50 volunteers from among their neighbors for the campaign.

With his force now numbering approximately 70 men, Mott headed north toward the town of Bennington, the hub of the Hampshire Grants and headquarters of Ethan Allen and his Green Mountain Boys. When Mott, Brown, and Easton arrived in Bennington they found Allen and his followers waiting for them. Allen, after a head count, insisted that he be appointed commander of the expedition because he controlled the largest number of men. Mott agreed, and Allen—who had no military experience—assumed command of the attack. With a force estimated at 270 men, Allen advanced to the village of Shoreham, which lay across Lake Champlain from Fort Ticonderoga.[19] One of Mott's men soon returned from a reconnaissance to report that the post was in disrepair, its garrison maintaining a peacetime routine.

The uncoordinated Connecticut and Massachusetts expeditions against Fort Ticonderoga were a breeding ground for trouble. Arnold, with his aggressive nature, short temper, and obsession with personal honor and dignity, was not the cool diplomat needed in this ticklish situation. Nor was the Connecticut faction any better in mediation, least of all the hotheaded, rowdy Ethan Allen.

An explosive confrontation between the leaders of the Connecticut expedition and Arnold took place in Shoreham. Arnold burst into the May 9 meeting between Allen, Mott, Easton, and Brown, who were absorbed in their final preparations for the attack. The Connecticut-managed assault on Fort Ticonderoga was scheduled for four o'clock the next morning. Upon learning that Mott had yielded command to Allen, Arnold confronted the frontier brawler with his commission as a colonel from the Massachusetts Committee of Safety, insisting that he was the senior officer present and therefore entitled to command the attack. Allen probably realized that Arnold's papers, issued by the powerful Massachusetts Provincial Congress, were more creditable than the commissions he and his officers held from a group of renegade Connecticut functionaries. He also saw the advantage of having a duly appointed Massachusetts officer (Arnold) with orders to seize Fort Ticonderoga along on the mission. Arnold's protests failed, however, and the best he could negotiate was a joint command with Allen.

With Allen and Arnold in the lead, the rebels assaulted Fort Ticonderoga during the early morning of May 10. The attackers quietly crossed the lake, reached the fort's gates at dawn, and found a lone sentry on duty. The startled guard momentarily resisted, then fled into the fortress' parade ground with Allen, Arnold, and about 80 Green Mountain Boys in hot pursuit. It was all over in 10 minutes; the attackers overpowered the small garrison and the fortress, and its valuable artillery and stores of gunpowder fell into rebel hands. After sending his prisoners off to Connecticut, Allen turned his men loose to ransack the place. Their efforts, reported a captured British officer, seemed "most rigidly perform'd as to liquors, provisions, &c whether belonging to his majesty or private property."[20]

It is amazing how quickly Arnold managed to estrange himself from the officers of the Connecticut expedition. Although he met them for the first time on May 9, by the time they sat down two days later to write their reports on their successful mission, it was apparent that they all hated Arnold. Easton and Mott, for example, sent a report to Arnold's civilian bosses, the Massachusetts Provincial Congress, in which they claimed that Arnold played no part in the capture of Fort Ticonderoga and recommended that "said Arnold's farther procedure in this matter highly inexpedient. . . ."[21]

Allen wrote his own letter to the Massachusetts officials, praising his fellow officers except for Arnold, who he did not mention. Mott wrote privately to that same body of officials denouncing Arnold's participation in the campaign. Calling him "Mr. Arnold," Mott said that after they had "generously told him our whole plan, [Arnold] strenuously contended and insisted that he had a right to command them and all their officers. . . ."[22]

Arnold quickly fired off his own version of events to his civilian bosses. His report included the following description of the situation in the fort following its capture:

> There is here at present near one hundred men, who are in the greatest confusion and anarchy, destroying and plundering private property, committing every enormity, and paying no attention to

publick service. . . . Colonel Allen is a proper man to head his own wild people, but entirely unacquainted with military service; and as I am the only person who has been legally authorized to take possession of this place, I am determined to insist on my right, and I think it my duty to remain here against all opposition, until I have further orders.[23]

Arnold's comment about Allen being "unacquainted with military service" is a bit of bravado, since the sum of Arnold's own military experience at the time was a brief prewar stint as a militia captain.

In the days that followed, the Green Mountain Boys slowly drifted back across the lake with their loot and returned to their farms. As Allen's gang left, Arnold's recruits started to arrive. Arnold now had the upper hand, and his situation improved further when his friend Oswald arrived with a small schooner seized from a wealthy loyalist named Philip Skene. The ship, named the *Katherine*, was captured at its berth on Lake Champlain by some of Allen's Green Mountain Boys, who did not know how to sail it. They turned it over to Oswald, who learned to handle boats from his seafaring father. Arnold quickly converted the *Katherine* to a warship by piercing her sides for four carriage guns and mounting eight swivel guns on her rail—those captured at Fort Ticonderoga and Crown Point.

Arnold christened his new warship the *Liberty* and used her to take the offensive. To Allen's amazement, his antagonist sailed the *Liberty* and two other boats down to the far end of Lake Champlain in search of a Royal Navy sloop named the *George III*. Arnold wanted the *George III*, the largest vessel on Lake Champlain, so as to secure control of the lake for the rebels. When Arnold found the sloop lying quietly at anchor near St. Johns (present day St. Jean), a British outpost 25 miles into Canada on the Richelieu River (also called the Sorel River), the colonel and his men silently boarded the ship and overpowered its crew of seven, all of whom were asleep at the time. Then, for good measure, the raiders captured the small British garrison at St. Johns, whose defenders consisted of a sergeant and 12 soldiers.

Learning that British reinforcements were en route, Arnold and his men gathered whatever military equipment they could carry and set sail with their booty and prisoners back toward Fort Ticonderoga. Arnold also pilfered the mail he found at St. Johns, which included a letter from

Governor Carleton to General Gage that stated there were fewer than 700 regular British troops to defend all of Canada.[24]

As they were returning up the lake, Arnold's men spotted a number of boats heading in the opposite direction. It was Allen and about 100 of his followers, who were trying to catch up with Arnold to share in the plunder of St. Johns. Although Arnold yelled across to them that British reinforcements were descending on the fort and they should return to Fort Ticonderoga with him, Allen and his men shunned the warning and continued north. Colonel Allen and his followers camped for the night in the woods near Fort St. Johns, where they were jolted awake by artillery fire from the British reinforcements Arnold had warned them about. Allen and his men raced to their boats and rowed with all their might back to the safety of Fort Ticonderoga.

This incident was an embarrassment for Allen and helped solidify Arnold's claim to command. Where Allen was brash and emotional, Arnold was organized and disciplined, and he emerged as the commander of American operations in the Lake Champlain region. By May 29, Arnold was able to write his civilian bosses: "Colonel Allen has entirely given up the command. I have one hundred and fifty men here, and expect in two or three weeks to have my Regiment complete, and believe they will be joined by a thousand men from Connecticut and New York."[25]

Arnold was proving to be a man of action who seemed destined for higher command. But he lacked influential friends to publicize his accomplishments and spawned a number of dangerous new enemies who were determined to wreck his fledgling military career. Arnold acknowledged his antagonists in a letter he penned anonymously to an Albany, New York, newspaper. Identifying himself as A.B. (a thin disguise), he wrote, "It appears that envy or self-interested views has created Colonel Arnold some enemies, who have . . . artfully endeavoured to misrepresent his conduct . . . ."[26]

Arnold's discord with Easton worsened when Arnold accused him of being a coward. Easton heard about the insult, stormed into Arnold's headquarters, and demanded an apology. Arnold responded by seizing the former tavern keeper by the collar and challenging him to a duel. Even though he was armed with a cutlass and a pair of loaded pistols, Easton refused to fight. Arnold then gave him a kick in the pants and threw him out of camp.[27]

While Arnold dashed around the Lake Champlain region, the Second Continental Congress was meeting in Philadelphia "to take into consideration the state of America."[28] Their distinguished ranks included John Adams from Massachusetts, a lawyer by profession; Samuel Ward from Rhode Island, a former governor of the colony; and Colonel George Washington from Virginia, a wealthy planter and veteran of the French and Indian War. The delegates convened under tense circumstances on May 10, with Boston already under siege by an ad hoc army of New England militia. While Congress had no authority over the American patriot forces surrounding Boston, its members were kept well informed about events there and encouraged, especially by the Massachusetts delegates, to take control of the army. The pressure on Congress to direct the rebellion escalated on the night of May 17, when John Brown arrived in Philadelphia with news that patriot forces had captured Fort Ticonderoga. Brown appeared before Congress the next day and gave a glowing account of the action. On the 31st, the delegates heard from Arnold, whose letter to the body was read aloud. Arnold claimed to have intelligence that the British in Canada were "making all possible preparation to cross the lake [Lake Champlain], and expected to be joined by a number of Indians, with a design of retaking Crown-point and Ticonderogo."[29] Unable to resist the war euphoria, Congress recommended that Governor Trumbull of Connecticut send rein-forcements to Ticonderoga.

Colonel Arnold's news, along with other intelligence pouring into Congress, convinced the delegates that they needed to take control of the insurrection and establish what they called the Continental Army (later renamed the United States Army), composed of troops from all the colonies. Having agreed to this step, the delegates turned their attention to selecting a commander in chief for their new army. On June 14, John Adams rose in Congress to say that he had one, and only one, person in mind to command the army—a Virginia gentleman with an independent fortune who was a skilled and experienced officer. Upon hearing these words, Washington left the room. The following day, the delegates unanimously elected the reluctant colonel commander in chief of the Continental Army.[30] Washington accepted the post declaring, "I beg it may be remembered, by every Gentleman in the room, that I, this day, declare with the utmost sincerity, I do not think myself equal to the Command I am honored with."[31]

A few days later, on June 17, another drama took place at Fort Ticonderoga when Connecticut's Colonel Benjamin Hinman arrived with reinforcements. Claiming to be the senior officer, Hinman informed Arnold that he, not Arnold, now commanded Fort Ticonderoga and Crown Point. Arnold refused to yield. The ensuing argument was resolved only after a committee from Massachusetts arrived with instructions for Arnold to put himself and his Massachusetts troops under Hinman's command. The committee explained that Massachusetts was hard-pressed to send any additional troops to the Fort Ticonderoga region and that Connecticut had agreed to provide reinforcements if its officers were put in charge. Rather than submit, Arnold ordered his troops to disband and resigned his Massachusetts commission, writing in his journal, "I have resigned my commission, not being able to hold it longer with honor."

Back in Philadelphia, Congress learned about this unpleasant episode and heard from Ethan Allen and John Brown on the subject of Benedict Arnold, who they depicted as a tempestuous glory seeker of low character. With the exception of Connecticut delegate Silas Deane, the members of Congress knew little about Arnold, who was not seriously considered for an appointment as an officer in the new Continental Army.

The final humiliation of Arnold's early military career occurred when James Easton, whom Arnold had booted out of camp, received a commission as colonel in the Continental Army and command of Arnold's old Massachusetts regiment. Easton arranged for his friend John Brown, whom Ethan Allen called his "able counsellor," to obtain an appointment as a Continental Army major. Benedict Arnold packed up his bags and left for home.[32]

Arnold's departure from the northern New York frontier did not go completely unnoticed. The civilians in the region, amounting to about 600 families, presented him with a testimonial scroll that included the following: "By your vigilance and good conduct, we have been, under Providence, preserved from the incursions and ravages of an enraged enemy. . . ."[33]

Arnold had organized the fledgling forces in the Lake Champlain region effectively. Allen, Mott, and Easton were bumbling incompetents by comparison, but they were experienced at playing politics and had influential friends to champion their careers. Had Arnold been more diplomatic and conciliatory during this time, his military career might have benefited when Congress absorbed the hodgepodge of New England soldiers and officers into the Continental Army.

On July 11, Arnold the civilian arrived in Albany en route to New Haven. One of the Continental army's new senior officers, former New York congressional delegate Philip Schuyler, was in Albany at the time. Schuyler's appointment to major general—one of only four such appointments made by Congress—was based largely on his military experience as a provincial officer attached to the British army during the French and Indian War. Schuyler's holdings included a sprawling country estate in Saratoga and a mansion in Albany. Because of his close connection with New York, Schuyler was placed in charge of all military operations in that colony, including Fort Ticonderoga and Crown Point. Following his appointment, Congress ordered Schuyler to invade Canada. Despite the controversy surrounding Arnold, Schuyler wanted to meet him, especially since he possessed first-hand knowledge about the military situation in the Lake Champlain region. At their initial meeting, which probably took place on July 10 at Schuyler's mansion on the outskirts of Albany, Schuyler and Arnold discovered they had a lot in common. Both were self-made businessmen with impressive family backgrounds. Schuyler, however, had inherited a substantial amount of property that he had shrewdly expanded into a vast agricultural and commercial empire. Prior to the war, he was involved in land speculation, rudimentary manufacturing, and colonizing his fertile upstate New York tracts with tenant farmers. Both Schuyler and Arnold had married wealthy women to further their careers. But Arnold's marriage to Peggy Mansfield paled in comparison to Schuyler's union with Catherine van Rensselaer. Schuyler's bride guaranteed him access to the lucrative business deals organized by the powerful Rensselaer family of New York. Also helping to cement their friendship was the fact that both men hated Ethan Allen and his crowd. Schuyler's loathing stemmed from his conviction that the Green Mountain Boys were trespassers, living on land claimed by New York.

Schuyler requested that Arnold write Congress a report on conditions at the upstate New York forts, and Arnold promptly complied. Dated July 11, Arnold's report described conditions at Crown Point, Ticonderoga, and Fort George, then summarized the overall situation at the three posts: "Great want of discipline and regularity among the troops. On the other hand, the enemy at St. John's indefatigable in fortifying, and collecting timber for building a vessel."[34] Schulyer, impressed with Arnold, invited him to join his staff as his adjutant general.[35] But before the offer could be discussed in detail, Arnold informed his new benefactor that he had received a letter from his sister Hannah in New Haven with terrible news—his wife Peggy, age 30, had died on June 19 from what was described as a "fatal illness."[36] The same missive reported that Benedict's ailing father-in-law and friend, Samuel Mansfield, had passed away three days later, probably the result of shock over his daughter's untimely death. Deeply distressed and anxious about his three little sons, Arnold cut short his discussions with Schuyler to hurry home.

Almost certainly among those who offered their condolences to the grieving Arnold was 37-year-old general Richard Montgomery, Schuyler's second in command. Montgomery was considered to be one of the brightest and most experienced combat officers in the infant American army. He was born in County Dublin, Ireland, on the country estate of his father, who was a baronet, a member of the Irish Parliament, and a retired British army officer. Baronet Montgomery educated his son in Ireland's best schools. While young Richard attended Trinity College, he decided, on the advice of his father and older brother, to leave his studies and join the British army. The Montgomerys had a long history of military service, and Richard wanted to maintain the family tradition. He also benefited from the fact that his father could afford to purchase an officer's commission for him.

Montgomery got to see much of New York, New England, and eastern Canada as his regiment moved from place to place during the French and Indian War. In early 1773, Montgomery arrived in New York and purchased a farm in Kingsbridge, just north of New York City. He then married Janet Livingston, a member of the wealthy and politically powerful Livingston family. Janet owned a beautiful parcel of land along the Hudson River near the town of Rhinebeck, and the couple was building a home there when the war started.

Montgomery's brother-in-law, Robert R. Livingston Jr., and his clan were at the forefront of the New York radicals, and Captain Montgomery, who was sympathetic toward the colonists' remonstrations, found himself immersed in his adopted family's anti-British politics.[37] In 1775, the Livingstons helped Montgomery get elected to the New York Provincial Congress, where his military experience made a big impression on his fellow delegates. They lobbied in the Continental

Congress for Captain Montgomery to be appointed a general in the new Continental Army. We can only speculate on the impression that Montgomery, an experienced, battle-scarred former British army officer, made on Arnold when the two men met for the first time in Albany. As a Massachusetts provincial officer, Arnold's brief military service had been mostly with amateur military windbags like Ethan Allen and Edward Mott. Even Schuyler had served as a lowly colonial auxiliary during the French and Indian War, working behind the lines as a paper-pushing administrator. Now Arnold was in the presence of a real soldier who had led elite British infantry in fierce combat against the Indians, French, and Spanish. Arnold must have admired Montgomery and envied his military experience and advantageous status with Congress.

Arnold's return to New Haven, in mid-July 1775, marked a low point in his life. Besides the recent death of his wife and father-in-law, he had to deal with his rejection by the rebel cause. Normally physically robust, Arnold's health took a turn for the worse, and he was periodically bedridden for days at a time with attacks of gout. He relied on his unmarried sister Hannah to care for his three sons, the oldest of whom was seven.

Arnold had used his own funds to pay for many of his expenses during his brief military service, and he wanted to be reimbursed by the Massachusetts Provincial Congress. Besides, despite his recent rebuffs in the Champlain Valley, Arnold believed in the patriot cause and viewed high command in the army as a means of restoring his family's honor and reputation.

With Hannah supporting him at home, Arnold made a trip to Watertown, where the provincial government was meeting, to submit his expense report in person and explore new command possibilities. Although he had lost his benefactor, Dr. Joseph Warren, who was killed at the Battle of Bunker Hill, Arnold now had the patronage of General Philip Schuyler. As later events would prove, Arnold decided that while in Watertown, he would travel a few miles farther east to Cambridge to seek an interview with General Washington and ask for a post in the new Continental Army. Arnold probably hoped that the commander in chief would remember meeting him the previous year in Philadelphia at one of the social functions connected with the First Continental Congress, which Arnold attended with his friend Silas Deane's Connecticut contingent.[38]

Arnold presented himself to the Massachusetts Provincial Congress on August 1. He submitted his expense account for his service as a Massachusetts officer to a committee headed by Dr. Benjamin Church Jr. Church's committee treated Arnold coldly, primed in part by inflammatory reports they previously received from James Easton. While waiting for the Massachusetts authorities to settle-up with him, Arnold rode over to nearby Cambridge in the hopes of getting an interview with Washington. Surprisingly, Arnold apparently had no problem meeting with the busy general, who was interested in talking to him about a secret plan to seize Quebec.

Chapter 2

The Distance and the Difficulties of the Way Were Much Underestimated [1]

eorge Washington had a lot on his mind when Benedict Arnold walked into his office in early August 1775. Among the complicated issues confronting the general was Philip Schuyler's invasion of Canada. Washington found the decision to invade a surprising one, and believed it exceeded Congress's proclaimed policy of conducting a defensive war. As Congress had stated as recently as June 1, "As this Congress has nothing more in view than the defence of these colonies. Resolved, That no expedition or incursion ought to be undertaken or made, by any colony, or body of colonists [New England] against or into Canada."[2] Despite the resolution, Canada proved too tempting a conquest to resist. Information and reports received in Philadelphia at the time depicted Canada as weak defensively, its people sympathetic to the rebel cause. Additionally, members of Congress viewed Canada as a potentially valuable negotiating tool in the expected reconciliation with Britain.

Victory in Canada seemed a simple task to the armchair generals in Congress, and so the decision was made to invade the colony. Since Schuyler was the senior officer in New York, Congress authorized him to command the invasion. Schuyler planned to use the long established route between New York and Canada for his attack: north on the military road from Albany to the south shore of Lake George, across Lake George and Lake Champlain, and down the Richelieu River to Montreal.

Few were willing to acknowledge it at the time, but providing support for Schuyler's newly designated Northern Department headquartered at Fort Ticonderoga, on top of maintaining Washington's Grand Army at Cambridge, was straining the resources of the infant nation. As a result, Schuyler was having problems recruiting and equipping his army.[3] Although Congress ordered him to invade Canada on July 1, a month later his campaign seemed stalled at Fort Ticonderoga. Schuyler found himself under intense pressure from the "chimney corner generals" in Congress (John Hancock and John Adams among them) who could not understand the cause of the delay, especially as the bills for the campaign were piling-up. One critic thought that Schuyler was "better qualified to lead a quadrille [a dance] than an undisciplined mob of men."[4] Washington, however, knew better and told his friend, "[M]ine must be a portrait at full Length of what you have had in Miniature."[5]

Washington wanted to help Schuyler, not only for the sake of the rebellion, but because the two men were friends. Their relationship stemmed from their days as fellow delegates in the Continental Congress, where they learned of their common interest in business. Both were highly principled family men (Schuyler had five daughters, and Washington was the stepfather to his wife Martha's two children from her first marriage). Both were experts in military administration, which they learned from the British army during the French and Indian War. Since they were the most experienced soldiers serving in Congress, Washington and Schuyler were appointed to committees involved with organizing the colonies for war.

Washington's large and inactive army was too far away to render any immediate assistance to Schuyler, but the commander in chief contemplated a diversionary move—a strike against Canada through the Maine district of Massachusetts—to help his friend. Washington probably came by this idea from New England officers who were aware that such a route existed. The logical objective of this second front was Canada's capital, the city of Quebec, which lay within striking distance from the Maine border. The scheme appealed to Washington because it would force the British to divert some of their troops away from Schuyler's thrust at Montreal in order to defend their capital. The occupation of Quebec would also give the Americans additional leverage in their anticipated negotiations with the British government to bring a quick end to the fighting.

A surprise attack on Quebec also appealed to Washington's love of military science and his bold imagination, and he soon went to work planning the campaign. He heard from the New England officers in his army that Colonel Jonathan Brewer of Massachusetts had proposed a strike against Canada via Maine prior to Washington's arrival in Cambridge. Brewer submitted his plan in May 1775 to the Massachusetts Provincial Congress, in which he volunteered to lead 500 men across Maine and capture Quebec in a surprise attack. The Massachusetts authorities liked the idea, titled "A Diversion of the Provincial Troops into that part of Canada," and gave it serious consideration. The attack was believed to be possible by following the courses of two rivers that nearly meet: the Kennebec in Maine and the Chaudiere in Canada. The bureaucrats heard that there was an easy portage between these two navigable rivers across three ponds (actually lakes) known as the Great Carry. Brewer's idea, however, was put on hold when he was seriously wounded at the Battle of Bunker Hill. Complicating the plan was that, while the existence of an inland water route from Maine to Quebec was common knowledge in New England, only a single white man was known to have made the trip.

The Maine-Quebec route had a long speculative history with the military when Washington first heard about it. The trail appeared on a 1682 French map. In 1697, Pierre Le Moyne d'Iberville, a French soldier and explorer, proposed attacking Boston by way of the Chaudiere River: "bursting from the woods with one thousand Canadians [militia] and six hundred regulars."[6] Five years later, French officers in Canada offered a plan titled "Premier Project pour L'Expédition contre la Nouvelle Angleterre" that recommended a coordinated attack against New England with warships sailing down the Atlantic coast joined by 2,000 "regulars, militia, and Indians, sent from Canada by way of the Chaudiere and the Kennebec."[7] There were several proposals to use the route during the French and Indian War, including a 1756 plan to send 2,000 British troops to attack Quebec via the Kennebec River. In 1758, Governor Pownall of Massachusetts wrote, "I should think if about 100 thorough wood-hunters, properly officered [sic] could be obtained in the county of York, a scout of such might make an attempt upon the [French] settlements by way of the Chaudiere River."[8] Over the years, Indians, army deserters, missionaries, and traders added bits of information about the route. Some made rough drawings, but much of what was known was speculation. Massachusetts sent a surveying party into Maine following the end of the French and Indian War, but it only traveled part of the route and completed its survey based on hearsay from locals.

Interest in the route reappeared at the start of the American Revolution, when the leaders of Falmouth (modern Portland), Maine, heard rumors that the British were preparing to launch an invasion of New England via the Chaudiere-Kennebec route. They sent a small scouting party, led by woodsmen Remington Hobby and John Getchell, with orders to "ascertain if any Frenchmen [Canadians] were in motion, or any of the savages were preparing to ravage the frontier settlements." According to those who knew him, Getchell was a respectable man known for his expert handling of Indian canoes. However, Hobby and Getchell never went beyond the upper Kennebec on their scouting expedition. The one man who had traveled and surveyed the entire route was living nearby, but he was not about to talk to Washington. His name was John Montresor, a British Army engineer bottled up in Boston with General Thomas Gage's army.[9]

Captain Montresor made the round trip from Quebec to the lower Kennebec River and back in 1761. His scouting and surveying expedition was ordered by General James Murray, who commanded at Quebec following its capture from the French. Murray heard there was a practical route from Quebec to the settlements in Maine and wanted someone to confirm its existence. He ordered Montresor to map it. Washington was given a copy of Montresor's journal and maps sometime after he arrived in Cambridge.

Montresor left Quebec on June 14, 1761, with 12 men, including Indian guides and expert canoe men, all lightly provisioned and planning to live off the land. The expedition arrived at Fort Halifax—located on Maine's Kennebec River, 60 miles from the sea—in 32 days. Montresor had purposely taken a long, roundabout route to Fort Halifax in order to explore various lakes and rivers in northern Maine. After resting at Fort Halifax for two days, they headed back on July 9, but this time using the direct Kennebec-Chaudiere route. Eleven days later, on July 20, they crossed the Canadian border and started down the Chaudiere River back toward Quebec City.

Since they included valuable military information, Montresor's original journal and maps were sent to London for safekeeping. The Americans had an official copy of the journal and maps—all provided to Washington some time after he arrived in Cambridge—but certain information had been purposely deleted when the items were copied, including some names, places, distances, and the date of Montresor's return to the capital. For example, here is the text in the rebels' copy of the journal entry for July 19, 1761: "Set out very early. Just by us we found a small lake bearing from the portage [word purposely missing]. Having passed it, we again entered on the carrying place. Our course was [word missing]. After walking about [word missing] we came to a very beautiful lake. . . ."[10]

Washington might have had second thoughts about the feasibility of the route if he could have talked with Montresor. The captain, who referred to his mission as "My discovery in 1761 of the unexplored Lands between Canada and Fort Halifax, on Kennebee River, with a party of savages," excluded his personal experiences in his official journal.[11] Writing years later about the mission, Montresor noted that he was "suffering from a loss of appetite from derangement of my System, for having been distressed by Famine for 13 days" during his 1761 trip across Maine.[12]

Fortunately, Washington had another source about the route. His informant was Ruben Colburn, a Maine businessman and militia captain who owned two-and-a-half square miles of land in the lower Kennebec Valley. Colburn also owned a saw mill and boat-building business, both located on his land. Colburn got into the boat building business by chance. He arrived in the Kennebec River Valley interested in entering into some profitable ventures. An English shipwright named Thomas Agry immigrated to the region in 1763 and settled near Colburn. The quantity of fine trees that grew in the region, including white oak and pine, impressed Agry. There were few similar trees in England, where many of the best had been cut down to build ships ages ago. Colburn and Agry became friends and decided to go into the shipbuilding business together. Colburn eventually built a sawmill upriver where felled trees were dragged and sawed into planking, which was then floated down the Kennebec to his boatyard.

Colburn and Agry were not the only ones building boats along the lower Kennebec River. In fact, a three-mile stretch of river front along the western shore of the lower Kennebec known as the Long Reach (modern Bath, Maine) was one of the best places in America to build ships. This area had a gently sloping shore on which to lay a keel and a channel that was wide and deep enough to launch a newly built ship. Ships were built along the Long Reach as early as 1743, when Jonathan Philbrick and his two sons constructed a schooner on the site. By the 1760s, several large shipyards were building full-rigged ships, including the *Earl of Bute* (built by shipbuilder William Swanton) and the 90-ton sloop *Merry Meeting* (built by John Patten, John Fulton, and Adam Hunter). In 1772, Patten, Fulton, and Hunter fabricated the ship *Industry*, which sailed from the Kennebec River for the West Indies with a cargo of boards, shingles, and ships masts. Kennebec yards were also turning out ships for English merchants, including the *Rising Sun* and the *Moon* for London businessman John Ayles. Once the war started, these same yards switched to making privateers (privately owned warships licensed to seize enemy merchant ships) like the *Black Prince*. Colburn and Agry's boatyard was farther upriver from the big operations along the Long Reach. Their yard specialized in the construction of fishing boats and small coastal trading ships.[13]

Colburn traveled to Cambridge, at his own expense, to promote the Kennebec-CaudiPre route when rumors reached Maine that such an attack was under consideration by the American high command. Colburn realized that a military expedition through the region would boost its infant economy. In particular, he wanted to get the contract to build the fleet of small boats that would be required for an American assault on Quebec via the Kennebec River. Colburn arrived in Cambridge on August 13, 1775, with spectacular proof of the feasibility of Montresor's route in the personage of a delegation of Canadian Indians, led by Chief Swashan, who had recently completed the overland trip from Quebec to Maine. Swashan and his followers were members of the Abnaki Confederacy who once lived along the coast of Maine and inland as far as Vermont and Quebec province. They knew the Kennebec and the other rivers in the region, "on whose banks they raised their rude harvests, and whose streams they ascended to hunt moose and bear in the forest desert of Northern Maine. . . ."[14] Staunch allies of the French during the period that preceded the American Revolution, disease had killed many of these Indians, and the rest withdrew to Canada when the French retreated from their outposts on the New England frontier. Seeking French protection, the displaced Abnaki took up residence in the Indian missionary village of St. Francis in Quebec, where the British erroneously started calling them the St. Francis Indians. The name stuck and was taken up by the Americans living in New England.

Some of these Indians, including Chief Swashan, were unhappy under British rule. The chief decided to offer his services to the Americans, and set out with four warriors for New England following the old Indian trail from Quebec to the coast of Maine.[15] This route passed through the lower Kennebec River Valley, home to some of their favorite camping places. They particularly liked Swan Island, a beautiful isle that split the lower Kennebec into two channels. The western channel—called Swan Alley by the first white settlers in the region—was the deeper of the two. Captain Colburn heard about the transient Indians and visited them while they were camped on Swan Island with an offer to help them complete their journey to Cambridge.[16] Colburn realized Chief Swashan and his braves, who had followed the passage described by Montresor, were proof that the route across Maine was practical. He decided to accompany Chief Swashan and his entourage to Cambridge so as to show them off at headquarters.

While the distance from Colburn's home to Cambridge seems great for the time, the trip could be made in 24 hours by sailing ship from the lower Kennebec River to one of the ports near British-held Boston (Salem, Gloucester, or Beverly, to name a few) and completing the trip by horse or carriage to Cambridge. Small American coastal sloops and schooners, operating alone and hugging the numerous bays and inlets along the coastline, were able to slip past the Royal Navy blockade of the region. It was a dangerous and expensive journey, but Colburn must have thought it worth the risk and expense, as he made the trek to headquarters three times in this manner to confer with Washington about the proposed attack on Quebec.[17]

Washington had other sources of information about the lower Kennebec River, including the people living along its shoreline. It was well known among these settlers (some of whom were serving in the Continental Army) that ocean-going ships could navigate the Kennebec for 43 miles inland to an old French and Indian military post called Fort Western. Washington's New England officers informed him of a long portage—the Great Carry—between the Kennebec and one of its branches known as the Dead River, so called because large sections of it had almost no current and was considered stagnant or "dead." Though few white men ever had seen the Dead River, it was known by the Indians who hunted in the area. Montresor's journal explained that the Dead River changed its character in upper Maine from a meandering waterway to a labyrinth of ponds, lakes, and streams called the Chain of Ponds. An army following its main channel, through the lower section of the Chain of Ponds, would reach a trail that headed up and over the Height of Land, the last ridge of mountains separating New England from Canada. Once in Canada, the trail led to Lake Megantic, a large body of water that was the source of the Chaudiere River, which in turn flowed north into the St. Lawrence River near Quebec City.

The route seemed straightforward, and advocates of the plan believed that a lightly equipped, fast-moving army without artillery could cover the distance in 20 days. In reality, with the exception of Captain Monstresor, the plan's advocates were pitifully ignorant of the terrain through which the route traveled, what the nineteenth-century historian Francis Parkman called the "unbroken forest" of Maine. "Only along the rocky seaboard or on the lower waters of one or two great rivers, a few rough settlements had gnawed slight indentations into this wilderness of woods," wrote Parkman. He continued:

> The rest was forest, pressed together in struggling confusion. Seen from above, the Maine forest was a sea of verdure basking in light; seen from below, all was shadow, through which spots of timid sunshine steal down among legions of lank, mossy trunks, toadstools and rank ferns, protruding roots, matted bushes, and rotting carcasses of fallen trees.[18]

Washington was awestruck by the stories he heard about the ease of attacking Quebec through Maine. He went ahead with the idea, referring to it early on as an expedition. The term expedition had a specific meaning at the time, which a contemporary military dictionary defined as "quickness, applied to time, motion, marching or attacking an enemy." It said that "the slow rules of a great war will not do in expeditions; the stroke must be struck with surprise. . . . Hence the very name of an expedition implies risk, hazard, precarious warfare, and a critical operation."[19] The nature of an expedition required a bold and courageous officer capable of operating independently and making decisions as events unfolded. Finding such a leader was a problem for Washington, who had a low opinion of many of the New England officers he inherited when he took command of the Continental Army. He revealed his sentiments in a confidential letter he penned to his cousin Lund:

Camp at Cambridge Augt 20, 1775 . . . their Officers generally
speaking are the most indifferent kind of People I ever saw. I have
already broke one Colo.[colonel] and five Captain's for Cowardice,
& for drawing more Pay & Provision's than they had Men in their
Companies. there are two more Colos. now under arrest, & to be
tried for the same Offences. . . . I daresay the Men would fight very
well (if properly Officered) although they are an exceeding dirty &
nasty people. Had they been properly conducted at Bunkers Hill (on
the 17th of June) or those that were there properly supported, the
Regulars would have met with a shameful defeat; & a much more
considerable loss than they did.[20]

Washington was contemplating a suitable commander for the
planned expedition when Benedict Arnold walked into his office for his
interview. The general likely was familiar with Arnold's assertive but
controversial command in upper New York, and he was curious to meet
him. The date of Arnold's meeting with Washington is a matter of
speculation, but it must have taken place on or about August 10. At the
time, Arnold's lone friend in Congress, Silas Deane, was part of a
congressional delegation that traveled to Cambridge to meet with
Washington and inspect the army. It is possible that Deane arranged the
initial meeting between Washington and Arnold. Other evidence
supporting the date of the first meeting as approximately August 10 is a
letter Washington wrote Schuyler on the 14th, in which he asked for
some lead (from which musket balls were made) that had been stockpiled
by the British at Fort Ticonderoga. Washington told Schuyler: "I am
informed it is very considerable, and that a part of it may be spared
without exposing you to any Inconveniency."[21] It is reasonable to assume
that Washington learned about the lead from Arnold, who had knowledge
of the stores captured at the fort.

Washington probably discussed his idea of a "sudden incursion
[sic]" into Canada during his first meeting with Arnold.[22] Arnold wanted
to resume his military career and used this opportunity to ask Washington
if he could participate in the mission. He offered to serve as a volunteer
but also let the commander in chief know that he desired a commission in
the Continental Army at a rank that would not compromise his honor.
Washington said he would think about it, and the two men parted. Arnold
returned to Watertown to press for the reimbursement of his expenses,
while the commander in chief continued to ponder the bold scheme to

surprise and capture the small garrison reported to be defending Quebec City.

Washington knew that there was only about a month of good campaigning weather left that year, and that he had to decide quickly if he was going to launch an attack against Quebec. After thinking over the situation for a few days, he decided to go ahead with the mission, and announced that he had selected the relatively inexperienced Arnold as its commander. It was not an impulsive decision—Washington liked Arnold from the start, and believed the former Connecticut businessman to be a bold, enterprising officer capable of leading an independent corps.

Washington had a knack for picking the right man for a job, a talent he acquired during his long-time experience as a businessman, politician, and army officer. He also possessed the imagination and self-confidence to shun conventional thinking and follow his intuition. Furthermore, Arnold's visits to Quebec before the war and his knowledge of the city and its approaches had worked in his favor. Arnold scored additional high marks when he sent Washington an operational plan for a Canadian expedition through Maine following their initial meeting. There is no known record of Arnold's report, but it must have impressed the commander in chief.[23]

As an obscure officer selected for high command by Washington, Arnold was not unique. Among Washington's other choices were Henry Knox and Nathanael Greene. Knox was a former Boston bookseller with a talent for artillery and Greene was a successful Rhode Island merchant with a genius for organization. Arnold, Knox, and Greene proved to be excellent choices for their respective assignments. In Arnold's case, he was a brilliant, courageous, and fast-thinking battlefield tactician.

Having found a commander for his Canadian expedition, Washington sought out Schuyler's approval of his plan before putting it into action. The general outlined his idea in a letter to Schuyler, dated August 20. "The design of this Express is to communicate to you a plan of an Expedition, which has engrossed my Thoughts for several Days," Washington wrote. "It is to penetrate into Canada by way of Kennebeck River, and so to Quebec. . . ." The letter included Washington's belief that a second assault on Canada in support of Schuyler's would force Carlton to divert troops from Montreal to defend Quebec: "He must either break up [abandon Montreal] or follow this party to Quebec, by which he will leave you a free passage or suffer that important Place

[Quebec] to fall into our Hands. . . . Not a Moment's Time is to be lost in the Preparation for this Enterprise, if the advices from you favor it."[24] Washington entrusted his letter to Arnold's friend Eleazer Oswald with instructions to wait for Schuyler's reply.

Increasingly concerned about the lateness of the season, Washington decided to launch his secret attack on Quebec without waiting for Schuyler's response. Plans were already underway when Oswald returned to headquarters on September 2 with Schuyler's reply, in which he gave his enthusiastic endorsement of the mission. "I thank your Excellency for the honor you have done me in communicating me your plan for an expedition into Canada," he wrote. "Your Excellency will easily conceive that I felt happy to learn your intentions, and only wished that the thought had struck you sooner."[25]

On the same day that he received Schuyler's reply, Washington wrote to Governor John Trumbull of Connecticut to inform him the assault aimed at Quebec was underway. "I may in Confidence inform you that I am about to detach 1000 or 1200 Men on an Expedition into Canada by Way of Kennebeck River from which I have the greatest Reason to expect either that Quebeck will fall into our Hands a very easy Prey or such a Diversion made as will open a very easy Passage to General Schuyler."[26] Military protocol at the time dictated that a force of this size be commanded by a colonel. This accounts for Arnold's commission as a colonel in the Continental Army.

Uneasy with the criticism he had heard of Arnold's derisive behavior toward some of his fellow officers, the commander in chief made it clear to Arnold that he must obey Schuyler when his expeditionary force reached Canada. Washington mentioned this point in a letter he wrote to Schuyler on September 8: "I shall take Care in my Instructions to Colonel Arnold, that in Case there should be a Junction of the Detachment with your army, you shall have no Difficult in adjusting the Scale of Command."[27]

It was possible, however, that the war would end before the Quebec expedition could take off. There were many influential Americans, both inside and outside of Congress, who felt that more should be done to seek a peaceful reconciliation with Great Britain before resorting to more bloodshed. They also criticized Congress' decision to order General Schuyler to invade Canada as an offensive step that went beyond the intent of the rebellion. On July 8, the moderates in Congress drafted what became known as the "Olive Branch Petition," a final statement of the colonists' concerns and hopes for a peaceful resolution of their grievances. Congress hurried Richard Penn and Arthur Lee to England to present their petition to the king. Typical of the comments at the time were those of North Carolina Congressman Joseph Hewes, who wrote to a business acquaintance in England in late July, "We do not want to be independent, we want no revolution. . . . Petition again; the eyes of our most gracious Sovereign may yet be opened and he may see what things are for his real interest before they are eternally hid from his eyes."[28] As he moved ahead with his secret attack against Quebec, Washington shared the hope that news would arrive from London that peace had been restored.

Washington's control of the planning phase of the Quebec campaign is evident from his extant orders and letters. For example, writing to Schuyler on September 8, Washington said, "I am much engaged in sending off the Detachment under Col: Arnold. . . ."[29] Washington, a brilliant organizer and administrator, was fascinated by military science. The commander had the opportunity to learn army administration when he served as an aide-de-camp to two of the greatest military administrators of the British army, Generals William Braddock and John Forbes, during the French and Indian War. Washington studied their administrative techniques to the point of copying their written orders for future reference. Among the planning decisions Washington made early on was that everyone on the perilous mission had to be a volunteer and in good physical condition.

Since the expedition was a temporary assignment, Washington organized it as two provisional (temporary) combat battalions of musket men (infantry) with the usual compliment of officers. In addition, three of the rifle companies recently arrived in Cambridge from the Pennsylvania and Virginia frontier would accompany the infantry, bringing the total force to about 1,150 men.

Three hundred miles northwest from Cambridge, another competent American military administrator, Philip Schuyler, was hard at work organizing an invasion of Canada. The key to Schuyler's thrust into Canada was transportation. He planned to use the interconnecting waterways of northern New York to reach Montreal. While some members of Congress criticized his seemingly stalled invasion, Schuyler actually was hard at work building a fleet of boats to carry his men and equipment into Canada. By the end of August, Schuyler had 60 vessels capable of carrying 1,300 men with a three-week supply of provisions.[30]

Most of the boats that Schuyler had constructed were called bateaux (the singular is spelled bateau), sturdy vessels developed by the French for use in the inland waterways of Canada. Simple in design and easy to construct by relatively unskilled laborers and soldiers, bateaux could be fitted with sails for operations in places like Lake Champlain or rowed in narrower, shallower bodies of water like the Richelieu River. Though Bateaux could be built in any size, they all shared similar characteristics: they were double-ended (pointed both bow and stern) with flat bottoms and slanting sides that allowed them to carry a large payload in relation to their size. The Americans adopted the bateau for a wide variety of military and civilian applications. Those Schuyler built were about 30 feet long, with a cargo capacity of three to four tons. Arnold's Canadian expedition planned to use a fleet of bateaux to transport its provisions, equipment, and supplies, and Captain Colburn wanted the contract to build them.

Colburn was making headway in his efforts to get the contract to build the bateaux for Arnold's invasion force. In a letter dated August 21, Arnold asked Colburn, on behalf of "His Excellency General Washington," for "particular information" about the route across Maine to Quebec City. Arnold was also interested in knowing if Colburn could build 200 bateaux on short order, which had to be "Capable of Carrying Six or Seven Men each with their Provisions & Baggage, (say 100 wt.[pounds] to each man)."[31]

It was probably sometime during this planning stage that Washington's planned intrusion into Canada began to be called the Arnold Expedition. The first known use of the term appeared in an October 4, 1775, letter Washington wrote to Schuyler, in which he noted, "Arnold's Expedition is so connected with your operations that I thought it most proper to detain him till I could give you the fullest account of his progress."[32] However, the commander's use of the term in his October 4 letter likely echoed the general acceptance of the name already being used to identify the independent corps. Also possible is that the term Arnold Expedition was adopted because it was vague and did not provide any clues to the size or objective of the mission.

Washington and his small headquarters staff continued to plan the campaign in concert with Arnold. They decided that Fort Western (present day Augusta, Maine), built by Massachusetts provincial troops during the French and Indian War, was the logical jumping-off point for the attack on Quebec, as it was located at the height of ship navigation (i.e., the farthest upstream point that a ship could sail) on Maine's Kennebec River and only a few miles upriver from Colburn's shipyard.

Washington next had to decide how Arnold's men would get from Cambridge to Fort Western safely, quickly, and well rested. A speedy passage was critical to the success of the operation, because winter came early to northern Maine and Canada and the expedition had to reach Quebec before the deep snow and cold weather made travel treacherous. Arnold's corps also had to move fast if it was to reach Quebec before the British could reinforce the place. Traveling overland was not an attractive option. Massachusetts, though settled 150 years prior to the start of the Revolutionary War, had a primitive road system. And while the Massachusetts roads were crude, those in Maine were much worse, resembling little more than muddy forest trails linking the region's sparsely populated coastal towns and isolated frontier settlements. In addition, almost all of the rivers along the land route to Fort Western would need to be forded by ferries, a painfully slow process for an army of over 1,000 men with equipment and personal baggage. It would take weeks for Arnold's corps to reach Fort Western using the available roads, and the men probably would arrive exhausted. Therefore, sailing by ship from the Cambridge area to Fort Western was the logical answer. The only problem was that the Royal Navy patrolled the New England coast and the Americans had no warships or armed merchant ships with which to oppose them. Even a small Royal Navy sloop posed a threat to a fleet of unarmed merchant vessels. The danger for American transports was heightened by the fear that a British spy or informer could tip-off the Royal Navy to the activity in the rebel camp.

The movement of 1,000 Continental troops along the New England coast by ship depended on secrecy and luck. Washington reduced the risk by ordering Arnold's men to sail for Fort Western on Maine's Kennebec River from an American-held New England seaport that was a safe distance from the Royal Navy base at Boston. At Fort Western, the expedition would off-load its men and equipment and follow Montresor's inland river route to Quebec in Colburn's bateaux.

Washington also decided that the expedition's prodigious supply of food, ammunition, tents, blankets, tools, medical supplies, and personnel baggage would be transported to Quebec by boat, while the troops would use the Indian paths and frontier traces that paralleled the route's waterways. This scheme eliminated any need for a cumbersome baggage train of horse-drawn wagons that typically accompanied an eighteenth century army. In fact, it is not by coincidence that all the battles fought during the American Revolution took place near roads; the armies of the time were dependent on their lengthy wagon trains of food and equipment in order to function.

The Arnold Expedition would be costly, and Washington had to find the money to finance it as he maintained his expensive blockade of Boston. His major source of funding were Continental notes (paper money) whose credibility was based on the people's confidence in Congress' ability to support the currency through taxes and other income.[33] The individual English colonies used paper money to provide a medium of exchange to finance their participation in earlier wars against France and Spain. The colonies pooled their experiences and resources in 1775 to issue their first emission of Continental notes, pledging the faith of the 13 colonies to its redemption. Congress printed two million dollars worth of paper money in June 1775 and another million in July, and Washington used some of it to finance the Arnold Expedition.[34] Continental notes were accepted at face value at this early stage in the conflict.

While we do not know the total cost of the Arnold Expedition, George Washington left a record of the amount of paper money issued to Arnold just before he left Cambridge. Washington was a meticulous record keeper, and a review of his headquarters papers shows that on September 10 he ordered James Warren, the paymaster general of the Continental Army, to give Arnold "so much Continental Money as will make up the whole Sum £1000 lawful [lawful indicates Massachusetts currency]."[35] Based on the daily wage of an unskilled laborer in Massachusetts in 1775, £1,000 had the equivalent buying power of about $115,000 in twenty-first century dollars. We also know that Washington signed pay warrants—money to pay his troops—to Arnold on September 13 for additional large sums of Continental money totaling £4,342 in Massachusetts currency.[36] This equals about an additional $500,000 in today's money.

Another medium of exchange provided Arnold were sterling bills of exchange, printed documents that functioned similarly to modern-day certified checks. The bills of exchange circulating in colonial America were drawn by Americans on British merchant firms who guaranteed to honor them at their face value. Though made payable to a specific individual, they could be endorsed and negotiated by whomever held them. Bills of exchange represented a safe and convenient way of transferring large sums of money from the colonies to Britain. There were still bills of exchange in circulation in America when the war started, and Arnold probably was given some with which to make large purchases when he reached Canada. Bills of exchange would disappear as the war continued and the money supply became tighter.

Additional financing for the expedition came from the personal fortunes or credit of the officers who led it. At one point during the campaign, for example, Arnold offered his personal credit to purchase clothing and food for his troops.[37] Men looking for the prestige and social status associated with command of a regiment had a better chance of receiving an appointment if they agreed to pay part of the cost of sending out recruiting parties and purchasing weapons, uniforms, tents, etc., for their soldiers. Several of the Quebec expedition's senior officers, including Arnold, were wealthy men who may have advanced some of their own money or credit to outfit the campaign.

The paper money issued by the Continental Congress or any of the individual colonies would not be accepted in Canada, where Arnold would need hard currency in the form of gold and silver coins to purchase food and other necessaries from the country folk and merchants. He also needed cash to pay for Indian auxiliaries and spies. We know that Arnold was carrying a quantity of coins with him from a letter written by Washington, in which he said that he had given Arnold "£1000 lawful money in Specie to answer his contingent Charges."[38] This important statement requires an explanation, especially since treasure hunters continue to scour Maine looking for Arnold's supposed lost chest of money. "Specie" refers to hard currency, which confirms that Arnold was carrying coins, probably in a sturdy box or chest in accordance with military practice of the day. Massachusetts had minted some coins in small denominations prior to the war, but these were scattered to the trade winds or had long since been melted down or lost by 1775. The specie that Arnold had with him was a variety of foreign coins still in circulation in the colonies: doubloons, silver dollars, pistoles, etc. The term "lawful" again indicates Massachusetts currency. Washington established the value of the hodgepodge of foreign coins he gave Arnold in terms of Massachusetts currency. Finally, "contingent charges" meant unexpected or unspecified costs. The word contingent is defined by a military dictionary in use during the Revolutionary War as "something casual or uncertain, that may or may not happen."[39]

Based on what is known about the financing of the Arnold Expedition, we can summarize that Arnold was carrying the modern equivalent of $615,000 in paper money issued by the Continental Congress to pay his officers and men and to purchase goods and services while he was in American territory, as well as a money chest containing the equivalent of $115,000 in today's currency in coins. In addition to paper money and cash, Arnold had with him an unknown dollar amount in bills of exchange with which to make large purchases from merchants when he reached Canada, plus his personal credit and/or the personal credit of his officers, who would guarantee payment against their own wealth and honor. Adding to the expedition's cost were a host of additional expenses—including Colburn's boat contract, clothing, tents, weapons, gunpowder, provisions, and transportation—paid for directly by the Continental Army. Since there is no record of a paymaster accompanying Arnold, the expedition's war chest was probably entrusted to Oswald, Arnold's volunteer aide-de-camp and trusted friend. Stories that the money chest was lost during the trek to Canada and still lies buried in the shifting sands of the Kennebec River are pure myth. There is no mention of a lost treasure chest in any of the known letters, diaries, or documents from the expedition. There are, however, numerous references to hard currency being spent throughout the campaign.

Financial historian Robert E. Wright has explained that money was scarce at the time, its buying power considerably greater than it is today, even after it is converted to current dollars. Wright argues that the Arnold Expedition was a costly undertaking, "especially when considered in terms of the colonies' total output of goods and services."[40] Washington, however, likely would have argued that the campaign was worth any cost; if victorious, it would spare the colonies the additional loss of blood and treasure by helping to end the war.

Washington entrusted the ocean transport phase of the campaign to Nathaniel Tracy (Harvard Class of 1769), a 24-year-old merchant residing in Newburyport, Massachusetts. Tracy was part of an elite pre-war commercial network made up of wealthy merchants and landowners who knew each other through reputation, recommendation, and cooperative business ventures. Businessmen like Washington and Tracy tended to cooperate on speculative land deals and other business ventures to protect their mutual interests and spread the risks among several investors. As one of the richest men in America, Washington may have known Tracy from his pre-war business transactions, or perhaps Tracy was recommended to Washington by Colonel John Glover, one of the general's advisors at the time. Glover was a successful ship owner and merchant from Marblehead, Massachusetts, who organized a regiment composed mostly of seamen at the outbreak of the war. His so-called "web footed regiment" was at Cambridge when Washington took command of the army. As fellow Massachusetts ship owners and merchants, it is probable that Glover and Tracy knew one another from business dealings or by reputation. Tracy's shipping empire was headquartered in the town of Newburyport, Massachusetts, a small but active seaport situated on the south bank of the Merrimac River about three miles inland from the Atlantic Ocean and 35 miles northeast of Boston.

Tracy's instructions from headquarters, in the handwriting of Joseph Reed, Washington's military secretary, were signed by the commander in chief on September 2. This is the earliest known document that moved the secret attack on Quebec from contemplation to reality, and marks the official start of the Arnold Expedition. Here is the key passage from Washington's instructions to Tracy: "You are hereby authorized & empowered to take up for the Service of the sd Colonies so many Vessels as shall be necessary for the transporting a Body of Troops to be detached from this Army on a secret Expedition. . . ."[41]

Reed sent a follow-up letter to Tracy alerting him that seven small ships had been located at the coastal towns of Massachusetts "fitted out for another Purpose, but will answer the Present equally well. . . . It will be a saving both in Time & Expence to make Use of these, You will therefore be pleased in your Transaction of this Matter to consider these seven Vessells as Part of the Transports, & only extend your Care to the Remainder."[42] Tracy was expected to make a modest profit for his efforts, which was customary at the time. The army's paymaster general sent Tracy a large cash advance to help finance the leasing of the additional boats, fitting them out as military transports and purchasing supplies and provisions.

The expedition moved further along the following day, when Ruben Colburn received the contract to build the boats it required. The most important part read, "You are to go with all Expedition to Gardnerstone [Gardinerston] upon the River Kenebeck, and without Delay proceed to The Constructing of Two Hundred Batteaus." Colburn was also instructed to hire a company of 20 men, "consisting of Artificers [unskilled laborers], Carpenters, and Guides to go under your Command to Assist in such Services as you & they, may be called upon to Execute."[43] In other words, Colburn was to hire a group of civilian boat builders, carpenters, and river men to accompany the expedition to help handle the boats and keep them in good repair. In the same contract, Colburn was directed to arrange for all the provisions he could muster in the Kennebec River region, including 500 bushels of Indian corn and 60 barrels of beef.[44]

Washington's request was probably beyond anything that Colburn had anticipated. The contract to build the boats, supply provisions for the army, and accompany it with a party of civilian workers and boatmen was a windfall for Colburn's business. Such an exciting opportunity to help the rebellion while earning some money elated him. Colonel Joseph Farnsworth received an appointment as Arnold's commissary officer at this time. As commissary officer, Farnsworth was responsible for "furnishing the army in the field with all sorts of provisions, forage, &c. by contract. . . ."[45] Farnsworth and Colburn left Cambridge together for Maine to prepare for Arnold's arrival. They stopped at Newburyport, where they purchased some provisions and equipment before sailing for the Kennebec.[46]

Another important aspect of the expedition's planning was the selection of officers. Washington probably allowed Arnold to pick his own. Giving Arnold such latitude was consistent with Washington's management style, which was to delegate responsibility to trusted subordinates. He likely gave Arnold some advice and guidance, recommending energetic, courageous officers for the expedition, and then allowed Arnold to choose the men he wanted, subject to Washington's veto.

By September 5, Arnold was actively recruiting for his secret mission. The General Orders for that date included a notice that a detachment would be selected the following morning "to go upon Command with Col: Arnold of Connecticut. . . . As it is imagined the

Officers and Men sent from the Regiments both here [Cambridge], and at Roxbury, will be such Volunteers, as are active Woodsmen, and well acquainted with batteaus; so it is recommended, that none but such will offer themselves for this service." The order specified that Arnold was raising a detachment consisting of two lieutenant colonels, two majors, 10 captains, 30 each of subalterns (junior officers), sergeants, and corporals, four drummers, two fifers, and 676 common soldiers (privates). The September 5 General Order also stated that Colonel Arnold was raising additional men for his expedition from the newly arrived rifle companies.[47]

The response for volunteers was overwhelming, partly because life in the Continental Army at the time was tedious and boring, but also because there was a martial passion in the rebel camp, with everyone eager for a chance to fight the Redcoats before the war was over.

Arnold selected his officers first, and seemed particularly interested in those who had distinguished themselves at the recently fought Battle of Bunker Hill. It is not by coincidence, therefore, that a number of his officers were veterans of that fight, including Samuel McCobb, Henry Dearborn, and Christian Febiger. A majority of Arnold's officers not surprisingly hailed from Massachusetts, since troops from that colony made up the bulk of the Continental Army at the time. However, Arnold also chose officers from New Hampshire, Rhode Island, and Connecticut for the mission.

The officers invited to join the expedition were allowed to select the common soldiers for the campaign, and they tended to pick men they knew from their former commands. For example, 24-year-old Captain Henry Dearborn selected men from his old New Hampshire detachment to serve under him. Arnold, perhaps on advice from Washington, encouraged this sense of community for the expedition; he wanted men who had worked together previously as neighbors, prewar militiamen, and soldiers in the Continental Army.

The call for volunteers also encouraged men experienced in the handling of small river boats to apply. It took experience to know how to load, trim, and maneuver the boats expected to carry from 100 to 200 pound barrels of food and supplies up the Kennebec River. Thus, soldiers who had experience with river boats were selected for the expedition and distributed among the various detachments. Three days after the call for volunteers went out, the names of those accompanying Arnold were removed from the duty rolls and told to report to Cambridge no later than Saturday morning, September 9.[48]

During this time, 19-year-old Aaron Burr was in Cambridge seeking a commission as an officer in the patriot army. Despite his distinguished family background and college education, young Burr was having difficulties finding an opening when he heard about the call for volunteers for a secret expedition. Burr and his friend Mathias Odgen, also in camp looking for a commission, sought out Arnold to see if they could join his corps as officers. Arnold told the two eager young patriots that he already had a full compliment of officers, but that they could accompany his corps as gentleman volunteers without military rank or official status.[49] This arrangement was common at the time—it gave aspiring young officers an opportunity to demonstrate their potential and, hopefully, to be rewarded with a commission. One young Revolutionary War gentleman volunteer accurately described his situation when he said, "I am neither an Officers nor a Soldier."[50] Since only generals were authorized to have a personal aide, lesser officers used these unpaid gentlemen as unofficial aides-de-camp to write orders and keep records. Gentleman volunteers were expected to pay all their own expenses while serving in the army.

With recruiting complete, 1,150 men, along with four women "belonging to the army," made up the Arnold Expedition. Arnold occupied the highest post, as commander, and relied a small headquarters staff to assist him. Most important among his staff was his adjutant, or administrative officer, Christian Febiger, a native of Copenhagen, Denmark. Arnold's staff also included a quartermaster—Benjamin Chatlin—whose job it was to organize and supervise transportation, locate forage, decide where to camp and distribute rations, ammunition, and clothing.[51] Chatlin, who came from Wethersfield, Connecticut, an important commercial center located on the Connecticut River, probably had a mercantile background, which was helpful in his position as quartermaster. A detail of private soldiers, known as the camp color men, assisted Quartermaster Chatlin.[52]

Eleazer Oswald, Arnold's prewar friend and confidant, acted as the commander's aide-de-camp, or personal assistant, though he was not listed officially as a member of Arnold's staff, because Congress dictated that only generals could have aides-de-camp on the army payroll. To circumvent this regulation, Oswald was designated an unpaid volunteer.

Arnold's headquarters staff also included a surgeon, Dr. Isaac Senter, and a chaplain, Samuel Spring. Senter, born in 1753, was a native of Londonderry, New Hampshire. He was studying medicine in Newport, Rhode Island, with Dr. Thomas Moffat when the war started. Senter joined the Rhode Island militia as a surgeon, marched with them to Cambridge, and remained with the army. He had several helpers, known as surgeon's mates, assigned to him during the expedition. Samuel Spring, born in 1746, was a recent graduate of the College of New Jersey (today's Princeton University).[53]

The expedition consisted of two provisional infantry battalions and three rifle companies.[54] The two infantry battalions—referred to throughout the campaign as the first and second battalions—contained a total of 886 men divided equally between them. A lieutenant colonel, with his own adjutant and quartermaster, commanded each battalion. Next to Arnold, these battalion commanders were the most important men on the expedition. Lieutenant Colonel Christopher Greene, age 38, led the first battalion. Born in 1737 in Warwick, Rhode Island, Greene was the son of a judge and a descendant of John Greene, a surgeon from England, who settled in Rhode Island in 1637. There is no known record of Greene's childhood or education, thought he must have been a person of some education, as he represented Kent County in the 1771 and 1772 sessions of the Rhode Island legislature. Greene earned his living in his family's ironworks and sawmills prior to the war. These enterprises, including the forging of ships' anchors, were located on the south branch of Rhode Island's Pawtuxet River. Active in the local militia, Greene was a lieutenant in Kent County's elite company, the Kentish Guards, which had answered the first alarm and marched off to Cambridge at the start of the war. Greene probably fought at the Battle of Bunker Hill. He was also politically well-connected and married to a daughter of Samuel Ward, who served three terms as Rhode Island's governor before he was elected as a delegate to the Continental Congress.[55] Christopher's cousin, Nathanael Greene, was a general in the Continental Army and one of George Washington's closest advisors.[56]

Christopher Greene participated in the siege of Boston and received a promotion to major in the newly organized Rhode Island Continental Line regiment commanded by General James Varnum. His second in command during the Arnold Expedition was Major Timothy Bigelow

(1739-1790), a former blacksmith and militia officer from Worcester, Massachusetts.

Arnold's second battalion was commanded by Lieutenant Colonel Roger Enos. Born in Simsbury, Connecticut, in 1729, Enos traced his American ancestry back to his great-grandfather, who came to Connecticut from England in 1646. At 46, Enos was one of the oldest members of the expedition. He also had the most military experience of any man on the mission. As a young man, Enos saw combat in Canada during the French and Indian War and participated in the arduous 1762 British campaign that captured Havana, Cuba. Following the Havana campaign, Enos was appointed captain in the regiment commanded by Israel Putnam, Connecticut's legendary Indian fighter, in the 1764 campaign against the Indians.   Enos was a lieutenant colonel commanding the 2nd Connecticut regiment when he joined the Arnold Expedition. Enos' second in command was Major Return Jonathan Meigs (1740-1823), a merchant from Middletown, Connecticut, and the son of Return Meigs, a hatter and member of the Connecticut General Assembly.[57]

Events would prove that, with the exception of Enos, Arnold made excellent choices in the selection of the expedition's senior officers. In fact, a surprisingly large number of them continued to serve following the Arnold Expedition and made important contributions to the winning of the war.

Both of Arnold's two battalions consisted of five companies, with a captain in command of each. Besides a captain, every company had two lieutenants, 12 non-commissioned officers (sergeants and corporals), and about 75 enlisted men. One of the most important company captains on the expedition was Henry Dearborn from New Hampshire, who led his militia regiment to Cambridge immediately following the Lexington alarm. Dearborn was educated to be a doctor and practiced with his father, Simon, until the start of the war, when he abandoned medicine in favor of a commission as a line officer. Dearborn survived the war and went on to be elected to the U.S. Congress (1792-1797), after which he served as the secretary of war throughout Thomas Jefferson's two presidential administrations.[58] Dearborn kept one of the most complete journals during the Arnold Expedition, which included a list of all of the officers ranked captain and above on the campaign. Below is the list of the officers on the Arnold Expedition as they appeared in Dearborn's journal:

Officers of the 2nd Battalion	Officers of the 1st Battalion
Lieut Colo Roger Enos	Lieut Colo Christopher Green
Majr Return J. Meigs	Major Timothy Biggelloe [Bigelow]
Captain Thomas Williams	Capt Saml Ward
Captain Henry Dearborn	Capt Simeon Thayre [Thayer]
Captain Scott	Capt John Topham
Captain Oliver Hanchett	Capt McCobb
Captain William Goodrich	Capt Jonas Hubbard[59]

The balance of the troops on the mission—outside of the two infantry battalions—were riflemen, whom Dearborn called light infantry. He used this term in his diary, when he noted that Arnold's "detachment consisted of Eleven hundred Men; Two Battalion[s] of Musket-men, and three Companies of Rifle-men as Lighte-Infantry." The term light infantry at the time referred to elite troops specially trained for scouting, raiding, and other dangerous assignments. Though the British army utilized special companies of light infantrymen at the start of the war, the Americans did not, believing at the time that riflemen could be substituted for light infantry. Washington and Arnold thought riflemen would be an asset to the expedition. Additionally, Washington was eager for a chance to rid himself of the riflemen, who he viewed as disruptive troublemakers.

Much of what has been written about rifles and riflemen during the American Revolution is romantic legend. Since riflemen played an important role in the Arnold Expedition, it behooves us to understand the rifle and the character of the men who used them.

The common civilian and military weapon of the time was a flintlock musket. Inexpensive to manufacture, it possessed a smooth bore (gun barrel) and could be loaded and fired three to four times a minute by an experienced soldier. Its sturdy barrel could also hold a bayonet. Rifles, in comparison, had grooved barrels, were costly to manufacture, and took an expert to fire accurately. Rifles existed throughout America, but the necessity of owning one outside of the frontier decreased by the time of the Revolutionary War, as most of the large game and hostile Indians in the settled area of New England had been killed or run off.[60] In addition, thrifty New England farmers had little interest in expensive guns.

A rifle could be fired accurately at almost three times the distance of a musket (300 yards for a rifle vs. 100 for a musket). Its grooved barrel, which fired the ball on a straight course at high velocity, was the reason for the weapon's accuracy and long range. American-made rifles at the time of the Revolutionary War were called long rifles, and some of the best were made by gunsmiths living in the vicinity of Reading and York, Pennsylvania. Although Revolutionary War-era rifles were crude by later standards (the long rifle reached its pinnacle of beauty and design as the Kentucky rifle 50 years after the end of the American Revolution), they possessed some of the slender, delicate characteristics of the postwar designs. A good rifle had a beautiful balance, allowing it to be carried comfortably in one hand.

People living on the frontier depended on their rifles to kill game at long range. Each rifleman knew the unique characteristics of his gun and how to fire it for maximum effect. However, rifles had several key drawbacks: they were complicated and time-consuming to load; their fragile barrels and stocks could not support a bayonet; and they were expensive, precisely constructed weapons that could be effectively handled only by a person who knew the unique characteristics of his gun.

The rifle's drawbacks became apparent to Washington, and he lobbied successfully for their limited use in the Continental Army. But at this early stage of the conflict, Congress was enthusiastic about raising companies of riflemen, and saddled Washington with hundreds of these restless frontiersmen with their precious rifles. Typical in his praise of riflemen was delegate John Adams, who told his wife, "These are an excellent Species of Light Infantry. . . . They are the most accurate Marksmen in the World."[61] On June 14, 1775, the Continental Congress authorized the formation of six companies of expert riflemen. These were the first units voted by Congress for the newly organized Continental Army. Congress resolved that the riflemen would serve for one year.[62]

The first rifle company to reach Cambridge was a Virginia outfit commanded by Captain Daniel Morgan. When the riflemen arrived, they went on the front lines and began picking off British sentries. When they were not taking long range pot-shots at the enemy, they were putting on shooting demonstrations for incredulous Yankee soldiers or provoking fights.

An assertive, natural-born leader, Daniel Morgan took unofficial command of the three rifle companies that marched with Arnold. He had no known formal education, a common law wife with whom he had two children, was short on conversation, and preferred to settle an argument with his fists (he stood six feet tall with broad shoulders and massive arms). However, behind his facade of frontier joking, drinking, and brawling was a serious, naturally intelligent tactician and superb leader. Morgan is credited with fighting the tactical masterpiece of the American Revolution, the 1780 Battle of Cowpens, South Carolina, where he gave the British a whale of a licking.

Little is known about Morgan's birth and early life. Several states— including New Jersey, Pennsylvania, and Virginia—claim him as a native son. He was probably born in New Jersey about 1735, the son of Welsh immigrants. His father was likely a poor farm laborer. Morgan never talked about his childhood, but it is believed that he had a bitter argument with his father and left home as a teenager. Young Morgan headed west, where there were opportunities and adventure. He followed a forest trace known as the Great Wagon Road, which began at Philadelphia, went southwest to Winchester, Virginia, and ended at the Yadkin River in North Carolina. Morgan stopped at Winchester, a lawless place on the edge of hostile Indian country, in the spring of 1753. He was 18 years old at the time, with nothing but the simple homespun clothing on his back. Morgan worked at various odd jobs until he saved enough money to purchase a team of horses and a wagon, then began hauling freight as an independent contractor. His outfit was one of many contracted by the British army during the French and Indian War. Morgan and his fellow frontier teamsters were a rough group. British officers, who viewed their disorderly behavior as a threat to discipline, detested them. After he got into a brawl with a Redcoat, a drum-head military court sentenced Morgan to receive 500 lashes on his bare back. Morgan later claimed that he retained consciousness throughout the ordeal, boasting that he kept count with the husky drummer who whipped him.[63]

In the early 1760s, Morgan became involved with a young woman named Abigail Curry, the daughter of a relatively prosperous farmer. By 1763, Morgan and Abigail were living together. Abigail bore Daniel two daughters, whom they named Nancy and Betsy. Morgan seems to have settled down in the years that followed. He bought a farm that prospered and by 1774 he owned ten slaves. He also served as a captain in the local militia. This obscure military command changed Morgan's life, as one the rifle companies authorized by Congress was to be raised in Frederick County, Virginia, where he resided. Morgan was offered the command of this newly established rifle company, which he promptly and enthusiastically accepted, and applied his enormous energies to recruiting his riflemen.

Though Congress stipulated that each rifle company would consist of 60 men, the response to Morgan's recruiting was so great that he accepted 96. One of Morgan's early biographers described his company as follows: "a finer body of men than those who composed the company were seldom seen. One that rendered better service, or than shed a brighter luster on the arms of their country, never existed."[64] Morgan's Frederick County men walked about 31 miles a day, arriving at Cambridge on August 6. Clergyman Ezra Stiles observed, "The Rifle Men commanded by Captain Daniel Morgan of Fredericks County Virginia, . . . 600 miles from Cambridge, arrived in three weeks."[65] This feat of endurance elicited considerable excitement among the New Englanders and made Morgan an instant celebrity in the American camp.

The other rifle companies authorized by Congress arrived in Cambridge behind the Virginians. One company, commanded by Captain William Hendricks of Cumberland, Pennsylvania, included private soldier George Morison, who recorded his war experiences in a journal that he kept throughout the Arnold Expedition. It begins with his account of the march his rifle company made from Carlisle, Pennsylvania, to Cambridge. Morison recorded that they walked fast, covering up to 29 miles in a day, and stopping only to enjoy the sites along their route or to tar and feather any British sympathizers who crossed their path. Traveling east from Carlisle, Hendricks' company stopped at Reading and Bethlehem. There was a convent at Bethlehem, and Morison wrote that "the nuns viewed us with apparent emotion. Many of them were young and beautiful. They expressed their concern that so many sprightly young men as we were should go face the enemy, perhaps never to return."[66] While crossing New Jersey, Hendricks' men collared a Tory, or British sympathizer, whom they tarred and feathered and "left . . . to ruminate on the quality of our manners." On July 30 they reached the Hudson River, where they stopped for a day to rest. Refreshed, they continued to Litchfield, Connecticut, where they further amused themselves by tarring and feathering another Tory. Following this ghastly ritual, they forced their naked antagonist, who was covered with feathers from head to toe, to drink to the health of Congress, after which they drummed him out of town. Having struck this latest blow for liberty, the Carlisle riflemen marched quickly to Cambridge, arriving on August 9. Despite their frequent stops, they too made incredible time, marching 441 miles in 26 days. Hendricks' rowdy Pennsylvania frontiersmen arrived at camp and promptly joined the other rifle companies in carousing and fighting with their New England brothers.

Washington believed in discipline, and insisted that the riflemen stand guard duty and dig trenches along with everyone else. The independently minded frontiersmen spurned these routine assignments, as their officers stood by unwilling or unable to control their men. One Pennsylvania riflemen was sent to the guardhouse for refusing to follow orders. A New England officer described what happened next: "[I]n about twenty minutes thirty-two of Capt. Ross' company, with their loaded rifles, swore by God they would go to the main guard and release the man or lose their lives, and set off as hard as they could run. It was in vain to attempt stopping them." The soldiers on duty "Sent word to Gen. Washington, who reinforced the guard to five hundred men with loaded pieces." On Washington's orders, the renegade riflemen were surrounded by New England troops "with their bayonets fixed, and ordered two of the ringleaders to be bound."[67] This ended the incident, but not the riflemen's defiant behavior.

There were six restless frontier rifle companies in Cambridge by September 1775. Washington determined that three of them should go to Canada with Arnold. The general realized that he would have a riot on his hands if he chose the three that would go, so it was agreed that a drawing of lots would decide the issue. This simple game appealed to the frontiersmen's sense of fair play. The lots were duly drawn, and the winners were Morgan's company from Frederick County, Virginia, and two Pennsylvania rifle companies; Captain William Hendricks'

Cumberland County unit and Captain Matthew Smith's Lancaster County men.[68]

The riflemen were an important component of the Arnold Expedition. An eyewitness noted that they carried "a rifle-barreled gun, a tomahawk, or small axe, and a long knife, usually called a scalping knife which served for all purposes, in the woods."[69] The riflemen usually dressed in a home-made hunting shirt, breeches, moccasins, or shoes. Their most distinctive piece of clothing was their hunting shirt, or frock, usually made of linen in colors and hues ranging from tan (the natural color of linen) to blues and reds. In most cases the rifleman's hunting shirt was fringed along the front opening, cape, and sleeves. Congressman Silas Deane saw some frontier riflemen in Philadelphia early in the war and he described their appearance in a letter to his wife, "They take a piece of Ticklenburgh [another name for linen derived from the German town of Tecklenburg, was famous at the time as a source for this fabric] . . . then they make a kind of Frock of it reaching down below the knee, open before, with a Large Cape, they wrapp it round them tight on a March, & tye it with their belt in which hangs their Tomahawk."[70]

There was no effort made to create a uniform, military appearance among the riflemen. They wore what they had, and their clothing was comfortable and practical. One rifleman on the expedition wrote that their clothing was "by no means in a military style." He also said they dressed "to ape the manners of savages."[71] While this statement suggests that the riflemen wore buckskin shirts, pants, and moccasins in imitation of the Indians, it is an incorrect assumption. Buckskin (clothing and shoes made from animal hides) was only worn when cloth was hard to come by or too expensive. The most common cloths available in Revolutionary War America were wool and linen. These fabrics were more durable, warmer, and dried faster than buckskin. It was especially impractical to wear clothing made of buckskin in the winter because it froze when wet.

The riflemen may have worn moccasins at times, particularly when they were hunting game over soft woodsy terrain in the summer. However, moccasins were impractical for long marches or extended military campaigns—they wore out quickly, and if they got wet, they stayed wet and clammy, or even froze in cold weather. Most riflemen wore shoes whenever they could get them. Some historians still insist that the riflemen carried extra leather with them and made new moccasins as their old ones wore out. Such a scenario is impractical. People in the eighteenth century, as today, used common sense. Why bother with the trouble of making moccasins during a campaign when shoes were sturdier, lasted longer, and were supplied for free by the army![72]

Turning to Arnold's New England musketmen, few of them had uniforms. A British spy observed some of Arnold's men prior to their departure from Cambridge and reported that the Americans "were most wretchedly clothed, and as dirty a set of mortals as every disgraced the name of a soldier. They had no clothes of any sort provided them . . . except the detachment . . . that are gone to Canada under Col. Arnold, who had each of them a new coat and a linen frock served out to them before they set out."[73] From this spy's report, and what we know about eighteenth century clothing in New England, it is probable that many of Arnold's enlisted men were issued sturdy, plain civilian short coats or jackets, most likely made from wool and dyed a brown or gray color. The jackets likely were cut short, falling a little below the hips, a popular style as it required less fabric and was faster to make than the traditional, longer coat of the era. These coats had been contracted from various sources months before for use by the army during the coming winter. Some were diverted from their original purpose in order to clothe Arnold's corps.[74] The other article of clothing mentioned in the spy's report was a frock, an oversized, simple pull-over work shirt. It was commonly made of linen and clasped by a single button at the neck. A belt was worn to cinch the frock at the waist.

Many of Arnold's infantrymen carried various types of small caliber civilian hunting guns known as fowlers, a name derived from the fact that they were used primarily to hunt birds and other small game. These guns were frequently brought from home, and were the personal property of the young men who carried them. The Americans tended to load these small-caliber muskets with double charges of ball to increase their firepower against the British, who were armed with larger-caliber muskets.

Most of the musket men on the expedition carried a variety of personal items with them, including a small knife or a hatchet, a haversack (usually holding two or three days' rations), and a knapsack or blanket roll.[75] The knapsacks or blanket rolls, carried slung over the men's backs, held spare clothing (such as an extra shirt, socks, undershirts, and drawers) and personal articles (razor, soap, comb, playing cards, fork and spoon, flint and steel to start a fire, etc.).

The musket men carried another common item—a leather cartridge box or pouch slung over the left shoulder and resting at the side just below the waist. The cartridge box held fixed ammunition, or rounds, for their muskets in the form of paper cartridges (consisting of a ball and enough gunpowder to fire the musket once). Given the frequent references in expedition members' diaries to making cartridges, it is likely that few, if any, of the infantrymen on the Arnold Expedition carried loose powder in horns. Since the Continental Army did not have the resources to supply muskets, knives, hatchets, haversacks, knapsacks, and cartridge boxes to its soldiers during this early period of the American Revolution, enlisted volunteers were expected to arrive in camp with their own. The result was an absence of uniform style, size, and quality in any of these items. The infantrymen tended to carry their belongings with them at all times (especially their personal articles and food) to prevent them from being lost or stolen.

Some of the officers on the Arnold Expedition may have had uniforms that they wore upon occasion. The Continental Army had yet to adopt clothing regulations for its officers, who were expected to provide their own clothing at their own expense. Arnold owned a uniform, which included a scarlet coat, from his prewar days as captain and commander of the 2nd Connecticut Footguards. He was spotted at a military event dressed in scarlet in April 1776, which means he probably was wearing his Connecticut Footguards uniform on important occasions during the Arnold Expedition.[76] However, Arnold likely wore less costly, more rugged and comfortable civilian clothing most other times.

It is likely that Arnold's officers were also wearing their old militia uniforms during the campaign. Uniforms were expensive and, since the war was expected to end quickly, most of Arnold's officers probably decided that their prewar militia uniforms were sufficient for the short campaign. New England militia uniforms usually consisted of a long coat that ended at the knees (called a regimental coat). The facings on the coat (collar, lapels, and cuffs) were in a contrasting color, and breeches usually matched the coat or facings. The color combinations varied according to the preference of each militia unit.

There were at least four women who accompanied the expedition. They were the wives of men in the ranks who joined their husbands for the campaign. The appearance of these women was not unusual, and women accompanied the Continental Army throughout the war. The presence of these women was frequently ignored by nineteenth century patriotic historians, who dismissed them as prostitutes. Today we realize that there existed a whole community of non-combatants who followed eighteenth century armies, the largest group of whom were the wives and children of soldiers. These women served a useful purpose by washing and mending clothing and acting as nurses, services for which they received pay, either from the army or individual enlisted men. Wives and children frequently received authorization to follow the troops along with other relatives, hired servants, and slaves. There were few camp followers on the Arnold Expedition, however, because it was expected to be so arduous. Still, four wives followed their husbands on the expedition. Two have been positively identified: Jemima Warner, the wife of Private James Warner, who accompanied her husband from Pennsylvania to Cambridge and joined him for the march to Quebec, and Mrs. Grier (first name unknown), the wife of Sergeant Joseph Grier.

There is a legend about a fifth woman on the campaign, described as a beautiful Indian princess named Jacataqua. She is one of the characters in Kenneth Roberts' popular novel *Arundel* about the Arnold Expedition.[77] Legend has it that Jacataqua was the descendant of a distinguished Abenaki sachem (chief) who lived on Swan Island. She is supposed to have taken-up with 19-year-old Aaron Burr during the expedition and, if the dubious story is true, Jacataqua was the second of Burr's alleged mistresses. His first lover is mentioned as being Dorothy Quincy, who was John Hancock's fiancee when she met Burr.

The other category of non-military personnel on the Arnold Expedition was gentlemen volunteer. Burr, Ogden, and Oswald have already been introduced as volunteers on the expedition, and four others—Charles Porterfield, David Hopkins, John McGuire, and Matthew Duncan—also served in this capacity. We know that Oswald served as Arnold's aide, Burr and Ogden were assigned to Lieutenant Colonel Christopher Greene's battalion, and David Hopkins (from Maryland) and Charles Porterfield (a Virginian) were assigned to Morgan's riflemen.[78] Porterfield rose to the rank of colonel later in the war. He was mortally wounded and captured leading his Virginia regiment at the Battle of Camden, South Carolina (August 16, 1780), and died from his wounds as a British prisoner of war.[79]

*   *   *

The diaries of Arnold Expedition members reveal tough young men, often in their teens, with little previous military experience. The men in the musket companies came from New England towns like Worcester, Stockbridge, Acton, Hadley, and Medfield in Massachusetts; New Haven, Stamford, and Middletown in Connecticut; Greenwich, Newport, Providence, and Tiverton in Rhode Island; and East Nottingham, Dunbarton, and Hillsborough in New Hampshire. They were mostly farmers and deep water sailors. A few knew how to survive in the woods. The more experienced woodsmen were the riflemen. They came from Carlisle and Lancaster in western Pennsylvania and along the Piedmont region of the Virginia frontier.[80]

Though diverse in their backgrounds, the men's eyewitness accounts of the expedition included a common theme: Benedict Arnold's exemplary courage and leadership.

Chapter 3

King Neptune Raised his Taxes
Without the Least Difficulty Where
King George Had Failed[1]

The members of Arnold Expedition were ready to leave
Cambridge on Monday, September 11, after only nine days of
planning and organizing. It was an extraordinary accomplishment for the fledgling Continental Army and its commander, George
Washington. Colonel Arnold also deserves credit for skillfully carrying
out Washington's instructions. In fact, Arnold had managed to get his
military career back on track in less than three months from the time of
his quarrel with Colonel Hinman over the command of the troops at Fort
Ticonderoga. Arnold was now a colonel in the Continental Army
commanding an independent corps, one of the most coveted assignments
in the army. He also had the support of Washington and Schuyler, two of
the most influential men in America.

But Washington still had lingering concerns about Arnold's
reputation for confrontation, warning him at the start of the expedition
that he must cooperate with Schuyler and put himself under that officer's
command if the two armies should meet in Canada. "Upon this Occasion
& all others, I recommend most earnestly to avoid all Contention about
Rank," Washington exhorted Arnold. "In such a Cause every Post is
honourable in which a Man can serve his Country."[2] Washington
paraphrased this advice to Arnold from his favorite play Cato and he used
it on other occasions. For example, writing to General John Thomas on
July 23, 1775, Washington said, "surely every Post ought to be deem'd
honourable in which a Man can serve his Country."

The first part of the 1,150-man Arnold expedition consisted of an overland march from Cambridge to the Massachusetts port town of Newburyport, where boats were waiting to transport the corps to Maine. Arnold did not assemble his army at Cambridge, to avoid drawing attention to the movement of so many men.[3] Instead, they left quietly in detachments following different routes to Newburyport. This plan also allowed the men to find better sleeping accommodations in the smaller towns and villages along their various routes. Dr. Senter liked the idea of dividing the expedition during the march to Newburyport "for the more convenient marching and lodging."[4]

Based on the existing roads at the time the distance from Cambridge to Newburyport was about 34 miles. The three frontier rifle companies were the first to leave, departing Cambridge on schedule on the morning of September 11. The two New England musket battalions were scheduled to follow later that day, but they refused to march until they were paid the one month's advance wages that had been promised them.[5] It is no wonder that Washington would later write privately about his New England troops, "such a dirty, mercenary Spirit pervades the whole, that I should not be at all surprizd [sic] at any disaster than may happen."[6] It took two days to get the money to pay the New Englanders, who left Cambridge on September 13, as the frontier riflemen were approaching Newburyport.

The three rifle companies traveled together. After months of dull camp life the men must have been pleased to be on the move and heading toward combat. The frontiersmen moved rapidly through the Massachusetts countryside and reached the outskirts of Newburyport by the evening of the 13th, but decided to stop and camp for the night so they could make a dramatic entrance into town the following morning.

The two New England infantry battalions also made good time. Both departed Cambridge on Wednesday, September 13, but at different times. Greene's battalion left in the morning while Enos' waited until evening. Major Meigs, second in command of Enos' battalion, wrote that his unit left Cambridge on Wednesday night and marched due north as far as the village of Medford before stopping. Their march resumed the next morning, and by taking country roads east through Malden, Lynn, and Salem they arrived at Danvers, where they camped for the night. A common soldier in Enos' battalion named Abner Stocking, from Chatham, Connecticut, wrote, "This morning we began our march at 5 o'clock and at sunset encamped at Danvers. . . . The weather through the day was very sultry and hot for the season of the year." Stocking mentioned the morale of the men during the trip: "We were all in high spirits intending to endure with fortitude, all the fatigues and hardships, that we might meet with in our march to Quebec."[7]

Enos' battalion resumed its march the following morning, passing through the Massachusetts towns of Beverly and Wendham to encamp at Rowley, where they spent the third night of their journey. From Meigs' account, we know that the battalion completed the final leg of the trip on Saturday morning, arriving in Newburyport at about 10:00 a.m. Arnold's entire corps was in Newburyport by Saturday night, September 16. However, the men were not all camped together. The riflemen bivouacked in a field in the neighboring village of Newbury, in an area known today as the upper common. The two divisions of musketmen bunked in Newburyport, where they occupied the town meeting house and two unused rope works.[8] Arnold and several of his senior officers were the guests of Nathaniel Tracy at his Newburyport mansion, located on Fish Street (today's State Street), a few blocks away from the town's bustling waterfront. Other officers found housing across the street from Tracy's mansion at an almost equally fine home owned by Tristram Dalton, another patriotic member of Newburyport's thriving business community.

Tracy and Dalton were gracious hosts. Major Meigs wrote that he spent two nights in Newburyport as the dinner guest of Mr. Tracy on one night and Mr. Dalton on the other.[9] The other officers lodged—not unpleasantly—down the street at the renowned Wolfe Tavern, which was owned by William Davenport. Dr. Senter mentioned in his journal that he "took lodgings at Mr. Devenport's [Davenport's], an Innholder." Senter said that he enjoyed his brief stay in Newburyport, and referred to it as "a very agreeable place."[10]

Arnold did not accompany his corps on its march from Cambridge to Newburyport. He assigned command of the routine trek through friendly country to Greene and Enos while he made the trip in a small rented coach, called a pantheon, accompanied by his aide Eleazer Oswald. They completed the trip in one long and busy day, during which they made some important purchases in the seaport town of Salem. Leaving Cambridge on Friday morning, Arnold and Oswald arrived in Salem at mid-day, where they purchased two hundred pounds of ginger "and engaged a teamster to transport that and two hundred and seventy blankets, received from the Committee of Safety."[11] Ginger, believed at the time to prevent scurvy, usually was sold in powdered form and mixed with drinking water. It was a popular food additive during the French and Indian War, especially among frontier troops, but its use as an anti-scorbutic declined during the course of the American Revolution.[12] Arnold and Oswald left Salem in the evening and arrived in Newburyport later that night.

The colonel spent the next day, Saturday, in Newburyport "buying a quantity of small stores" and attending to some other last minute details.[13] This is an important statement to note, because it shows us that a wealthy man such as Arnold had enough money and the access to transportation to take personal items with him on the expedition, the most important being additional foods. Arnold shopped in Newburyport for provisions for his personal use on the expedition: wine, preserved jams and jellies, sugar, coffee, tea, dried beef, pickles, salted pork, portable soup (bouillon), tinned butter (preserved between layers of salt), and spices to supplement his army rations. His purchases were not unusual, since wealthy officers tried to make life as pleasant as possible for themselves in the field. Officers could bring anything they could afford with them, including wagon loads of elegant tents, furniture, clothing, food, liquor and wines, and servants. Since the Arnold Expedition was traveling light and fast in small boats, the amount of personal baggage an officer could carry with him was limited. There are clues; however, in the diaries from the expedition that Arnold's officers brought some stocks of personal food with them. For example, Dr. Senter wrote on October 20, 1775, in his journal, "I was obliged to draw forth my small butter box containing about half a dozen pounds [of butter]," and Major Meigs reported losing his kettle, butter, and sugar in a boating accident.[14] Some enlisted men also purchased food but were generally confined by their budgets and limited space to taking few nonessential items with them.

Arnold's corps paraded in an open field early on the morning of Sunday, September 17. A number of the diarists recorded the event, including Ebenezer Wild, who wrote in his journal, "This day [September] 17th had a general review, and our men appeared very well and in good spirits, and made a grand appearance. . . ."[15] Seeing Arnold's command lined up in formation must have been a stirring sight for the pro-rebellion population of Newburyport, who turned out to witness this proof of the 13 colonies' determination to fight.

Arnold's corps assembled in full martial array: serried ranks of sturdy young men, many of whom were still teenagers. Few, if any, wore uniforms. They dressed in civilian clothing, and only their shouldered firearms and cartridge boxes made them resemble soldiers. An onlooker could make out the figure of Colonel Arnold with his small headquarters staff facing his corps of 1,150 men. Rifleman John Joseph Henry was in the ranks and remembered Arnold long after as "a short handsome man, of a florid complexion and stoutly made." Henry called him "a remarkable character . . . brave, even to temerity and beloved by the soldiery."[16] But despite his bulky, athletic look, Arnold's eyes— described as marvelously strange like those of an animal or some predatory bird, pale as ice, unblinking—were likely his most distinguished feature.[17]

The public was treated to watching Arnold review his troops lined up facing him from right to left. The three rifle companies were probably on the right in the position of honor, with the 1st Battalion, commanded by Green next to them, followed by Enos' 2nd Battalion on the extreme left. During his inspection, he would have seen the only known black soldier on the expedition. His name was Benjamin Butcher and he was a private in Captain Hubbard's company.[18] Butcher was probably a free black man who volunteered for the mission.

Since few of Arnold's officers were wearing uniforms, their military ranks were identified by a rosette or gathered piece of ribbon, known as a cockade, displayed on their hats. Cockades were in fashion at the time among most European armies, and the Americans copied the idea from the British. The wearing of colored cockades was a rudimentary system implemented by Washington at the start of the war. The regulation authorizing the use of cockades appeared in the army's General Orders for July 23, 1775, that recommended "some Badges of Distinction may be immediately provided."[19] The orders specified red or pink cockades for field officers (colonels, lieutenant colonels, and majors), yellow or buff for captains, and green for subalterns (lieutenants and other low-ranking officers). Sergeants, according to the General Orders, "may be distinguished by an Epaulette, or strip of red Cloth, sewed upon the right shoulder; the Corporals by one of green."

A few of Arnold's officers might also have been wearing a crimson-colored sash, which served as a badge of office or function (such as adjutant or officer of the day). Some other officers may have worn a small plume or decorative feather in their hats to further distinguish themselves from the common soldiers. The variety of symbols to indicate rank and function during this early period of the American Revolution existed because the army had to make do with whatever was available.

A careful observer to the parade at Newburyport would have noticed that Arnold and his officers carried a diversity of weapons. Most officers carried swords, and though a wealthy officer might have owned several different types, the majority would likely have carried a practical, short-bladed sword known as a hanger (or cutte) on the expedition. Arnold and his officers also armed themselves with a variety of pistols and a European pole-arm known as a spontoon, a six- to eight-foot-long wooden pole with a spear-like metal tip. Washington favored this weapon for his officers as a symbol of rank and as a signaling device. It also freed the officers to focus on leading their troops rather than being distracted with the loading and firing of a musket or pistol.[20] Even if they were wearing civilian clothing, it was easy to distinguish Arnold's officers from the enlisted men because the officers usually had the money to afford a better quality of cloth and tailoring than the enlisted men.

There is no mention among extant documents of flags on the expedition. The main army at Cambridge had them, and it is likely Arnold's corps brought along a few, which were unfurled and flying when the complete expedition mustered at Newburyport. The Americans had no national flag at this point in the war, and the flags they flew were more or less square in shape and festooned with painted patriotic slogans.

The colonists felt at this time that theirs was a "loyal protest" and that they fought to redress their grievances with their mother country. The rebels liked flags and standards with patriotic and martial images, and slogans that expressed their sentiments. Popular designs at the time were a red flag with the word *LIBERTY* written across in bold letters or the outline of a pine tree above the words *An Appeal to Heaven*.[21] Sometime late in 1775, General Washington unfurled an unofficial national flag, called the Grand Union or Continental flag, at Cambridge. It represented the 13 rebelling colonies with 13 alternating red and white stripes. There was a canton (a square or rectangular section in the upper-left corner of the flag next to the staff) in the form of a British Union Jack to represent the colonists' fundamental allegiance to their mother country.[22] There is a slim possibility that the Arnold Expedition had a Grand Union flag with them.

Music was played during the campaign, and we can envision Arnold's fifes and drums grouped together during their muster at Newburyport for maximum impact. The musicians had the practical role of relaying commands to the troops through specific fife and drum calls. Our visualization of Arnold's force at the Newburyport muster should also include a number of dogs that became attached to Arnold's corps. Soldiers throughout history have loved having dogs with them, and the Arnold Expedition was no exception.

The overall effect of Arnold's assembled army at its Newburyport parade was a practical earthy look with splashes of color and military organization. "We passed the review with much honor to ourselves," Abner Stocking penned in his journal, "and went through with the manual exercise [drilling with their muskets] with much alacrity."[23] The common soldiers in Arnold's corps were healthy young men who had been drawn to Cambridge by a common dislike of the British and a sense of adventure. Although Arnold's army may have appeared somewhat unsoldierly when it mustered at Newburyport, it was a potent fighting force. Similarly armed and equipped colonists had already dealt the British deadly blows at Concord and Bunker Hill.

Following their Sunday morning muster in the field, the expedition's members marched into town. Newburyport was situated in a commanding location on the south shore of the Merrimac River with easy access to the sea. The town had a commercial look about it, with numerous warehouses and merchants' homes lining its streets.[24] The corps proceeded to the First Presbyterian Church to attend a special service as patriotic townsfolk lined the way. As many soldiers as possible marched into the church with the expedition's colors flying and drums beating.

The men formed two ceremonial lines inside the church and presented arms. As drums rolled, Chaplain Spring solemnly walked between the lines of soldiers to the pulpit. The men stacked their arms in the aisles, after which the chaplain preached extemporaneously. Following the service, the church sexton led Chaplain Spring, Colonel Arnold, and his senior officers down a flight of stairs to the crypt below the sanctuary, where the remains of charismatic English evangelist

George Whitefield lay entombed. The sexton removed the lid from Whitefield's coffin, and Arnold and his officers gazed upon the remains of the great cleric. Whitefield's body had decayed, but some of his clothing remained intact. The sexton solemnly reached into the coffin and removed the clerical collar and wristbands from the corpse. He cut them into small pieces with a pair of scissors and gave a piece of the precious relic to each officer to take with them to Quebec. As the coffin was closed, they prayed for the success of their enterprise.[25]

Nathaniel Tracy arranged for the transport of Arnold's army from Newburyport to Fort Western in 11 fishing boats and small merchant ships provisioned and waiting at the wharves on Water Street. Tracy gathered an assortment of single-masted sloops, double-masted fishing boats, and coastal traders normally used to transport loads of lumber, salt fish, and animal hides along the coast. One diarist described them as "dirty coasters and fish boats."[26] They carried no cannons nor did the rebels have any warships to serve as escorts. Enemy warships were known to patrol the area, and Arnold's unarmed ships would be easy prey if they were intercepted by even the smallest Royal Navy vessel. Washington anticipated this danger when he warned Arnold to use caution before putting out to sea. The general instructed him, "When you come to Newbury Port you are to make all possible Inquiry what Men of War or Cruizers there may be on the Coast to which this Detachment may be exposed on their Voyage to Kennebeck River. . . ." Washington told Arnold to march his troops overland to Maine: "if you shall find that there is Danger of being intercepted. . . ."[27] For all the Americans knew, a flotilla of Royal Navy warships could be just over the horizon, waiting to pounce on Arnold's defenseless fleet.

Tracy also worried about the American military activity taking place at Newburyport in anticipation of the expedition's arrival. Writing to Joseph Trumbull on the subject, Tracy said, "[T]he place they are destined for, may be kept a Secret, but it is impossible to prepare so many Vessells, without having it known, they are bound on some expedition."[28] Tracy helped by sending three patrol boats on Saturday to search the coastline as far as the Kennebec River for British warships. The boats returned on Monday, September 18, with assurances that the waters between Newburyport and the Kennebec were clear of the enemy.

Since Arnold's troops were getting restless, this news came at an opportune time. Based on the favorable reconnaissance report, Arnold began sending his men on board the transports late that afternoon. They remained on board ready to sail on the first salutary wind. The expedition's troops were evenly distributed among the 11 vessels, with about 100 men per ship. Tuesday morning, September 19, saw a favorable wind blowing, and the flotilla raised anchor. An enthusiastic crowd gathered at the waterfront to shout huzzahs as the expeditionary force sailed out of the harbor with their drums beating, fifes playing, and colors flying.[29] By 11:00 a.m., all the ships were safely out to sea, except for the schooner *Swallow*, which ran aground on a sandbar in the entrance to the harbor. The expedition lost valuable time as the soldiers aboard her transferred to other ships. The crew remained on board, and Arnold instructed them to proceed to the Kennebec River with their cargo as soon as possible. Then, the little unarmed flotilla sailed out into the open sea and plotted a course for Maine. A worried Arnold scanned the horizon for enemy warships. He had every reason to be concerned, as the Royal Navy knew all about his expedition, including its exact location.

The first known British reference to the Arnold Expedition was a note dated September 8, 1775. General Thomas Gage, who commanded the British army in North America (with the exception of parts of Canada), wrote the memo to Vice Admiral Samuel Graves, his counterpart in the Royal Navy, asking for warships to intercept the rebels at sea. Mr. Washington's so-called secret expedition had not even left Cambridge when Gage moved to destroy it.[30] Gage's message to Graves read as follows:

Boston September 8th 1775—

I have certain Advices by two Deserters, that about 1500 Men have Marched from Cambridge which are said to be gone to Canada, and by way of Newberry [Newburyport], but by that Route they may be intended for Nova Scotia; I should therefore think it exceedingly necessary some small Vessel should be immediately sent to Watch their motions, . . . I should hope that the Naval Force you have in that Province would with timely Notice be able to defeat any Attempts the Rebels can make at Sea for a Descent there.[31]

The fact that information from two American deserters, who crossed into British lines somewhere around Boston, reached Gage's headquarters was not a bit of luck, but the result of meticulous intelligence work, the scope of which we probably will never know because of the secrecy surrounding it. Both the British and Americans were obtaining useful information by methodically interrogating deserters and prisoners. Both sides were also getting input from civilian sympathizers, spies, double agents, and paid informers. They employed other techniques such as intercepting enemy dispatches, or writing false dispatches that were allowed to fall into enemy hands. The British also were trying to turn American officers with bribes or promises. Other favorites in the British bag of tricks were printing counterfeit money and adding false paragraphs to authentic letters that they planted in newspapers to discredit or embarrass Washington and other rebel leaders. The capture of an enemy vessel at sea was a valuable coup, every piece of paper aboard scrutinized for useful information. Anything interesting, gathered from any source, made its way to headquarters for evaluation and review by trusted officers and civilians who performed this work in addition to their other duties. General Washington, for example, preferred to work behind closed doors, probably evaluating intelligence information with his military secretary (Joseph Reed at the time) and his aides-de-camp.

The British scored an intelligence triumph in the early months of the war, while the Arnold Expedition was still being organized, when they got Dr. Benjamin Church Jr. to pass them information about rebel plans.[32] Church had a mansion and a mistress and he turned to providing General Gage with information in order to finance his expensive life style. Church's treason was uncovered in October 1775, but we do not know the extent of the damage. Equally dangerous to the Americans at the time was Major Benjamin Thompson, a New Hampshire militia officer who worked as a British undercover agent. Thompson was observing the American camps and fortifications around Boston and reporting everything he saw to General Gage in Boston via innocent-looking letters that included intelligence data written in invisible ink.[33] The Americans staged their own intelligence tour de force when they stole all of General Gage's official papers from his Boston headquarters.[34]

The next known item in the paper trail of British documents concerning the Arnold Expedition is a follow-up note from General Gage to Vice Admiral Graves dated September 27, which showed that Gage knew that the rebel expedition had sailed in a flotilla of boats to Maine's

Kennebec River. Gage, however, still believed that its objective was Halifax:

> Boston September 27th 1775
>
> Sir, Since Conversing with you this Morning on the Subject of the Rebels Embarking a Number of Men at Newberry, I have again considered that matter, and think it absolutely Necessary you should Immediately send some Ships of War to look after them. It is possible they may be some Days about Kennebec, or Mechias [Machias, Maine] to try to augment their Force, and to procure more Boats, to land their Men in the Province of Nova Scotia. . . .[35]

That the authorities in Halifax had been alerted to the possibility of a rebel attack by October 17, 1775, is evidenced by a report written by Nova Scotia's Governor Francis Legge to his superiors in London, which included: "I am inform'd that Fifteen hundred of the Rebels had marched Eastward under the Command of General Thomas [John Thomas, an American general, which was incorrect]. . . that their design is to destroy the Navy Yard here. . . ."[36]

The British realized their mistake about the objective of the Arnold Expedition by mid-October, as demonstrated by an excerpt from a November 27, 1775, summary report from General William Howe to London. Howe replaced Gage, who was recalled to England in September 1775. Although Howe's comments were dated late November, they prove that he had knowledge of the Arnold Expedition much earlier. In this report, Howe referred to a British raid on the coastal town of Falmouth (modern Portland), Maine, that took place on October 18, 1775:

> On the return of this detachment, the 5th instant [November 5], I received confirmation, that the party from the Rebel Army, under the command of a Colonel Arnold, of which I presume your Lordship would have advice from General Gage, had gone up the Kennebec River, intending to enter Canada by the River Chaudiere; that they had got to Fort Halifax, about sixty miles from the mouth of the Kennebeck, from whence they had sent back about two hundred sick; nothing further has been since heard of them.[37]

With the above intelligence in hand and knowledge of the movement of Schuyler's northern army, the British in Boston tried to reinforce Quebec City during October 1775. But a lack of cooperation from the Royal Navy, whose ships were the only way to get reinforcements quickly from Boston to Quebec, frustrated their efforts.

The most revealing document in the exchange of notes between the army and navy is an October 12 missive from Vice Admiral Graves to General Howe, in which the admiral explains why he refused to provide transportation for troops bound for Quebec. Because of its importance, Graves' note is presented in is entirety:

> Boston 12 October 1775
>
> Sir,
>
> From different Conversations I have had on the subject of navigating in the River St. Lawrence at this time of the year, and on the probability of Vessels getting to Quebec, I have been led to take the Opinions of Captains Hartwell and Macartney upon the likelihood of the Cerberus [a Royal Navy frigate] and Transports arriving at Quebec, supposing they were now ready to depart: these Gentlemen assure and authorize me to say, the Attempt is extremely dangerous and that to persevere after getting into the River will be fatal to the whole, and that they look upon the Scheme to be impracticable: the reasons they have given me are so forcible, that I am intirely of their Opinion, and think it not adviseable [sic] to attempt it.
>
> I am Sir &c
>
> Sam Graves[38]

In the end, the Royal Navy did nothing to help get reinforcements from Boston to Quebec. But the question that remains is why Graves did not send warships to destroy Arnold's unarmed transports while they were vulnerable at the wharf in Newburyport or at sea en route to Maine? The accepted explanation is that Graves was sadly handicapped by the small number of ships assigned to him and that none were available to intercept Arnold's unarmed flotilla. Graves only had a handful of ships designed to fight on the open seas, and with them he was expected to patrol the labyrinthine American coastline from the mouth of the St.

Lawrence River to the Florida Keys. Graves was saddled with fifty-gun double-deckers in a situation that required a fleet of easily maneuverable, shallow-draft warships.[39]

But there is another explanation for Graves' failure, one that begins with his background. Graves, though a competent sailor, had never held a high post prior to his appointment to command the North American Station in 1774. He seemed befuddled with this great responsibility and incapable of figuring out how to use his resources to his best advantage. One official report described Graves as "a corrupt Admiral without any shadow of capacity."[40] In another appraisal, a British officer wrote home about Graves' lack of initiative, saying, "[H]e was not supporting in material points the dignity and terror of the British Flag."[41]

With some imagination and determination, Graves could have stretched his resources to take advantage of the golden opportunity he had to crush Arnold's unarmed transports, either at Newburyport or while they were sailing unprotected along the New England coast. The Royal Navy finally dismissed Graves in a curt letter from the admiralty, dated February 22, 1776, which read: "The service on which you have been employed being at an end, you are hereby required and directed to strike your flag and come on shore."[42] But all was not lost for the British—the Arnold Expedition had within its ranks a spy, a man posing as a deserter from the British army.

*   *   *

Arnold's fleet sailed unmolested by British warships from Newburyport to the Kennebec River. Faced with favorable weather and a good breeze, the fleet traveled the roughly 100 miles in about 24 hours.

Captain Dearborn included in his journal a list of six flag signals supplied by Arnold, to be used to communicate instructions to the flotilla. Signal number five, for example, was an "Ensign [flag] at the Main-Top Peak." This was the signal "for dispersing and every Vessel making the Nearest Harbour."[43] Major Meigs' journal entry for September 19 (the day the flotilla sailed from Newburyport) shows that he also recorded the signals, adding "I was very sea-sick."[44] His ailment was common among the expedition's soldiers—who were unaccustomed to the sea—and the situation was aggravated by sailing in small, overcrowded ships that reeked with the smell of dead fish or animal hides. Arnold, however, was an experienced sailor who must have enjoyed his temporary job as commodore of the fleet. He was aboard the schooner *Broad Bay*, designated the flagship of the flotilla, and sailing in the lead. The colorless transports sailed along briskly but hove to (slowed down) when they sighted two fishing schooners. A sailor on the *Broad Bay* shouted across the open sea, asking if they had seen any ships of the Royal Navy. The reply was an agreeable "no," and the fleet sailed on.

As the day wore on, the weather turned foggy and the seas became rough, causing most of the troops, according to Dr. Senter, "to disgorge themselves of their luxuries [good food] so plentifully laid in ere we embarked."[45] Gale-force winds ensued, adding to the men's misery and the difficulty of keeping the ships on course. At midnight, Arnold gave the signal to anchor for the night off Wood Island, which lay a little southwest of the intricate entrance to the Kennebec River. The foul weather continued into the following morning, "very thick and foggy, attended with rain," but the ships groped their way along the coast and began arriving at the mouth of the Kennebec River around 9:00 a.m. on September 20. Meigs, who was aboard the sloop *Britannia*, recorded his arrival in his journal:

> In the morning we made the mouth of Kennebeck, right ahead, which we soon entered. . . . We were hailed from the shore by a number of men under arms [local militia], which were stationed there. They were answered, that we were Continental troops, and that we wanted a pilot. They immediately sent one on board. . . . I would mention here, that this day makes fourteen only, since the orders were first given for building 200 battoes, collecting provisions for and levying 1,100 men, and marching them to this place. . . .[46]

Major Meigs was fairly accurate in his calculation. The expedition commenced only 18 days earlier, on September 2, when Washington wrote out instructions to Tracy to assemble transports at Newburyport. Therefore, in less than three weeks a corps of over 1,000 armed, equipped, and healthy men sailed up the Kennebec River. It was an incredible achievement for Washington, Arnold, and the fledgling Continental Army.

Not only is it difficult to comprehend how the British failed to intercept Arnold's unarmed transports at sea, but it is equally puzzling to understand Washington's long delay in informing the Continental Congress of the existence of the Arnold Expedition. Washington first informed Congress of the mission in a report he wrote them on September 21, by which time the expedition was already in Maine. His deliberate delay in informing Congress—who were his civilian bosses—of the strategically important and costly campaign can be justified as part of his effort to keep the Arnold Expedition a secret. However, the real reason for Washington's wait was that he had decided, at the outset of his command, to maintain tight control of the army and allow little outside interference from Congress in matters of strategic planning and troop deployments. In other words, his delay in notifying Congress of the expedition was part of an intentional policy of withholding information from them.

While Washington was an astute politician who worked diligently to maintain a good relationship with Congress and other government officials, he was determined to make his own decisions, and report them after the fact. Congress aided Washington in establishing his independence by issuing vaguely worded instructions to him. In their directive to Washington, dated June 22, 1775, Congress said, "many things must be left to your prudent and discreet management, as occurrences may arise upon the place or from time to time fall out."[47] Congress had granted Washington discretionary powers because they had no experience in operating an army and trusted their new commander: they believed he was a dedicated member of Congress and an experienced soldier.

Washington decided to adopt a broad interpretation of his instructions, and began establishing his independence from Congress within a few days of his arrival in Cambridge. He did this in a shrewdly worded statement, included in his first report to them, dated July 10, 1775. The text is complicated but well worth comprehending, as it shows how Washington eliminated any sort of shared command of the army with Congress:

> My best Abilities are at all Times devoted to the Service of my Country, but I feel the Weight, Importance & Vanity of my present Duties too sensibly, not to wish a more immediate & frequent Communication with the Congress. I fear it may often happen in the Course of our present Operations that I shall need that Assistance &

Direction from them, which Time & Distance will not allow me to receive.[48]

Washington's report to Congress about the Arnold Expedition included some additional insights regarding his decision to launch the mission. For example, it emphasized Washington's belief that he could spare the men from his army for an intrusion into Canada because the British in Boston showed no signs of stirring from their elaborate fortifications. Here is the text of Washington's report to Congress, in which he gave them the electrifying news that he had sent an expedition to capture Quebec:

I am now to inform the Honbl. Congress, that encouraged by the repeated Declarations of the Canadians & Indians, & urged by their Requests, I have detached Col. Arnold with 1000 Men to penetrate into Canada by Way of Kennebeck River, &, if possible to make himself Master of Quebeck. By this Manoeuvre I proposed, either to divert Carleton from St Johns, which would leave a free Passage to General Schuyler, or, if this did not take Effect, Quebec in its present defenseless State must fall into his Hands an easy Prey. I made all possible Inquiry as to the Distance, the Safety of the Rout[e], & the Danger of the Season, being too far advanced, but found nothing in either to deter me from proceeding, more especially, as it met with very general Approbation, from all, whom I consulted upon it. . . . They have now left this Place [Cambridge] 7 Days, &, if favoured with a good Wind, I hope soon to hear of their being in Kennebeck River. . . .

I was the more induced to make this Detachment, as it is my clear Opinion, from a careful Observation of the Movements of the Enemy, corroborated by all the Intelligence we receive by Deserters, & others, of the former of whom we have some every Day, that the Enemy have no Intention to come out, until they are re-inforced. They have been wholly employed for some Time past, in procuring Materials for Barracks, Fuel & making other Preparations for Winter. These Circumstances, with the constant Additions to their Works, which are apparently defensive, have led to the above Conclusion, & enabled me, to spare this Body of Men, where I hope they will be usefully & successfully employed.49

On September 20, while Washington was writing his report to Congress, Arnold's flotilla began its passage up the Kennebec River to

Fort Western. After entering the Kennebec, Arnold's flag ship, the *Broad Bay*, sailed six miles upriver to a small cove called Parker Flats, where it anchored and waited for the rest of the flotilla to arrive. Arnold called the place Eels Eddy and said that many of his men were extremely seasick from the rough voyage from Newburyport. He sent some of them on shore for "refreshments" (typical of his concern for the welfare of the soldiers under his command). But, after waiting six hours, only eight out of the 11 ships in the convoy reached the rendezvous. The colonel could only account for the *Swallow*, which had run aground on a shoal in Newburyport harbor. Worried about the fate of his two missing ships, the sloops *Conway* and *Abigail*, but unwilling to wait any longer, Arnold ordered the assembled fleet to weigh anchor, break out their sails, and continue upriver. It turned out that the missing sloops had sailed past the entrance to the Kennebec in the morning fog and rain and up the nearby Sheepscot River, mistaking it for the Kennebec. Luckily, river pilots were able to navigate the two stragglers through the maze of interconnecting small rivers and channels, where they rejoined the fleet on the following day.

As Arnold's ships began their passage upriver, members of the expedition stood at the rails to look at the passing shoreline. What they saw were farms—sliced out of a curtain of stately spruce, hemlock, and pine trees—hugging the shoreline and an occasional village or country inn nestled in the forest. Autumn came early to this region; the trees showed the first signs of fall colors as Arnold's convoy threaded its way into Maine's interior. Feeling safe from the Royal Navy, at least one of Arnold's ships probably triumphantly unfurled a rebel ensign from its mast: a scarlet flag with the word *LIBERTY* painted in bold white lettering. Another of his ships likely hoisted a scarlet ensign with the words *An Appeal To Heaven* blazed in large white letters.

The arrival of Arnold's flotilla was an exciting event for the people of this remote region, and those on shore stopped what they were doing to watch the ships sail past. Most locals sided with the rebellion and were thrilled to see these shiploads of American troops brandishing their weapons in defiance to British rule. Some of the men on the expedition came from this part of Maine. They had traveled to Cambridge at the start of the war and now were passing through their homeland as volunteers in Arnold's corps. They recognized the landscape and started looking for family and friends among the people excitedly running down to the shore. Coasters, fishing boats, and bateaux sailed by, exchanging greetings and huzzahs with the men on the transports. Almost everyone in the Kennebec Valley knew the stories of the ancient Indian trail from Maine to Quebec, and reckoned that these American soldiers were coming up the Kennebec to follow that fabled route to Canada.

The river valley that the flotilla entered had been largely unsettled just 25 years before, and much of its development was due to the efforts of Dr. Silvester Gardiner. Gardiner was a Rhode Islander by birth who went to London and Paris to study medicine when he was a young man. After completing his education, Gardiner returned to America and settled in Boston, where he used his European contacts to branch out into the pharmaceutical trade, importing medicines for distribution and sale. Gardiner also opened a chain of successful apothecary shops in Boston and got involved in land speculation in 1753, becoming the principal investor of the Kennebec Purchase Company. Founded in 1661, this firm owned a huge land grant in Maine that extended for 15 miles on both sides of the Kennebec River. But the company had been unable to attract many settlers to the region due to its remote location and opposition from the local Indians. Gardiner took charge of the business and successfully lobbied for the construction of Fort Western in the middle of the land grant, to provide security against Indian attacks and convince settlers that the valley was a safe place to live.

Having solved the problem of security, he turned his attention to attracting settlers to his property. Gardiner did this by offering free land to new settlers in British and American newspapers. A 1761 newspaper advertisement, for example, promised 200 acres in the Kennebec River Valley "to each family who shall become Settlers on Condition that they each build a house not less than 20 feet square, and seven feet stud; clear and make fit for tillage five acres within three years, and dwell upon the premises personally, or by their substitutes for the term of seven years or more. . . ." The glowing ad claimed that the Kennebec River and nearby sea abounded with various kinds of fish, and that the land along the Kennebec was fertile, with "plenty of meadows and intervale, that many settlers have carried with them 20 head of cattle which they have been able to keep year round. . . . It is well stored with great quantities of the best and most valuable timber."[50]

Gardiner's final claim was that settlers living on his land had easy access to the Boston market by ship, "which was 24 hours with favorable wind." His promotion brought settlers into the region, and Gardiner and his fellow investors made money by charging them for a variety of services, including milling their wheat and selling choice parcels of land at an immense profit. The Kennebec Land Purchase Company also allocated parcels of land to be used for towns, which they sold at premium prices.

The bulk of Arnold's men came from Massachusetts, New Hampshire, and Connecticut, and marveled at the development in this remote region. Where they expected to see forests with a few primitive cabins, they gazed instead upon a luxuriant valley dotted with neat farms. They even viewed some stately homes, frequently situated on well-chosen high ground overlooking the beautiful river. This lowermost section of the Kennebec River Valley was called Georgetown (the area today includes the towns of Bath, West Bath, Georgetown, Phippsburg, Woolwich, and Arrowsic Island). The most populated place in the Georgetown region was expansive Arrowsic Island, whose intricate shoreline included many attractive coves and inlets. Major Meigs from Connecticut commented favorably about the island's "handsome meeting-house, and very good dwelling houses."[51] For sport, the men aboard the schooner *Betsy* shot at seals they spotted in the coves along the island's coastline.[52]

One of Arnold's ships anchored at Arrowsic Island to rendezvous with Captain Samuel McCobb, who was waiting there with 20 additional men for the expedition. McCobb, who made his home on the island, was active in local politics. Inspired by the first news of the fighting around Boston, he organized a company of his fellow residents, who marched under his command to Cambridge, where they were assigned to Colonel John Nixon's Massachusetts regiment. McCobb's company was among the patriots who boldly occupied Bunker Hill and Breeds Hill on June 16, 1775. In the ensuing Battle of Bunker Hill, 2,500 British troops dispatched from nearby Boston forced the rebels off the hilltops but with terrible casualties; more than 1,000 British attackers were killed or wounded in the effort.

Due in large part to his courage at Bunker Hill, McCobb was invited to join the Arnold Expedition. Many of McCobb's veterans joined him for the campaign, but he needed additional recruits to complete his company, and he rushed back to Georgetown to enlist more men with the understanding that he would rendezvous with the expedition at Arrowsic Island.[53]

Though Arnold was glad to have McCobb's additional men, he was upset with the slow progress of his convoy. The local pilots who came on board at Parker Flats warned him that the water level upriver was low at this time of the year, and there was danger that his heavily laden transports would run aground in the shallow water. It is surprising that Arnold, an experienced New England-based sailor, did not consider this problem beforehand. Fearful of attempting to navigate the tricky river in the dark, Arnold ordered his ships to drop anchor at dusk just upriver from Arrowsic Island, near the present site of the town of Bath, which had several shipyards. Some of the officers, including Captain Dearborn and gentleman volunteer Burr, went ashore for the night to get away from the foul-smelling, overcrowded transports and enjoy the hospitality of the enthusiastic local residents. Dearborn, who had fought at Bunker Hill, must have thrilled his hosts with an account of the battle, while young Burr could describe his college days at Princeton. There were few college graduates in the colonies, especially in an area as remote as the Kennebec River Valley, and the cultured Burr must have been a favorite guest.

At dawn on September 21, Arnold's convoy resumed its historic passage up the Kennebec. As the day progressed, the ships gradually separated in the tricky currents until they were out of sight of one another. Farms and hamlets could still be seen on both sides of the river, whose rock-strewn shoreline and waters were teeming with geese, gulls, ducks, and many kinds of fish. Despite their slow progress, everyone aboard was in good spirits and eager to buy potatoes and pork from the cash-starved farmers who were hawking food to the troops as they rowed their boats alongside the convoy.

After passing through a narrow stretch of the river dotted with small islands, the transports filed into Merry Meeting Bay, a wondrous phenomenon of nature located 20 miles from the sea.[54] In truth, this large, shallow bay is a tidal riverine, but the earliest colonists called it Merry Meeting Bay and the name stuck. Arnold's men passed tidal marshes along the bay's shoreline that were a haven for migrating water fowl. Five miles farther upstream from Merry Meeting Bay was Swan Island, a favorite camping ground of the Indians who once inhabited the region. The schooner *Betsy* sailed through this section of the river on the afternoon of September 21 while the officers aboard feasted on "Salmon and Lobsters in *Betsyes* cabbin."[55]

The *Swallow* rejoined the others during the day, reporting that she had passed two of the transports (the *Houghton* carrying 120 troops and the *Eagle* 84) that had run aground in shallow Merry Meeting Bay.[56] Arnold ordered the *Swallow* to take aboard some extra men and go back to help the two stranded ships off the shoals by attaching ropes and towing them off with row boats. Several of Arnold's ships anchored near Swan Island on the night of September 21. The officers went ashore that night, and the island's residents fed and entertained them. Aaron Burr was believed to have been among the men who visited Swan Island, where he first met, as the legend goes, the beautiful Indian princess Jacquetta. After a night together, the young woman agreed to accompany Burr as his concubine.

Continuing upriver, the ships next passed another settlement on the west bank of the Kennebec, named Richmond, where they saw the remains of an old military post (Fort Richmond) built on the site in 1721. This fort was a reminder of how the early colonists of Maine needed to defend themselves against surprise attacks from the French and Indians. However, some of the men aboard the ships were probably too busy shooting at the cranes that inhabited this section of the river to pay much attention to the dilapidated structure. Sailing farther north, the transports passed Pownalborough (now Dresden) on the east side of the river. Captain Dearborn reported seeing "a Court-House and Goal [jail]—and some very good Settlements" at this place.[57] Some men went ashore at Pownalborough to a tavern, where they drank egg rum and "Lt. Lyman [from Capt. Hubbard's company] held a young woman in his Lap."[58]

A little farther north brought Arnold's ships to another settled area called Gardinerston (also called Gardiner's Town, Gardinerston Plantation, and Gardinerstown, the place named in honor of Dr. Silvester Gardiner), where the ships sailed between "a more level flat country" covered with pine trees and a scattering of spruce and hemlocks.[59] There also existed some cleared pastureland in this region, as well as fields of Indian corn, "Dwelling houses," two saw mills, a liberty pole erected by the local rebels, and Reuben Colburn's boatyard.[60]

The plan was to take delivery of the expedition's 200 bateaux at Colburn's boatyard while the transports continued nine miles farther upriver to Fort Western, which had been designated by General

Washington as the advance base for their ascent into the wilderness. Colburn's bateaux were critical to the success of the mission to capture Quebec before it was reinforced or winter—which came early to this region—trapped the expedition in the wilderness. The *Broad Bay*, which had raced upriver, reached the vicinity of Gardinerston on September 21 just as the wind died. Arnold was so anxious to reach Colburn's that he ordered a longboat to row him the rest of the way.

As Arnold's longboat raced on, everyone on board her strained their eyes, looking upriver for Colburn's boatyard and the promised flotilla of bateaux. Suddenly the men in the longboat cheered as they saw hundreds of boats, "all Lying on Shore ready to receive our Detachment."[61] In all likelihood Reuben Colburn was standing alongside his splendid little armada waving triumphantly to an elated Colonel Arnold. So far, all of General Washington's planning had gone reasonably well. Despite some mishaps and delays, all 11 transports carrying the expeditionary force arrived safely at Gardinerston by Saturday, September 23. Everyone aboard the vessels was healthy and rested, and Colburn's 200 bateaux were ready to take them the rest of the way to Quebec.

The construction of the Arnold Expedition's bateaux was a minor miracle and a testament to Yankee ingenuity. Colburn received his contract at Cambridge on September 3 and Arnold arrived at Gardinerston 18 days later to find his 200 boats waiting for him. The actual construction time was something less than 18 days, since it took at least two days for Colburn to travel from Cambridge to Gardinerston after receiving his contract.[62]

A full description of how these boats were built is in order. The term *bateaux* describes any boat with a flat bottom and sharply pointed bow and stern. There were many ways to build a small boat, and Colburn probably used the simplest technique, called clinker-built construction. In this type of boat building, the sides of the vessel are created by overlapping planks of wood, as opposed to carvel construction, where the edges of the planks meet to form a smooth surface. The long, wide planks used to form the sides of clinker-built boats are called strakes. Arnold's bateaux were probably three strakes high. Narrow curved pieces of wood called "ships knees" attached to the bottom of the boat and held the strakes together. This part could be fabricated quickly from curved tree roots and branches. Another shortcut used by Colburn was to build his boats with what are called hard clines. In boat parlance, this means that there is a sharp edge instead of a graceful curve, where the sides and the bottom of the boat are joined.

It was a monumentally difficult task to build 200 clinker-built, hard cline boats in less than three weeks using the tools available at the time. There is no known record of how Colburn built his fleet, but modern-day boat builders believe Colburn created what may have been the first assembly line in America in order to produce 200 boats in less than eighteen days. Colburn probably divided his work force into specialized teams who kept making the same part. One team, for example, cut and nailed planks together for boat bottoms. This was the first step in the building process. The assembly line came into play when a finished bottom passed to another team that nailed three ships knees onto each side. This gave Colburn the skeleton of his bateaux. The upright, unsupported ships knees were held in position with braces, after which it is believed the bottom of the boat was turned upside down and raised onto saw horses. The ships knees then faced downward, making it easy for another team of workers to nail the strakes to them. The ends of the strakes were curved to form the pointed ends of the bateau. This was possible to do quickly because the strakes were supple green lumber. Oakum, a caulking material made from rags, loose hemp, and jute fibers soaked in tar or creosote was used to seal to the seams along the bottom of the boat and between the strakes. Workmen forced the oakum into the seams using primitive caulking guns. With the addition of a few details, such as thole pins (oarlocks), Colburn had a finished bateau. He and his workmen must have worked around the clock to get them finished so quickly.

Arnold walked through Colburn's wood chip littered boatyard, examining his freshly made flotilla of bateaux. The colonel was familiar with boat construction from his pre-war days as a merchant in New Haven and captain of his own ships. Passing along rows of bateaux, Arnold was able to make an expert inspection of Colburn's work. He knew immediately that his bateaux were constructed from green timber, which emits a distinctive strong odor because it is still full of sap. The colonel also knew that Colburn's bateaux would leak as the unseasoned wood planking lost its moisture and shrank, opening the seams between the planking. He recognized that the boats were too small. While the contract did not specify the length of the bateaux, Arnold stated in his letter to Colburn dated August 21, 1775, that he wanted boats that could carry six or seven men. Arnold's instructions in this regard were clear: "Two hundred light Battoes Capable of Carrying Six or Seven Men each with their Provisions & Baggage (say 100 wt to each man)."[63]

Colburn knew that this size payload required a bateau that was at least 30 feet long. However, he built boats that were probably no more than 26 feet in length. Colburn was right in building smaller boats than specified in Arnold's instructions, because he knew something about the rough conditions that the expedition would face on the upper Kennebec River. He built sturdy boats for the campaign, with thick sides and bottoms that were capable of withstanding a lot of knocking around. He also knew that the boats would have to be lifted or dragged around rapids and waterfalls. Even so, each of the 26-foot-long boats weighed almost 400 pounds empty. This was a lot of weight for teams of men to carry around slippery, rock-strewn rapids and waterfalls. Thirty-foot boats would have been even heavier and almost impossible to carry over the portages that lay upstream. Granted, boats built from seasoned wood would have been lighter, but Colburn had to work with the materials he had on hand. His experience told him that a 400-pound boat was the maximum weight load that the men could handle.

The bateaux that Colburn built were crude by any standards. However, both Arnold and Colburn knew that expensive, well-built boats were unnecessary in this situation, since they only would be used for a short time, on a one-way trip to get Arnold's provisions and equipment as far as the St. Lawrence River. Arnold was not expected to return via the same route, and he would have no further use for this fleet of shallow river bateaux once he reached Canada. Colburn had done his job well; he had built 200 inexpensive and durable boats in less than three weeks.

A careful reading of Arnold's letters and journals reveals no condemnation of Colburn's work. Arnold was a wily businessman who understood that Colburn was running a small business on the edge of the wilderness and it was unreasonable to expect him to have had enough seasoned wood on hand to build 200 boats on short notice. Arnold's familiarity with business also made him wise to the fact that Colburn would never build hundreds of boats without a contract. Still, the boats that Colburn built were too small to accommodate all the cargo that the expedition had to transport to Quebec. Arnold judiciously solved this problem by negotiating with Colburn to build an additional twenty boats at a reduced price to compensate for the shortage of load capacity specified in the contract. It is interesting to see, as our story continues, that Arnold was better at interacting with businessmen than with his fellow army officers. Arnold expected his boats to leak at their seams; thus Colburn's original agreement also specified that he would accompany the expedition with a company of boat builders to help keep the flotilla afloat.

Colburn kept his word, built the additional bateaux, and accompanied the expedition up the Kennebec with 20 workmen. He never received full payment for his boats or services from Congress, who disputed his invoices. Colburn relentlessly pursued his unpaid bill for years and went so far as to visit General Washington's home at Mount Vernon, arriving apparently unannounced on December 15, 1799, to ask the retired general (and former president) to help him get his money. But when he knocked on the door, he was told that Washington had died the previous day. Colburn petitioned the United States Senate as late as 1824 for payment on his 1775 boat contract. His appeals were denied because he could not produce any records or receipts to support his claim. Colburn years earlier had foolishly turned over his supporting documentation to the government, which had lost or misplaced his paperwork. Some other records pertaining to his contract were destroyed when the British burned Washington D.C. during the War of 1812.[64]

Part of Colburn's claim against the government, reaching back to 1775, was that Washington and Arnold instructed him to send a scouting party along the Quebec expedition's intended route and submit a written report upon their return describing everything they had seen. Arnold wrote to Colburn on August 21 asking him to organize the reconnaissance:

> you will Also get particular Information, from those People who have been at Quebec, of the Difuculty attending an Expedition that way, in particular the Number, & length, of the Carrying Places, wheather [whether] Over, Dry land, Hills, or Swamp. . . all which you will Commit to writing & Dispatch an express to his Excellency as soon as possible, who will Pay the Charge & expense you may be at in the Matter.[65]

Colburn promptly complied with Arnold's request by employing two experienced river men named Dennis Getchell and Samuel Berry to reconnoiter the intended route. Getchell and Berry lived along the Kennebec in a settlement called Vassalborough, located a short distance upriver from Fort Western. With their contract from Colburn in hand, Getchell and Berry headed for the wilderness in a canoe on September 1. They hired an Indian guide to accompany them as well as three other white men, one of whom was Dennis Getchell's brother Nehemiah. The intrepid rivermen returned in two weeks, feeling lucky to be alive. As agreed, they submitted a written report to Colburn of their reconnaissance, dated September 13, which they gave to him along with their bill.

In their report, Getchell and Berry said they traveled up the Kennebec, crossed the Great Carry, and, by their own reckoning, paddled an additional 30 miles up the Dead River. While traveling through this lonely, desolate country distinguished by marshes and mountains and infrequently visited by small Indian hunting parties, they met a Norridgewock Indian named Natanis living alone in a cabin. The Indian claimed that he was being paid by Governor Charlton to watch for spies or a rebel army trying to enter Quebec via the Kennebec-Chaudiere route. Getchell and Berry reported this story along with other information given to them by Natanis, who said that British lookouts were stationed at the headwaters of the Chaudiere River and a detachment of Redcoats were quartered just over the Canadian border.

After hearing these stories, the Indian guide leading Getchell and Berry refused to go on, and they took the chance of paying Natanis to take them farther upriver. With Natanis in tow, the little scouting party continued their hurried inspection until they ran into some shallow water and decided to turn back. Their decision not to continue, as specified in their instructions from Colburn, to the headwaters of the Chaudiere (Lake Magentic) was also based on information from an Indian woman they met en route who told them that "at Shettican [Sartigan] the uppermost Settlement on the Chaudiere there was a great Number of Mohawks that would have killed us."[66] Colburn handed their alarming report to an apparently skeptical Arnold who, as we shall see, sent his own scouting party upriver under the command of a reliable officer, with orders to kill Natanis and see if there were actually any hostile Indians or British troops along his intended route.

Colburn also gave Arnold a map of the expedition's route drawn by Samuel Goodwin (1716-1802), an early settler to the region who originally worked as a surveyor. He subsequently became the owner of an inn and general store in Pownalborough. Goodwin had traveled extensively in Maine as a surveyor and claimed he had journeyed to Quebec following the legendary Kennebec-Chaudiere route. Colburn approached Goodwin prior to Arnold's arrival, asking him to make a map of the route. Goodwin complied, as evidenced by a letter he sent to General Washington in which he described his services to Colonel Arnold and encouraged the Continental Army to build a military road between Fort Western and Quebec. The following excerpts from Goodwin's letter confirm the existence of his map and describe its contents:

> Pownalborough, District of Maine, Octor 17th 1775
>
> According to your Excellencys Verbal orders to Collo. Benenedeck Arnold I supplyd him with A Plan of the Sea Coast from Cape Elizabeth to Penobscut and the River Kennebeck to Ammeguntick Pond [Lake Magentic], and Shaddair River [Chaudiere River]. . . which Shaddair, Emptys into the River St Lawrance about four miles above Quebeck[,] and the Passes and Carrying Placeses [places] to Quebeck, and also made Several Small Plans for Each Department [Arnold's principal officers] for their Guid, [guidance or perhaps copies for guides or scouts], and also Gave him [Arnold] a Copy of A Journal which Represeted all the Quick watter & Carrying Places to & from Quebeck. . . .
>
> Mr Ruben Coalborn informed me you wanted a Plan I begain it about three weeks before Collo. Arnold Arived or I Could not have Gott it Redy for him. Please to Excuse the Smallness of the paper for there is a famin [famine; shortage] of it here.
>
> I am Sir with all Due Respects your most Obedeant Devoted and very humbl. Servtt
>
> Samuel Goodwin[67]

There are no references to Goodwin's map in any of the extant diaries, letters, and reports from the expedition. Everyone on the march seemed to be using copies of Montresor's map and journal, which was probably more accurate and detailed than whatever information Goodwin supplied.

General Washington selected Fort Western as the staging place for the expedition because it was the farthest point upstream an oceangoing ship could travel (the height of deep water navigation) on the Kennebec River. The old fort sat on a strategic bluff overlooking the Kennebec about 10 miles upriver from Colburn's shipyard and a total of 45 miles from the sea. Upon arriving at the fort, Arnold made his headquarters at the nearby home of Esq. Howard and his family, whom Dr. Senter described as being "an exceeding hospitable, opulent, polite, family."[68]

Fort Western had been an important frontier post during the early years of the French and Indian War when it was feared that the French might attempt to invade New England via the Chaudiere-Kennebec route. This threat ended when the British army captured Quebec City in 1759, making Fort Western unnecessary. What Arnold's troops found there on September 23, 1775, was a run-down trading post located in the wreck of an abandoned military post at the edge of civilization. The old fort's wooden barracks, blockhouses, palisades, and storehouses had fallen into disrepair and were rotting.

The expedition's stay at this depressing place was busy and frustrating because of the low water level in the river. Either Washington and Arnold had been misled, or they had overlooked making inquiries about the water level of the Kennebec, which was especially low at this time of the year. The problem was that melting snow, which fed the regions waterways, had ended until the following spring. Only after his arrival did Arnold realize that the river was too shallow to allow his heavily laden ships to sail beyond Gardinerston. He tried off-loading some of the ship's cargo into his new fleet of bateaux and other boats hired from the locals so as to get his transports to float higher in the water. But the effort failed: the river was still too shallow for the larger ships to reach Fort Western even after some of their cargo had been transferred. As a result, Arnold and his men lost precious days of good weather as they transported tons of provisions and supplies from Gardinerston to Fort Western in small boats.

Just how much freight was the expedition carrying? Dr. Senter left an accurate record of the cargo that Arnold had accumulated at Fort Western, which he estimated to be a total of 100 tons. Senter included the weight of the bateaux, food, weapons, ammunition, equipment, and supplies. He started by figuring the heaviest category first, which were the bateaux. He calculated that they weighed 400 hundred pounds each, for a total of 40 tons. He estimated that the basic food for 43 days for each man weighted 35 tons. This did not take into account other commissary stores, which included sugar, salt, yeast, and butter. Senter next calculated the expedition's ammunition and weapons. He knew that 100 rounds of ammunition were brought for each man. He estimated their combined weight at four tons, plus another five-and-a- half tons to account for the weight of the rifles and muskets. Then there were tents, blankets, and all kinds of camp equipment, which added another 10 tons to the load. He figured that the hundreds of shovels and axes being taken added another ton to the baggage.

Senter next added all the personal baggage of the officers and common soldiers (extra shoes and clothing plus personal belongings), which he estimated at 10 pounds per man, equaling a total of six tons. In addition there were medical supplies, nails, black smith tools (to repair weapons), and other miscellaneous items. When Senter added it all up he came to a grand total of 100 tons, all of which had to be carried around waterfalls and rapids on the river and portaged overland from one river to another. Since time was against them, Arnold's corps needed to carry all their baggage with them. There was no time to move provisions forward and establish advance supply bases. Speed was essential, and all the expedition's men, food, and equipment had to move along together.

When Arnold's provisions and equipment finally were assembled, the scene at Fort Western must have been impressive. We can picture Dr. Senter walking along the bluff alongside Fort Western among the rows of stockpiled food and equipment. All of the expedition's food was packed into large wooden casks (the preferred cargo container of the time) because they could be sealed tight and moved easily by rolling them along the ground. The armies subsisted on three food items: beef, flour, and biscuits. The beef was cut up into four-lb. sections that were heavily salted and packed in tightly sealed casks filled with brine. Each cask of beef weighed 220 pounds. The flour destined for the expedition was also packed in casks. It could be used to bake bread, but an army on the move did not stop long enough to build ovens and bake bread, so they used the flour to thicken stews and chowders. While there is some speculation that the expedition carried portable iron bake ovens with them, this is not logical, because the weight of the ovens, even if they were available, were too heavy for the bateaux and inconsistent with how armies in the field had used flour for centuries prior to the American Revolution.

The third basic food item carried by Arnold was bread, and the expedition's journalists use the word constantly—which adds to the belief that the men were baking bread en route. However, what these men called bread was actually biscuits. The word is derived from the Latin words *bis* (twice) and *coctus* (cooked).[69] Flour prepared in this manner was known by many names, including ship's bread, sea biscuit, hard bread, biscuit marin, and hardtack. The biscuit baked during the Revolutionary War was a dense, tough product whose greatest attribute was its long-lasting nature. Biscuits were baked prior to a military campaign and packed in casks. The biscuits supplied to Arnold were probably thin and oval shaped.

While the expedition moved through developed areas, the men supplemented their diet with food purchased from local farmers and merchants. When the civilians living in the vicinity of Fort Western heard the jingle of money, they rushed to sell the 1,000-plus soldiers fresh meat, smoked fish, vegetables, liquor, cider, bread, pies, cakes, and dairy products. However, this situation changed once the expedition got beyond the frontier and had to subsist mainly on the beef, flour, and biscuits they carried with them.

Once Arnold reached Fort Western, he began to apply his considerable energy and talent to the exact route that his corps would take to Quebec. Arnold's knowledge of his route consisted of a copy of Montresor's map and journal, the fresh report from scouts Getchell and Berry, Goodwin's map and journal, plus some scraps of information given to him by the local settlers. This accumulated knowledge gave Arnold some idea of the course and the obstacles blocking their path. He knew the route was difficult, and called for maneuvering the boats through rapids and portaging past several waterfalls. He also was aware that, far upriver, the Kennebec narrowed into a shallow, fast-moving highland stream. In this region the corps would leave the river and follow an overland shortcut across three ponds (the Great Carry) that would take them to the Dead River. Montresor's journal entry for July 13, 1761, explained the reason for striking overland to the Dead River:

> We came this day to where we were to begin our portage across the country westerly to the western branch of Kennebec river, called the Dead River, which western branch [swings to the north just before joining the Kennebec] . . . the eastern branch of the

Kennebec, has a great many windings, is full of islands, shallow and rapid. To avoid these inconveniences it is usual to carry the canoes through the woods till you meet the river [the western branch of the Kennebec called the Dead River], where it is of great depth and its current hardly perceivable. This portage is divided by three different lakes, each of which is to be passed before you can arrive at the Dead River.

Montresor commented that the local Indians, called the Abenaquis, had left no trail markers, and disturbed the land as little as possible to hide the way. "No nation, having been more jealous of their country than the Abenaquis," Montresor wrote in his journal, "they have made it a constant rule to leave the fewest vestiges of their route."[70]

Arnold knew that the Dead River led to a series of lakes, called the Chain of Ponds, located in a mountainous region of western Maine that would take the expedition to a ridge of mountains called the Height of Land, which separated New England from Canada. The expedition would emerge from this barren mountain region onto a beautiful meadow from which Lake Megantic could be seen, the source of the Chaudiere River. Arriving on the south shore of the lake, they would launch their bateaux, follow it down the Chaudiere to the French-Canadian settlements, where they expected to get a warm reception. The expedition would then push on to the southern shore of the St. Lawrence River. Arnold's plan was to cross the St. Lawrence in their bateaux at night, and rush into Quebec City and overpower its small, disheartened complement of British troops with the help of American sympathizers. He believed that the route would be fast and easy once he got to the Great Carry.

Arnold was out of contact with General Schuyler's Northern army by the time he reached Fort Western. The last reliable news he had about them was based on a letter from Schuyler written from Fort Ticonderoga on August 31.[71] Schuyler's communiqué reached headquarters on or about September 8, as Arnold was in the final stages of preparing to leave for Canada.[72] According to Schuyler's report, his 2,000-man army was moving north toward the Canadian border, where spies had informed him that Governor Carlton had concentrated his best troops at St. Johns. The garrison at St. Johns was reported to consist of about 475 British regulars from the 7th and 26th Regiments plus 38 gunners from the Royal Artillery and some Canadian volunteers. Arnold knew the place because he had raided it in May, after capturing Fort Ticonderoga. He recalled that it sat on the west bank of the Richelieu River, approximately 26 miles southeast of Montreal.

Fort St. Johns was the gateway to Canada from Lake Champlain and the key to taking Montreal, which was a poorly protected commercial city of 8,000 whose prosperity depended predominantly on the fur trade with the western Indians. There was another fort between St. Johns and Montreal called Chambly. However, Schuyler had reports from spies, sympathizers, and informants that the British used it as a military depot. They described Fort Chambly as more of a hotel than a fortress, because it housed many women and children belonging to the British troops defending St. Johns.[73]

Schuyler could have circled around St. Johns and headed directly for Montreal, but that would only encourage the troops at St. Johns to attack his army from the rear. Furthermore, to ensure that Schuyler would not go around his stronghold, Carleton had an armed schooner named the *Royal Savage* strategically stationed in the Richelieu River near the fort. It was the largest warship in the region, and if Schuyler dared to bypass St. Johns, the *Royal Savage* could sail onto Lake Champlain and sever his supply line from Fort Ticonderoga. Schuyler was aware of the situation and determined to capture St. Johns before moving on to Montreal. His August 31 communiqué sounded positive, containing the first news of his army's movement north into Canada with a force believed to be almost three times the size of the garrison at St. Johns. "Gen. Montgomery leaves Crown Point to day with twelve hundred Men, and four twelve pounders [a reference to artillery], I follow him this Evening. . . . I Shall then be near two thousand Strong," Schuyler wrote.[74]

Schuyler's intelligence gathering included an interview with Captain Richard Jenkins (perhaps a ship's captain), who had been in Quebec in July. In a report dated September 10, Jenkins described the situation there. The interview and report are a further indication of the intensive intelligence gathering activities carried out by both sides during the Revolution. Jenkins' report confirmed that Quebec's garrison had been stripped to reinforce St. Johns, leaving the city virtually unprotected.

Here are the highlights from Jenkins' intelligence report, a copy of which likely made its way to Washington's headquarters, adding to the commander-in-chief's conviction that the Arnold Expedition was a smart move:

Information of Capt. Jenkins, Rec'd September 10, 1775

> Capt Richard Jenkins, arrived at Quebec sometime in July . . . left it
> the 21st—found six or seven Transports there, from Boston loading
> with Provisions & Wood for General Gage—That the Brig. Gaspee
> the only Armed vessel there. . . . That there are not more than twenty
> five Soldiers in Garrison, & Chief of the Artillery gone to St. Johns,
> where the Soldiers have hard Duty in preparing floating Batteries,
> intending to retake Ticonderoga [an exaggeration]. By the best
> Information the Canadians are much in favor of the Colonies.
> Quebec easily taken. Governor Carleton, has between 5 & 600
> hundred Soldiers. Indian Sachems declare their hatchets are buried
> and will not take them up. . . . The addresses and petitions of the
> Congress & others has got among the Canadians & that the
> Governor was much enraged at it.[75]

Arnold launched his invasion of Canada on Sunday, September 24, believing that Schuyler's army quickly would reduce St. Johns and continue north toward Montreal. However, unknown to Arnold at the time, Schuyler's novice Northern army had tried twice in mid-September to capture St. Johns but was repulsed each time by the tough British garrison defending the place. The failure to seize St. Johns by a direct assault forced Schuyler to undertake a time-consuming and costly siege to capture it, which made a quick link-up between Schuyler's and Arnold's forces out of the question. Arnold did not know it when he left Fort Western, but his expedition headed toward Canada with no possibility of help from Schuyler's paralyzed Northern army.

The Arnold Expedition was officially launched when the colonel ordered Morgan's riflemen to advance up the Kennebec River from Fort Western. Rifleman George Morison wrote in his journal on the eve of his departure with Morgan that he knew he faced a difficult journey: "111 miles through frightful wilds, craggy and almost impassable hills and mountains, obstructed with falling tress, thickets and quagmires."[76]

Morison's appraisal was way off on all counts. The journey was far more difficult than anything he imagined, and the actual distance between Fort Western and Quebec, using the route that Arnold planned to follow, was more than twice as long, at 270 miles.[77] What followed is one of the greatest adventure stories in American history.

Chapter 4

All About Them Stood the Forest Primeval,
Dark, Silent and Mysterious [1]

Beyond **Fort Western**, Benedict Arnold was on his own and responsible for the lives of more than 1,000 men and women. Washington's planning and orders had taken the expedition this far, and its continued success rested with Arnold until he reported to General Schuyler. Arnold's corps was transporting 100 tons of freight through a virtually trackless wilderness deep into enemy-held territory. By necessity, they had no artillery with them to breach the walls of Quebec, which meant that the success of the mission depended largely on surprise and help from sympathizers within the city's walls. [2]

Arnold was particularly counting on the collaboration of John Mercier, his prewar business friend and pro-rebel supporter who resided in Quebec. He believed that the city's reported weak garrison would lose heart as Mercier and his partisans opened the gates of the city for the American patriots. The success of the operation depended on timing and luck, but the prize was worth the effort, as Washington mentioned in a confidential letter to his brother, John Augustine Washington, written from Cambridge on September 10: "[I]f the Detachment I am sending (though late in the Season) from hence should be able to get possession of Quebec the Ministry's Plan, in respect to that Government will turn out finely." [3]

Where did Washington get the idea that a small army—with no artillery or naval support—could capture a fortified city surrounded on three sides by deep water? The answer is that behind Washington's temperate, conservative demeanor was a daring and vigorous warrior who thought in terms of audacious action.

As commander-in-chief of the Continental Army, Washington was willing to take risks, especially if they would help bring the war to a speedy and successful conclusion. He expressed this idea in a letter to Governor Nicholas Cooke of Rhode Island early in the war: "[W]e are in a Situation which requires us to run all Risques—No Danger is to be considered when put in Competition with the Magnitude of the Cause."[4]

When he sent Arnold forth with a lightly armed army in the wilderness, Washington believed that he was taking a calculated risk based on his perception of the military and political situation in Canada at the time. His best intelligence was that Quebec was poorly defended and that its civilian population was friendly to the American cause.

Washington also was counting on Colonel Arnold, whom he had hand-picked to lead the hazardous mission, to handle any unforeseen situations and boldly lead his army to Quebec. Washington would later describe Arnold as "a judicious—brave Officer—of great activity—enterprize & perseverance."

The Arnold Expedition was not a conventional campaign because of its secretive nature and its emphasis on speed and surprise. The term guerilla warfare did not exist at the time of the American Revolution; the contemporary term for hit-and-run tactics was partisan warfare or petite guerre (small war). However, the Arnold Expedition was not envisioned as a raid against Quebec City. Arnold's mission was to seize and hold the place until he could rendezvous with Schuyler's army. The Arnold Expedition is best defined as the equivalent of a modern deep attack.[5] Its aim was to support the Northern army's main Canadian offensive by capturing and holding Quebec, the key position along the St. Lawrence River that was Canada's essential line of communication and supply.

The fact that the campaign came early in the war is important, because it shows that Washington was trying new ideas and learning as he went along. He picked up some important lessons from the Arnold Expedition; the most significant probably being that a relatively large operation sent deep into enemy territory was risky and expensive.

Another explanation for Washington's organizing such a bold exploit early in the war was his fascination with military science. He was an avid reader of military textbooks (the presentation of the principles of a subject) and treatises (a detailed discourse on a specific subject) and was anxious to employ what he had learned. Washington was not alone in his interest in reading military textbooks and treatises. With few experienced European-trained officers available to instruct them, Americans tended to educate themselves on military subjects by reading, especially in the years just prior to the American Revolution. The most popular military book in America at the beginning of the Revolutionary War was Humphrey Bland's *Treatise of Military Discipline; In Which is Laid down and Explained The Duty of the Officer and Soldier.* . . . First published in England in 1727, Bland's was the basic primer for new officers and included information on how to drill troops and fire muskets in platoon formations.[6] Washington included Bland's *Treatise of Military Discipline* in a recommended reading list that he included in a letter of advice to a newly appointed Continental Army officer written at the time of the Arnold Expedition. The other books on Washington's 1775 "must read list" are more interesting to our story, because they help us understand his decision to launch his daring and novel assault on Canada. The books are: (1) *An Essay on the Art of War*; (2) *Military Instructions for Officers Detached in The Field*; (3) *The Partisan: or, The Art of Making War in Detachment* (originally published in France in 1759, the first English language edition appeared the following year); and (4) *Manoeuvres, or Practical Observations on the Art of War.*[7]

These four books were advanced texts on warfare with "how to" ideas about seizing enemy fortifications and enlisting the aid of non-combatants. For example, there is a chapter about seizing enemy posts in *Military Instructions for Officers Detached in the Field* that could have been Washington's inspiration for his attack on Quebec:

> A surprize in war is an unexpected attack by suddenly assaulting the enemy when he least expects it. . . . We may refer all sorts of surprizes to two kinds; the one is, by means of ambuscades to attack the enemy on his march. . . ; the other, by making sudden irruptions into the posts of the enemy and seizing them by open force. . . .

The text explains how to capture an enemy post and includes the following advice:

> All the environs that have any relation to the place the enemy occupies must be known; on what side lie the avenues, morasses, rivers, bridges, heights, woods, and all covered places that are in the neighbourhood without which it is scarce possible to regulate approaches prudently.[8]

Military Instructions for Officers Detached in the Field also includes practical information about attacking an enemy position including using bad weather to your advantage:

> [I]f the storm forms, and the wind increases, direct your approaches in such a manner, that you may always have the wind on your back, because if you have it in your face, the enemy's centries [sentries] can look forward and discover you; . . . You need be in no uneasiness about the enemy's centries seeing you, or hearing the noise of your march, because the severity of the weather obliges them to enter their boxes [sentry boxes], and turn their backs to the wind . . . [9]

Arnold likely shared Washington's interest in reading military textbooks and treatises. He only had a few months of experience as an officer prior to his appointment by Washington to lead the corps assigned to capture Quebec. The majority of Arnold's military contacts at the time were with New England merchants and farmers who, like himself, became full time soldiers for the first time when the Revolutionary War started. It seems logical that Arnold acquired some of his military education from the same books that Washington had read. Perhaps with one or two of his military textbooks in his personal baggage, Arnold was ready to strike out from Fort Western for Quebec.

Arnold agonized over the recent report from Colburn's scouts that enemy lookouts, hostile Indians, and British Redcoats were stationed along his intended route. He selected Lieutenant Archibald Steele of Smith's Pennsylvania rifle company, one of his best young officers, to command a scouting party whose mission was to follow the expedition's planned route as far as Lake Magentic and return to meet the advancing army with their findings. This was a dangerous assignment, but Steele was suited for the job from his prewar life on the Pennsylvania frontier, where he had learned wilderness skills that included how to move stealthily through hostile Indian country. Steele left Fort Western on Sunday morning, September 24, with 12 men in two birch bark canoes. His orders included capturing or killing the Indian Natanis who told scouts Getchell and Berry that he was a lookout for the British.

That afternoon, Arnold dispatched a second party from Fort Western commanded by an officer identified as Lieutenant Church. This party consisted of a guide, a surveyor, and seven soldiers. Their mission was to measure and map the army's route as far as the Dead River.[10] The chapter titled "Reconnoitring" (Reconnoitering) in *Instructions for Officers Detached in the Field* stressed the importance of sending a surveyor in advance of the main army:

> Parties ordered to reconnoiter, are to observe the country or [sic] the enemy; to remark the routes, conveniences and inconveniences of the first & the position, march, or forces of the second. In either case, they should have an expert geographer [surveyor] capable of taking plans readily. . . . All parties that go for reconnoitering only, ought to be but few in number. . . . It is incontestable, that a numerous party cannot guide along so imperceptibly as a small handful of men.[11]

Historians frequently have ignored the important role that surveyors played in the American Revolution. No army at the time would move without a surveyor, and General Washington, who was one in his youth, was aware of their value. The surveyor in Lieutenant Church's party is of special interest, because he kept one of the most accurate and detailed journals of the expedition. His name was John Pierce, and he was a native of Worcester, Massachusetts. He earned his living as a surveyor before the war and was a corporal in the Worcester militia company commanded by Timothy Bigelow, a neighbor and friend. Pierce marched off to Cambridge with his militia company at the start of the war, agreeing to stay on active duty for five days. He reenlisted for an additional six months, during which time he volunteered to join the Arnold Expedition. Pierce was 30 years old at the time he became the expedition's surveyor and engineer, a dual title he received because the word "surveyor" described his occupation, while "engineer" stated his function in the army. The title of engineer did not come with any particular military rank, but indicated that the title-holder was responsible for laying out fortifications, selecting routes, and mapping terrain. The British army had excellent engineers, many of whom were graduates of the Royal Military Academy at Woolwich, England. The Americans, however, had no formally schooled men but appointed experienced surveyors like Rufus Putnam and John Pierce to the position.[12]

These men learned their trade by working as apprentices and reading textbooks, such as Samuel Wyld's *The Practical Surveyor* (London, 1725, with numerous subsequent editions) or John Love's *Geodaesia: Or*

The Art of Surveying and Measuring Land Made Easy (first published in London in 1688). Eventually, skilled engineers from France arrived to assist and train the Americans. These foreign engineers played an important role in designing the field fortifications that helped win the decisive actions of the war, including the surrender of Burgoyne at Saratoga in 1777 and Cornwallis' defeat at Yorktown in 1781.

The diarists on the Arnold Expedition seldom mentioned Pierce because his surveying activities were a common occurrence in colonial America. However, Pierce was important to the success of the Arnold Expedition and interesting to modern historians. The British and American armies were always accompanied by surveyors, whose responsibilities included determining the routes for the army to follow, where rivers and streams should be forded or bridged, and where the army should camp. Pierce went ahead of the Arnold Expedition, laying out the exact route for it to follow and posting direction signs. Typical of Pierce's signs was one that read, "Gentlemen these are to inform you that I have Discovered a much Better Landing Place about 20 Perches up the river on the Left which you may find by advancing."[13] More about perches in a moment.

Pierce probably possessed the standard surveying instruments of the day—a surveyor's compass, a pole, and an iron chain. His compass determined direction by reading a pointer on the dial of the instrument that showed orientation from magnetic north. His compass was a large instrument mounted on a sturdy tripod and equipped with a hairline sight that allowed him to take precise readings by aiming at a specific distant object or landmark. An assistant would stand at a distance with a pole that had a painted ball on top for Pierce to sight on if there was no object at which to aim, such as in a featureless open field or a forest. Pierce used his sixty-foot long surveyor's chain made up of one hundred precisely made iron links. It was divided into various measurements, including a perch (also called a rod), which was sixteen and one-half feet long. The surveyor's standard sixty-six foot chain can be equally divided into four perches. Pierce's assistant would physically run out the chain on the ground and push a metal pin, called an arrow, in the ground at the far end of the chain, after which the chain could be run out as many times as necessary to measure a specific distance. One chain equals four perches, and eighty chains equals one mile.

It is evident that Pierce was measuring some distances with his surveyor's chain from a sign that he posted at the expedition's first portage. It included the direction that the army was to follow on their hand-held compasses, which Pierce stated as 23 degrees west from magnetic north. The sign read:

> 1st Carring [carrying] Place, W. 23 degrees N. 9 perches on the Left hand the river. Please to let this Paper Stand that all may Know the Course and Distance and you'll oblige Gentlemen. Yours to Serve Jno. Pierce Surveyor.[14]

Pierce could also take several sightings from the same position with his compass and use geometry to determine distance in rough terrain over which it was not possible to run out a chain. However, there is no indication that Pierce carried out extensive surveys or drew any maps during the expedition, because the army was moving quickly and had no plans to return over the same route. His principal function was to use his experience and common sense to find the best route for the army to follow.

After taking the prudent steps of dispatching reliable scouts and a surveying party, Arnold turned his full attention to the organization of his expedition. At Fort Western, Arnold divided his army into four divisions instead of the two infantry battalions and one rifle detachment under which his corps had thus far been operating. He opted for four divisions to have smaller units whose departures from Fort Western could be staggered to prevent bottlenecks at the portages and campsites en route. Arnold designated his three rifle companies as his first division, which he put under the field command of Captain Daniel Morgan, who would spearhead the expedition's march to Quebec. He put the riflemen out in front because they were his strongest and most able-bodied men. Arnold also wanted his riflemen in front because, like other American officers at the time, he viewed them as his light infantry—the best troops he had—and he wanted them to be the first to face any attack by the enemy. Their skills as woodsmen and frontier warriors made them best suited to blaze a trail, clear campsites for the infantrymen, and detect and repel any potential Indian ambush. By comparison, many of Arnold's musket men were from long-settled towns along the coast, where they worked as farmers, tradesmen, and laborers before the war. These men had less pre-war experience in the use of weapons than the riflemen, as much of the larger wild game had been hunted in the settled areas of the colonies and the hostile Indians killed or forced to move farther west or to Canada.

Colonel Arnold initially assigned Lieutenant Colonel Greene and two musket companies to the first division. But Morgan was unhappy with this arrangement, as Greene outranked the rifle company's officers. Morgan confronted Arnold, complaining that the New England musket companies would only slow down his riflemen. He also insisted that Washington had assured him that the rifle companies on the expedition would only be subject to Arnold's orders. The story was a bluff; Washington had never made any such promises to Morgan, but Arnold could not risk any further delays and removed Greene and his two musket companies from the first division.[15]

Greene was given command of three musket companies designated as the second division. Arnold put Major Meigs in command of the third division, which consisted of four musket companies. Meigs' company commanders included Henry Dearborn, who kept one of the most important diaries of the expedition, and 19-year-old Samuel Ward Jr., a recent graduate of the College of Rhode Island (today's Brown University). His father, Samuel Ward, one of the founders of the college and former governor of Rhode Island, currently represented his colony in the Continental Congress. Arnold gave the fourth division to Lieutenant Colonel Enos. It consisted of three musket companies plus Captain Colburn's company of 20 boat repairmen. Arnold placed a special trust in Enos because his fourth division would be bringing up the rear, as well as carrying a disproportionally high percentage of the expedition's food and equipment. The thinking in giving Enos' division extra provisions and equipment to carry was that they would have the benefit of following a cleared trail, with campsites and shelters left behind for their use by the three divisions that proceeded them.

The expedition's gentlemen volunteers were distributed throughout the divisions as officer assistants. Burr was assigned to Greene's second division. The future vice president of the United States wrote his sister a letter from rustic Fort Western on September 24. "We are necessarily detained here a Day or two," he explained, but assured her that his next letter would be written from Quebec. He also told her that he was enjoying the hospitality of the neighborhood people, "falling on roast Chickens and wallowing if I please in a good feather Bed. . . . But adieu to these soft scenes—tomorrow I traverse the Woods." Young Burr closed his letter with a pledge to write again from Quebec in "three Weeks or less."[16]

Nine Indians accompanied the Arnold Expedition. Four of them were the St. Francis braves who came from Quebec with Chief Swashan earlier in the year. After arriving in Cambridge with Colburn, Chief Swashan met with the local military and civilian authorities and answered their questions, especially those regarding efforts being made by the British to recruit Indians to fight the rebels. Following their meetings it was agreed that "the said Chief, with his Interpreter . . . would proceed to Fort Ticonderoga" to assist Gen. Schuyler, "while the four braves who came down with him should remain in Cambridge, under the direction of his Excellency General Washington."[17] These four Indians eventually joined the Arnold Expedition, traveling to Fort Western on their own.[18]

The other five Indians on the campaign were members of the Penobscot tribe who had chosen to remain in a remote section of Maine rather than flee to Canada. Once the principal tribe of the Abenakis confederation, the Penobscots had been numerous and powerful at the start of the seventeenth century, inhabiting some of the best locations along the coast and hunting in the interior of Maine.[19] But the English settlers had taken most of their land, and disease and warfare had sharply reduced their numbers, so that by the time of the American Revolution there were but a few hundred people living along the banks of the Penobscot River near the present-day city of Bangor. Especially devastating to the Penobscots was their alliance with the French against the British during the colonial wars that preceded the American Revolution. A proclamation by Massachusetts' royal governor at the start of the French and Indian War helps explain the tribe's demise:

> [W]ith the Advice of his Majesty's Council thought fit to issue this Proclamation and to declare the Penobscot Tribe of Indians to be Enemies, Rebells and Traitors to his Majesty King George the Second. And I do hereby require his Majesty's Subjects of this Province to Embrace all opportunities of pursuing, captivating, killing and Destroying all and every of the aforesaid Indians.[20]

The Penobscots did not formally side with the rebels in the Revolutionary War, but allowed their young men to join the American military, without committing the tribe as a whole. The five Penobscots known to have been recruited for the Arnold Expedition are identified as Soncier, Eneas, Sebatis, Metagone, and Sewanockett.[21]

There are only a few brief references to the Indians on the expedition by the various diarists, and the majority of them likely crewed the large canoe carrying Arnold and Oswald. Arnold needed mobility to move quickly between the advancing divisions, and he opted to travel in a canoe manned by Indians who knew how to handle it. Since the Indians almost certainly were inexperienced in handling batteaux, Arnold hired veteran Kennebec rivermen, including Samuel Berry, the four Getchell brothers, and a French-speaking Huguenot named Jaquin, who were dispersed throughout the corps to teach the soldiers how to handle the clumsy boats and navigate the river. The expedition did not need the Indians as guides or scouts; they had Montresor's map and diary and experienced frontier riflemen to move ahead of the army. Arnold also wanted to keep his Indians with him to use as couriers and for special assignments.

The majority of each division marched on land and followed the Kennebec, while the bateaux carried the bulk of the expedition's provisions, gunpowder, musket balls, tents, and other heavy equipment. Arnold could move rapidly between the various divisions in his canoe to supervise the operation and give orders. Couriers deployed to maintain communications among the four divisions. Thus, Arnold was not alarmed that Enos' fourth division was still at Colburn's boatyard with a party of men off-loading the last cargoes from the ships on the same day that Morgan's first division started upriver from Fort Western. Enos had time, because his division was not due to depart Fort Western until three days later.

Arnold allowed his four divisions to spread out and advance at their own pace to the Canadian border. Once they entered Canada, they faced a greater possibility of being attacked and would have to advance in a close formation, prepared to defend themselves. The rendezvous point for the expedition was Lake Magentic, the large body of water that lay just over the border (according to Montresor's map). "I design Chaudiere Pond [Lake Megantic]," Arnold wrote Washington, "as a general Rendevouze, and from thence to march in a Body."[22] All four division commanders received copies of Montresor's map, which showed the location of the lake.

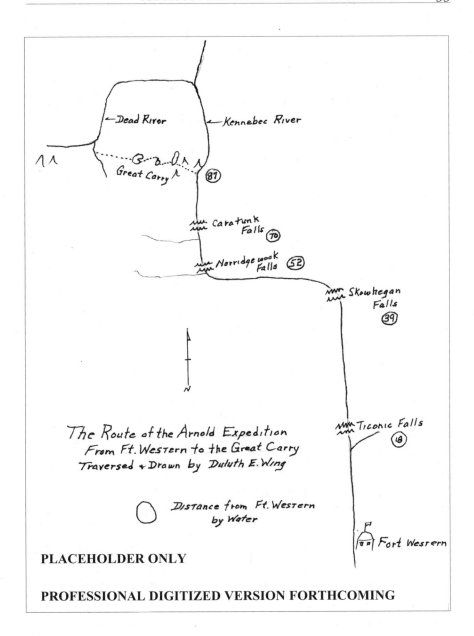

The Route of the Arnold Expedition
From Ft. Western to the Great Carry
Traversed + Drawn by Duluth E. Wing

Distance from Ft. Western
by Water

PLACEHOLDER ONLY

PROFESSIONAL DIGITIZED VERSION FORTHCOMING

The expedition was launched from Fort Western with the help of local people, who descended on the post with their wagons and teams of animals. They offered to transport some of Arnold's freight along the first leg of the route, which was an old military road that ran between Fort Western and another abandoned military post upstream called Fort Halifax. The local population's enthusiasm was not wholly patriotic, as they expected to be paid for their work. Money was scare in the region, and the arrival of Arnold's army to this edge of civilization was an economic boon.

Arnold quickly put his plan for advancing on Quebec into action, as evidenced by a report he penned to Washington dated September 25. The colonel's communiqué included news of his safe arrival in Maine and the scouting party he had dispatched under Lieutenant Steele. Arnold also informed the commander-in-chief that he had sent Lieutenant Church and "seven Men with a Surveyor & Pilot [expert river man], to take the exact Courses & Distance to Dead River so called, a Branch of the Kennebec."[23]

Each division left Fort Western on schedule. The three rifle companies, comprising the first division, started out on Monday, September 25, with a 45-day supply of food. Captain Dearborn recorded the riflemen's departure in his journal: "Captains Morgan, Smith and Hendricks, with their Companies of Rifle Men embarked on Board their Batteaus, with orders to proceed up the River as far as the great Carrying place. . . ."[24] With the riflemen leading the way, the balance of the army, unevenly but eagerly, followed in the coming days. Meigs' diary confirms the departure of the second division a day behind the riflemen: "[September] 26th. [Lieutenant] Colonel Green embarked on board battoes, three companies of musketmen,...on their tour to Canada."[25] The third division left the following day under the command of Major Meigs, who wrote in his diary on the date of his departure, "I embarked on board my battoe with the third division of the army, consisting of 4 companies of musketmen, with 45 days' provision, and proceeded up the river, hoping for the protection of a kind Providence."[26] The fourth division, commanded by Lieutenant Colonel Enos, consisted of three musket companies and Colburn's boat repairmen. Their job included picking up stragglers from the divisions ahead of them and providing a rear guard.

Arnold remained at Fort Western to supervise the departure of his entire corps. He was there on the morning of September 29 to watch two of Enos' musket companies depart. Arnold then wrote out orders for Enos, who was bringing up the rear with the third company in his division: "Leave two or three men with the Commissary [Joseph Farnsworth] to assist him, and hurry on as fast as possible without fatiguing the men too much. Bring on with you all the carpenters of Capt. Colburn's company, and as much provision as the batteaux will carry."[27]

Having done everything possible at Fort Western, Arnold and his aide Oswald boarded a large birch-bark canoe manned by some of the expedition's Indians and started upriver to join his advancing army. However, Arnold soon discovered that his canoe leaked, and rather than lose time making repairs, he switched to a sturdier pirogue (a dug-out canoe made from a single tree trunk) at Vassalborough and quickly closed in on the men ahead of him.[28]

In his letter to Washington, Arnold noted that the distance between Fort Western and Quebec City was 180 miles, and that his corps would make the trip in 20 days. "I have engaged a Number of good Pilots, & believe by the best Information I can procure, we shall be able to perform the March in twenty Days—the Distance about 180 Miles," he wrote.[29] Arnold knew that there were 87 miles of rapids and waterfalls from Fort Western to the Great Carry, after which he believed the route became easier, allowing his army to quickly advance to Quebec.

Out on the river, the inexperienced boat crews were having a difficult time. The Kennebec was unpredictable, because its depth, width, and current changed with the seasons and weather. The water level was at its lowest point of the year, which added to the number and length of places where the boats had to be manhandled through shallow water and exposed rocks. But the low volume of water in the river also provided some advantage, in that the intensity of the rapids diminished.

A three-man crew usually manned each boat—two men handling the oars or poles and the third in the rear steering with a pole or oar. The number of crewmen varied with river conditions, and up to five men might be used at times to work the boats. The expedition was moving against the current, which required continuous rowing of the bateaux with oars or, more commonly, propelling them upstream with long, iron-tipped poles—called setting poles—that pushed the boats against the flow. In a strong current, ropes had to be thrown to the shore and the boats dragged upstream by teams of men, a technique called cordelling. Common soldier George Morison mentioned the hazards of such an effort in his diary: "[W]e were often obliged to haul the boats after us through rock and shoals, frequently up to our middle and over our heads in the water; and some of us with difficulty escaped being drowned."[30]

Morgan's riflemen came to the end of the old military road and emerged at Fort Halifax, situated on a high plateau where the Sebasticook River flowed into the Kennebec. This strategic site was first fortified in 1754. The British army and militia had connected it by road to Fort Western so that the two forts could reinforce one another. When Montresor arrived at Fort Halifax from Quebec on July 9, 1761, he found it to be a busy place. "Fort Halifax was built by Mr. Shirley in 1754, to awe the Indians and cover the frontiers of New-England," he recorded in his journal. "The fort is garrisoned by a company of New-Englanders and supplied from the settlement below [Fort Western]." Montresor noted that the fort's defenses were "more than sufficient against an enemy who has no other offensive weapons than small arms."[31] This probably was a reference to the fact that, following his journey across Maine, Montresor realized it would be impossible to transport artillery over the route. The fort did not endure, however, and Morgan's riflemen arrived there 15 years after Montresor to find nothing but an abandoned, decaying relic from the past.

Morgan's riflemen began arriving at Fort Halifax on the evening of September 27, with the rest of the army struggling into the decrepit fort over the next four days. It took each division an average of two-and-a-half days to travel the 18 miles between Fort Western and Fort Halifax. The exhausted boat crews did not realize that the stretch of river they just traveled was smooth compared to what lay ahead on the tempestuous Kennebec. This first portion of the trip was easier because the men did not have to portage their boats. Also, the boats were not fully loaded, as part of the expedition's freight had been transported by wagons and carts along the old military road. But Arnold had reasons to feel optimistic: Monstresor had recorded that it took him only 12 days to travel from Fort Halifax to Lake Magentic.[32] Also, scouts Getchell and Berry had informed Arnold back at Fort Western that the Kennebec and Dead Rivers were pretty passable, "the water, in general., shoal., on account of the late dry season. The trees were well marked, as far as we went, and the way is so direct as may be easily found."[33]

The men fully loaded the bateaux at Fort Halifax and resumed their voyage upstream. There was no road beyond Fort Halifax, and the men marching on land had to be guided along a rough trail on the eastern side of the river. The heavy boats did not have far to go to meet the Kennebec's next challenge, which was a half-mile of swift water cascading over a series of rock ledges called Ticonic Falls. This was the expedition's first portage. The men poled and dragged the boats as far as possible into these rapids. When they could advance the boats no farther, they muscled them to the western bank of the river for portaging, and tons of food and equipment—plus the heavy bateaux—were carried around the rapids. Meanwhile, the men in the land party were being led up the east side of the Kennebec. They had to wade across the river to the west side, where the best portage lay. Once across, they helped to carry the freight and boats around the rapids. Local farmers arrived with teams of horses and oxen to help. The fully loaded bateaux were too heavy to drag ashore, so the men waded into the cold water to unload their cargoes. Everything in the boats was off-loaded and carried to dry land. Even empty, the heavy bateaux were hardly manageable. The men pulled and dragged them out of the water and onto dry land, where they turned them over and carried them across the portage on their shoulders. Diarist Morison noted how some of the men aided their efforts by passing handspikes under the bottoms of the bateaux at the portages.[34]

A minimum of four men were needed to lift the 400-pound empty boats using this technique, one man on each corner. There was a trail to follow, but it traveled over rough terrain, resulting in the men weaving and stumbling over inclines, declines, and slippery rocks. "Our progress under these immense burthens," Morison wrote in his journal, "was indeed slow, . . . having to lay them down at the end of every few rods to rest."[35]

The tons of food, tents, gunpowder, weapons, medical stores, and other miscellaneous equipment and supplies had to be portaged beyond the falls, where the men put the boats back into the water and carefully reloaded their cargoes. The length of the portage around Ticonic Falls was about three-fifths of a mile, and it took the better part of a day for each division to portage around this first obstacle. Though members of the expedition continued to receive help from civilians as they moved upriver, the number of people they encountered diminished as they continued upstream.

Ticonic Falls provided an indication of what lay ahead. Five Mile Ripples, a long stretch of swift water, was the next dangerous section of the river that the bateaux navigated fully loaded. Captain Dearborn described the passage on September 30:

> Proceeded up the River this Morning, found it exceeding rapid and rocky for five miles, so that any man would think, at its first appearance, that it was impossible to get Boats up it, I fill'd my Battoe to day [Dearborn's boat filled with water], and wet all my Baggage, but with the greatest difficulty, we got over what is call'd the 5 mile ripples, and then encampt, and dryed my Cloathing as well as I could.[36]

Wet clothing and bodies had serious implications; winter came early to the region, and the men made huge fires at night to dry their belongings. William Humphrey wrote on September 28 that "it now begins to grow uncomfortable."[37] Two days later, he recorded an apparent sharp drop in the nighttime temperature: "last night it froze so hard as to freeze our wet clothes. . . and ice was as thick as window glass."[38] The men on the boats could not keep dry, and colder temperatures exacerbated the problem. The plummeting nighttime temperatures were a reminder that the expedition had been racing against the weather since its inception. A speedy arrival at Quebec before the region became encased in ice, snow, and freezing temperatures was critical.

The Kennebec River turned tranquil beyond the Five Mile Ripples, giving the men a much needed respite. They now were in a section of the river that the settlers had named Canaan. Arnold's bateaux must have made a spectacular scene as they passed by the small settlements and isolated farms that dotted the shoreline of this northern paradise ablaze with autumn colors. This pleasant stretch of the river ended abruptly as the expedition approached Skowhegan Falls.

Spelled differently by nearly every one of the diarists (Arnold called it Souheagen Falls, Major Meigs wrote it as Scohegin Falls, and Morison reported it as Cohegan Falls), Skowhegan Falls brought misery and danger to the expedition. It was the expedition's second portage. This dangerous section of the river began with a right angle into a narrow gorge of rapidly moving water. One moment the bateau men were gliding along tranquilly and the next they were poling their boats with all their strength through a raging chasm. Protruding ledges of rock surrounded them on both sides, making it impossible to get ropes to men on the shore.

The crews poled their boats through this torrent, fighting against the current, and when they could pole no farther they got into the cold, foaming river and pulled the bateaux through the raging water with ropes. The rapids continued beyond the gorge, but at least lines could be thrown from the boats to men on shore who helped pull them upriver against the swift current. Still, no one rested easy, because they could look upriver and see the menacing waterfalls that blocked their passage. As they neared the 20-plus-foot-high Skowhegan Falls, they could see that there was a rocky island in the middle of the waterfalls surrounded by cascading water. The best portage around the falls was up and over the rocky island, which extended upriver to calmer water.

The Indians had showed the first white settlers the way—they maneuvered their canoes to the base of the falls and then hoisted them with ropes to the summit of the rocky island. Arnold's men planned to use this old Indian portage, but instead of lifting lightweight birch bark canoes up and over the precipice, they had to haul 220 clumsy bateaux plus the tons of food, guns, ammunition, tents, and medical supplies up to the rocky island with dangerous white water all around them. The scene must have been incredible as the men used ropes and pulleys to lift the boats up the steep face of the island with the waterfalls pummeling around them. The Indians had cleared some ground on the far end of the island, which they used as a camping ground. Arnold's men found this place and were happy to rest for a while after their long ordeal. The portage at Skowhegan Falls continued for days, as each division made its way up and over this formidable obstacle.

Some of the crews had to stop for almost a week above Skowhegan Falls to repair their battered boats. "Could we have then come within reach of the villains who constructed these crazy things, they would fully have experienced the effects of our vengeance" noted Private Morison.[39] Historian Justin Smith echoed these sentiments when he wrote, "Without a doubt the feebleness of the bateaux was a vital defect in the preparations for Arnold's enterprise. . . . The need of strong boats could not have been understood at Cambridge. . . ." Smith blamed the mistake on "haste and scanty knowledge of the conditions."[40]

Today's historians continue to blame the bateaux for the problems of the expedition, with comments like, "Why canoes were not used on an expedition up a river so full of rapids and falls is not clear,"[41] and, "Perhaps the greatest mistake in Arnold's Expedition was the use of the heavy bateaux instead of light canoes, which could have been carried easily across the portages and maneuvered more surely in the rapids of the rivers."[42] The 220 clumsy bateaux take on a growing importance as Arnold's men stopped beyond Showhegan Falls to scrutinize the damage.

A strong indictment against the bateau is the fact that those members of the expedition who were using Indian canoes seemed to move quickly and easily along. Arnold, for example, appeared to be gliding effortlessly back and forth among his divisions in a dug-out canoe. The decision to use bateaux was Washington's. He had experience on the frontier, especially as a young surveyor navigating the rivers of western Virginia and Pennsylvania. Even if Washington did not know about river craft, Arnold certainly did. He saw the big canoes commonly used as transports on the St. Lawrence River during his prewar business trips to Canada. However, a close examination of the situation reveals that Washington made the right decision in using bateaux instead of canoes, despite the comments of the inexperienced men on the expedition and numerous historians.

Arnold loaded his Indian canoe lightly, with only a few personal items. Canoes were easier to handle in rough water, provided they were lightly loaded. However, a heavily loaded canoe, lying low in the water, was difficult to control. In fact, a heavily laden bateau was more seaworthy than a similarly loaded canoe. The secret of the bateau's seaworthiness is the angle of its flared sides, which makes it almost impossible to overturn.

Washington opted for bateaux because they could be built quickly and cheaply by semi-skilled labor.[43] They were plentiful on the lower Kennebec, where the river flowed comparatively wide and deep, and where carpenters and tools were available to build them. In addition, the expedition's boats were disposable, to be used to get the army's freight to Canada after which they would be abandoned. Bark canoes were expensive and time-consuming to build, and few white men knew how to construct them. In addition, the rock formations in the Kennebec had shale ledges with sharp-edged rocks that could tear out the bottoms out of bark canoes. Only a lightly loaded and skillfully handled canoe had an advantage over a bateau on the Kennebec River.

Another problem that became evident as the expedition moved upriver was the inexperience of the boat crews in handling the craft.

Some of the men may have lied about their experience with small boats in order to secure a place on the expedition. This resulted in numerous accidents, as boats smashed against rocks or stranded in shallow water. It also took a lot of experience and skill to load and trim small boats with heavy cargo. Thus, the inexperienced crews caused some of the mishaps attributed to the boats. Aaron Burr acknowledged this problem in one of his letters: "Imagine to yourself 200 Battoes managed by men—two thirds of whom had never been in one. . . ."[44] The idea of relieving the boat crews with fresh men from the marching column did not work. The problem was that Arnold did not have enough experienced men to relieve his tired crews, and it was not logical to replace men who had mastered the rudiments of handling the boats with beginners from the marching column. One historian claims that the short and frail-looking Burr was one of the best boatmen on the expedition. He learned to handle small boats while growing up near the Elizabeth River in New Jersey.[45]

Emergency repairs were made to the bateaux by Colburn's crew at Skowhegan Falls, and the journey resumed. The changing character of the Kennebec continued as the expedition moved upstream. Along one stretch of the river north of Showhegan Falls the men were running their boats through rapids called the Bombazee Rips that ended abruptly in a majestic stretch of calm river surrounded by beautiful countryside. One of these tranquil places occurred where the Sandy River emptied into the Kennebec from the west. This was the landmark that warned the river guides that the expedition was approaching its next formidable obstacle: a one-mile series of rapids and waterfalls known as Norridgewock Falls. The river climbed 90 feet during this one-mile stretch, and no boat could possibly survive in the torrent. The expedition approached the falls via an old Indian village—Norridgewock—that stood about a mile below the cataract. Norridgewock was once a large Indian settlement and the site of a French Catholic mission.

Contemporaries described the Indians who once lived here as "fierce denizens of the wilderness": they came from various tribes and sub-tribes of the Abenakis who had left their native haunts to live under the direction of missionaries.[46] The last French priest at the site was Father Sebastien Râle (pronounced *Rall* by most of the New Englanders), whom the English colonists believed was encouraging his Indian converts to attack settlements in Maine and New Hampshire. Many people in New England at the time of the Revolutionary War knew the story of how a party of colonial militia had attacked the village in 1724, burned it to the ground, and killed many of its inhabitants, including Father Râle. Some of the Indians returned to bury Râle and erect a cross over his grave. Arnold's men arrived at the site to find a large open tract of land where the village had stood. They did some sightseeing among the ruins of the village, viewing the remains of the Catholic Church built by Father Râle as well as his grave, which was marked by a large wooden cross. The story served as a reminder that the majority of Canada's white population was Catholic, while the liberating American rebels were staunch Protestants.

Norridgewock Falls was the expedition's third portage. The expedition hired all available teams of horses and oxen in this sparsely settled region to help haul the boats and baggage past this obstacle. Even the oxen brought along for beef were pressed into service. Like the two previous portages, the work was arduous and time consuming. But the job got done, and the divisions, each in turn, arrived safely upriver from the falls.

Norridgewock Falls was an important landmark on the Kennebec River, and every diarist mentioned the date they arrived there. We can get a sense of how spread-out the expedition had become from the dates that each division reached the falls. According to Arnold's journal, he arrived on the morning of October 2, only to find that Captain Morgan's first division had just completed portaging their boats and baggage around it.[47] Greene's second division was just approaching the falls on that same date, while Meigs' third division, accompanied by some of Colburn's company of civilian carpenters, did not reach the site until the night of October 4.[48] Enos' fourth division was two days behind Meigs, arriving at the falls on the 6th and not clearing it until the night of the 7th.[49] Arnold spent almost a week at Norridgewock supervising the passage of his entire command past this formidable obstacle before resuming his journey upriver.

Arnold used the opportunity of the Norridgewock portage to take an inventory of his army's food supply. The results were shocking, as he realized that a large quantity of food had spoiled from water damage. The bateaux were taking a terrible beating with water shipping (the nautical term for seeping) into them through gaps in their seams and from the spray flying into the boats as they traversed the rapids. As the expedition's medical officer, Doctor Senter's responsibilities included

the inspection of food. His journal entry from Norridgewock Falls, dated
October 5, describes how the river water ruined their provisions:

> The fish [dried cod] lying loose in the batteaux, and being
> continually washed with the fresh water running into the batteaux.
> The bread casks not being water-proof, admitted the water in
> plenty, swelled the bread, burst the casks, as well as soured the
> whole bread. The same fate attended a number of fine casks of peas.
> These with the others were condemned. We were now curtailed of a
> very valuable and large part of our provisions. . . .

The hasty preparation of provisions at Gardinerston at the start of the
expedition accounted for additional spoilage. Senter mentioned this
problem in his same October 5 journal entry: "A few barrels of salt beef
remained on hand, but of so indifferent quality, as scarce to be eaten,
being killed in the heat of summer, took much damage after salting, that
rendered it not only very unwholesome, but very unpalatable."[50] In
addition, the men had wasted some of their provisions along the march,
believing that they had an abundant supply. Arnold supervised the grim
task of inspecting the expedition's dwindling food supply and dumping
spoiled and rotten provisions. He should have taken action to impose
food rationing when he realized the expedition was falling behind
schedule and much of the food had been ruined.

Hunting game to supplement their food supply seemed a logical
solution to the problem. But the noise and smells created by over 1,000
men had frightened away almost all of the game along the route. Besides,
there were orders not to fire any weapon for fear it would give away the
expedition's position to any Indian war parties that may have been
dispatched from Canada to watch and listen for signs of rebel movement
from Maine. However, despite the food shortage, there was no talk of
turning back. Everyone tightened their belts and resumed the trek, hoping
that the worst was behind them.

For the moment, the spirits of the men improved as they continued
upriver. They now traveled in a beautiful wilderness that few white men
had ever seen. The Kennebec flowed broad and smooth through this
region of lush vegetation. Dearborn called this area "exceeding good,"
but the pleasures of the passage were soon spoiled by a cold rain that
drenched the men and their baggage. Greene's second division and
Meigs' third division passed the mouth of Seven Mile Stream (today's

Carrabassett River) in the rain. Mountains became visible in the distance for the first time, giving the Kennebec—now devoid of the rivers that fed it—the appearance of a mountain stream. But one more obstacle remained to be conquered before reaching the Great Carry: Carritunk Falls.

Carritunk Falls, known today as Caratunk or Solon Falls, actually was a series of rapids when Arnold's army ascended the Kennebec River. After seeing the place, diarist Greenman called it "Hell Gate Falls"; Humphrey referred to it as "Devil's Falls."[51] Even the Indians respected this place: the word Carritunk means "rough." What prompted these names was a series of ledges composed of dark rocks with sharp edges at an upward angle. The portage around Carritunk Falls was about a quarter-mile and Morgan's riflemen led the way, arriving at the falls on October 4.[52]

Dr. Senter portaged around Carritunk Falls on October 10 and camped for the night about a mile above the place. His diary entry for the following day is rich in the details of the march. According to Senter, he "Decamped the usual time, viz., at the rising sun and that he continued his march mostly by land this day and that the men were now scattered up and down the road [route] at the distance of ten or twelve miles. At 7 in the evening we quit the water," he continued, "and with the greatest difficulty procured a fire. . . . Sprung our tents and made an exceeding luxurious bed with the blue joint grass, which this river land produces in great plenty."[53]

The diaries show that the individual companies within the four divisions advanced at their own pace, as there were few open spaces along the upper Kennebec where large numbers of men could camp together. The selection of campsites normally was the responsibility of the quartermaster, who selected sites based on a variety of particulars, including defense, open ground for tents, and accessibility to fresh water. Surveyor Pierce probably selected and marked the campsites on the Arnold Expedition, leaving little for the quartermasters to do. In addition, as the rest of the army moved upriver, they utilized the campsites established by Morgan's riflemen.

Dusk was the signal for the scattered companies to stop for the night and make camp. Most of the men were trekking on land while the bateaux transported their equipment and most of their provisions. The marching column carried two days' rations with them, consisting of salted beef (which may or may not have been cooked) along with some flour and biscuits. The expedition followed the rough Indian trails, which tended to weave in and out from the shoreline, as much as a half-mile inland, following the best terrain. The rifle companies who led the way marked the route for the other divisions to follow. They used axes to clear the rough, narrow trail. The possibility of a surprise attack existed, particularly by Indians sent from Canada, so the men kept their weapons with them at all times. Some of the experienced frontiersmen on the expedition wrapped a greased or waxed cloth around the lock (firing mechanism) portion of their weapon to keep it dry, clean, and ready for action.

At dusk, if everything went well, the men headed down to the riverbank, where they met their boats and camped for the night. The forest frequently came down to the banks of the river, making it necessary for the men to camp among the trees. Some unloaded the bateaux while others organized their campsite and prepared the evening meal. Everyone, including the officers, probably slept in small "A" or wedge tents, made of canvas held upright by two wooden poles. The soldiers looked for a level, smooth patch of ground with strategically placed trees from which to string their tents, and a company-size campsite was sometimes scattered over one or two acres. Each tent slept five or six men who bundled together to keep warm.[54]

The expedition's officers slept in these same small tents, but with fewer men per tent. One advantage that many officers enjoyed was the services of a private soldier drawn from the ranks to act as a servant. This practice was wide-spread in the British army, and the status-conscious Americans copied this custom as a convenient way for an officer to have a personal servant, also called a "waiter."[55] The soldiers encouraged this practice as a way of being exempt from ordinary duty, and apparently did not mind acting as a combination valet, butler, cook, and groom for their officer. There are clues that Arnold and his officers had servants, including an entry in surveyor Pierce's diary that reads, "my waiter remains at Point Aux trembles"; diarist Stocking mentioned that "a waiter of Captain Morgan was drowned."[56]

Captain Dearborn's journal entry for October 25 also indicates that personal servants were on the expedition: "This Night I was Seized with a Violent Head-Ach and fever, Charles gather'd me some herbs in the woods, and made me Tea of them."[57] The "Charles" mentioned by

Dearborn was Charles Burget, a French youth who enlisted in Dearborn's company at Fort Western and was known to have been the captain's servant. Dearborn mentions Arnold's waiters in a later entry: "I met one of Col. Arnolds Waiters."[58] And then there is Stocking's journal, in which he notes, "A servant of Colonel Arnold's who had been taken prisoner. . . ."[59] Slave-owning southern officers frequently brought a slave with them to act as their servant, and it is possible that Daniel Morgan, who was from Virginia and owned slaves, had a slave attending him on the Arnold Expedition.[60] Morgan's officers, all of whom were from Virginia, might also have brought slaves with them from home to attend to their feeding and grooming on the trek to Canada.

The five or six enlisted men who shared a tent also cooked and ate their food together. They were called an eating mess, or mess, and this arrangement was common in both the British and American armies during the Revolutionary War. There were no common kitchens or eating places. The commissary officer or his assistants issued the messes their uncooked rations. The campfires that Arnold's men made each night were probably huge affairs. Lieutenant Humphrey gives us a clue when he wrote on September 29, "we made large fires and refreshed ourselves."[61] Each mess had its own campfire, started in an open area with the small, dry pieces of wood that littered the forest floor. A handful of birch bark was the preferred kindling because it ignited quickly and flared fiercely. Small dead tree trunks and branches were added once the fire got going. The men piled the wood lengthwise and cris-cross on the fire. As one end of the pile burned down, a fresh length was pushed into the fire. This method saved a lot of time and effort, and provided a long-lasting fire for men who had been working hard all day. As soon as they could, the men would strip off their wet clothing which they dried on ropes strung near the roaring fire.

The messmates cooked their food in their camp kettle. No stone fire rings have been found in any of the campsites known to have been used by the Arnold Expedition. If anything, they would have moved some rocks around to serve as seats. Instead, to save time and labor, they cooked their food on a bed of hot coals over which they suspended their kettle. Salted beef or pork was a basic food, along with flour and biscuits. Dried peas (also spelled pease) were issued if available. The messmates poured some of their flour into their kettle to thicken their food, which they called stew. If they added fish to their other ingredients, they called it chowder. There were plenty of brook trout and round whitefish in the Kennebec. Atlantic salmon could also be found in the upper section of the river in September prior to spawning. Or, the soldiers could make chowder using the dried fish issued by the commissary. They poured their stew or chowder over some of their biscuits and subsisted on this simple diet day after day.

There probably was little activity in camp after the food had been cooked and eaten. The men, exhausted from their labors during the day, went right to sleep and awoke at dawn to begin the long process of loading their bateaux and continuing their march toward Quebec.

The terrain became rougher beyond Carritunk Falls, as the foothills of the mountains reached down to the riverbanks. The river was still wide and impressive, but tangled growths of trees and bushes now hugged the shoreline, giving the river a wild and rough appearance. The Kennebec is formed deep within this rugged country by two smaller meandering rivers named the East Branch and the West Branch. Montresor had explored both branches in 1761 with his Indian guides and indicated their labyrinthine courses on his map. He followed the meandering East Branch on his trip from Quebec to Maine, starting from its source, which was Moosehead Lake, deep in northern Maine. On his return trip, Montresor took the West Branch (which was also called the Dead River). The Dead River was so named because it was a tranquil stream that seemed to have no current. Like its sister the East Branch, the Dead River also serpentined through northern Maine.

The Indians showed Montresor a short-cut between the Kennebec River and the Dead River, which made it the shortest and most practical route between Quebec and Maine. Known as the Great Carry, this shortcut was a 11-mile portage from a point above Carritunk Falls on the Kennebec across three lakes to the Dead River. The Dead River was easy to follow to its source, a chain of ponds near the border between Maine and Quebec. The Indians showed Montresor the way among the numerous ponds and streams in the region, and he marked the route on his map. After crossing the chain of ponds, Montresor's guides took him through a pass in the Appalachian Mountains that brought him to Lake Megantic in Canada. The intrepid British engineer's map and journal was the key to crossing from Maine to Quebec. By 1775, few white men living in Maine had been curious enough to trek across the Great Carry to the Dead River. The anticipation of reaching the portage increased as the expedition drew closer to it. They believed that they would have an easier time as they moved rapidly across it and emerged onto the tranquil and deep Dead River, which pointed due north to Canada. By this time they had fought their way 87 miles up the Kennebec from Fort Western.

Morgan's rifle company reached the Great Carry on October 6. Its men recognized the place by locating a mountain peak that looked like a sugar loaf, directly below which a stream flowed into the Kennebec. The source of this stream, called Carrying Place Stream, was the first of the three ponds that comprised the Great Carry. It had taken the expedition much longer than expected to reach this milestone on their march to Canada, but morale was high despite the hardships and delays, and everyone expected the worst was behind them as they neared the overland portage. Morgan's riflemen beached their boats among dense underbrush and trees, and rested after their long and arduous ordeal.

Back in Cambridge, Washington was unaware of the expedition's position when he wrote Schuyler that Arnold must be nearing Quebec. The commander-in-chief hoped that the colonel would "have no Difficulty in regulating your Motions with Respect to him."[62]

Little did he know that Arnold's corps was still 200 miles from its destination.

The Sky Looked Down Through the Dense Forest . . . Upon a Broad Arrow Struck Through its Very Heart [1]

The members of the Arnold Expedition did not receive the relief they had hoped for when they arrived at the Great Carry. In fact, their labors increased as they began to inch their way along the lengthy and difficult portage. With food running low, and the weather continuing to deteriorate with plunging temperatures and piercing gusts of wind, the men became increasingly anxious as they advanced deeper into the Maine woods and farther away from any chance of rescue from the outside world.

The Great Carry, described as being an easy short-cut between the Kennebec and the Dead Rivers, turned out to be a twelve-and-a-half-mile nightmare. As promised, it consisted of three navigable lakes separated by long, rough, and muddy trails, and camouflaged by the Indians who kept them just wide enough to accommodate small parties of lightly equipped men and their slender canoes. The Arnold Expedition arrived at the site with 1,100 to 1,150 men, 220 heavy boats, and tons of ammunition, equipment, and food—all of which needed to be carried between the three ponds and what turned out to be a final, miserable portage through a swamp from the third pond to a stream that flowed into the Dead River. The corps remained resolute throughout the ordeal, however, partially due to Colonel Arnold, who moved confidently among his troops, assuring them that the worst was behind them and that they soon would be in Canada, whose people would welcome them as

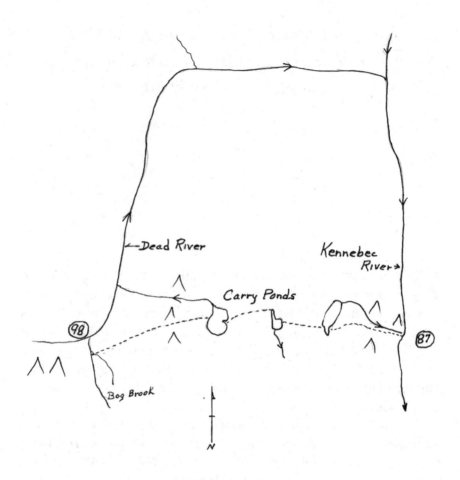

THE Route of the Arnold Expedition
"The Great Carrying Place"
From the Kennebec to the Dead River
Traversed and Drawn by Duluth E. Wing

⭘ Distance from Ft. Western
   by water

PLACEHOLDER ONLY
PROFESSIONAL DIGITAL MAP FORTHCOMING

liberators. The other officers imitated their commander's confidence, especially Morgan, whose charismatic personality, common sense, and endurance had elevated him to the unofficial command of the expedition's three rifle companies. But in the rear of the column and beyond the notice of the expedition's other senior officers, Lieutenant Colonel Enos was losing heart. His division carried the bulk of the army's food reserves, and his growing pessimism threatened the expedition's success.

An advance party of riflemen and pioneers (a military term for men provided with leather aprons, hatches, saws, spades, and pick-axes) led by Morgan were the first to reach the Great Carry, arriving at the site on October 6 after 17 days of slogging up the Kennebec from Fort Western.[2] Morgan's pilots knew the trick of finding the entrance to the portage, camouflaged among the dense brush and trees, by locating a large mountain in the shape of a sugar loaf (today's Henhawk Ledge) then finding the place where the river turned eastward within site of this mountain. The guides knew that they were abreast of the Great Carry when the sugar-loaf-shaped mountain seemed to rise out of the river. There was also a rock-strewn brook (present day Carrying Place Stream) that emptied into the Kennebec just above the entrance to the portage.[3]

Heavy rain fell on Sunday, October 8, and Morgan decided to give his tired men a day of rest at the entrance to the Great Carry before pushing inland. Private Morison was with Morgan and grateful for the chance to relax, writing in his journal that the riflemen were worn out from days of hauling their bateaux "through the shoals, being mostly wet. . . . Providence however sent us a day of rest, for we were detained in our tents all this day by reason of great rain."[4]

Morison and his fellow troops would have been heartened to know about a letter that had been found aboard the captured British brig *Dolphin*. This unarmed British merchant ship had been seized off the coast of Massachusetts en route to Boston from Quebec. All the letters, reports, and documents found aboard the *Dolphin* were rushed to General Washington's headquarters for evaluation. Among the correspondence was a letter written by Captain Thomas Gamble, a British quartermaster officer stationed at Quebec, to his counterpart in Boston. In his letter Gamble explained that the residents of Quebec would not fight if the Americans attacked their city:

> I am apt to think the Canadians will lay down their arms and not Fire a shot, their minds are all Pioson'd by Emissarys from New England & the Damn'd Rascals of Merchants here and at Montreal . . . the Canadians talk of that D—d abused word liberty.[5]

Morgan's riflemen were eager to accommodate the people of Quebec, but they had to get there first. They awoke in their tents on the morning of October 9 to find that the rain had stopped. Anxious to proceed, the riflemen broke camp and started trekking up the narrow Indian trail that marked the entrance of the Great Carry. Hatchet marks made on trees by the scouting parties dispatched from Fort Western by Arnold helped them locate the route. The trail paralleled shallow Carrying Place Stream for a short distance before veering northeast to the first pond. The path the riflemen found was disappointing—too narrow and rough for all the men, boats, and equipment behind them. They required a path that was at least eight-feet wide, so as to accommodate the boats and baggage going in one direction and the men returning the opposite way to pick up another load. This meant cutting and chopping down trees and underbrush to widen the route. Rifleman Morison described their slow progress in his journal:

> This morning [October 9] we hauled out our batteaux from the [Kennebec] river and carried thro' brush and more, over hills and swamps to a pond. . . . This was by far the most fatiguing movement that had yet befel us.[6]

The rest of the army arrived slowly at the Great Carry and followed the trail being widened by the riflemen and pioneers.[7] Arnold reached the portage on the morning of October 11 to find the bulk of his force already there and hard at work transporting the boats and baggage over the rough, narrow trail. He ordered three additional companies under the command of Captain Oliver Hanchett to hurry forward to help Morgan's men improve the route. The 34-year-old Hanchett hailed from Sheffield, Connecticut, and had held a captain's commission in the 2nd Connecticut Regiment before volunteering for the Arnold Expedition. Hanchettt was one of Arnold's favorite officers, and the colonel often chose him for difficult assignments.

It was around this time that a courier arrived with a message from Washington's headquarters. The dispatch, dated October 4, 1775, was written by Colonel Reed, Washington's military secretary. Reed was an educated man who had been a successful Philadelphia lawyer prior to the war. We can picture Arnold sitting on a folding camp stool, with men moving bateaux and baggage all around him, excitedly opening the dispatch. "I have his Excellency's directions," Colonel Reed told Arnold, "to acknowledge your favor of the 25th September, by Lieutenant Gray [the letter Arnold wrote Washington from Fort Western]. He approves of your disposition, and the order of your march, and hopes you will keep ever in your mind the lateness of the season, and the necessity of making the utmost dispatch."[8] Reed continued with an update on the last known position of Schuyler's Northern army, based on a letter written by Schuyler on September 20.[9] Schuyler reported that he was "waiting for artillery and supplies of men and provisions" before resuming his attack on St. Johns, which was still stubbornly resisting. Reed followed with a summary of the latest information about the situation in Canada.

As Washington's confidant, Reed was well informed on the latest intelligence at headquarters, which was based on evaluating information gathered from spies, paid informers, sympathizers, deserters, prisoners, and intercepted British dispatches and letters. He confidently assured Arnold, based on information received at headquarters and reports from Schuyler, that "the Canadians and Indians are extremely favourable, and we are every moment in expectation of hearing something decisive," meaning Schuyler was expected to capture St. Johns very soon and continue his march toward Montreal. Reed also shared the latest American intelligence with Arnold concerning Quebec, which offered great prospects for an American success in that quarter. Here is the complete text of Reed's comments concerning this matter:

> By a brig from Quebeck for Boston (taken eight days ago, in three weeks from the former) [Reed was referring to the letters and documents found on the captured brig Dolphin] we understand that the whole force is drawn from Quebeck to St. John's, and that, in its present situation, it [Quebec City] must fall into your hands without firing a shot; that there is a great magazine of powder and other warlike stores at Quebeck, and the French inhabitants and English merchants most favourably disposed to the American cause. We have also some intercepted letters from some officers at Quebeck to Gen. Gage and others, confirming our former accounts [pro-American disposition] of the Canadians.

We hope this delay by General Schuyler will be a happy circumstance for you, as it may keep Carleton engaged at St John's; whereas, by his returning from thence, and throwing himself into Quebeck, your enterprise would most probably be defeated. At present there is not a single Regular at Quebeck; nor have they the least suspicion of any danger from any other quarter than Gen. Schuyler.

Wishing you all possible honour to yourself, and success to your Country, I remain, Sir, your most obedient and humble servant,

J. Reed.[10]

This was great news from headquarters, but Arnold first had to get his corps to Quebec, which was proving to be a greater challenge than he or General Washington had imagined.

When he arrived at the Great Carry, Arnold had other important news from Lieutenant Church. Following their orders, Church's party traveled as far as the Dead River, which they reached on October 6 before turning back the following day to rejoin the main army. Church's surveyor, John Pierce, kept a journal of their experiences in which he reported a relatively easy trip, during which they were able to supplement their army rations with fresh game and fish. For example, on October 4 he wrote, "Landed at Indian Carring Place [The Great Carry] about 11 O'clock and went over to ye first Pond . . . our Party Killed 2 Partridges—and I Killed one musquash [muskrat] and Catched a Plenty of Trouts and Chubbs [the name given to large minnows that grew up to a foot in length]—had a fine Chowder for Supper Slept Peaceably." His entry for October 6, written while camped along the Dead River, included, "Poor Land—Drank what is Called running tea [probably soldier's slang for liquor mixed with tea]. . . . Tried for fish in the Dead river but Caught none—Saw Some Partridges but it being windy we Killed none this Day—but the inconveniency of not having fresh meat for Supper was Supplied by the above mentioned Delicate Dish of Tea."[11]

Church successfully completed his mission and reported to Arnold that he had traveled and measured the intended route as far as the Dead River, including an accurate survey of the Great Carrying Place. He said that the first lake or pond on the portage, named East or Big Carry Pond, was irregular in form, one-and-a-quarter miles long, and half-a-mile wide. He explained that the distance between East Carry Pond and the second lake, called Little Carry Pond, was a half-mile over rough but hard ground. The lieutenant noted that Little Carry Pond was a half-mile across and a muddy, unwholesome piece of water with a tangle of dead, moss-covered trees at its far end.

The portage between Little Carry Pond and the third lake, named West Carry Pond, was through a mile of hazardous swampy ground choked with exposed roots. Church said that West Carry Pond was the largest of the three lakes and that beyond it lay a difficult three-mile portage to the Dead River. The first two miles of the distance, Church explained, consisted of a steep ascent to the top of a hill followed by an easy descent. But the final mile of the portage from West Carry Pond to the Dead River was through a savannah, which from a distance looked like a beautiful flat plot of firm ground covered by moss, groves of spruce and cedar trees, and bushes. But one step into this greenery would reveal it to be a muddy, treacherous swamp. Church related that a man would sink eight or ten inches into the mud and constantly step upon the unseen sharp snags of dead trees. However, past this obstacle was a stream (modern Bog Brook) that seemed to be a straight and smooth man-made canal that the bateaux could navigate onto the Dead River.

Church also reported that he had used several campsites made by Lieutenant Steele's advance scouting party, but had not seen or heard from them since he watched them depart Fort Western on September 23. Colburn's scouts, Gretchel and Berry, had been told that there were Indians loyal to England watching the Dead River, and there was fear that Steele's party may have been ambushed by them or attacked by the British soldiers rumored to be lurking near the Canadian border.

With Church's rough survey in hand, three companies of musket men took the lead from the riflemen and continued widening and improving the Indian path. Arnold put Christian Febiger in charge of the project. Febiger was one of Arnold's best officers and also one of the most interesting men on the expedition. Born in Denmark, he was 29 years old when he joined the Arnold Expedition. Febiger's father traded horses and lumber in the Caribbean and was probably a pre-war business acquaintance of Benedict Arnold.[12] Young Febiger had attended a military academy in Denmark before joining his uncle, who was the governor of the Danish Virgin Islands as well as a horse trader. Febiger next toured the British American colonies in 1772 as the representative of a Danish West Indian merchant firm. He traded lumber, fish, and horses up and down the American coast, eventually establishing his business in Boston, where he was living when the Revolution broke out. Febiger joined the rebels within a week of the start of the war by enlisting in Colonel Samuel Gerrish's Essex and Middlesex militia. Appointed the regimental adjutant in May 1775, with the rank of captain, Febiger fought at Bunker Hill, where he successfully rallied the reserves and led them into action. Arnold met Captain Febiger at Cambridge and invited him to join his expedition as his adjutant with the rank of major. The young man agreed, and probably helped Arnold select the 1,100 volunteers who accompanied the expedition from among the 4,000 applicants who desired to go.

As they stumbled across the Great Carry, one wonders if the men who signed on for the expedition at Cambridge remained as eager as they had been for adventure. Everyone was dirty and cold, and it was impossible to find a dry place to camp. Great gusts of wind and snow squalls followed the recent heavy rains, adding to their misery. The pioneers were now in the lead of the slowly advancing column, swinging their axes to widen and improve the turbid trail between West Carry Pond and the Dead River, when suddenly they discerned several hideous figures coming toward them from the opposite direction. Fearing danger, the men dropped their tools and grabbed their loaded muskets, pointing them at the freakish human shapes that drew closer. A moment later, the men working behind the advance party heard yelling and cheering. Febiger ran forward with his pistol drawn to see what the commotion was all about. He arrived on the scene to find that the ragged, gaunt figures coming up the Indian path from the Dead River were members of Lieutenant Steele's scouting party and included John Joseph Henry from Smith's Pennsylvania rifle company. Though the scouts had made it to the Canadian border with no signs of the enemy, they otherwise had a miserable experience and felt lucky to be alive.

Young Henry was shocked by what he witnessed when he returned to the main army. He had last seen his fellow soldiers at Fort Western and remembered them as a high-spirited band of robust young men, well-equipped and provisioned and eager to surmount the wilderness. Reunited with this same force 26 days later, he found everyone worn out, ailing, dirty, and hungry. He learned that conditions were so bad that Colonel Arnold had ordered the construction of a temporary hospital, which was immediately occupied by ten seriously ill soldiers. A surgeon's mate named Matthew Irvine was placed in charge of the place.[13] Arnold also sent instructions back to Enos to select a junior officer with 15 or 20 men who were "not so well able to proceed, yet capable to taking care of the sick," to help Irvine and keep a bateaux at each pond to ferry the afflicted back to Irvine's hospital. Doctor Senter blamed bad drinking water as a major cause for sickness among the men. He described the problem in his journal entry for October 15, which he penned while encamped along the shoreline of swampy Middle Carry Pond. "Many of us were now in a sad plight with the diarrhoea. Our water was of the worst quality," noted Senter. "With this we were obliged not only to do all our cooking, but use it as our constant drink."[14]

Arnold ordered the speedy construction of a second building between East Carry Pond and the Kennebec to serve as an emergency food depot. He believed that there were still 100 barrels of provisions at Fort Western, and he sent a messenger to Colonel Farnsworth with orders to hire civilians to bring up this food to stock the depot. Arnold explained his decision in a letter to Washington: "The expense will be considerable, but when set in Competition with the Lives or Liberty of so many brave Men, I think it triffling."[15] If there were 100 casks of provisions at Fort Western, they never reached the Great Carry, probably because Farnsworth did not have the manpower or boats to get them upriver.

The construction of the food depot was part of Arnold's improvised plan for his attack on Quebec. His intention was to drive his army in scattered units to Lake Magentic, where he would reassemble them and march closer to Quebec with hoped-for fresh intelligence from American sympathizers inside the city. However, since the expedition had fallen way behind schedule, and everyone was sick and hungry, Arnold decided that a food depot on the Great Carry was necessary in the event he was forced to turn back.

Arnold finally addressed the serious food shortage as the expedition trekked across the Great Carry. On October 15, Arnold's headquarters party camped at the edge of the sinister savannah that separated West Carry Pond from Bog Creek. While he believed that his corps had 25 days' provisions, enough to get to Quebec, the companies near Arnold were on the verge of starvation.[16] The colonel ordered a reduction of rations to three-quarters of a pound of pork and three-quarters of a pound of flour per man per day. Arnold ordered the few oxen still being herded along as work animals killed at once to provide food. Dr. Senter described the fate of the last of these animals: "I had almost forgot to mention the sufferings of a poor ox, who had continued the march with us, through all our difficulty." Senter said that two men were responsible for driving the animal along. "[W]henever we came to a pond or lake he was drove round it. Rivers and small streams he swam and forded without any difficulty." This ox was butchered on October 20, and each man received a pound of its meal as he passed. "This was a very agreeable repast," wrote Senter, "as we had been principally upon salt pork for twelve days."[17] There were also trout in the ponds, and the men gorged upon them for as long as possible.[18] A few moose had also been shot. Major Meigs noted that four had been killed to date, adding that the meat made excellent eating.[19]

The Great Carry portage had taken much longer than expected. In an effort to make up lost time, Arnold instructed Lieutenants Church and Steele to take twenty "axe men" (pioneers) plus surveyor Pierce, move up the trail as fast as possible, and start clearing the portage from the upper Dead River to Lake Magentic. He also instructed Steele to go beyond the lake and travel down the Chaudière "near the Inhabitants & examine the falls, portages, &c—and return to the Pond [Lake Magentic] as soon as possible."[20] Arnold expected to meet them near the lake in about eight days. Nature, it seems, had a different timetable in mind for Arnold's army.

The expedition had survived the rain and mud, putrid water, and short provisions, only to stand on the edge of a vast open area near the end of the Great Carry portage that appeared to be beautiful grasslands with scattered trees. In reality, however, this was hazardous marshland. Captain Dearborn described the area as "a spruce swamp knee deep in mire all the way" with an "almost impenetrable" thicket.[21] Dr. Senter verified the difficulty of this portage: "[W]e rose to a great height, then a sudden descent into a tedious spruce and cedar swamp, bog mire half knee high. . . ."[22] Darkness forced some of the men to spend a night in the swamp, camped in mud and stagnant water amid a tangle of bushes, rushes, and rotting tree trunks.

In spite of all their difficulties, if we believe the contemporary accounts, every man remained in high spirits. Boosting morale was Lieutenant Steele's report that the army was on course to Canada and that he had found no signs of Indians or British troops during his scouting mission. Steele also reported that the Dead River was a smooth, deep stream with only a few small waterfalls and rapids. Arnold mentioned the high morale of his corps in a letter he wrote to Washington from Middle Carry Pond on October 13:

> A person going down the river presents the first opportunity I have had of writing your excellency since I left Fort Western. . . . Three divisions are over the first Carrying place, and as the men are in high spirits I make no doubt of reaching the Chaudiere River in Eight Days.

In this same letter, Arnold took care to summarize his situation for Washington:

> Your Excellency may possibly think we have been tardy in our March, as we have gained so little, but when you consider the badness & weight of the Batteaus and large Quantity of Provisions &c. we have been obliged to force up against a very rapid Stream, where you would have taken the Men for Amphibious Animals, as they were great Part of the Time under Water, add to this the great Fatigue in Portage, you will think I have pushed the Men as fast as they could possibly bear.[23]

We know that this letter arrived at Cambridge on November 5 because General Nathanael Greene mentioned its receipt in a letter he penned on that date.[24] Arnold's estimate of reaching the Chaudière River from the Great Carry in eight to ten days proved wrong.

Eight days after he wrote Washington, Arnold's corps would still be in Maine, lost and starving.

Colonel Benedict Arnold on the Arnold Expedition. *Author's Collection*

Captain Daniel Morgan on the Arnold Expedition. Note that Morgan is wearing shoes and not moccasins. *Author's Collection*

Gentleman volunteer Aaron Burr on the Arnold Expedition. This illustration is based on a letter Burr wrote to his sister from Fort Western at the start of the campaign. In his letter, 19-year-old Burr described his clothing, weapons, and accoutrements. Burr's face is based on his earliest known portrait painted by Gilbert Stuart in 1794. *Author's Collection*

A middle-class farmer/Continental Army soldier on the Arnold Expedition.

Author's Collection

Illustration by George C. Woodbridge

A lower-class laborer/Continental Army soldier on the Arnold Expedition.

Author's Collection

Chapter 6

A Direful Howling Wilderness Not Describable[1]

Arnold knew that he was almost 200 miles from Quebec City when he wrote Washington on October 13 that he expected to reach Lake Magentic in eight days. The colonel made this bold assertion because he was a hands-on, hard-driving field commander who excelled at motivating his men and achieving his goals. Although Arnold moved confidently among his troops, it must have been unnerving for him to realize that his army had traveled less than 100 miles since leaving Fort Western two weeks earlier and, as he admitted in his letter to Washington, "we have had a very fatigueing Time."[2]

Adding to his problems was a dearth of fresh and reliable information about the situation inside Quebec and the location and size of Schuyler's army. Arnold mentioned his lack of information in his communiqué to Washington: "I have had no intelligence from Gen. Schuyler or Canada [a reference to Arnold's contacts in Quebec City], and expect none until I reach Chaudière pond [Lake Magentic]."[3] The colonel's reference to the expectation of news from Quebec or Schuyler when he reached Lake Magentic is interesting because, barring a miracle, the only way Arnold was going to get information was to dispatch swift couriers to his prewar friends in Quebec, who could rendezvous with him at the lake. This is precisely what Arnold did, calling upon two of his Indians for the job who, until now, had been manning his canoes.

Arnold penned an urgent letter on the night of October 13 to his friend John Mercier in Quebec, "or in his absence to Captain Wm. Gregory, or Mr. John Maynard," while his Indians made preparations to leave on their vital mission early the following morning. In his letter to Mercier, Arnold said, "I am now on my march for Quebec with about

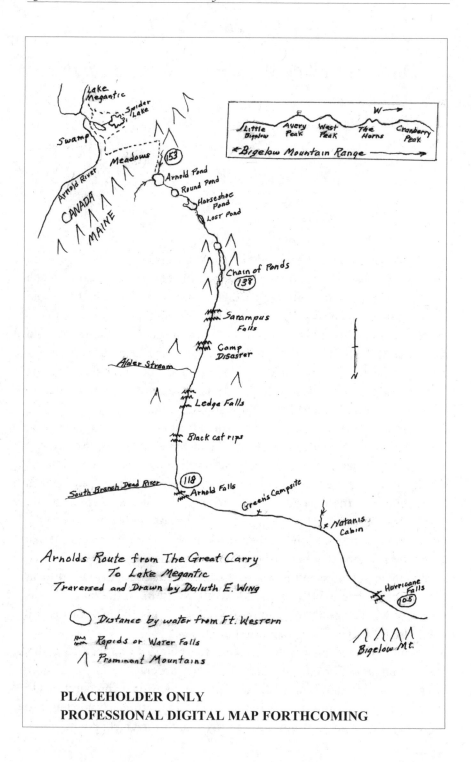

Arnolds Route from The Great Carry
To Lake Megantic
Traversed and Drawn by Duluth E. Wing

Distance by water from Ft. Western
Rapids or Water Falls
Prominent Mountains

PLACEHOLDER ONLY
PROFESSIONAL DIGITAL MAP FORTHCOMING

2000 men [a deliberately exaggerated number], where I expect to have the pleasure of seeing you soon. This detachment is designed to co-operate with Gen. Schuyler to frustrate the unjust and arbitrary measures of the ministry and restore liberty to our brethren of Canada." The colonel explained that the person delivering the letter was "a faithful Indian," who would carry back a message with the number of troops in Quebec, "and in short what we have to expect from the Canadians and merchants in the city." Arnold added that anyone who came out of the city to meet him on the road "would be received with pleasure and handsomely rewarded." He enclosed a second letter asking Mercier to send it to General Schuyler by express. In this letter, Arnold wrote that "after a very fatiguing and hazardous march over a rough country up the Kennebec river. . . we have at last, arrived at the Dead River, which we have examined to the Chaudière pond; and hope in a fortnight of having the pleasure of meeting you in Quebec. Any intelligence or advice you can communicate will be gratefully received. . . ."[4]

Arnold entrusted two of his Penobscot Indians, Eneas and Sabatis, to carry his letters to Quebec.[5] A French-speaking soldier named John Hall accompanied them. Hall was a deserter from the British army who had joined the Continental Army in Cambridge and volunteered for the expedition.[6]

As Arnold expectantly watched his couriers leave camp, he must have thought about the present location of Schuyler's army. He wondered if they had already taken Montreal while his expedition was falling behind schedule. He may have felt better about his own circumstances if he knew the sad condition of General Schuyler.

Unlike his friend Washington, who had a robust constitution, Schuyler was not a healthy man. He suffered from rheumatism of the joints and was prone to intestinal and malarial fevers. Advancing from Fort Ticonderoga, Schuyler's army camped on a swampy island (Ile aux Noix) that commanded the entrance to Lake Champlain. Directing his army from a tent in the cold and damp ground brought on his ailments. In a letter to Washington, Schuyler confided that he had been "much indisposed with a billious Fever," a term loosely applied at the time to a complex of symptoms comprising nausea, abdominal pains, headache, and constipation.[7] Schuyler's condition worsened on the night of September 10. "[M]y Disorder reattacked me with double Violence and every fair Prospect of a speedy Recover vanished," noted Schuyler, whose wife was summoned to help care for her husband.[8] On September 16, with his wife at his side, the general was carried in a litter from his tent and gently placed on board a boat that took him back to Fort Ticonderoga. Schuyler eventually recovered his health, but his frail constitution prevented him from rejoining his army in the field. Schuyler turned over the command of his army to Montgomery, the former British army captain who had been commissioned a general by Congress and appointed as Schuyler's second in command.

As the siege at St Johns wore on, Montgomery's problems increased. Disease, cold weather, harsh living conditions, and stiff resistance from the post's defenders weakened his army and eroded discipline. While the general remained outwardly patient with his troops, he vented his frustration in his personal correspondence. To his brother-in-law, Robert R. Livingston, he confided, "The New England troops are the worst stuff imaginable. There is such a equality among them, that the officers have no authority. . . . The privates are all generals, but not soldiers." In this same letter Montgomery referred to the New Yorkers he commanded as "the sweepings of the New York streets."[9]

Back at Cambridge, an outwardly cool-headed Washington was penning similar confidential letters about the New England troops he commanded. Writing to his confidant Joseph Reed, who was visiting Philadelphia at the time, the general grumbled:

> Such a dearth of Publick Spirit [patriotism] & want of Virtue, such stock-jobbing, and fertility in all the low Arts to obtain advantages, of one kind or another. . . and such a dirty, mercenary Spirit pervades the whole, that I should not be at all surprizd at any disaster that may happen. . . . [C]ould I have foreseen what I have, & am like to experience, no consideration upon Earth should have induced me to accept this Command.[10]

Despite all his problems, Montgomery was the bright spot in the Northern army's assault on Canada. He was resourceful and relentless in his siege against St. Johns, during which he cut off all supplies into the fort to starve the garrison into surrendering. His tactics also included sending several detachments deeper into Canada to create mischief in the British rear and to recruit French-Canadians for the rebel army. One of his units succeeded in capturing Chambly, the British supply depot 12 miles north of St. Johns.[11]

Washington was aware of the problems with the Northern army, which seemed to be advancing into Canada at a much slower pace than the Arnold Expedition. Based on the reports he was receiving from Schuyler, the commander-in-chief realized that the Northern army had run into unexpectedly strong enemy resistance and might have to retreat back down Lake Champlain. The general expressed his concerns in a letter to Schuyler dated October 6, in which he asked that if the Northern army abandoned its invasion of Canada, "I beg it may be done in such a Manner that Arnold may be saved by giving him Notice." Washington then told Schuyler that, no matter what happened, "your Army to keep up such Appearances as may fix Carlton and prevent the Force of Canada being turned wholly upon Arnold," and stressed the importance of keeping pressure on the enemy "that Arnold may have Time to retreat."[12]

From his little tent deep in the Maine forest, Arnold was unaware of Schuyler's illness, of his relinquishing the field command of his army to Montgomery, whose advance into Canada was stalled at St. Johns, or of Washington's troubled letter to Schuyler expressing the possibility that Carlton could continue to delay Schuyler's Northern army at St. Johns while he sent troops to intercept Arnold's intrusion. On the other hand, neither Washington, Carlton, Schuyler, Montgomery nor anyone else from the outside world knew that by mid-October Arnold's intrepid corps of volunteers had finally broken out of the muck and mire of the Great Carry and were rapidly advancing up the Dead River toward Quebec. The corps continued to move in company-size detachments, with the majority of the troops marching on land, weapons at the ready, while their provisions and baggage were transported on the remaining serviceable bateaux. As always, each division was responsible for its own provisions, and according to Arnold's reckoning there existed a reserve supply of food with Enos' fourth division.

The Dead River proved to be everything that had been promised by the scouting parties—a narrow, deep river, smooth and almost black in color, with few obstacles to impede a rapid advance toward Canada. "The river is so remarkably still and dead, that it is difficult to determine which way it runs," noted Private Abner Stocking.[13] The river, almost uniform in width with steep shores rising eight or ten feet on either side, appeared like a man-made canal. Low, clinging vegetation overlapped the river-banks and spread out onto the flat land to form a broad flood plain broken by stands of trees. Mountains dominated the view. They were later

The Bigelow Mountain Range, as seen from the upper Dead River.

Amy Lawrence

referred to as the Bigelow Range, Bigelow Mountain, or simply the Bigelows, in honor of Major Timothy Bigelow.[14] Private Stocking from Captain Hanchett's company took time to write a graphic description of the region in his journal:

> On our right and left were excessively high mountains, the summits of which were covered with snow and ice. Could I have ascended to the top of one of these mountains I thought I could have overlooked all creation. The land between the mountains appeared to be very rich and fertile—wild grass covered the ground, four or five feet in height, and served us a good purpose for covering for the night.[15]

Arnold's men were feeling that the worst was behind them even as they struggled with a new problem: the shortage of oars to row their bateaux. The expedition had started out with a plentiful supply of oars, but the boatmen had relied on long setting poles to push the bateaux up the shallow Kennebec River. As a result, the men discarded many of the oars by the time the expedition reached the Dead River, where their sturdy setting poles were too short to reach the river bottom. With oars in short supply, the boatmen had to push their bateaux along by grabbing at the bushes and underbrush along the riverbanks.

Adding to the men's frustrations was that the Dead River meandered through the countryside; despite their constant labors, they always seemed to be looking at the Bigelow Mountain Range. A few rapids and waterfalls on the Dead River, though shorter and gentler than anything the boatmen had experienced on the wild Kennebec, also created problems. The first of these small waterfalls, or ledges, was located about eight miles from where Arnold's men launched their boats into the Dead River. Although the river only fell about eight feet through these cascading ledges of rock, it was impossible to drag or push the bateaux over them, and everything had to be off-loaded and portaged. This obstruction would later be named Hurricane Falls. According to Lieutenant Steele, who had commanded the expedition's scouting mission, the cabin of the Indian Natanis lay a few miles beyond the falls, surrounded by a lovely meadow. Dearborn, marching with Meigs' third division, mentioned the cabin in his journal entry for October 17: "[I]t Stands on a Point of Land Beautifully situated. . . . [T]he river is very Still, and good Land on each side of it a Considerable part of the way. . . ." The passing expedition found the cabin abandoned with no sign of its former occupant, who had concealed himself in the nearby forest and observed their every move.

"[W]e proceeded up the River 5 miles farther," continued Dearborn in his entry for the 17th, "and found Colo: Arnold and [Lt.] Colo: Green with their Divisions, making up Cartridges, here we Encampt."[16] Dearborn's company was managing to move faster than the rest of their division when they came upon Greene's entire division, in camp on the south shore of the Dead River and busying themselves making cartridges for their muskets while they waited for Enos' fourth division, with the food reserve, to catch up with them.

Much had happened to Greene's division in previous days. Greene and his men took the lead from Morgan's division on the Great Carry when the riflemen were delayed with clearing and widening the trail. Maintaining their position at the head of the main army, Greene's men portaged around Hurricane Falls on October 16 before camping for the night a few miles farther up the trail, near the site of Natanis' cabin. Colonel Arnold, in a buoyant mood after a day of good progress up the Dead River, arrived at their camp that night. As promised by his scouts, he found the river relatively easy to navigate, and believed that the expedition could now advance quickly to the Canadian border. However, Arnold's mood changed when Greene informed him that his division was almost out of food and had stopped to wait for Enos' rear division to come along with the expedition's reserve supply. The colonel had a quicker remedy and ordered Major Bigelow (Greene's second in command) to go back with some men and boats to retrieve food from Enos. Bigelow set out for Enos' column early the following morning (October 17), taking 12 bateaux and a detachment consisting of three lieutenants, six sergeants, and 87 men. Not knowing exactly how far back Enos was, but expecting Bigelow's relief party to return shortly with food, Arnold told Greene to stay where he was. Greene was keeping his men busy making cartridges while they waited for Bigelow's return. Meanwhile, at mid-day on the 17th, Morgan's division passed through Greene's camp and reclaimed the lead.

Although motionless, Greene's division continued to consume food. "[V]ery short of provisions," wrote one of Greene's worried officers. "[O]ur company had not five or 6 lb. of flour to 50 men."[17] This information contrasted starkly to a missive Arnold wrote just a few days earlier to commissary officer Farnsworth, in which he claimed, "The three first divisions have twenty five days provision[s]. . . ."[18]

How could Arnold have been so mistaken about his army's food supply? The answer may be that, while Arnold was an excellent combat officer, he was a careless administrator.[19] He was also inexperienced at this early period in his military career and oblivious of the need to impose strict discipline, tighten-up his straggling column, and get better control of his remaining provisions. There is, for example, no mention in Arnold's journal, letters, or the journals of any of his officers or enlisted men that he made any effort to get an accurate tally of his provisions during the expedition, and he implemented rationing only when his men were on the verge of starvation. Though they acknowledged his courage, even the common soldiers on the expedition noted Arnold's lack of military organizational skills. One of the enlisted men called him "our bold though inexperienced general."[20]

The men in Greene's hungry division caught trout and tried hunting for game, especially moose, as they impatiently waited for Bigelow's return. When Montresor traveled through this region 14 years earlier, he had reported seeing many animal footprints on the sand near the Dead

River and concluded that the area was full of game.[21] Lieutenant Steele's men had killed several moose along this section of the river when they passed through it earlier in the month during their scouting mission. But the arrival of colder weather, heralding the onset of winter, and the smell and movement of 1,000 men through the region, had frightened off the animals.

Such was the cheerless state of things when Captain Dearborn and his company, from Meigs' third division, stopped at Greene's campsite. Meigs arrived at the campsite the following day with the rest of his division, which spent the night before moving out, accompanied by Dearborn's company, the following morning.

There was no thought of Morgan or Meigs sharing their divisions' provisions with Greene. It was understood from the outset of the expedition that each division was responsible for its own provisions, and Meigs' men were already on half rations and needed every ounce they had. However, based on their rapid progress up the Dead River, everyone was optimistic that they would soon reach the French Canadian settlements, where they would find a warm welcome and a plentiful supply of fresh provisions. Besides, there were extra provisions in Enos' slow-moving rear division, which carried the expedition's huge food reserve.

Certain that Bigelow would soon return to Greene's encampment with provisions, Arnold left Greene to catch up with Meigs and Morgan. But Major Bigelow still had not returned from his mission by the evening of the 19th. Unknown to Greene at the time, Enos' slow-moving division was much farther behind than expected; they were still crossing the Great Carry on the morning of the 17th when Bigelow left Greene's camp to find them.

Returning to Captain Dearborn for a moment, his diary entry for October 19 included a casual but significant reference about the weather: "The weather Rainy." On the following day, October 20, he reported more rain in his diary: "Weather rainy all day we Suppose this days March to be 13 Miles." The heavy downpour continued during the night of the 20th and into the following day; Dearborn described its menacing consequences: "[October] 21, . . . it Rained very fast all [last] Night, the River rose fast." Historians and meteorologists have concluded that Arnold's corps was in front of a late-season hurricane, which had crossed over 1,000 miles from the Caribbean to upper Maine, with heavy rains driven by winds strong enough to uproot trees. The Dead River had risen several feet by October 21, but the expedition kept moving through this raging tempest, except for the men of Greene's hungry division, who remained huddled at their camp waiting for Bigelow's return. The rain-soaked men of Morgan's and Meigs' divisions forced their way up the swollen Dead River, their route often blocked by uprooted trees that had crashed into the stream. They portaged their boats around rapids and small waterfalls that had grown in size and intensity from the steady rainfall. Despite the bad weather, Morgan's division pushed on and increased its lead over the others.

Meanwhile, Greene's division remained in its Natanis' cabin camp during almost three days of heavy rain and wind, keeping an anxious lookout for Major Bigelow's return. At about 11:00 a.m. on October 21, Greene's men finally spotted some bateaux coming toward them from the direction of the Great Carry. Surely it was Bigelow's relief party returning with food from Enos' much-publicized reserve supply! But as the boats drew nearer, they turned out to be carrying Lieutenant Colonel Enos with some men from his division. Enos landed and told Greene that he had hurried ahead of his division to find Arnold. Greene informed him that the colonel had gone ahead. But where was Major Bigelow and the stockpile of extra food? Enos noted that Bigelow was coming along, but that Arnold was mistaken—Enos had no reserve supply of food and was on half-rations himself. Enos said that he had given Bigelow everything his division could spare, which was only two barrels of flour. With that the conversation ended, and Enos, disappointed not to find Arnold and concerned for the welfare of his men, went back downriver to find his division.

Another drama was about to take place farther up the Dead River. It began when Morgan, Meigs, and Arnold made their separate camps on the night of October 21 on the cold, rain-soaked ground. The army was, as usual, strung out for miles, mindful of Arnold's instructions for each company to proceed at its own pace. The rain finally stopped during the night, but the winds continued to gust. Many of the men decided it was safer to camp in the open ground near the river, since the high winds were toppling trees and it was dangerous to sleep in the woods. The men managed to kindle fires and attempted to get some sleep.

On the night of October 21, the van of the army consisted of the two Indian couriers and the French-speaking soldier (John Hall), en route to

Quebec with a letter announcing the imminent arrival of Arnold's army. Next in line were Lieutenants Steele and Church, with 20 pioneers and surveyor Pierce, somewhere on the Height of Land clearing the trail. Arnold's headquarters party was behind them, using a pirogue for speed and mobility. Based on the descriptions in his journal, Arnold camped on the night of October 21 near what today is called Ledge Falls, located 15 miles upriver from Greene's camp. Morgan's rifle division was camped about a mile behind Arnold. Meigs' third division was farther downstream. Behind them were Greene's division, whose men were still camped near Natanis' cabin, and bringing up the rear was Enos' division. As a point of reference, Arnold's camp at Ledge Falls was 127 miles from Fort Western and 143 miles from Quebec.

During the night of October 21-22, the Dead River suddenly came alive. Arnold said that he was wrapped in his blanket when a distant rumbling noise woke him from a comfortable sleep. Though he could not spot anything in the darkness, the sound kept getting louder. Suddenly, a torrent of water overran his little camp; the heavily swollen ponds and streams of the Chain of Ponds had overflowed and swept down the Dead River in a tidal wave. Precious food casks, equipment, and guns were swept away in the surge, which crashed downriver, striking each sleeping detachment in succession. All were caught by surprise and scrambled for higher ground, grabbing whatever they could carry.

The next morning the Dead River Valley appeared as a flat, featureless flood plain as far as the eye could see. All the landmarks had disappeared under the voluminous water. The flood waters had stranded many men on scattered pockets of dry land, surrounded by a four-foot-deep torrent of terrifying rapidity and overwhelming force. Some of the men reached safety in the remaining boats, but the bulk of the troops had to wait for the floodwaters to subside enough for them to walk to dry land. Even then, they had to make large circuits to avoid flooded areas. Rifleman Henry called it "one of the most fatiguing marches we had as yet performed, though the distance was not great in a direct line."[22]

It seems that the violent flood stunned everyone on the expedition, and kept them occupied for most of the day trying to retrieve and dry their provisions, weapons, ammunition, clothing, tents, cooking utensils, and blankets. Despite the catastrophe, the riflemen and Meigs' division managed to travel a few miles on that and the next day. Morgan's proud Virginians left the two Pennsylvania rifle companies and went ahead on their own, even passing Arnold's headquarters party and reaching the beginning of the labyrinth of lakes and streams known as the Chain of Ponds before making camp on the night of the 23rd. They found the ponds overflowing from the heavy rain, but were somehow able to navigate this maze of waterways by finding a few of the features described by Montresor and locating marks left by Lieutenant Steele's scouting party.

Fearing the worst, Arnold turned back and linked up with Smith's and Hendrick's Pennsylvania rifle companies and Meigs' third division during the 23rd, all of whom camped at a series of ledges called Shadagee Falls that night. The group felt lucky to be alive and camping on a dry piece of land, which would come to be known as Camp Disaster. Given the grim situation, Arnold asked the officers in camp with him to attend a council of war. On everyone's mind was the catastrophe of the previous two days—days they had thought would be among their easiest. The run-off from the heavy rains had transformed this normally tranquil section of the Dead River into a funnel of dark, raging water running between the mountains that caused at least seven bateaux to overturn. The men on foot were also in danger, becoming confused and losing their way among the swollen streams and brooks that flowed into the narrow river valley. They sensed that, as they moved farther upstream and the Dead River valley became narrower, their situation would grow worse.[23] But there was no time to wait for the river to subside, as the expedition was now racing against starvation, the approach of winter, and the fear that Quebec would be reinforced.

Arnold held his council of war that dreadful night with the officers present at Camp Disaster: Major Meigs, Captains Smith and Hendricks, and their subordinates. Captain Morgan may also have attended, coming downstream from his camp site. This is the first known record of Arnold calling a council of war since the start of the expedition, but their circumstances were bleak and Arnold, who never would yield to turning back, wanted to measure his officers' resolve in this crisis.

Arnold and his subordinates discussed their situation, including the fact that they had no news from the French-speaking settler named Jaquin who had been dispatched to make contact with the nearest Canadian settlements, the Indian couriers sent to Quebec, or the 20-man advance party commanded by Lieutenants Steele and Church. They also were unsure of the condition of Greene's and Enos' divisions, but assumed they were not far behind and were coming up with large reserves of food. The men camping with Arnold were dangerously low on provisions. The flooding also had ruined their chances of catching fish.

Despite their problems, Arnold was optimistic throughout the meeting; inspired by his commanding presence and courage, his officers voted unanimously to proceed. Bold action was necessary to make up the time lost, and the council decided that Captain Hanchett of Meigs' division would temporarily relinquish command of his company to take charge of 50 of the best men drawn from the different companies in camp. This choice detachment would push ahead to the nearest Canadian settlement and return with fresh provisions. Americans at the time referred to such elite troops as picked men, and they were the forerunner of the Continental Army's Corps of Light Infantry.

Arnold believed the closest inhabitants were at a cluster of small, scattered settlements along the ChaudiPre River known collectively as Sartigan. However, he had no idea of the exact location or size of this community of peasant farmers, whether they had any food to sell, or if there were any enemy troops stationed there. Arnold and his officers also decided that Greene's and Enos' divisions had to move faster. Believing that Greene's division had been well provisioned from Enos' reserves, Arnold and the officers with him decided that these two laggard divisions should advance with as many troopers as they could supply with rations for 15 days, and that the others should return to Fort Western with their sick and feeble men. The council also agreed that anyone at Camp Disaster who was ill or too exhausted to proceed—amounting to 26— should start back the next morning toward the Kennebec settlements under the care of an officer. Having made their decisions, the group did its best to get some sleep.

Arnold awoke the next morning and promptly put the council's plan into action. He wrote out instructions to Enos and dispatched a courier to find him. His directive read, in part,

> Dead River, 30 miles from Chaudiere Pond [Lake Magentic; Arnold's calculation of his distance from the lake was fairly accurate], Oct. 24, 1775. We have had a council of war last night, when it was thought best, and ordered to send back all the sick and feeble with three day's provisions, and directions for you to furnish them until they can reach the commissary [a reference to the stock of provisions that Arnold ordered Colonel Farnsworth to establish

at the Great Carry] or Norridgewock; and that on receipt of this you should proceed with as many of the best men of your division as you can furnish with 15 day's provision; and that the remainder whether sick or well, should be immediately sent back. . . .[24]

Arnold sent a separate note with similar instructions to Greene, unaware that Enos and Greene were camping near each other. Having completed this task, Arnold exchanged a few final words with Captain Hanchett and watched, along with everyone else at Camp Disaster, as his 50 picked men headed upriver for the Canadian settlements. Everything depended on their reaching the French villages and returning with food before the army died of starvation. Arnold then supervised the loading of the invalids onto bateaux for their return trip to the Maine settlements. He also gave part of the gold and silver coins he was carrying to Major Meigs, the senior officer present, for safekeeping, with instructions to split the money with the other division commanders when they reached Canada.

Arnold maintained a bold command presence throughout the crisis. According to Morison, he walked among the troops to quiet their fears before pushing on: "[O]ur gallant Colonel himself, after admonishing us to persevere as he hitherto had done, set out with a guide for the inhabitants in order to hasten the return of provisions."[25] Having done everything he could, Arnold departed Camp Disaster late in the morning of the 24th with nine men, including his aide-de-camp Oswald, and swiftly pushed on to catch up with Hanchett's detachment, which had left camp earlier in the day.

Greene and Enos never received Arnold's orders. Disappointed by Enos' failure to provide his division with food, and lacking any instructions, Greene pondered whether to push on toward Canada where there was the promise of food, or retreat back to civilization while there was still time. Greene decided to keep going and try to find Arnold, who might be able to order some food for his hungry men. His decision was no surprise; Greene was a tough officer who later in the war (1777) would successfully defend Fort Mercer, New Jersey, with 400 men against an assault by 1,800 determined Hessian troops.[26]

Greene's division broke camp on the morning of October 22, leaving behind an apparently less courageous and bewildered Lieutenant Colonel Enos and his unhappy division. Greene's famished men traveled about 15 miles in two days before camping for the night (October 24) near Adler Stream. After attending to his division, Greene started upriver that night in a bateau, hoping to find Arnold. Lieutenant Humphrey wrote in his journal that the last of the provisions were distributed that night. "We are absolutely in a dangerous situation, the men are very much disheartened and desirous to return; however, if their bellies were full, I believe they would rather go forward," said Humphrey.[27] Greene was gone that night and most of the next day, while his division remained in camp. He rejoined them on the afternoon of the 25th empty-handed. Arnold, of course, was far ahead, following Captain Hanchettt's party toward the French Canadian settlements. Even if Green had found him, Arnold had no food to provide.

Having returned to his division, and lacking any orders or information from Arnold, Greene decided to send all of his sick men back to the Kennebec settlements and push on as quickly as possible with the rest. There were 48 men sick, and Greene left them in the care of a junior officer with orders to make the return trip in three bateaux. It was impossible, however, to fit so many men in just three bateaux, and some of the sick apparently were expected to walk. Greene also dispatched two men from his division as couriers. One headed upriver to report their situation to Arnold, while the other went downstream to find Enos and ask him to parley. Adding to everyone's misery and gloom was the fact that six inches of snow fell on the night of the 24th, "attended with very severe [cold and windy] weather."[28]

On the verge of starvation and in an inhospitable wildness far from civilization, Major Bigelow wrote his wife Anna a melancholy letter that he entrusted to an officer who was returning to the Maine settlements with the sick:

October 25, 1775

On that part of the Kennebec, Called Dead River 95 miles from Norridgewock.

Dear Wife,

I am at this time well, but in a dangerous situation, as is the whole detachment of the Continentals with me. We are in a wilderness, nearly one hundred miles from any inhabitants, either French or

English. . . . We are this day sending back the most feeble, and some that are sick. If the French are our enemies, it will go hard with us, for we have no retreat left. In that case, there will be no alternate between the sword and famine.

May God in his infinite mercy protect you, my more than ever dear wife and my dear children.[29]

After sending back his sick and frail men, and dispatching couriers to find Arnold and Enos, Greene ordered the remainder of his downhearted division to advance. His men managed to trek about three miles along the riverbank before stopping for the night at Arnold's old campsite at Shadagee Falls, where they waited for their bateaux with their remaining equipment (probably consisting mostly of their tents) and established camp for the night. They must have had some information, probably from the trickle of sick and feeble men returning from the front, about what had happened to Arnold, Morgan, and Meigs, because Lieutenant Humphrey knew that the colonel had sent Captain Hanchett ahead "with a party, the number I do not know, to purchase of the French if possible and to clear the roads."[30]

We are fortunate that Dr. Senter—who kept one of the most accurate diaries of the expedition—was traveling with Greene at the time. Senter said that Greene's men were "almost destitute of any eatable whatever, except a few candles, which were used for supper . . . by boiling them in water gruel."[31] But their forlorn camp suddenly came to life when the courier sent downriver returned with news that Lieutenant Colonel Enos was on his way with his officers for a council of war with Greene.

Senter said Enos arrived with five officers from his division, the most important of whom were his three company commanders, identified by Senter in his journal as Williams, McCobb, and Scott. The first officer mentioned was Captain Thomas Williams, who served in Colonel John Paterson's Massachusetts regiment prior to volunteering for the Arnold Expedition. The second was Captain Samuel McCobb, a resident of Arrowsic Island, Maine, who had fought at the Battle of Bunker Hill. There is no known information about Enos' other company commander—identified only as Captain Scott—or the other two officers who accompanied him, identified as Lieutenant Peters and "adjutant Hide" (David Hyde, the adjutant of Enos' division).[32] Senter called the lot "grimacers," because they arrived for the council with cheerless faces.[33] Attending the council from Greene's division were Lieutenant Colonel Greene, Major Bigelow, and their three company commanders, Captains Topham, Thayer, and Ward.

Senter was an observer to the parley that followed, and he described the event in his journal. He noted that the council began with Enos claiming the right to chair the meeting as senior officer present. Following this, the officers debated whether to proceed or turn back. Enos' officers were in favor of returning, stating that even if all the remaining provisions were evenly divided, there still was not enough food to feed the men in the two divisions for five days. The matter was put to a vote with predictable results. Greene and his officers voted that all remaining provisions should be divided up equally and as many men as possible should advance, while any sick or "timorous" men should turn back. The officers with Enos disagreed, and voted in favor of everyone turning back. The big surprise was Enos, who cast his vote in favor of proceeding. But Senter felt that Enos had conspired with his officers beforehand and that his vote masked his true intentions, which were to abandon the expedition and return to Cambridge. Senter's suspicions were confirmed when Enos declared, after hearing the vote of his officers, that it was his duty to remain with his men and to lead them home. Greene and his officers retorted that they were "determined . . . to go through or die," and asked him to share his provisions with them, to which Enos replied "that his men were out of his power, and that they had determined to keep their possessed quantity whether they went back or forward."

After a heated discussion, Enos agreed to share his provisions with Greene. With that, Enos started back for camp while Greene ordered his men to abandon their tents and all other camp equipment and head upriver toward Quebec.[34] At the same time, Captain Thayer and gentleman volunteer Ogden headed downriver in several bateaux to Enos' camp to pickup the promised food. Thayer expected to receive at least four barrels of flour and two barrels of pork, but when they arrived at the 4th division's camp, they were given only two barrels of flour. Despite their entreaties, Thayer and Ogden were told that the 4th division was destitute and could spare nothing more. Thayer, however, was convinced that Enos' division was "overflowing in abundance of all sorts and had much more food than what was necessary for their return." As a very angry Thayer prepared to depart, Captain Williams stepped forward and bid him an emotional farewell, saying that he never expected to see Thayer alive again. Then Enos advanced, with tears in his eyes, to say his last farewell to Thayer and Ogden. With that, the two intrepid warriors started back upriver to catch up with Greene, while Enos and his division folded their tents and silently stole away back toward civilization.[35]

There were probably soldiers in Enos' division who would have opted to go on if given the chance. However, Enos was in command, and he ordered everyone to turn around and head for home. The situation was just the opposite among Arnold's other divisions, whose commanders were determined to go on and whose men caught their officer's spirit, optimism, patriotism, and courage and followed them. If Arnold was half-crazy for pushing on, then Greene, Morgan, Bigelow, and Meigs were as mad as their commander.

Enos defected on the night of October 25, taking with him his three understrength companies—about 150 men—plus another 150 invalids and stragglers, including the 48 sick from Greene's division.[36] The boat repair crew commanded by Reuben Colburn turned back with him. Thayer and Ogden camped in the snow that night, "without the least to cover or screen us from the inclemency of the Weather," and caught up with Greene and Bigelow the following morning with their two precious barrels of flour.[37] They found them in a region called the Chain of Ponds, with the mountains that separated New England from Canada looming in the background.

It took several days for the news to spread up the line that Enos' division had turned back with the army's reserve supply of food. Captain Dearborn heard about it on October 27 and wrote in his journal:

> Our men made a General Prayer, that Colo: Enos and all his men, might die by the way, or meet with some disaster, Equal to the Cowardly dastardly and unfriendly Spirit they discover'd in returning Back without orders, in such a manner as they had done, And then we proceeded forward.[38]

Ephraim Squier, a private in Captain Scott's company of Enos' division, kept a diary during the expedition. He mentions only that Scott returned from a meeting on October 25 and his company started back toward the Kennebec settlements. They reached Norridgewock Falls four days later and were back at Fort Western by November 4. Squier mentioned a shortage of food only once in his diary, when he wrote that a barrel of flour was lost while one of their bateaux was running some rapids on their return trip. "The loss of the flour much lamented," wrote Squier, "we being short of provisions."[39]

When they got to Fort Western, there were no boats available to take them back to Massachusetts. The fishing boats and coastal freighters that had transported the expedition from Newburyport to Fort Western had returned weeks earlier, forcing Enos' men to walk back to Cambridge. Typical was Squier's entry for November 16: "Set out this morning; very bad walking, snow almost knee-deep here. Went-to-day to Wells, 17 miles. Here we got cider and apples plenty."[40] On November 23 they arrived back at Cambridge, where Private Squier said his company was disbanded and he returned to his old regiment.

While Enos' men where making their way back to Fort Western, Arnold's three remaining divisions were in a life-and-death struggle to reach the Canadian settlements. They were moving through the numerous ponds, lakes, and streams that made up the Chain of Ponds with no accurate maps or experienced scouts to show them the way. In addition, the few landmarks in the region, such as a particular stream or portage, had been obscured when the waterways overflowed their banks. Trail markers, left by scouting parties, were sometimes missed as a result of damage and debris left behind by the recent storm and flood. The men knew that they faced a long overland trek over the Height of Land, which lay beyond the Chain of Ponds, but were unsure of the distance to the closest Canadian settlement and what kind of reception they would receive when they got there.

Washington moved quickly to court-martial Enos, especially since his commission as an officer expired at the end of the year. The commander-in-chief ordered a Court of Inquiry to investigate the circumstances of his defection. The court met on November 29 with Major General Charles Lee as president and completed their business in one day, recommending that "a court martial should be immediately held for his trial."[41] A court-martial was convened a few days later. This was serious business, and the prescribed 13 officers were appointed to try Enos on charges of abandoning the expedition without the permission of Colonel Arnold.

Enos established his defense strategy in a letter he wrote on November 9 to Washington while en route back to Cambridge. Enos stated that he was short of provisions but shared what he had when he overtook Greene's division. He stated that a meeting of all the officers present took place, and claimed it was decided that "it was thot [thought] best for my Whole Division to Return & furnish those that proceeded with all our provisions, Except 3 Days to bring us back, wch I did without Loss of time."[42]

The court-martial heard testimony from Enos and his officers, all of whom found themselves in the same uneasy position as their commander. Typical was the testimony of Captain McCobb, who swore:

> About fifty miles up the Dead River we held a Council of War, at which I assisted as a member; and it was agreed that the whole division under Col. Enos should return [a lie], there not being sufficient provision to carry both divisions through. Colonel Greene's division being some way ahead [another lie], it was found that we should save two days' time by letting that division go forward, and time was too precious and provision too scarce to enter into disputes. It was thought best for the service, that Colonel Greene's division [the weakest division on the expedition] should proceed, and we left them with about five day's provisions, and returned with three ourselves.[43]

The situation would have been very different if some of the men Enos abandoned on the Dead River were able to speak out at his court martial, including Private Abner Stocking, whose journal includes a bitter criticism of Enos' defection:

> To add to our discouragements, we received intelligence that Colonel Enos, who was in our rear, had returned with three companies, and taken large stores of provisions and ammunition. These companies had constantly been in the rear, and of course had experienced much less fatigue than we had. They had their path cut and cleared by us; they only followed, while we led. That they therefore should be the first to turn back excited in us much manly resentment.[44]

It is unclear just how much food Enos' division possessed when it turned back.

The court acquitted Enos because there was no one present to speak out against him. In his ruling, General Sullivan said that the colonel was perfectly justified in returning with his troops because he had sent forward so much of his provisions to support the other divisions, "as left them so small a quantity that their men were almost famished with hunger on their return. . . and that their going forward would only have deprived the other division [Greene's] of a part of theirs. . . ."[45]

Unsatisfied with Enos' explanation, Washington referred to his action as "a great defection" in a letter to John Hancock, the president of the Continental Congress.[46] In another letter to his confidant Lieutenant Colonel Joseph Reed, Washington said that Enos had abandoned Arnold without that officer's "privity or consent."[47] Washington also understood that Enos' defection reduced the chances of Arnold's success. Writing Schuyler on November 30, he mentioned the impact of Enos' action to the success of the mission: "Colonel Enos who had the Command of Arnold's Rear Division is returned with the greater part of his Men, which must weaken him so much as to render him incapable of making a successful attack on Quebec without assistance from General Montgomery."[48]

Washington's observation was correct; Enos' imprudent action had weakened the expedition's strength by three companies.

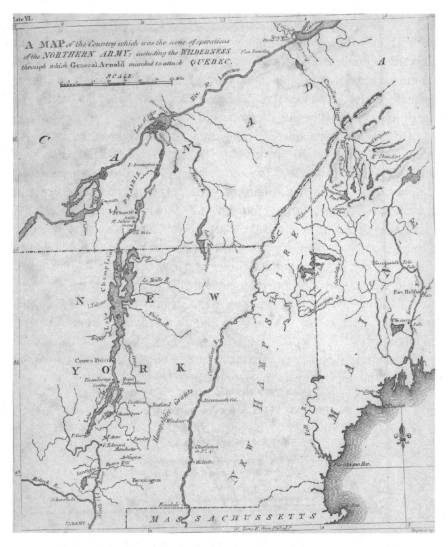

A Map of the Country which was the scene of the operations of the Northern Army; including the Wilderness through which General Arnold marched to attack Quebec.

This map is Plate VI from the atlas that accompanied the five volume, first American edition of John Marshall's *Life of George Washington* (1804-1807). The map is generally accurate except that the three ponds (lakes) that comprised the Great Carry between the Kennebec River and the Dead River are missing. Note also that modern Vermont is part of the colony of New York. *Author's Collection.*

Chapter 7

All Regard For Order Lost[1]

rnold reached the Chain of Ponds with his headquarters party during mid-day on October 25 and immediately started across this wondrous six-mile-long string of lakes, marshes, and streams carved by nature through the Appalachian Mountains in northern Maine. Lower Pond was the first pond in the course, followed by a short portage to Bag Pond. In similar fashion Arnold traveled the glimmering chain across Long Pond, Pocket Pond, Little Pocket Pond, Natanis Pond, Round Pond, Lost Pond, Horseshoe Pond, Mud Pond, and Moosehorn Pond (renamed in the twentieth century to Arnold Pond), which Montresor called "the last and most considerable lake" when he traveled through the region in 1761.[2]

Arnold's little party was moving fast through the area, and his journal shows that he was making good progress despite the difficulties of the route and the miserable weather. In fact, the course was more challenging than anything the men had experienced to date. Arnold's journal entry for the day recorded numerous hardships and bad luck, including losing his way several times in the labyrinth of mountain-shrouded waterways that had inundated the adjoining land from the recent heavy rains:

> Here we were, a long time at a Loss for the Portage [from Round Pond]—at length we found a small brook [modern Horseshoe Stream] which we entered & rowed up abt 1-1/2 miles with much difficulty being obliged to Clear away the drift Loggs in many places—Snowed and blowed very hard. . . . All this day in the last Lake the Sea ran so high we were obliged to go on shore several times to Bail our Battoes, which was with much difficulty kept above the water—Night coming on & we being much fatigued and

chilled with the cold, we were obliged to encamp without being satisfied whether we were right or not as our guides gone forward [Lt. Steele's party with surveyor Pierce] had made no marks or we have missed them—We made it 11 o clock before we could get comfortable to lie down.

Arnold believed he had traveled a total of 14 miles that day, "but as we rowed agt [against] sea & wind we might possibly be deceived 3 or 4 miles in the distance."[3]

Note that Arnold said he was navigating through the Chain of Ponds in "Battoes" (bateaux) and not pirogues or Indian canoes, which he had been using to facilitate rapid movement up and down the river between his advancing divisions. He probably switched from canoes to bateaux before departing Camp Disaster, as there was a dangerous current in the Dead River from the recent rains that was carrying uprooted tress and other debris in its wake. Fragile Indian canoes would never stay afloat in this gauntlet of fast-moving flotsam.

Arnold's party traveled late into the night of October 25 before making camp in the darkness. They awoke the next morning to discover that a deep snow covered the Appalachian Mountains. The day that followed turned out to be a long and exhausting one for Arnold and his companions. The colonel was traveling with nine men: his aide Oswald, woodsman Nehemiah Getchell, and his seven remaining Indians.[4] The water levels in the surrounding streams and lakes continued to swell from the recent rains, enlarging and distorting every waterway and making it impossible to follow Montresor's map or otherwise determine which waterway led to the next lake along the Chain of Ponds.

Arnold sent out a scout (probably one of his Indians) early on the morning of the 26th to survey a promising stream while he and the others prepared a sparse breakfast and packed their baggage. The scout returned with no useful intelligence, nor had he seen any markers or signs from the men ahead of them. There were two detachments ahead of Arnold's headquarters party. One consisted of the 50 picked men, commanded by Captain Hanchett, who had left Camp Disaster two days earlier. The other group, hopefully somewhere up the trail, was the reconnaissance–surveying party commanded by Lieutenants Church and Steele, which included surveyor Pierce and 20 enlisted men from the expedition. The Steele party left the Great Carry almost two weeks earlier with orders to "clear the Portages & take a survey of the Country."[5] Arnold found welcome evidence that Steele's party had traveled through the area from some markers and direction signs left by Pierce to identify the trail, including one that read, "9 perches on the Left hand the river[.] Gentlemen Please to let these Lines remain where they are that each and every may Discover the Course and Distance and you'll Greatly oblige your Humble Servt [Servant] Jno. Pierce Sur [Surveyor]."[6] The best hope the expedition had was that Steele's advance party had made contact with the French Canadians and was returning with food. But on the morning of October, Arnold's party could find no trail markers from Pierce or Hanchett. Arnold broke camp and started up a narrow, crooked, and rapidly moving brook that looked promising.[26]

Arnold's luck held, and he reached strategic Moosehorn Pond on the upper Chain of Ponds that afternoon. A description of the lake in Monstresor's journal reinforced Arnold's judgment that he was in the right place: "a short portage brought us to the last and most considerable lake. . . it is about three fourths of a mile in length and almost five hundred yards wide. Our course over it carried us its full length."[7]

But the colonel's party had no time to admire the lake's beauty. They were in a race against time, fighting off the increasingly cold weather, snow, and starvation. The men quickly launched their boats on Moosehorn Pond and rowed to its northern end, which they reached around 4:00 p.m. The northern shoreline of the pond turned out to be a dense curtain of trees and brush that Arnold and his companions searched in the fading daylight, looking for a brook marked on Montresor's map that emptied into the lake from the north. The brook was the key to finding the portage that would take them over the last summits of the mountains and into Canada. Although this final portage was called the Great Carrying Place or the Boundary Portage, a more vivid and accurate name given to it was the Terrible Carrying Place.[8]

Montresor's map showed that the entrance to the Terrible Carrying Place was near the brook. Arnold's men found the stream, probably aided by Pierce's markers, and despite the fading daylight, they decided to push on. Arnold knew that they faced a long portage over the mountains, and he told his men to hide their bateaux in the brush along the shoreline of Moosehorn Pond and follow him inland on foot. After following the stream for about two miles they turned and began to ascend a mountain. The route had been marked for them by Pierce. Unknown to Arnold at the time, Captain Hanchett's men were ahead of him carrying bateaux on their shoulders, a staggering feat of physical strength and endurance, especially for cold and hungry men.

The Terrible Carrying Place portage turned out to be a dense carpet of foliage and underbrush that ascended a mountain (later named Louise Mountain) whose peak was 1,800 feet above sea level. Other mountains paralleled it, and Montresor named this section of Maine's Appalachian range the Height of Land in his journal: "July 19, 1761, . . . Bidding adieu to the southern waters [Moosehorn Pond] we entered on the portage of the height of land." Missing from the copies that the British had made of Montresor's journal were key mileage and direction data, such as how far to travel along the brook in the Terrible Carrying Place portage before turning, and in which direction. The entry describing the Terrible Carrying Place portage in Arnold's pilfered copy of Montresor's journal read, "Our course was nearly [distance and direction missing] the ascent very considerable. After walking two miles we gained the greatest height and began to descend."[9] The boundary separating these two British possessions, though unmarked at the time, was easily determined by observing the flow of any mountain stream or river in the area. Any water that flowed north toward the St. Lawrence River was thought part of Canada and, conversely, water that flowed south toward the Atlantic Ocean was deemed part of New England. The same principle applied in establishing this section of the modern border between the United States and Canada.

Unbeknownst to the members of the Arnold Expedition, there was a second pass through the mountains at a lower elevation. It had no name then, but would ultimately come to be called Coburn Gore. The Indians explored Coburn Gore before Montresor or Arnold arrived on the scene and found it virtually impassable because of rough terrain and dense vegetation. Despite its higher elevation, the Terrible Carrying Place was the easier and shorter of the two routes.

Surveyor Pierce had come to the expedition's rescue by figuring out the distances and directions of the Terrible Carrying Place portage. He marked the difficult route, which followed the brook from Moosehorn Pond north for two miles to the summit of Louise Mountain—one of the mountains comprising the Height of Land—before turning west for another two miles to Seven Mile Stream. While ascending Louise Mountain, Arnold stumbled onto Pierce and the 20 men from Lieutenant

Steele's advance party, who were working to improve the trail when Arnold came upon them. After exchanging warm greetings, Pierce told the colonel that Lieutenants Steele and Church were ahead, probably scouting the Chaudière River in an Indian canoe that they had taken with them. Meanwhile, Pierce said he had already been over the entire portage from Moosehorn Pond to Seven Mile Stream (today's Arnold River), which he calculated to be four-and-a-half miles. When asked about Seven Mile Stream, he explained that it was a short, narrow waterway that flowed into Lake Magentic. Pierce added that the distance from Seven Mile Stream to Lake Magentic was only a half-mile on a straight line, but three times that distance following the course of the meandering stream.

Darkness prevented Arnold's party from advancing any farther along the trail, and they camped for the night with Pierce and his party on the Height of Land. There was little to eat that night, and everyone went to sleep hungry, dirty, wet, and cold. They had traveled 152 miles since leaving Fort Western, but were still 118 miles from Quebec City. During the night they became apprehensive when they spotted fires in the distance on the Canadian side of the portage. Fearing that it might be a British patrol, Arnold ordered sentries to guard the camp against a possible enemy attack. Adding to their problems was that there was no sign of Captain Hanchett's 50-man detachment.

Arnold had other things to worry about. He was troubled by the severity of the route he had traveled in recent days and, after making camp on the Height of Land with Pierce's party, he instructed Getchell to go back down the trail in the morning to help guide the army over the difficult and dangerous route. Arnold ordered Getchell to tell the division commanders that, because they faced numerous debris-clogged portages in the Chain of Ponds, plus a long and hazardous trek up and over the Height of Land, they should abandon their boats and proceed on foot. To ensure that there would be no confusion in this matter, Arnold gave Getchell a note for his senior officers that read, "The Carrying-places from lake to lake [a reference to the Chain of Ponds] are so many and difficult, that I think the whole will get forward much sooner by leaving all the batteaux."[10] The bulk of the army had been marching on land since the start of the expedition anyway, and there were few provisions and equipment left to transport by water, making the bateaux useless. The new plan was for everyone to carry whatever they could and to walk the rest of the way to Quebec.

The next morning, Getchell headed back down the trail to find the remainder of the army while Arnold's enlarged party descended through the blow downs and dense underbrush of the Height of Land onto a lovely meadow of tall grass. During their descent they stumbled into Hanchett's detachment, whose campfires, it turned out, they had seen from the Height of Land during the night. After comparing their routes, it was decided that Hanchett had cut his own trail, at a lower elevation, across the Height of Land that he had crossed with four bateaux. Everyone traveled together, following the trail across the meadow to Seven Mile Stream.

It would seem that Arnold had achieved a major victory as he descended from the Height of Land into Canada. He was on the Canadian frontier with a force consisting of over 80 men with their weapons, ammunition, and four bateaux. On closer examination, Arnold had little to celebrate, as his men had abandoned or lost all of their other equipment. Worse still was that the men traveling with Arnold—and the hundreds of others coming up the trail behind them—had no food or warm clothing, and at least 60 miles to travel on foot through an increasingly cold and inhospitable wilderness to reach the nearest settlement. Many of Arnold's men were sick and frightened at the grim prospect of dying from illness or slowly starving to death in this dreadful wilderness. Arnold's determination and leadership had brought them to Canada, but at a terrible cost in human suffering. There was no turning back now, and Arnold decided to get the men with him to Lake Magentic before deciding his next move. He also wanted to find Captains Steele and Church, who may already have made contact with the French-Canadians.

Anxious to reach Lake Magentic, Arnold commandeered the four bateaux that Captain Hanchett's detachment had laboriously carried over the Height of Land and loaded them with as many men as possible. He instructed Hanchettt, who was the senior officer present next to Arnold, to proceed on foot with the rest of the men along the banks of Seven Mile Stream and rendezvous with him at Lake Magentic. With that, Arnold started for the lake. He floated past the meadow and through a bleak, half-frozen bog that extended from the edge of the meadow to the south shore of Lake Magentic. Arnold was maneuvering his bateaux through this morass when he saw Lieutenants Church and Steele coming the other way in an Indian canoe. There was a third man with them, a French-speaking Huguenot who Arnold recognized as Jaquin, the river guide he had recruited back at Fort Western. Jaquin told Arnold that he was returning alone from Sartigan when he ran across Arnold's two lieutenants and decided to continue his trip back to the main army with them.

We can picture the little flotilla of American boats bobbing in Seven Mile Stream, surrounded by an ice-coated morass, as Jaquin told Arnold the first good news that the colonel had heard in weeks. "the French Inhabitants," Jaquin said, "appear very friendly & were rejoiced to hear of our approach, [and] that there are very few Troops at Quebec. . . ."[11] Jaquin had more good news: General Schuyler had captured St. Johns after killing or wounding nearly 500 of the enemy's troops.[12] Jaquin's report was exciting, but based on rumors from a remote village. Arnold needed confirmation of the story, which he would get when his couriers returned from Quebec. Meanwhile, he wrote an inspiring message to his field officers with Jaquin's news, which he sent back to the army the following morning.

A little farther down Seven Mile Stream lay Lake Magentic, a considerable body of water in a beautiful setting of rolling hills and trees. Seven Mile Stream flowed into Lake Magentic near its southern end, and the colonel's party glided their boats into this extraordinary lake guided by Lieutenants Steele and Church, who took them to a deserted Indian camp they had found along the eastern shoreline of the lake. Arnold's detachment came ashore here and established headquarters in what was described as a large Indian wigwam or bark house, where they lit a fire as a signal to Hanchett and settled in to await the arrival of his detachment. The distance from where the colonel left Hanchett on Seven Mile Stream to the wigwam camp was only two-and-a-half miles on a straight line. However, the short trip quickly turned into a catastrophe for Captain Hanchett and his detachment.

Hanchett's plan was to march his detachment along the shoreline of Seven Mile Stream to Lake Magentic. Following that route, however, led them into the miserable bog that bordered the southern end of the lake. Hanchett and his men grew disoriented as daylight faded and the river split into several branches, as well as a small lake (Lake Rush). They did not know that Lake Rush actually was a flooded section of Seven Mile

Stream whose main channel passed through the lake before resuming the guise of a short river (the Rush River) that emptied into Lake Magentic. Hanchett had a copy of Montresor's map, but it did not show any of these details.

Arnold became alarmed when Hanchett's party failed to arrive at the bark house. Darkness already had fallen when the colonel dispatched his bateaux into the night to look for the missing men. They were discovered hopelessly lost, but still floundering onward in some marshy ground almost three miles from Arnold's camp, and had to be ferried in small groups to the wigwam shelter. It was midnight before all of Hanchett's exhausted men reached the safety of the bark house, where they learned that Arnold planned to make the final dash to Sartigan in the bateaux that they had laboriously carried over the Height of Land. Hanchett, who had been one of Arnold's most loyal officers, resented the colonel's presumptuous decision. Arnold's brash and indelicate behavior had added another enemy to his growing list, which included Ethan Allen, James Easton, and John Brown, who were now Continental Army officers serving under General Montgomery.

Although it was late at night, Colonel Arnold turned his attention to writing a letter to General Washington. In it he informed the commander-in-chief that he had arrived safely at Lake Magentic with 70 men. He also related the story of Jaquin's visit to Sartigan, including his being told by the local farmers that there were only a handful of British troops guarding Quebec who were unaware that a rebel army was approaching the city. The colonel closed his letter with a sobering appraisal of his mission to date. "Our march has been attended with an amazing Deal of Fatique," he wrote. "I have been much deceived in every Accout of our Rout [route], which is longer, and has been attended with a Thousand Difficulties I never apprehended. . . ."[13] Among the "thousand difficulties" was the lack of contact with his army that Arnold had experienced over the last three days.

Arnold awoke early on Saturday morning, October 28, and immediately went to work to save his men. The experiences of the previous day, including Hanchett's miserable time in the swamp, were proof that Montresor's map of the region was inaccurate and incomplete. The explanation for these deletions can be found in the British engineer's own journal, which stated that the Indians took him down Seven Mile Stream in the dark. His journal entry for July 19, 1761, mentions this point: "We had gone down the river [Seven Mile Stream] . . . when night overtook us, but being resolved to reach the lake [Lake Magentic], we still pushed on."[14] Montresor was unable to see the features of the land at night, which explains why several critical landmarks were missing from his otherwise superb map. Montresor's major omission was his failure to realize that he was being taken through a bog that bordered the southern shore of Lake Magentic and that Seven Mile Stream splits into several branches as it approaches the lake, similar to the way the Mississippi River divides and re-divides as it approaches the sea. The branches of Seven Mile Stream are known today, from west to east, as the Black Arnold, the Dead Arnold (collectively called the False Arnolds), and the Rush River. The False Arnolds are choked with wood debris and terminate in a bog that cannot be navigated by boat. The main channel of Seven Mile Stream flows into Lake Rush before it resumes the appearance of a river (the Rush River), which empties into Lake Magentic.

Montresor also failed to see a large lake northeast of Lake Magentic, which the Indians called Nepiss Lake (today's Spider Lake). Arnold knew that the four divisions coming up behind him were all following Montresor's map, which did not show the False Arnolds, Lake Nepiss, and Lake Rush. Montresor, who had made the chart in 1761, was ignorant of these defects in his map and probably would have been thunderstruck to learn in 1775 that over 600 of Washington's military amateurs were crossing into Canada and secretly advancing on Quebec.

Arnold took action to make sure that his main army did not walk into the bog as Hanchettt's detachment had done the previous day. He instructed a lieutenant named Isaac Hull, a young officer in Hanchett's detachment, to turn back and guide the army across the narrow split of dry land that traversed the swamp.[15] How this dry land route was discovered is unrecorded. Arnold also entrusted Hull with two important letters. One he addressed to his four division commanders, with a warning to keep to the east side of Lake Magentic, along with the great news of Jaquin's warm reception at Sartigan. The other was his report to General Washington, which Arnold instructed Hull to deliver to his most dependable officer, Lieutenant Colonel Enos, who would arrange for someone to deliver it to Cambridge. Arnold still had no idea that Enos had deserted with a quarter of the army.

Arnold next took Hanchett's four bateaux and Lieutenant Steele's Indian canoe to race down the Chaudière River to the French settlements. His relief party consisted of Lieutenants Steele and Church, Oswald, Jaquin and some men from Hanchett's detachment. Before leaving the wigwam camp, Arnold instructed Hanchett to proceed on foot with his remaining men and follow the eastern shore of Lake Magentic to the headwaters of the Chaudière River. Hanchett then was to march along the banks of the river until succor arrived from Arnold's relief party. After seeing Hanchett's detachment off, Arnold's contingent left "to proceed on to the french Inhabitants, & at all events send back provisions to meet the rear."[16]

The "hands on" manner in which Arnold took personal charge of getting food for his starving men is typical of his aggressive, assertive character. Arnold was a leader, not a follower, with a genuine concern for the welfare of the troops under his command. Other members of the expedition, notably Aaron Burr, interpreted Arnold's action differently, and believed that he took charge of the relief party as a selfish act to ensure that he would be among the first to reach food at the French settlements.

It was now time for the rest of the army to make the difficult trek over the Terrible Carrying Place into Canada. Arnold did not record the details of his crossing of the portage but others did, including Private Morison, who wrote that after Moosehorn Pond his detachment came to:

> the Terrible Carrying Place; a dismal portage indeed. . . . The ground adjacent to this ridge is swampy, plentifully strewed with old dead logs, and with every thing that could render it impassable. Over this we forced a passage, the most distressing of any we had yet performed.[17]

To this point, the men of the Arnold Expedition had experienced great suffering and displayed tremendous courage in the face of almost certain death. The sick and faint of heart already had turned back, leaving about 600 men, divided into ten understrength companies and accompanied by two female camp followers. A review of the companies and their division assignments will help in tracing their march, as they became separated and reached Lake Magentic from different directions.

As previously noted, each company was identified by the name of its captain, a system widely used by the American Army during the Revolutionary War. Morgan's, Smith's, and Hendricks' rifle companies comprised the first division of the army. Morgan was the division's senior captain and commander. Lieutenant Colonel Greene commanded the second division, with Major Bigelow his second in command. This division consisted of three infantry companies under the command of Captains Thayer, Topham, and Hubbard. Major Meigs commanded the third and biggest division, comprised of four infantry companies commanded by Captains Dearborn, Ward, Goodrich, and Hanchett. Since Hanchett was on detached duty as commander of the picked men, his company fell under Meigs' personal command.[18] Following Enos' defection, Lieutenant Colonel Greene was second in command of the expedition under Colonel Arnold. As usual, the companies operated independently of each other, with responsibility for their own bateaux, tents, and provisions.

Not surprisingly, Morgan's rifle company led the way over the Terrible Carrying Place portage. They arrived at its entrance on Friday morning, October 27, about a day's march behind Arnold's headquarters party. Ignoring Arnold's recommendation, and still engaged in a rivalry with the New Englanders, Morgan's Virginian's lifted their serviceable bateaux on their shoulders and crossed the Terrible Carry in one horrendous day's march. Smith's and Hendrick's rifle companies were next in line, and Morison's diary provides a graphic account of the difficulties they faced on October 26 as they trekked through the Chain of Ponds toward the Height of Land: "The day was very cold, and the ground covered with a pretty deep snow which had fell in the night of the 25th; in consequence, our progress was much impeded by reason that we could not distinguish ground sufficiently solid to march upon with our burdens; some of us frequently slipped into bogs."[19]

Upon reaching the Terrible Carry, Smith's and Hendricks' companies were more realistic—or perhaps more tired—than Morgan's, and they abandoned their bateaux and tents before attempting the portage, as confirmed by Morison, who said, "[We] took out our guns, with everything that was portable, from the bateaux, and got ready our packs."[20] Their decision to forsake their heavy bateaux made the trek easier, but it meant they were committed to sleep in the open and carry everything all the way to Quebec. The companies commanded by

Dearborn and Ward from Meigs' third division were the next to cross the divide, and they also left their bateaux and tents, but not before cutting up some of the canvas tents to sew bags with which to carry their remaining provisions.

Many of the farmers and laborers on the Arnold Expedition knew how to sew and could make simple duffel-type bags quickly by folding a piece of fabric and sewing two sides closed. They tied the open side with a piece of cord after they loaded "*provisions*" (the term meant either food or supplies) into the bag. The men carried the bags by slinging them over their shoulders. Canvas does not make a good blanket; however, it is probable that many of these resourceful men created simple canvas capes to cover their shoulders and wrapped a piece of canvas around each leg, from knee to ankle, to protect their legs from being bruised by the thorny underbrush. Called country boots, these primitive leggings were held in place with rope or strips of leather tied just below the knees, as well as around the ankles.

Dearborn's and Ward's companies camped on the Height of Land on the night of the 27th and completed their passage over the divide and down to the meadow the following day. The scene was spectacular, with the meadows framed by the Appalachian Mountains in the background. Greene's division occupied the rear, with each company moving at its own pace. Goodrich's company from Meigs' division was the last party to cross the Height of Land. Lieutenant Colonel Greene accompanied them, and they camped on the night of October 27 in the Chain of Ponds. Goodrich's band started across the Terrible Carry early the following morning, and arrived at the beautiful meadow in mid-afternoon to find the rest of the army waiting for them. They soon learned that everyone else knew that Enos deserted with his three companies, along with what they believed was the army's reserve supply of food. The divisions gathered in the meadow were destitute, with no hope of being furnished with food from the rear.

The army assembled in the meadow and enacted the ancient ritual of dividing the remaining food. Every company put whatever provisions they had into a common pool, the contents shared equally among all present. There was so little meat to divide that the officers decided not to take any. Humphrey recorded in his diary that each man received "5 pints of flour and 2 oz. of meat."[21] It is frightening to realize that this small amount of food would have to sustain each weak and starving soldier until succor arrived from the French settlements. Four of the companies—Goodrich's, Dearborn's, and Ward's companies from Meigs' division and Smith's Pennsylvania rifle company—elected to keep moving while there was still some daylight, and they took off immediately following the food distribution. With no information about their route other than copies of Monstresor's map, these men left the meadow and started following the Seven Mile Stream in the direction of Lake Magentic. Their hastiness would cost them dearly, when Lieutenant Hull arrived at the meadow a few hours later with the written warning from Arnold to avoid following Seven Mile Stream. Arnold instructed his corps to return to the edge of the high ground at the end of the Terrible Carry and "strike off to the right hand . . . which will escape the low swampy land and save a very great distance." Arnold also reported that he expected to send back food from Sartigan in three days. His letter included the story of Jaquins' warm reception at Sartigan by the French-Canadians, who "rejoiced to hear we are coming and that they will gladly supply us with provisions. He says there are few or no regulars at Quebec."[22] The men raised a cheer and, according to one account, the whole valley rang with their exaltations at these good tidings.[23]

A joyous Major Bigelow penned a hurried letter to his wife with the glorious news:

Dear Anna,

I very much regret my writing the last letter to you, the contents were so gloomy. It is true our provisions are short (only five pints of flour to a man, and no meat), but we have this minute received news that the inhabitants of Canada are all friendly, and very much rejoiced at our coming, and a very small number of troops in Quebec. We have had a very fatiguing march of it, but I hope it will soon be over. The express [the courier carrying Arnold's report to Washington] is waiting, there fore must conclude.[24]

Another distribution took place in the meadow, where Major Meigs parceled out some of the gold and silver coins he was carrying, which he split with Lieutenant Colonel Greene and Major Bigelow. They would need this hard currency to make purchases, especially food, when they reached the French settlements. Major Meigs reported giving 500 dollars to Greene and a similar amount to Bigelow. The major also said he gave "Mr. Gatchel" (Nehemiah Getchell) 44 dollars and "Mr. Berry" (Samuel Berry) £4.5 "lawful money."[25] The term "lawful money" meant that Berry was paid in Massachusetts currency. We cannot rule out that civilians like Getchell and Berry—who were hired by the army—may have received what was called country pay, which meant that they received goods for their services instead of money. However, this form of barter was unlikely at this point in the campaign, because desirable commodities such as gunpowder and lead were in short supply and needed by the army.

The officers and men in Morgan's Virginia rifle company were exhausted when they finally reached the meadows. They were the only company to carry all of their bateaux into Canada, but paid a terrible price for their feat, as evidenced by John Joseph Henry, who saw them and wrote, "It would have made your heart ache to view the intolerable labors of his fine fellows." Henry said that the flesh had worn from their shoulders, even to the bone, from hauling their bateaux over the Terrible Carry.[26] The Virginians, who carried seven bateaux over the pass, rested for a while before proceeding down Seven Mile Stream toward Lake Magentic. This left five companies at the meadows—Thayer's, Topham's, and Hubbard's (comprising Lieutenant Colonel Greene's entire division), Hanchett's company from Meigs' division, and Hendrick's Pennsylvania rifle company. These five companies followed Arnold's advice and headed, under the direction of Lieutenant Hull, back to the high ground near the Terrible Carry, where they camped for the night.

A few miles to the northwest, the impulsive companies commanded by Dearborn, Ward, Goodrich, and Smith were also resting for the night before resuming their uncharted trek to Lake Magentic by following the course of Seven Mile Stream. All four companies eventually marched straight into the bog that bordered the southern end of Lake Magentic. They had a few bateaux and Indian canoes with them, which were used to transport their remaining provisions to the birch bark hut for safekeeping before returning to help the men across the uncharted rivers (the false Arnolds) and bogs that blocked their passage to the dry land on the southeast side of Lake Magentic, the site of the wigwam camp.

Captain Dearborn described how he used his canoe to help the trapped men reach dry land: "Capt Goodrich was almost perished with the Cold, having Waded Several Miles Backwards, and forwards, Sometimes to his Arm-pits in Water & Ice, endeavouring to find some place to Cross this River [the Dead Arnold]," he wrote. "I took him into my Canoe, and Carryed him over. . . ."[27] It was dark before Dearborn got Goodrich to safety, and they decided to spend the night at the wigwam camp before rounding up other boats in the morning and going to the relief of their stranded men, who had managed to find a bit of dry land and make a fire by dragging some wood from the surrounding swampland. A small flotilla of bateaux and canoes worked all the next day to get the men to the wigwam camp, where everyone rested for the night. They arrived at the site to find that their unguarded larder had been raided by Captain Morgan's Virginians, who had come down Seven Mile Stream, stopped briefly at the wigwam camp, and stolen some of the New Englanders' food.[28]

John Joseph Henry was among the men struggling through the bog. His narrative includes an account of one of the women who made the crossing with Captain Goodrich's company. She is identified as the wife of Sergeant Grier, a member of that company. Henry said that he saw Grier's wife, whom he described as "a large, virtuous and respectable woman." Henry continued, "My mind was humbled, yet astonished, at the exertions of this good woman. Her clothes more than waist high, she waded before me to firm ground. No one, so long as she was known to us, dared to intimate a disrespectful idea of her."[29] Mrs. Grier was soon reunited with her husband, who was helping to handle the boats.

The companies commanded by Dearborn, Goodrich, Ward, and Smith somehow arrived in the wigwam camp by the evening of October 30 and continued their march the following day, reaching the place where the Chaudière River flows from Lake Magentic. They passed the shattered remnants of Morgan's shipwrecked company sprawled out along the riverbank. The Virginians said that they had started down the Chaudière with the fast-moving current, and were making good progress until their bateaux catapulted into fierce rapids. Working frantically, the riflemen hopelessly tried to keep control of their boats, and their bateaux smashed on the rocks. One man was killed, and they lost all of their bateaux and most of their provisions. A soldier who saw them said, "Their condition was truly deplorable, they had not when we came up with them a mouthful of provisions of any kind, and we were not able to relieve them, as hunger stared us in the face."[30]

Morgan and his men learned the hard way how this river got its name. The word Chaudière is French for caldron, and the title aptly describes this virtually unnavigable river of boiling rapids and foaming waterfalls. The Chaudière races north from Lake Magentic to the St. Lawrence River, dropping 1,100 feet during its 100 mile course, the northern portion of which consists of treacherous rapids littered with huge rocks that can smash a boat to bits.

The five companies being guided cross country by Lieutenant Hull were in no better shape than the others. The young lieutenant managed to get lost and march the men following him into another section of the bog. Lieutenant Humphrey was with them and recorded what happened in his diary:

> October 29, 1775, This day we proceeded in front on our way to Sartigan; the traveling is very bad so that almost every step we sink in half leg high, but we have encouragement by our pilot [Lieutenant Hull] that it is better ahead. Lost one man belonging to Capt. Topham's company, viz. Samuel Nichols, who must inevitably perish; we now find the pilot knows the way no better than we do; we traveled about 5 miles and encamped.[31]

Private Stocking, of Hanchett's company, was another member of the detachment who followed Hull into the bog, and he wrote a graphic account of this life-threatening experience:

> We began descending towards an ocean of swamp that lay before us. We soon entered it and found it covered with a low shrubbery of cedar and hackmetack, the roots of which were so excessively slippery, that we could hardly keep upon our feet The top of the ground was covered with a soft moss, filled with water and ice. After walking a few hours in the swamp we seemed to have lost all sense of feeling in our feet and ankles. As we were constantly slipping, we walked in great fear of breaking our bones or dislocating our joints. But to be disenabled from walking in this situation was sure death. We traveled all day and not being able to get through this dismal swamp, we encamped. I thought we were probably the first human beings that ever took up their residence for a night in this wilderness—not howling wilderness, for I believe no wild animals would inhabit it.[32]

Hull compounded his error by leading his wards toward Nepiss Lake, thinking it was Lake Magentic. Dr. Senter was with them, and called their wanderings "a state of uncertainty. . . with the conjoint addition of cold, wet and hunger, not to mention our fatigue—with the terrible apprehension of famishing in this desert."[33] Lieutenant Hull, now referred to as the "pretended pilot," was as frightened as the rest, in addition to suffering "the severe execrations he received from the front of the army to the rear," which Senter said "made his office not a little disagreeable."[34] They headed way off course and all around Nepiss Lake before finding some footprints in the snow that they decided to follow. The footprints led them to Lake Magentic, whose shoreline they traced to the Chaudière. Somehow, by November 1, everyone who was left on the expedition was walking along the shore of the Chaudière River.

It is possible that the expedition's diarists exaggerated the food shortage up to this point in their journey. Private Stocking, for example, wrote on October 27 that he caught "plenty of trout" in Moosehorn Pond.[35] Some of the men had eaten their portion of the food dolled out in the meadow in one meal and counted on luck and providence to see them through. Dr. Senter mentioned this ongoing problem in his diary: "That several of the men devoured the whole of their flour the last evening, determined (as they expressed it) to have a full meal., letting the morrow look out for itself. . . ."[36]

But even the men who conserved their small rations were soon wanting, and it is clear from all the diaries that the soldiers on the Arnold Expedition were starving and near death as they struggled along the snow-covered, uncharted banks of the Chaudière River. With the big game having been frightened away, men were reduced to eating soap, lip salve, shoe leather, and cartridge boxes—all of which went into their pots to make soup—along with some small forest creatures and at least two pet dogs. Abner Stocking described their perilous situation in his diary entry for November 1: "Our fatigue and anxiety were so great that we were but little refreshed the last night by sleep. We started however very early, hungry and wet."[37]

Private Stocking said he marched all day before encamping in a fine grove of trees, where he found some men from Captain Goodrich's company feasting on a dog. The animal belonged to Captain Dearborn, who had given up his pet labrador to feed the starving men. "My dog was very large and a great favourite," Dearborn noted. "I gave him up to several men of Capt Goodrich's company, who killed him and divided him among those who were suffering most severely with hunger. They ate every part of him, not excepting his entrails; and after finishing their meal, they collected the bones and carried them to be pounded up and to make broth for another meal."[38]

Several diarists also told of butchering and eating a Newfoundland dog belonging to Captain Thayer. Private Henry mentioned Thayer's dog in his journal, claiming that he came across some men sitting around a fire and sat down to join them, "absolutely fainting from hunger and fatigue. . . . Death would have been a welcome visitor." The men had a kettle of broth cooking over their fire and offered Henry a cup full of the simmering brew. Though they told him it was made from the flesh of a bear, one taste of the smelly greenish broth convinced young Henry that it was dog. Henry claims he only had one taste before continuing his march. He camped that evening with his messmates, with whom he shared a good fire, but no food.[39]

By November 2, the army was crawling along the banks of the Chaudière. All pretensions of military order were now gone, the army scattered up and down the river for miles. Some of them stopped to search with their fingers for edible plant roots along low, sandy stretches of the river.[40] There was no trail to follow and everyone stayed close to the river bank, their progress slowed by the low, swampy land, steep river banks, and cold streams that flowed into the Chaudière from all directions. The men had been advised to save themselves and not try to help a starving or fallen comrade. Companies attempted to stay together, but had to leave their weakest comrades behind, allowing the strongest men to reach Sartigan and send back help. "Cooking being very much out of fashion," penned Dr. Senter, the men had little else to do than stagger as quickly as they could toward relief.[41] The doctor said that the army had arrived at the zenith of its distress.[42]

Somewhere in this frigid wilderness, a woman camp follower named Jemima Warner watched her husband die. He was a member of Goodrich's company, and diarist Abner Stocking told how Warner and his wife loved each other and were inseparable. Jemima lagged behind with her soldier husband when he became too sick to continue walking and comforted him, as best as she could, until he died. "Having no implements with which she could bury him," Stocking said, "she covered him with leaves, and then took his gun. . . and left him with a heavy heart."[43]

Captain Samuel Ward was among the famished, dirty, and cold young men staggering through the snow toward Quebec. Only 19 years old, he was the son of the wealthy merchant and high rebel Samuel Ward Sr. His father had arranged for his son to receive a commission in the newly organized 1st Rhode Island Regiment when the Revolution started. Young Ward volunteered for the Arnold Expedition and received command of a company. How different circumstances had been just 45 days earlier, when this proud teenager paraded with the rest of the army to the cheers of the people of Newburyport. Did this young man, facing death from starvation and frigid temperatures, regret his decision to march to Quebec with Arnold? Assuredly not, because Ward believed—as did the other officers and common soldiers on the expedition—that the British government was conspiring to take away his liberties.[44] Ward felt he had to draw the line against the increasing intrusion by the king and his henchmen into his life, and that his offspring would be enslaved by arbitrary taxes, alien armies and officials, false religion, distant trials, and pervasive corruption if he did not take a stand now with Colonel Arnold, his respected and beloved commander.[45] Ward would survive the Arnold Expedition, rise to the rank of lieutenant colonel, and eventually become a prosperous New York City merchant. He was among the first Americans to open trade with China, and arrived in Canton in 1788 aboard his merchant ship *George Washington.*

In a twist of irony, on the same date (November 1, 1775) that young Ward was staggering through the Canadian woods, Congressman Samuel Ward, Sr., his obviously much misinformed father, wrote home from Philadelphia, "[B]y the best Accts. from Colo. Arnold He had got near Quebec without any Opposition, the Canadians were very friendly, there were no Soldiers in Quebec & few or no Guns mounted on the Walls, the Troops were in good Health & high Spirits & expected to take the Place easily."[46]

Where was Arnold during these critical days in early November? His location can be traced from the diary entries and letters written during this period: he was at the wigwam camp on Saturday, October 28, with 15 men in four bateaux and one Indian canoe. His party reached the source of the Chaudière River that same day, and started down it with their baggage lashed to their boats. The first seven miles were easy, but the river became progressively rougher and they soon found themselves fighting for their lives in the rapids. Arnold and his crew bravely committed themselves to run the raging waters in their clumsy bateaux, but courage was not enough, as their boats were tossed against the rocks. Two of the bateaux and the canoe smashed to pieces and capsized, the other two damaged.[47] Provisions and weapons were lost in this watery deathtrap, and six men pitched into the frigid waters only to be saved by the greatest exertions. This place would later be known as the Devil's Rapids. Somehow everyone got to shore safely and salvaged what they could. They built campfires to warm themselves and divided the remaining food. Arnold took stock of their situation and decided that he would continue with the two serviceable bateaux. He could only take six men with him and the others, including surveyor Pierce, he left behind to walk to the French settlements.

Arnold portaged his remaining boats around the Great Falls and resumed his drive toward the settlements. Pierce and the others, who were left behind, watched the bateaux until they disappeared from sight before picking up their packs and weapons and walking along the river bank. Pierce wrote in his journal that they estimated it would take four days for the men left behind to reach the French settlements, "and each man had not more Provision for the 4 Days than he Could Comfortable eat at one meal[. I]n this miserable Condition we Comforted our Selves as well as we Could Resolving to go through or Die in the Attempt."[48]

Chapter 8

The Heartrending Entreaties
of the Sick and Helpless[1]

On November 2, 1775, Dr. Isaac Senter was slowly threading his way through the rocks and underbrush that bordered the Chaudière River when he saw strange creatures coming toward him. "[F]our footed beasts, &c.," he said, "rode and drove by animals resembling Plato's two footed featherless ones."[2] Senter wondered if he was seeing a mirage brought on by extreme fatigue and hunger. But as the shapes drew closer, he recognized the one in the lead as his indestructible comrade, Lieutenant Archibald Steele, who was riding on horseback and leading a small herd of cattle being driven by some French-Canadians. Senter and the other soldiers with him cheered as loudly as their feeble condition would permit.

The men butchered a heifer on the spot, each of them receiving one pound of beef that they quickly cooked and ate. Additional relief parties arrived to distribute mutton, meal, and other foodstuffs along the line of march and to help the exhausted stragglers to safety. Colonel Arnold was responsible for organizing the succor that saved their lives. He had raced ahead from the Terrible Carry, promising his men to send relief as soon as he reached the first French-Canadian settlements. Arnold and a small party arrived by boat at Sartigan on the night of October 30, and relief parties, heavily laden with provisions, left early the following morning to locate what remained of the expedition.

All military organization had been abandoned in the final days before relief arrived, as the starving soldiers headed for the closest French-Canadian farms. Several companies, including Morgan's and Goodrich's, had lost all their provisions when their remaining bateaux smashed to pieces in the treacherous rock-strewn rapids of the Chaudière. Some members of the expedition were traveling in company size formations, while others were shuffling along in small groups or alone. Private Morison said he was instructed not to stop to help the weak or sick but to "shift for himself, and save his own life if possible."[3]

The relief parties reached the first men on November 2 and worked their way up along the river, bringing food and comfort to everyone. Those too sick or feeble to walk to Sartigan were transported there on horseback. Captain Dearborn noted that the three days prior to the arrival of help had been the worst. During this time he witnessed dead men along the route of march, and spotted some of those still living walking barefoot in the snow. Knowing how his men were suffering, Dearborn said that he was moved to tears when he saw the relief parties coming upriver from Sartigan.[4] The last feeble stragglers were found and cared for as the remains of Arnold's ragged, dirty army began limping into the village, thankful to be alive. Hanchett's detachment probably was the first to arrive, and reached Sartigan on October 31.[5]

Dearborn's company were among the next, reaching the settlements at about 5:00 p.m. on November 2. Captain Smith's rifle company came in with them. Some members of Ward's company reached the hamlet on the afternoon of November 3. William Hendricks' Pennsylvania rifle company arrived that evening, along with men from the companies commanded by Thayer and Topham. Rifleman Morison said he arrived on the morning of the 4th with some others, looking "more like ghosts than men, issuing from a dismal Wilderness."[6]

Meigs was among the last to arrive. He reached Sartigan on November 4 with the remnants of Hanchett's company, and wrote in his journal that he had finally arrived in civilization after spending 31 days in an uninhabited wilderness.[7] Two Indians found Lieutenant John McClellan of Hendricks' Pennsylvania rifle company in the woods and carried him to Sartigan in a canoe.[8] Sick with pneumonia, he died shortly after reaching the settlements. Rifleman John Joseph Henry lamented McClellan's death, remembering him as a young man "endowed with all those qualities which win the affections of men."[9]

The arrival times of the other men in Sartigan were not recorded, but Morgan's rifle company, in particular, must have had a terrible ordeal after losing all their provisions when their bateaux were destroyed in the rapids above the Great Falls. The best evidence is that Morgan's men reached the settlements on November 3.[10] Bookish little Aaron Burr, who seemed so frail and unsuited to wilderness life at the start of the campaign, turned out to possess a surprising capacity for enduring fatigue and privation. Rifleman Henry said he saw him hiking along the Chaudière looking fit and encouraging the others to keep moving.[11] One biographer attributed Burr's surprising stamina and skills to a childhood spent fishing, hunting, and boating in the rivers and marshes that surrounded his New Jersey childhood home.[12] Another said that Burr's indomitable will, rather than his physical strength, sustained him through the terrible ordeal.[13]

By the evening of November 4, 1775, about 600 men had made it to the French settlements. They had walked the last 60 miles through trackless forests, following the course of the river from Lake Magentic to the cluster of peasant farms and Indian tepees known as Sartigan. An estimated 40 to 50 Americans had died trying to reach Sartigan from a combination of hunger, sickness, and fatigue.[14] One veteran returned to Maine over the same route a year later, where he saw the remains of some of his comrades, "human bones and hair scattered about the ground promiscuously."[15]

Sartigan was not much of a place, just a motley collection of small farms hacked out of the forest and Indian wigwams scattered along the banks of the Chaudière River. There were not enough buildings to shelter all of Arnold's men, which forced them—in their already weakened state—to build crude lean-tos and constantly tend fires to keep warm.

Their enthusiastic welcome at Sartigan largely was due to the fact that the American rebels—or *Les Bostonnais* as they were called—arrived with cash and were willing to pay dearly for everything. Many of the officers had money, as evidenced by a message that Arnold wrote to Major Meigs (who apparently had assumed the role of the expedition's paymaster): "Sartigan, 1st Nov. 1775. You may let each Captain have about twenty or thirty dollars out of the money I gave you, as I suppose they will want a little pocket money for present use, and to supply their men."[16] "The people are civil," penned Lieutenant Humphrey, "but very extravagant with what they have to sell."[17] Morison also mentioned the high cost of goods in his November 5 journal entry: "[T]he people very hospitable; provisions plenty, but very dear—milk one shilling per quart—bread, one shilling per loaf. . . ."[18] Captain Dearborn voiced a similar sentiment: "[T]he inhabitants appears to be very kind, but ask a very Great price for their Victuals."[19]

The squalor of the peasant farmers they met upon reaching Sartigan surprised many of Arnold's men, who tended to come from prosperous farming communities and busy coastal towns in New England. Pierce wrote one of the most interesting descriptions of these people in his entry for November 3, 1775:

> all their Farming Tools and household furniture is very Poor—They draw their Oxen by the horns—their Houses and Barns are Chiefly Thatched and very Poor—they Lodge Chiefly on Straw Beds which are Raised on Bedsteads about 2 feet 1/2 [two and a half feet] high—their Windows are Chiefly Paper but Some Glass—A Good Chunked Breed of horses—Small Cattle—Poor Hogs—very Good Fowls of all Sorts—No Chairs to Set on—All Set [sit] on Blocks & Stools. . . . I Slept between two Frenchmen in a French house—it was very odd to hear them at their Devotion.[20]

Two days later, Pierce made another entry in his journal about the locals:

> November 5 1775, . . . It is to be Observed that the French in these Back Settlements are very Stupid not one to 400 that could read one word but were very Precise in Saying their Prayers Counting their Beads and Crossing themselves.[21]

After organizing succor for his men, Arnold turned the relief work over to his officers and directed his attention to other problems.[22] The colonel seemed inexhaustible—"with ability and fortitude rarely if ever surpassed," was how one of Arnold's nineteenth-century biographers put it—a trait that helped him earn a reputation as one of America's best field officers during the Revolutionary War.[23] One of Arnold's highest priorities was to discover what had happened in the war since he departed Fort Western.

Now in British-held territory, Arnold needed to know the situation in Quebec as well as the location of General Schuyler's northern army. Access to reliable information became critical when the villagers told Arnold that the British knew about his army and a warship had arrived at Quebec to help defend the city. This intelligence contradicted the last information he had received from headquarters (Colonel Reed's letter dated October 4) that said, "At present there is not a single Regular at Quebeck; nor have they the least suspicion of any danger from any other quarter than Gen. Schuyler."[24]

If the peasant's information was true, then Arnold had lost the critical element of surprise. Was his mind racing as he wondered what had happened to the messages he sent a month earlier to Mercier and Schuyler from the Great Carry? He should have received replies from both by now, especially since common soldier Hall, the French-speaking British army deserter, assured Arnold that he had watched the two Indian couriers depart from Sartigan on the road to Quebec. In fact, the Indians had returned, insisting that they delivered Arnold's letters to Mercier. The colonel did not know what had gone wrong, but suspected his Indian couriers either had not reached Quebec or had betrayed him. Arnold thought about the contents of the letter that he had written to Mercier from the Great Carry. If it had fallen into enemy hands, he had at least inflated the number of men with him as being 2,000, which might intimidate the reportedly small garrison at Quebec into surrendering. He might already have been thinking about disguising the actual size of his command, if necessary, by marching his men around blazing campfires at night, accompanied by the sounds of shovels digging and officers screaming orders, so as to persuade Quebec's defenders that he had arrived with a formidable army. General Washington was a master of such deception, which he used successfully later in the war to fool the British into believing that he was digging in to defend Trenton while he slipped away in the night with the bulk of his army to surprise the enemy garrison at nearby Princeton.

But before attempting any tricks, Arnold decided to send another letter to Mercier from Sartigan using a different courier. His second letter shows how eager Arnold was to know the situation inside Quebec. The colonel's ability to express himself clearly and concisely was much admired by Washington, who wanted his senior officers to be good communicators. Note that the name of Arnold's courier has been deleted from the letter. This is because the text of the letter comes from the retained, or file copy, which, for security reasons, did not mention the messenger's name:

Sartigan, November 1, 1775.

Dear Sir,

As I make no doubt of your being hearty in the cause of liberty and your Country, I have taken the liberty to inform you that I have just arrived here, with a large detachment from the American Army. I have several times, on my march, wrote you by the Indians, some of whom have returned and brought no answer. I am apprehensive they have betrayed me. This will be delivered you by _____ on whose secrecy you may depend. I beg the favour of you, on receipt of this, to write me, by the bearer, the number of troops in Quebeck and Montreal; how the French inhabitants stand affected; if any ships of war are at Quebeck, and any other intelligence you may judge necessary for me to know. I find the inhabitants very friendly this way, and make no doubt, they are the same with you. I hope to see you in Quebeck in a few days. In the mean time, I should take it as a particular favour if some one or two of my friends would meet me on the road, and that you would let me know if the enemy are apprized of our coming; also the situation that General Schuyler is in.

Your compliance will much oblige, dear Sir, your friend and humble servant,

B. Arnold[25]

This letter never reached Mercier, who was suddenly arrested at Quebec on October 28 and thrown into jail.[26] Lieutenant Governor Hector Theophilus Cramahé, a Swiss-born retired British career officer, commanded at Quebec in Governor Carleton's absence. Despite the fact that Carleton had declared martial law in Canada, a delegation of merchants petitioned Cramahé, demanding to know why Mercier had been detained. Cramahé replied, "[T]hat in the present shape of the Province he was not at liberty to acquaint them with his reasons."[27] In truth, a copy of Arnold's October 13 letters to Mercier and Schuyler, or a summary of their contents, had been delivered to Cramahé, and he and the authorities in Quebec wanted to keep knowledge of Arnold's approaching army from the city's residents, who already were unnerved by the news of Schuyler's advance toward Montreal.

It is unclear how Cramahé learned about Arnold's letters to Mercier; the traditional story is that one or both of Arnold's Indian couriers were responsible. But it is more likely that the information came from common soldier John Hall, the French-speaking, alleged British army deserter who volunteered for the Arnold Expedition.[28] Hall was a double agent, posing at Cambridge as a deserter but actually working for the Crown. With his soldiering experience and knowledge of French, Hall was a natural for selection by the Americans for the Canadian campaign. Double agent Hall gained a coup when Arnold instructed him to accompany the two Indians carrying his October 13 letters addressed to Mercier and Schuyler. Hall's instructions from Arnold were, upon reaching Sartigan, to arrange for a Canadian to escort the two Penobscots (Eneas and Sebatis) to Quebec, after which Hall was to gather information from the local people and return to the advancing army.[29] Ironically, Arnold sent Hall along because he did not trust the Indians.

Hall probably went as far as Sartigan, per Arnold's instructions, where he was able to get word to the British authorities in Quebec City (perhaps via the French-Canadian guide he selected at Sartigan to accompany Arnold's two innocent Indians), alerting them to the rebel column advancing on Quebec and informing them that Mercier was Arnold's principal contact in the city. The lack of any known published record of John Hall's activities is not unusual, because he would instantly have been hanged as a spy if the rebels discovered his true identity.

Mercier's arrest caused concern among Quebec's inhabitants, who were given no explanation for his apprehension and for why he was not charged with any crime. Mercier was a British citizen and an important merchant in Quebec, and his detention caused a stir as far away as London, where the following anonymously written account of his tyrannous arrest was published in the newspapers:

> On Saturday, the 28th of October, Mr. John Dyer Mercier, as he was going into the upper Town, was laid hold of by the Town Sergeant, and conducted to the main guard and there confined, and his papers were seized and examined merely by the order of the Lieutenant-Governour, without any crime or accusation alleged against him, and at daybreak the next morning he was put on board the Hunter sloop-of-war. This was very alarming to the citizens of Quebeck, who there-upon had a meeting, and appointed three of their number to wait on the Lieutenant-Governour, to know the cause of so

remarkable step. He made answer, "that he had sufficient reasons for what he had done, which he would communicate when and to whom he should think proper." But nothing was found that had proceeded from him, or that could serve as proof to convict him of any crime.

The newspaper story, which provided other accounts of the arbitrary detention and mistreatment of Canadians, concluded by saying that the king had surrounded himself with powerful but poor advisors who had become "instruments of arbitrary power over their fellow-citizens. . . . [T]he King was told he was reduced to this alternative: he must part with his Ministers or his Colonies. He has made his choice. He has kept his Ministers, and lost America."[30]

It was inevitable that rumors began to circulate inside Quebec that a rebel army, commanded by a Colonel Arnold, had crossed Maine and was marching on their city. Lieutenant Governor Cramahé was a nervous man who did what he could to improve Quebec's neglected defenses while there still was time.

The Royal Navy sloop *Hunter* (a small warship armed with ten guns and a crew of 80), Captain Thomas Mackenzie commanding, arrived at Quebec from Boston on October 12 with orders to proceed to Montreal "or to any other part up and down the River as shall be thought best for the Kings Service, endeavouring in all things to demonstrate your Zeal for it by an active and steady discharge of your Duty."[31] Mackenzie decided to anchor his ship at Quebec when he discovered that the city was virtually undefended. The *Hunter* was the warship that Arnold heard about from the French-Canadian peasants. Although she was small, the *Hunter*'s ten cannons represented a formidable hurdle for Arnold, whose expedition had neither artillery nor naval support. An even bigger problem for Arnold was that his corps was marching across Quebec province toward the south shore of the St. Lawrence River. Quebec stood on the north side of the river, and the British would undoubtedly use the *Hunter* to discourage the rebels from trying to cross, or to blow them out of the water if they made the attempt.

On November 5, 1775, Arnold's problems multiplied with the arrival of the *Lizard* at Quebec. She was a small Royal Navy frigate (three masts and cannons mounted on two decks), carrying 28 guns and a crew of 160.[32] Her arrival meant that Arnold would have to dodge two enemy warships when he reached the St. Lawrence. But there was even more bad news in store for Arnold, who learned that the *Lizard* had escorted two store ships (the *Elizabeth* and the *Jacob*) from England, both of which were loaded with munitions, uniforms, and money.

The arrival at Quebec of H.M.S. *Lizard* and her consorts was no accident, but rather the result of urgent reports from Governor Carleton for help. Carleton had been sending dispatches to his superiors in London throughout the summer, informing them of Schuyler's military build-up on Lake Champlain. At the time, Carleton believed he could defend Canada with an army recruited from the local population. With this idea in mind, he asked the home government to rush him weapons, ammunition, uniforms, and money. The *Elizabeth* and the *Jacob* were London's rapid response to Carleton's urgent pleas. The two heavily laden, unarmed merchant ships sailed from England on August 16, 1775, escorted by the *Lizard* and with orders to proceed to Quebec, where Governor Carleton would provide them with additional instructions.[33]

Congress learned about the two supply ships even before they sailed from England. Their information came from American sympathizers in Britain, who tipped off the rebels about the valuable cargo aboard the *Elizabeth* and *Jacob* and its destination. Apparently unaware that the two ships were being escorted by the *Lizard*, or hoping to snag the merchantmen despite the escort, the rebels raced to try and intercept the two unarmed merchantmen at sea. The New England colonies had armed some merchant ships, but because they were embroiled in politics and bureaucracy, they failed to respond to Congress' plea. John Hancock, the president of the Continental Congress, then informed Washington about the two Quebec-bound store ships in a letter dated October 5, in which he wrote, "The Congress having this day Rec'd certain Intelligence of the Sailing of Two. . . Brigantines, of no Force [unarmed] from England on the 11th of August last, loaded with Six Thousand Stand of Arms, a large Quantity of Powder & others Stores for Quebec, without Convoy [incorrect intelligence], and as it is of great importance if possible to intercept them."[34] Washington, who received Hancock's letter at Cambridge on the 11th, jumped at the chance. He was in the midst of converting two coastal merchants' ships, named the *Speedwell* (renamed *Hancock*) and the *Eliza* (christened *Franklin*).[35] Washington immediately informed his military secretary, Joseph Reed, who was in charge of refitting both ships with cannons at Beverly, Massachusetts, of this great opportunity, ordering him to accelerate the work on the *Hancock* and *Franklin* and to get them to sea as soon as possible. Reed's efforts included instructing the officers on the scene, "You will immediately set every Hand to Work that can be procured & not a Moment of Time be lost. . . ."[36]

The two refitted warships sailed from Beverly on October 22 under the overall command of Nicholson Broughton, an experienced sea captain. Washington gave Broughton sealed orders with instructions not to open them until his squadron was out of sight of land. The sealed orders were part of Washington's efforts to keep the mission a secret from the British, who had spies and informers everywhere. Upon reaching the open sea, the cankerous Broughton read his orders and decided it was too late in the season to sail into the waters off the mouth of the St. Lawrence River and that he probably had missed the Quebec-bound store ships anyway. Broughton ignored Washington's explicit orders, deciding instead to raid Charlottetown, the capital of St. John Island (now Prince Edward Island), which he heard was undefended and contained shops and warehouses filled with valuable goods.[37] Thus the two store ships, crammed with enough equipment to outfit a small army, safely cleared the North Atlantic and sailed into the St. Lawrence River.

The *Lizard* carried two additional valuable assets to assist Quebec: a strongbox full of gold and silver coins that would help buy the fidelity of Quebec's militia, and John Hamilton, the ship's captain. This capable and experienced officer had been handpicked by the admiralty for what they expected to be a difficult assignment requiring a man of good judgment and independent action. Hamilton lived up to their expectations.

The *Lizard* reached Quebec on November 5 with the *Elizabeth* and *Jacob*. Captain Hamilton hailed the city with a 15-gun salute from the *Lizard*'s great guns then moored his ship and went into town to confer with Lieutenant Governor Cramahé and Captain Mackenzie, commander of the sloop *Hunter*. After being briefed on the situation, including the approach of Arnold's Expedition toward Quebec, Hamilton decided to remain at Quebec rather than proceeding farther upriver to Montreal. As the senior naval officer at Quebec, Hamilton took command of the *Hunter* and several smaller-armed vessels in the river. He also used the valuable resources of his frigate to help defend the city. The *Lizard*'s log entry for November 7 gives some of the particulars: "Disembarked our

Marines to Assist the Garrison. They being in want of regulars. . . sent on shore 100 Hand Grenades and 10 Fuses for the Use of the Garrison [. S]ent the Sail maker & 2 men On Shore to make sand Bags to Repair the walls."[38] Eventually, Hamilton off-loaded all of his ship's cannons, which were strategically placed on shore.

Another boost to Quebec's morale arrived in the person of Colonel Ethan Allen, the famous ringleader of the Green Mountain Boys. This arch-rebel passed through the city in chains en route to stand trial for treason in London. Allen was captured when he made a reckless, premature attack on Montreal with 250 Canadian recruits. His apprehension impressed the French-Canadians and helped boost the morale of Quebec's defenders. Arnold may have heard rumors of Allen's capture, which would have come as no surprise, since Arnold had first-hand experience of his behavior. Meanwhile, the American propaganda machine back in Cambridge and Philadelphia had a field day with images of the courageous Colonel Allen being taken away in chains in an effort to convince the people that they were subject to the same brutal treatment by the depraved and tyrannical British government.[39]

Despite the presence of two Royal Navy warships, the military and political situation in Quebec remained perilous. There were not enough dependable men defending Quebec to man the extensive fortifications that circled the city. Besides, much of Quebec's seemingly impressive defenses were in disrepair after years of neglect, and could easily be assaulted by a determined attack. In addition, most of the civilian population was apathetic in their loyalty to Britain and indifferent to who occupied the city, so long as their lives, homes, and businesses were safe. The merchants, in particular, were nervous that their wharves and warehouses—stuffed with goods—would be burned by the rebels. They wanted the city to surrender at the first sign of Arnold's approach. The final straw was Cramahé, who despite his military career, proved to be a government functionary who lacked the determination and enterprise of Governor Carlton. Cramahé seemed resigned that the rebels would take the city and was not interested in getting advice from Captain Hamilton.[40] For example, in a letter to General William Howe in Boston, Cramahé wrote, "[I]f attacked before Gen. Carleton's arrival [return to Quebec with troops] there is too much reason to apprehend the affair will be soon over."[41]

While feckless Cramahé went through the motions of defending Quebec, Arnold was 60 miles away in Sartigan, making as much trouble as he could for his opponent. He recruited for his army about 50 Indians, who demanded cash for their services.[42]

One of the Indians who joined the expedition was Natanis, previously thought to be as "big a rogue as ever existed under heaven."[43] It turned out that he had been shadowing the Americans since their arrival on the Dead River, helping them in small ways without showing himself for fear of being shot. He finally stepped forward at Sartigan, and shook the hand of Lieutenant Steele, whose scouting mission had been ordered to kill him. From that moment onward, Natanis proved to be a friend and ally to the Americans.[44]

Arnold was also handing out broadsides encouraging the French Canadians to join his army. His proclamations, printed in French, were probably composed back in Cambridge by Major General Charles Lee's aide-de-camp, William Palfrey, who was conversant in the language. General Lee corrected the French grammar in the original draft of the proclamation.[45] The proclamations were printed at headquarters and shipped to Arnold in Maine with a covering letter from Joseph Reed, Washington's military secretary. The bundle of proclamations caught up with the expedition at Fort Western, and Arnold mentioned their arrival in his September 27 report to Washington: "I have received a Letter from Col. Reed, with the Manifesto's. . . ."[46] The proclamation, titled "Address to the Inhabitants of Canada," were probably entrusted to Eleazer Oswald, who oversaw their safe arrival in Canada along with most of the expedition's money and headquarters papers. These broadsides, which arrived in Canada with the expedition's headquarters baggage, read in part:

Friends and Brethren,

The Great American Congress have sent an army into your province under command of General Schuyler, not to plunder but to protect you. . . . To cooperate with this design. . . I have detached Colonel Arnold into your country, with a part of the Army under my command. . . . I invite you therefore as Friends and Brethren, to provide him with such Supplies as your Country affords; and I pledge myself not only for your Safety and Security, but for ample Compensation. The Cause of America and of Liberty is the Cause of

every virtuous American Citizen; whatever may be his Religion or
his Descent, the United Colonies know no Distinction but such as
Slavery, Corruption and arbitrary Domination may create. Come
then, you generous Citizens, range yourselves under the Standard of
general Liberty—against which all the Force and Artifice of
Tyranny will never be able to prevail.[47]

The proclamation that Arnold distributed was part of a stream of
American propaganda engineered to bring the Canadians into the war as
allies. There were compelling reasons for the Canadians to join the
rebellion as the fourteenth colony, especially the fact that their country
had been conquered by the British just 12 years prior to the start of the
Revolutionary War. But there were other circumstances in Canada
working against *Les Bostonnais*, one of which was the loyalty of
Canada's clergy to the British. Canada's white population of 100,000
was primarily Roman Catholic, and the British did not interfere with the
Catholic religion after annexing the former French colony. The Quebec
Act of 1774 guaranteed religious toleration, which helped secure the
good will of the Catholic clergy, who had great influence over the people,
reminding them that the American invaders were Protestants—a religion
they considered to be the devil's work. Washington was aware of the
domination of the Catholic Church in Canada and warned Arnold to
respect the people's religious beliefs. The general mentioned this point in
the set of written instructions that he gave Arnold before the expedition
left Cambridge. Washington told Arnold, "[A]s far as lays in your Power
you are to protect & support the free exercise of the Religion of the
Country & the undisturbed Enjoyment of the Rights of Conscience in
religious Matters with your utmost Influence & Authority."[48]
    Another problem that Arnold confronted with the civilian population
of Canada was that they had no experience with self-government and
seemed content to continue living in the highly stratified, class-based
system in which the majority of the people were *habitants*, French-
Canadians who rented their land from the rich and powerful *seigneurs*
who owned large estates originally held by feudal grants from the king of
France. Thus the richest farmlands in Canada at the time—the acreage
along the St. Lawrence, Richelieu, and Chaudière rivers—were divided
into large estates controlled by the *seigneur* class. The merchants and
tradesmen living in Montreal and Quebec were more liberal and
pro-active in their politics. Some of these urbanites were businessmen

who had immigrated to Canada from New England following the British conquest. Called the "old subjects" (as opposed to the French-Canadians, who were called the "new subjects"), these transplanted New Englanders tended to side with the rebellion, but were estimated to be only 2,000 in number and unable to influence the French-Canadians, who were under the control of the priests and *seigneurs*. Thus, despite all of Arnold's overtures, promises, and proclamations, he was only able to recruit a handful of Canadians for his army, and had to continue to rely on gold and silver to buy food, labor, shelter, and to hire boats, horses, and wagons from the local civilians. Washington also provided Arnold direction on this point in his written instructions:

> You are to endeavor. . . to conciliate the Affections of those People & such Indians as you may meet with by every Means in your Power—convincing them that we Come at the Request of many of their Principal People, not as Robbers or to make War upon them but as the Friends & Supporters of their Liberties as well as ours.[49]

From the moment that he arrived at Sartigan, Arnold realized that this scattered settlement could only serve as a temporary stopping place to collect and rest his army before moving on. Even if he wanted to camp there for an extended period of time, the area lacked food and shelter to support his men. Arnold himself only stayed at Sartigan for one day before advancing six miles down the river, closer to Quebec City, where on the morning of November 1 he established his headquarters in a wayside tavern. Lieutenant Steele and another officer named John Taylor, from Smith's Pennsylvania rifle company, were among those who accompanied him and assisted in the purchase and transportation of additional food for their hungry men.

Arnold moved farther down the river valley to St. Joseph, the first real village along the Chaudière, and then to another, larger village named Ste. Marie, which he reached November 5, leaving a trail of cash and proclamations behind him. The land that Arnold was passing through was owned by seigneur Gabriel Elzear Taschereau, who managed his vast acreage in feudal splendor from a manor house located near St. Marie. Like the other seigneurs, Taschereau was a loyalist. He vacated his mansion at the approach of the Americans and ran off to Quebec, where he joined the militia. Arnold occupied Taschereau's vacant home and enjoyed the comforts of the manor house for one night before advancing closer to Quebec on November 6.

The road north from Ste. Marie paralleled the Chaudière River for four miles, at which point the river cut off sharply to the left and the road angled to the right. Arnold followed the road, which took them through a bleak, almost uninhabited 12-mile stretch of woodlands called the Forest of Sertigan. The village of St. Henri, situated along the banks of the Ethemin River at the northern edge of the forest, was in a thickly populated region only ten miles from Quebec City with a good road connecting it to Pointe de Lévy (also called Point de Lévis, Point Levis, and Point Levi), the name given to the area along the southern bank of the St. Lawrence River directly across from Quebec. Traffic going to Quebec could cross by ferry from Lévis (a village near Pointe de Lévy) to Quebec City, but the British had long since halted this and other ferries along the river and removed all boats from the south side of the St. Lawrence in anticipation of Arnold's arrival. Some troops caught up with Arnold at St. Henri, which allowed him to dispatch a lieutenant with a detachment of riflemen to reconnoiter the road between St. Henri and Pointe de Lévy. He also sent spies into Quebec City, but its defenders anticipated this move by the Americans and questioned any strangers who entered. Arnold's spies were discovered in this manner and promptly arrested. Arnold, though dangerously close to Quebec, still only had rumors about the military situation in the city and the position of Schuyler's northern army. A joining up with Schuyler was a definite option now that it was apparent his expedition had lost any chance of surprise.

The letter Arnold had been hoping for finally came on November 8, when an Indian courier arrived at St. Henri with a message from General Montgomery, Schuyler's second-in-command. Reliable news from the Northern army at last! Arnold anxiously broke the seal of the dispatch, unfolded it, and started to read its contents. Montgomery's letter, dated October 29, 1775, was written from St. Johns, Canada. Sadly, there is no known copy of Montgomery's letter, but we can speculate on its contents based on the last reliable news he had about Arnold's position and on his own situation at St. Johns. The last information he had about Arnold was from a letter Washington wrote Schuyler, in which he said that Arnold had arrived at Fort Western. Washington included a copy of Arnold's report from the two scouts who traveled as far as the Dead River.[50]

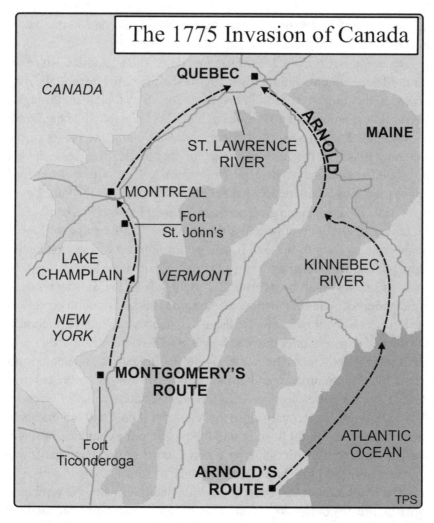

There was the possibility that Arnold already had captured Quebec. Whatever the case, Montgomery asked Arnold to report his position and the exact number of men under his command. Montgomery probably explained his situation, as well as Schuyler's illness and return to Fort Ticonderoga to regain his health. He may have described how he arrived before St. Johns in early September to find the place well fortified with artillery and garrisoned with what informants told him were the majority of the regular troops in Canada plus some militia and Indians, amounting to about 700 men. Arnold knew St. Johns because he had raided the place in May and understood the dangers of bypassing it and moving on to

Montreal. The general may also have explained that he commanded 2,000 Connecticut and New York troops, few of whom had any military experience, and how he had lost valuable time waiting for sufficient artillery and mortars to arrive from Ticonderoga to reduce St. Johns. Montgomery recommended that Arnold send him a reply via the two Indians who had delivered his letter.

Arnold immediately responded to Montgomery. In his reply, dated November 8, 1775, the colonel described his little army's horrendous trek to Canada: "I cannot at present give you a particular detail, but can only say we have hauled our batteaux over falls, up rapid streams, over carrying places; and marched through morasses, thick woods, and over mountains, about 320 miles [a miscalculation, the actual traveled was approximately 270 miles]—many of which we had to pass several times to bring our baggage." Arnold next told how Enos returned from the Dead River, "contrary to my expectation, he having orders to send back only the sick, and those that could not be furnished with provisions," and how he had written General Schuyler on October 13 but he was betrayed and the enemy was aware of his movements. The colonel said that all the canoes around Pointe de Lévy had been destroyed, and there were two frigates and several small armed vessels "lying before Quebec, and a large ship or two lately arrived from Boston." Waiting for Schuyler to arrive, retreating or surrendering were unthinkable options for Arnold. Instead he told Montgomery, "I propose crossing the St. Lawrence as soon as possible . . . otherwise shall endeavor to join your army at Montreal."[51]

Arnold wrote a similar letter addressed to General Washington and entrusted both dispatches to Montgomery's courier, who was intercepted en route by the enemy.[52] Arnold's letters did not give any information about the number of men with him, their weak physical condition, and his shortage of weapons and warm clothing. This type of sensitive information was intentionally excluded as a precaution against dispatches falling into enemy hands. So the British learned little from these latest intercepted dispatches.

Arnold now knew, from Montgomery's letter, that the northern army could not give him any immediate help. He was on his own in hostile territory with around 600 sickly, poorly armed and equipped soldiers and 50 Indian mercenaries, all of whom were strung out for several miles. Arnold reread the instructions Washington had given him at Cambridge on September 14, in which the general required him to put his corps under Schuyler's command: "[I]f he should be in Canada upon your Arrival there, you are by no means to consider yourself as upon a Separate & Independant Command but are to put yourself under him & follow his Directions."[53]

The prudent course of action was to abandon his attack on Quebec and head west to link up with the northern army. A lesser man might have taken this tact, which could be justified with honor. But Arnold was an assertive, tough officer, and his only thoughts were to ford the St. Lawrence and assault Quebec. To do this, he had to consolidate his corps and get it across the river, no matter how sick, threadbare, and footsore the men were from their terrible ordeal. He therefore sent back an order on the 6th that instructed "every captain to get his company on as fast as possible, and not to leave a man behind unless unfit for duty."[54] The dauntless Colonel Arnold had already worked out a way to get his force across the river under the guns of the two Royal Navy warships. His solution was to wait for a dark, windless night and then silently slip past the enemy warships and patrol boats in Indian canoes.

The scouting party Arnold dispatched from St. Henri on the night of November 6 returned the next morning and reported the enemy had consolidated all their forces at Quebec City. Based on this information, Arnold advanced along the road on the morning of November 7 to Pointe de Lévy to await the arrival of his troops. Pointe de Lévy had been chosen by Arnold, in part, because there was a flour mill at the site with a supply of wheat at hand that could be ground into flour.

The bulk of Arnold's corps pulled out of Sartigan on November 3 and marched on foot toward the St. Lawrence at the rate of 10 to 20 miles a day. Food was plentiful but expensive, however there was no warm clothing or shoes for sale from the peasants at any price. Unknown to Arnold at the time, ammunition was in short supply, and there were not enough muskets and rifles for all the men; about 100 had lost their weapons during the numerous bateaux accidents that had befallen the expedition along the Kennebec, Dead, and Chaudière Rivers. The sick and feeble soldiers, 96 in number, were too weak to walk and required transport down the Chaudière from Sartigan in rented or purchased canoes. Major Meigs and Captains Topham and Thayer were responsible for the care of the invalids. Captain Dearborn was among the sick, probably suffering with some form of pneumonia. He wrote in his journal that it was snowing when he left Sartigan and that he saw a great number of men who were marching barefoot and "in poor circumstances."[55]

And thus the locals observed a rawboned column of American patriots—some without weapons and wrapped in tattered, dirty coats and blankets—marching resolutely toward Quebec. One of the Americans described the scene in his journal: "[O]ur clothes were torn in pieces by the bushes, and hung in strings—few of us had any shoes, but moggasons [moccasins] made of raw skins—many of us without hats—and beards long and visages thin and meager. I thought we much resembled the animals which inhabit New-Spain [South America], called the Ourang-Outang."[56] The Americans' destitute appearance increased the reluctance of the French Canadians to join them. The locals must also have wondered how these invaders planned to capture Quebec without any warships or artillery.

Arnold's ragged, poorly equipped men began arriving at Pointe de Lévy, through gusts of snow and strong winds, on November 7, the same day that the smartly dressed and well-armed Marines from the *Lizard* disembarked to help defend Quebec. The British gained another small advantage on November 9 as evidenced by the log of the *Lizard*, which reported the arrival at Quebec of "his Majestys Schooner Magdelin Lt. Joseph Nunn [commanding] from Portsmouth [England] with Dispatches[.]"[57] The *Magdelin*'s six cannons added to the defenders' firepower. Across the river, Arnold and his companions bought extra provisions and supervised the construction of scaling ladders that they were paying the French-Canadians to make. Officers forayed back into the interior, to the villages along the Etchemin and Chaudière, to buy or rent additional boats and canoes, while soldiers made crude shoes from the hides of butchered animals. Dr. Senter arrived on this busy scene on November 8 with "snow over shoes. In open sight of the enemy naught but the river divided us."[58]

The British were watching the Americans on the south shore of the St. Lawrence at the same time. The log of the *Lizard* recorded that "the Charlotte Armd Ship [a sloop with a crew of twenty] made the Signal for the Approach of the Enemy."[59]

A man named John Halstead arrived in the rebel camp about this time. Senter described Halstead as a man formerly from "the Jerseys" (New Jersey) who "followed merchandise [a merchant] in Quebec" and an individual the British suspected was "holding a correspondence with the Bostonians."[60] As a precaution, Lt. Governor Cramach ordered Halstead to leave the city immediately, so as to prevent him from aiding the rebels. Halstead headed across the river, where he was welcomed as a "friend of liberty," while loyalists back at Quebec were calling him "a great scoundrel."[61] Since Halstead knew the river and surrounding terrain, Arnold decided to use him as a pilot for his planned dash across the river.[62] Just how many troops Arnold had at Pointe de Lévy by mid-November is uncertain, since Dearborn noted at the time that "a Considerable number of our men are left on the road Sick or woren [worn] out with fatigue & hunger."[63]

The men of the Arnold Expedition who reached the St. Lawrence had the exhilaration of viewing their objective for the first time. Death had stalked them over almost 300 miles of waist-high freezing water, dense swamps, torrential rains, raging floods, falling trees, thickets, quagmires, wind, ice, snow, and near starvation, and those who survived the journey were ecstatic about their triumph. "When we halted [we] were within sight of Quebec," penned private Morison, "the river St. Lawrence between us and the town. We were filled with joy at this event, when we saw ourselves at the end of our destination; and at length freed from the misery we endured in the woods."[64] It was also a personal victory for Arnold who, despite unanticipated obstacles and inaccurate information about his route, had led his men across 270 miles of muck and mire. As a result, their fellow Americans soon would celebrate Arnold as the "American Hannibal" and his officers and men as the "famine proof veterans."[65] General Washington expressed his admiration for their accomplishments in a letter to General Schuyler in early December:

> It gave me the highest Satisfaction to hear of Colonel Arnold's being at point Levi, with his Men in great Sprits after their long and fatiguing March, attended with almost insuperable Difficulties, and discouraging Circumstances of being left by one third of the Troops nearly that went upon the Expedition: The Merit of this Gentleman is certainly great and I have every wish that Fortune may distinguish him as one of the her favorites.[66]

Even the enemy admired the expedition's achievement, as evidenced by the following extract from an anonymous letter from Quebec subsequently published in British newspapers:

A View of the City of Quebec, the Capital of Canada. This etching was published by Robert Sayer in London in 1768.

Historic Urban Plans, Inc.

Quebeck, November 9, 1775.

There are about five hundred Provincials arrived on Point Levi, opposite to the Town, by the way of Chaudiere, across the woods. Surely a miracle must have been wrought in their favour. It is an undertaking above the common race of men, in this debauched age. They have traveled through woods and bogs, and over precipices, for the space of one hundred and twenty miles, attended with every inconvenience and difficulty, to be surmounted only by men of indefatigable zeal and industry.[67]

Having endured great hardships, the expedition's members experienced one bit of good luck when they discovered that the British had failed to destroy the flour mill at Pointe de Lévy when they withdrew behind Quebec's walls. Major Henry Caldwell, a retired British officer and reportedly the richest man in Quebec, owned the mill, and he may have interceded to prevent it from being destroyed, hoping he could reclaim it at some future date. Caldwell had recently come out of retirement to command the British residents in the city who had organized into a militia. The rebels not only occupied the working mill, but found a supply of grain on the site from which fresh bread could be made. Halstead knew how to operate the mill, as he once had managed the place for Caldwell.

Captain Mackenzie, who commanded the *Hunter*, saw the rebel activity on the south shore and decided to send some men to reconnoiter and, if possible, to snatch some boat oars from the rebels. Mackenzie selected his younger brother, a 15-year-old midshipman (apprentice naval officer) for the job. The youngster took a cutter (ship's boat) loaded with heavily armed sailors from the *Hunter* and quietly rowed to a secluded section of the shoreline. Their boat made it ashore, but Arnold's watchful sentries discovered—and shot at—them. Realizing what had happened, Captain Mackenzie began firing his ship's guns in support of his brother's landing party. In the melee, the sailors returned to their cutter and hastily rowed out of range, inadvertently leaving behind their commander. Young Mackenzie hid in the underbrush for a while before making a dash for the boat by plunging into the cold water and swimming toward safety. Some of Arnold's Indians spotted him, jumped into the river after him, and took him prisoner. Mackenzie was the first prisoner

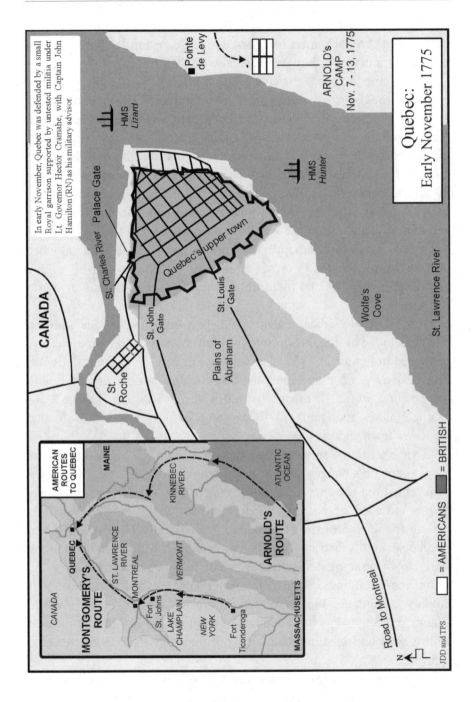

In early November, Quebec was defended by a small Royal garrison supported by untested militia under Lt. Governor Hector Cramahe, with Captain John Hamilton (RN) as his military advisor.

Quebec:
Early November 1775

CANADA

St. Lawrence River

Pointe de Levy

ARNOLD's CAMP
Nov. 7 - 13, 1775

HMS Lizard

HMS Hunter

Palace Gate

St. Charles River

Quebec's upper town

Wolfe's Cove

St. Roche

St. John Gate

St. Louis Gate

Plains of Abraham

Road to Montreal

AMERICAN ROUTES TO QUEBEC

MAINE

KINNEBEC RIVER

ATLANTIC OCEAN

MONTGOMERY'S ROUTE

CANADA

QUEBEC

ST. LAWRENCE RIVER

MONTREAL

Fort St. Johns

LAKE CHAMPLAIN

VERMONT

NEW YORK

Fort Ticonderoga

MASSACHUSETTS

ARNOLD'S ROUTE

N

JDD and TPS

☐ = AMERICANS   ■ = BRITISH

of war that Arnold's men had seized since carrying the war into the enemy's country, and they were elated with their prize.[68]

Determined to cross the river and attack the city, Arnold observed Quebec through his spyglass from across the river.[69] The city stood on a promontory in a bend of the St. Lawrence. He could see the two Royal Navy warships (*Hunter* and *Lizard*) strategically anchored in the river. Commanding the view was the spectacular rock formation called Cape Diamond, which rose more than 300 feet above the river and dominated the landscape. A smaller river, named the St. Charles, flowed into the St. Lawrence above the city. Deep water surrounded Quebec on three sides, and the only land approach was from the west toward the high ground dominated by Cape Diamond. This unique combination made Quebec one of the best natural fortresses in the world, and worthy of the nickname given it in the nineteenth century—"the Gibraltar of North America."

Arnold put together a plan of Quebec from his various sources, which included his recollections of his prewar visits and a map of the city published in France in 1755. Although out of date, this map, titled *Plan de la ville de Quebec*, indicated the major features of the city, including the position of its fortifications and gates.[70] The map showed, for example, that Cape Diamond divided Quebec into two sections, called the lower town and the upper town.

Lying beneath Cape Diamond, the lower town was located along the river's edge on a narrow strip of land. Arnold knew that the lower town represented the commercial heart of the city; shops, offices, and warehouses crowded its narrow, winding streets. John Mercier, Arnold's prewar friend and business associate, had recently built a wharf and warehouse in this district. The poorer people of the city also lived in the lower town, crammed together in small houses scattered among the commercial buildings. Though the lower town possessed no particular military advantage, the upper town, situated on the crest of Cape Diamond, occupied a natural defensive location and had been improved with a wall and bastions (fortified positions) that faced all the land approaches.

The unprotected lower town was relatively easy to conquer with its hodgepodge of narrow streets at the water's edge. Getting into the upper town was the problem. The only way up from the lower town was to climb hundreds of narrow stone steps or to travel on a steep, circular road.

Plan of the City and Environs of Quebec with Its Siege and Blockade by The Americans. (London, September, 1776), by William Faden. *Author's collection*

"A View of Quebec From the East," by Joseph F. W. Des Barres, ca. 1781.

Library and Archives Canada / C-080270

This dirt road (later paved in 1785) was called the Cote de Montagne, and a barrier blocked the approach of potential invaders from ascending from the waterfront. Approaching the upper town from the land side was also problematic. Although Quebec's defenses were considered to be in disrepair, they were still substantial, consisting of 30-foot-high, 50-foot-thick earthen ramparts faced with stone. The stone had fallen away in some places, but the earthen walls remained intact and protected every land approach to the city. Less strategic sections of Quebec's walls (facing the sea) were constructed of wooden stockades. Artillery in the upper town faced the river and controlled the passage of ships sailing up or down the St. Lawrence, which narrowed sharply in front of Cape Diamond.

There were three gates into the upper town from the land side, and Arnold probably knew their locations from his prewar business trips to Quebec. Perhaps the most important of these gates was Porte St. Louis (St. Louis Gate), located near the river. This portal, lined with numerous shops and taverns, opened onto St. Louis Street, the commercial center of the upper town, and ended at the center of the upper town at the Place d'Armes (parade ground). Nearby was the military headquarters of the city, called the citadel (or Fort St. Louis), and the governor's place, called the Chateau St. Louis, which sat on the crest of Cape Diamond with a spectacular view of the river below. Chateau St. Louis was also known as the government house, as it was the nerve center of the British administration of Canada. The only approach to the palace was past the citadel and through an extensive garden. Inside the palace were a luxurious council chamber on the ground floor and a large room for holding official receptions and banquets. Nearby were the city's cathedral, government offices, hospitals, and a Jesuit college. During his prewar trips, Arnold probably strolled along St. Louis Street and frequented its coffee houses, where he transacted business and talked politics with his friends. To the north of Porte St. Louis, another gate, called Port St. Jean (St. John's Gate), rested near some houses and shops, called the suburb of St. Jean, which lay outside the city's walls. Farther north, another gate opened into the city. Called the Palace Gate, it faced the St. Charles River and two other suburbs called St. Roch and Palais. Abatis (an entanglement of tree branches) and cannons protected all three gates.

Arnold next turned his attention to the ships in the St. Lawrence. He noticed that, besides the two stately warships anchored in the river, there were armed boats patrolling up and down, watching for any attempt by the rebels to get across. Arnold had no intention of letting this formidable naval array interrupt his plans. He would have been further encouraged to make the crossing and attack the city if he had read the confidential report John Hamilton, captain of the *Lizard*, sent to his superiors in London on November 10. In his report, Hamilton expressed pessimism, saying that he expected Quebec to fall to the Americans:

> Lizard at Quebec the 10th Novemr 1775
>
> Please to inform my Lords Commissioners of the Admiralty of the Arrival of The Magdalen Schooner at Quebec this day [according to the log of the Lizard, this ship actually arrived at Quebec on the 9th], with dispatches for General Carleton, which was delivered to the Lieut. Governor, but am afraid they will share the same fate of mine [dispatches brought by Captain Hamilton from England for Governor Carleton], that of being brought back again, the Communication being entirely cutt off by the Rebels, between this Place and Montreal where General Carleton is, but cannot learn any Certain intelligence concerning him;—I have offerr'd my Service to the Lieut. Governor several times;—This Evening we are inform'd there is an advanced Party of the Rebels on the South Shore [Arnold's men] & I fear the Town will soon be invested, their [Quebec's] defense is weak and the Inhabitants not to be depended on—If it should be necessary to stay here the Winter for the Protection of the Garrison I am greatly afraid I shall lose His Majestys Ship Lizard but I should not hesitate a Moment if I think it will be the Means of saving the City.
>
> The Ships & Vessels of Force [warships] here are—Lizard, Hunter, Magdalen and an Arm'd Vessel of Six Guns & Sixty Men appointed by the Governor—The Weather is already set in severe and if some unforeseen assistance does not speedily arrive I am afraid this City and Province will soon be in the Hands of the Rebels as there is no Military force nor Provisions for carry on a siege—Their Lordships may depend on my Care & Attention and ready Service to co-operate with the Governor on all Occasions for the good of the Service and hope the steps I may be obliged to take will meet their approbation.
>
> I am Sir, John Hamilton, R.N.[71]

How many men were defending Quebec when Captain Hamilton wrote his report on November 10? There is an accurate "Return of Men for the Defense of Quebec," dated one week later, that stated there were 63 officers and 1,248 men protecting the city.[72]

Compared to Arnold's 600, this is an overwhelming number. But a closer examination of the November 16 British strength report reveals fewer available defenders, since it includes 500 civilians only recently pressed into service as militia, 11 officers and 132 soldiers and sailors who were still en route to Quebec from Montreal, 100 new recruits belonging to the Royal Highland Emigrants, plus numerous sailors onboard the warships (too far away to render any prompt assistance if the city were attacked from the land side). The actual number of dependable troops defending the city's walls, gates, and barricades remains unclear. The Americans believed that the bulk of Quebec's defenders were indifferent militia who would throw down their weapons and run if attacked. Their sentiment was vocalized in a popular doggerel, circulating at the time in Canada, which lampooned the colony's compulsory militia service: "Let us take arms, my dear friends, A march to Boston is but a pleasant walk. . . . And cheerfully go and get our throats cut."[73]

The rebels also felt that many of Quebec's residents sympathized with their cause and would join them once the fighting started. But the reliability of the Quebec militia was a matter of opinion and speculation. Some of Quebec's British and French militiamen were as patriotic as the rebels camped across the river. They were defending their families, homes, and businesses against the Americans. It is probable that some members of the Quebec militia were retired French or British soldiers, or militia, with military experience from the French and Indian War. Such men constituted a dangerous enemy. The military situation inside Quebec remained a mystery to Arnold, who continued to observe the city, watching the endless pacing of armed patrol boats while he waited for the weather to clear.

High winds and rough water between November 10 and 12 deterred the rebels from attempting to cross the St. Lawrence in their canoes. Certain that the weather would soon improve, a restive Arnold held a council of war late on the night of the 12th. During the meeting he confirmed that they would cross the river, under cover of night, at the first opportunity. Then Arnold had Halstead brief them on Quebec's layout and his conviction that its garrison, composed largely of conscripted militia, would not fight.[74]

As Arnold had predicted, the weather cleared by midday on the 13th, with the prospects of a dark night and calm water. Morale in Arnold's camp soared that day when news arrived that St. Johns had surrendered to Montgomery, whose army already was advancing on Montreal.[75]

With his corps in a conquering mood, Arnold reassembled his officers to finalize their plans for the hazardous crossing they would attempt that night. Attending the meeting were Lieutenant Colonel Greene, Majors Meigs and Bigelow, and Captains Thayer, Topham, Morgan, Dearborn, Hanchett, and Ward. Arnold reported that the expedition had accumulated 40 canoes and dugouts that were hidden in a cove just behind the mouth of the Chaudière River. They agreed that these boats would quietly be moved to the St. Lawrence from their hiding place as soon as darkness fell. Arnold explained that, because there were not enough boats, the troops would have to cross the two-mile-wide river in several trips. He said that 60 men would have to stay behind to guard the baggage and protect their camp if they had to retreat back to Pointe de Lévy, and he selected Captain Hanchett to command this rear guard.

Having made their preparations, the meeting ended, and every man readied himself for the big mission. Crossing in small, open boats in the face of two Royal Navy warships and heavily armed patrol craft was reckless and hazardous, but Arnold's vocabulary did not include words like caution or retreat, and his bravery infected every man in his corps. Hanchett, however, already resentful of Arnold for denying him the honor of being the first to reach Sartigan, now felt additional hostility toward his commander for being denied a place in the climactic river crossing.

The first American boats started crossing the river at about 9:00 p.m. on November 13, accompanied by the sounds of British patrol boats passing to and fro.[76] Arnold, Halstead, Morgan, and a few riflemen occupied the lead boat, followed by Indians with their muskets at the ready. Silently, the boats crossed the river with muffled oars (a figure of speech), passed the British patrols, and set a course for a cove just west of the city. The cove that Arnold and his men quietly paddled toward was the same place where, in 1759, British general James Wolfe landed 4,500 troops for his attack on French-held Quebec. A narrow path leading from the cove, up a steep embankment, ran to pasture land called the Plains of

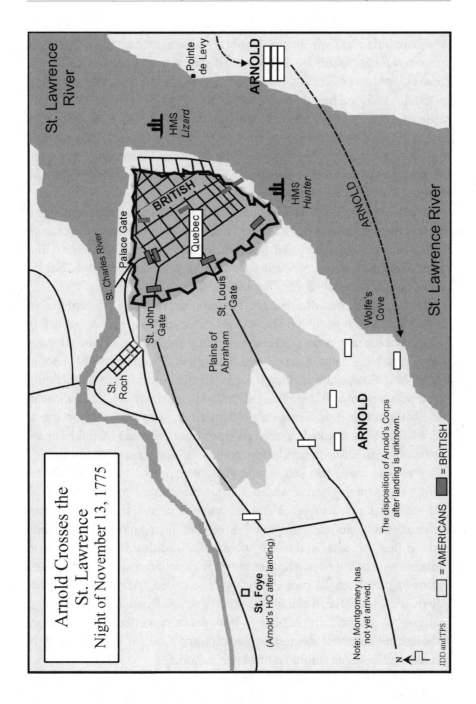

Arnold Crosses the
St. Lawrence
Night of November 13, 1775

St. Lawrence River

St. Charles River

St. Lawrence River

Pointe de Levy

ARNOLD

HMS *Lizard*

HMS *Hunter*

BRITISH

Quebec

Palace Gate

St. John Gate

St. Louis Gate

Plains of Abraham

Wolfe's Cove

St. Roch

St. Foye
(Arnold's HQ after landing)

ARNOLD

ARNOLD

The disposition of Arnold's Corps
after landing is unknown.

Note: Montgomery has
not yet arrived.

N

JDD and TPS

= AMERICANS   = BRITISH

Abraham (also known as the heights), which extended to Quebec's ramparts and St. John's Gate. The total distance from the cove (called the Anse au Foulon or Wolfe's Cove) to Cape Diamond was one-and-a-half miles. In 1759, General Wolfe defeated 5,000 French soldiers (who sallied forth from their encampment to confront the British rather than risk a continued siege) on the Plains of Abraham in one of the world's most decisive battles. The Battle of the Plains of Abraham represented the climax of the French and Indian War and secured Quebec for the British.

Arnold's first boats came ashore with no enemy sentinels in sight. Their passage, however, had not been without incident. Stocking mentioned in his journal that "Several of the bark canoes in crossing upset, by which accident we lost some muskets, and baggage, but no lives, though some of us very narrowly escaped."[77]

Once ashore, guards were posted and everyone else was ordered to stay quiet and out of sight. The second wave of soldiers made it safely across. But the men were cold and wet, and some built small fires to keep warm. A passing patrol boat spotted the light and headed toward shore to investigate. Seeing the craft approach, Arnold emerged from his hiding place with a number of his men, their muskets at the ready. The sailors in the boat saw the dim forms on the shoreline, who started shooting at them. The boat backed away, rowing frantically as Arnold's men continued firing; they later claimed to have killed three of the enemy.[78]

The boat made its escape, and Arnold expected to hear Quebec's church bells ringing out a warning at any moment. But quiet returned, and the third wave of rebel canoes made it across the river without incident. The boats had completed three round trips by 4:00 a.m. when bad weather forced an end to the operation. The colonel had 500 men on the north side of the river who already were clambering up the cliffs to the Plains of Abraham.[79] Upon seeing what he called "Abraham's Plains," rifleman John Joseph Henry called it "an extensive chaimpaign [campaign] country" and compared it to places in western Pennsylvania, although he admitted the terrain surrounding Quebec was "on a more gigantic scale" to anything he had seen at home.[80]

A road across the heights led to St. John's Gate. Due to the carelessness of the garrison, some stories claim, St. John's Gate was open and unguarded on the night that Arnold crossed the river. Private Fobes tells the story best: "The city was completely exposed, St. John's gate was open. We stopped a man that had just come out of it, and could have entered, with nothing to hinder."[81] This tale is repeated in several other contemporary accounts, including a letter written by Lieutenant John Strake, an officer on the *Lizard*. Writing in early November, Strake explained that "[T]he Inhabitants were in a state of despondency expecting that the Army under General Arnold, which having crossed the River St. Lawrence . . . wou'd advance and enter the gates without resistance, for such was the consternation, that the gates were not shut."[82]

Aaron Burr insisted, even 50 years after the fact, that "there were not 100 soldiers in Quebeck upon the arrival of Arnold's party on the northern shore of the St. Lawrence," and that all of the gates were open "and the city might have been entered with perfect ease."[83]

While the situation inside Quebec during the early morning hours of November 14 remains a mystery, in retrospect, Arnold should have taken the chance and tried to storm the city immediately after crossing the river. Despite the gunfire and noise near Wolfe's Cove, Cramahé did not know that the rebels had crossed, and would not until the following morning.[84]

Lacking any accurate information about the situation inside the city, and with his men cold and exhausted, Arnold decided not to risk an assault. Instead he posted guards near the ramparts and proceeded to the nearby suburb of Ste. Foye, over a mile away from Quebec, where he established his headquarters in the mansion of Major Caldwell, who commanded the British militia.[85] Arnold arrived at Caldwell's, surprising several of his servants who had arrived the previous day with carts and wagons to haul away some of their master's household goods and livestock. Arnold chased them away and seized everything on the property, causing an angry Caldwell to write, "[T]hey lived on my beef and potatoes for a week."[86] Major Meigs noted that the troops occupied "other houses adjacent [to Caldwell's mansion], which were fine accommodations for our troops."[87]

In a surprise maneuver, later that morning a British party sallied out from the city to snatch a drowsy American sentry.[88] The incident infuriated Arnold, who decided to test Quebec's resolve without delay. His first move was to write out a summons for the city to surrender, assuring its residents that they would be safe. Here is the key passage from his warrant:

I am ordered by his Excellency Genl Washington, to take Possession of the Town of Quebec, I do therefore in the Name of the United Colonies, demand immediate surrender of the Town, Fortifications &c of Quebec, to the Forces of the united Colonies under my Command. . . . On surrendering the Town, the Property of every Individual shall be secured to him, But if I am obliged to carry the Town by storm you may expect every Severity practised on such Occasions, and the Merchants who may now save their property will probably be involved in the general Ruin.[89]

Arnold picked Matthais Ogden to deliver his demand to Lieutenant Governor Cramahé. This youngster, who joined the expedition as a gentleman volunteer with his friend Aaron Burr, had conducted himself admirably during the march across Maine. The colonel wanted to present his terms of surrender in a ceremony contrived to terrorize Quebec's governor and citizens. He hoped that Quebec's inhabitants would listen to his generous terms and pressure Cramahé into capitulating, especially since it was known that the British garrison at St. Johns had surrendered to Montgomery. Arnold began by parading his Kennebec veterans to within 800 yards of the St. Louis Gate, where they gave three huzzahs. Then young Ogden marched closer to read the terms of surrender in front of the city's walls, now lined with curious onlookers. "According to the custom," Ogden later wrote in his journal, he was carrying a white flag and accompanied by a drummer, who "beat a parley" (from "parler," the French verb meaning "to speak"). Militiamen, members of the Royal Highland Emigrants, and marines from the *Lizard* could be seen on the ramparts as Ogden advanced. Lieutenant Governor Cramahé was among them, accompanied by an imposing man in uniform. As Ogden approached the walls, the officer standing next to Cramahé waved his hand, and a moment later a cannon bellowed forth. Its projectile hit the ground near Ogden and his drummer, "spattering us with the earth it threw up."[90] The cannon shot was followed by three cheers from the city's ramparts, as the dumbfounded rebel emissary scampered back toward his comrades.[91] One observer on the ramparts described the scene: "[T]hey huzza'd thrice—we answer'd them with three cheers of defiance, & saluted them with a few cannon loaded with grape & canister shot—they did not wait for a second round."[92]

Arnold scowled at the British officer who fired on the white flag. The man stared back. He was a tough, battle-hardened Scotsman named Allan

Maclean. Arnold had heard about Maclean from informers and hearsay, but now studied this quixotic figure through his glass for the first time. He saw a barrel-chested, middle-aged man dressed in a smart red uniform and the distinctive bonnet of a Scots Highlander regiment. The Kennebec men would hear a lot more from Maclean in the days ahead, as this charismatic soldier, described by a fellow officer as "brave, indefatigable and experienced," took control of Quebec's defenses from the paralyzed civilian authorities.[93]

Who was Allan Maclean, and how did he manage suddenly to appear at Quebec at a most unfortunate time for Arnold? To appreciate Maclean, we must trace his life up to his hasty arrival at Quebec. He was born in Mull, Scotland, in 1725, the son of Donald Maclean, the 5th Laird of Torloisk and head of the Clan Maclean. His clan supported Prince Charles Edward (known to history as Bonnie Prince Charlie) in his bid to regain the ancient throne of Scotland from the English. The clans rallied to Charles Edward's side, culminating in the great battle of Culloden Moor in 1745. Young Allan was the second in command of Clan Maclean at the battle, in which the Scots charged massed English infantry with the din of the clan's bagpipes bellowing out their blood-curdling war chants. The clans, heavily outnumbered, were defeated by an army commanded by the Duke of Cumberland, whose victory the English honored by naming a flower in his honor ("Sweet William"), which the Scots called "Stinking William." Maclean managed to escape the decimation of Scotland that followed Culloden and fled to the Netherlands, where he joined the Scots Brigade of the Dutch army. He received a lieutenant's commission and fought at the Battle of Bergen-op-Zoom in 1746.

Maclean returned to Scotland in 1750 after the King of England declared a general amnesty for all former rebels. He settled in Edinburgh, where he lived for a few years before purchasing a lieutenant's commission in the 60th (Royal American) Regiment, which fought in North America throughout the French and Indian War. Maclean fought the French during the siege of Fort Carillon (renamed Fort Ticonderoga by the British after its capture) in 1758, where he was severely wounded. He recovered from his wounds in time to fight the French again at Fort Niagara in 1759. Promoted to captain in the 3rd Independent Company of New York, Maclean fought in 1759 at the decisive Battle of the Plains of Abraham. Returning to Britain, he raised his own regiment of Scots Highlanders, to be called the Royal Highland Volunteers or Maclean's

Highlanders. However, the war ended soon after Maclean's regiment reached America. The ministry ordered the regiment disbanded, but rewarded Maclean with a large land grant on St. John Island (today's Prince Edward Island) and half the annual salary of a major.

Maclean decided to return to Britain, where he lived until the start of the American Revolution. In the summer of 1775, a few months after the start of the war, he received permission from the government to return to America to raise a new regiment of loyal Scotsmen, to be called the Royal Highland Emigrants. Maclean received the rank of lieutenant colonel in the new Loyalist regiment.[94] He sailed for America and landed in Boston, where General Gage welcomed him. From Boston, Maclean sent out recruiting officers to enlist men from among the former members of British Highland regiments that had settled in America at the end of the French and Indian War. His recruiting parties raised some troops from among the Scots veterans in upstate New York and the Maritime provinces, and probably reached Quebec in early September with 120 men from his new emigrant regiment.[95] Maclean's stay at Quebec was brief, as he left the city commanding a force consisting of his own men, 60 fusiliers from the 7th Foot, and a detachment of French militia to support Governor Carleton, who was organizing a relief party at Montreal to break Montgomery's siege of St. Johns, still stubbornly defended by Major Charles Preston.[96]

Montgomery learned of Maclean's move toward St. Johns and dispatched a strong detachment north to intercept him. Heavily outnumbered, Maclean hurried back to Quebec, which sat virtually defenseless in the face of the sudden appearance of another rebel force (the Arnold Expedition).

Having beaten off every British attempt to reinforce St. Johns, Montgomery allowed recent prisoners-of-war to confer with Major Preston at St. Johns. These prisoners were proof that there was no hope of relief, and Preston surrendered while Maclean and his Highlanders raced back toward Quebec. Maclean reached the town of Trois Riveres, on the St. Lawrence, on November 8 in an armed brig (a two-masted ship) named the *Fell*, where he was stalled by the same gale-force winds that prevented Arnold from crossing the river. Realizing that time was critical, Maclean decided to continue his journey by land and reached Quebec City on November 12, just hours ahead of the rebels.[97]

En route, Maclean intercepted the two Indian couriers carrying Arnold's November 8 letter (written at the village of St. Henri) to Montgomery. This interception was not as unlikely as it seems. Long-distance travel was confined to waterways like the St. Lawrence, or to a few roads. Maclean's men literally bumped into Montgomery's Indians. Maclean read Arnold's letter, which gave him valuable information about the rebel situation as well as this sobering passage: "I propose crossing the St. Lawrence as soon as possible; and if any opportunity offers of attacking Quebec with success, shall improve it. . . ."[98]

Maclean got to Quebec just ahead of Arnold with 80 men from his Highland regiment. The Highlanders were the only Regulars in Quebec other than *Lizard*'s marines and a handful of artillerymen. Maclean augmented this small force with 120 new regimental recruits who arrived in Quebec during his absence. Captain Malcolm Fraser enlisted these men from among the Scots living in Newfoundland and Prince Edward Island, bringing Maclean's Royal Highland Emigrants—at Quebec on November 12—to a total strength of more than 200 officers and men.[99] Although authorized to wear the distinctive Highland uniform of the Black Watch, including kilts, these uniforms were slow in arriving; Maclean's Highlanders instead donned simple green and buff uniforms.

Lieutenant Governor Cramahé gladly allowed an officer of Maclean's experience to take charge of Quebec's defense and put some starch into the people's will to resist. Maclean got to work immediately.[100] Besides chasing off Captain Ogden, he disrupted a gathering of some of the city's residents to discuss negotiating with the Americans. He burst into their meeting, thundering that there would be no talk of negotiating with the rebels, whom he characterized as thieves and looters.[101] He continued his theme of appealing to the self-interests of Quebec's residents by portraying the Americans as banditti who had come to plunder and pillage their homes and businesses. It was better, he reasoned, for Quebec's 5,000 inhabitants to help defend their homes and businesses rather than risk the consequences of supporting the half-starved, ill-clothed rebel army trying to seize the city's riches. Maclean took other measures, including evacuating residents from the exposed lower town to the safety of the walled upper section and leveling buildings near the city's walls to give his artillerymen a clear field of fire. This move also prevented the rebels from using these vacant buildings as observation or sniper posts. Maclean's measures seemed to have worked, as evidenced by a letter written by a young Royal Naval officer on November 20, in which he noted that Quebec's population was more optimistic about defending their city since Maclean's arrival. "His activity and exertions contributed to give spirits to the people, and rouse them from their despondency," the officer wrote.[102]

Although Benedict Arnold was a courageous, tenacious, and natural-born leader, these traits alone were not enough to counter Maclean's military experience. While Arnold was counting pills in his uncle's Connecticut apothecary shop, Maclean was commanding British infantry against the flower of the French army in America. Arnold's slim military experience became evident once the Quebec expedition got underway. For openers, the wily Daniel Morgan duped him at Fort Western, insisting that his rifle companies could not be commanded by any of Arnold's New England officers. Arnold also failed to maintain tight control of his provisions—imposing rationing only after his supplies had dwindled to dangerously low levels—while his best officer, Lieutenant Colonel Roger Enos, who was no coward, turned back from the Dead River with a third of the expedition's manpower when he realized they were facing starvation. Many commended Enos' decision to quit, including William Gordon, who published an eyewitness history of the Revolution in 1788. "A number of officers of the best character," Gordon wrote, "are fully satisfied, and persuaded that his conduct deserves applause rather than censure."[103] Only through raw determination and willpower did 600 of Arnold's volunteers make it to Quebec.

Maclean was responsible for the sortie that captured the sleepy American sentry on the morning of November 14, and he chased off Ogden from St. John's Gate with a burst of grapeshot. Maclean also refused to accept a letter from Arnold protesting the firing on his unarmed envoy. Maclean then tricked Arnold into believing that he was going to come out of the city and attack his camp. This alleged British plan included transporting 200 men at night in boats behind Arnold's position. Alarmed by the news of a British attack, Arnold ordered an inspection to be made of his corps' arms and ammunition. Apparently this was the first time he checked on the amount of ammunition he had since investing Quebec. The result was shocking, as Arnold discovered that most of his gunpowder had been lost during the march from Maine, leaving only enough for five rounds per man. He also determined that numerous muskets and rifles had been damaged or lost during the long ordeal. Short of weapons and ammunition, and fearing a British attack, Arnold ordered a hasty retreat 18 miles upriver to the town of Point aux Trembles (modern Neuville) to await Montgomery's arrival. News arrived that Montgomery had captured Montreal a few days earlier (November 13), and the outwitted Arnold withdrew from within site of his goal (Quebec) to await the arrival of the victorious veteran Montgomery with reinforcements and artillery.

The Kennebec corps' depressing retreat began on the afternoon of November 18, when they abandoned their campfires surrounding Quebec and started down the frozen road that ran along the northern bank of the St. Lawrence River. It was a bitter defeat for Arnold, who abhorred failure. Rifleman John Joseph Henry recalled years later that the army retreated from Quebec "through a severe winter . . . in a slovenly style, accompanied, probably, by the maledictions of the [Canadian] clergy and nobility." The men walked and slid along the thin sheets of black ice that littered their route, arriving the following evening at Point aux Trembles, where Arnold reported that he had 650 men (including Canadian Indians), of whom 550 were fit for service.[104]

Henry described Point aux Trembles "a straggling village . . . where quarters were obtained in the village and farm houses, dispersed over a space of some miles, up and down the river."[105] Burr wrote his uncle from there: "I expected some Weeks ago to have had the Satisfaction of writing you a Letter from Quebec—when that Time will be is now very uncertain."[106] After arriving in the village, Arnold's men spotted a ship on the river heading in the opposite direction. Unknown to them at the time, it was the brig *Fell* bringing Governor Carlton back to Quebec.

The governor was passing by Point aux Trembles under humiliating circumstances. He had hurriedly abandoned Montreal on November 11 in the face of the approaching rebels. There was a chaotic scene at Montreal's waterfront, as workers hastily loaded a small flotilla of ships with the doomed city's most valuable military cargo and its small garrison of regular troops, amounting to about 100 men. Governor Carleton then boarded the armed schooner *Gaspe*, the flagship of his little fleet. According to one eyewitness account, the scene had the atmosphere of a funeral, as the *Gaspe*, two other small warships, and eight transports cheerlessly slipped away from the docks, setting a course for Quebec, which lay 150 miles upriver. The rebels triumphantly entered Montreal two days later after negotiating for the city's peaceful surrender with a delegation of local businessmen. As Montgomery was entering Montreal, Carleton was slowly working his overloaded flotilla down the St. Lawrence toward Quebec.

Carleton, who thought he had escaped Montgomery, was surprised to run into the American artillery that blocked the St. Lawrence River at the village of Sorel. Anticipating that the troops at Montreal would try to flee to Quebec, Montgomery had guns posted at Sorel to blockade the river. The enterprising rebels had even constructed a floating gun battery to block the channel.[107]

Trapped and reluctant to run the rebel gun batteries (especially with a ship loaded with gunpowder), Carleton decided to escape on his own and leave the rest of his men to their fate. Disguised in peasant clothing, Canada's distinguished governor-general eased over the side of the *Gaspe* during the night and slipped past the rebels in a small boat, whose crew paddled with their hands to avoid making any noise. Once by the blockade, oars moved the boat upriver until they happened upon the brig *Fell*, which took Carleton to Quebec. Back at Sorel, Carleton's befuddled flotilla surrendered to the rebels with all their valuable military cargo.[108]

Schulyer reported Carleton's shabby getaway to his friend Washington, stating that Canada's illustrious governor, "disguised En Canadien & accompanied by six Peasants, found Means to make his Escape."[109] The garrison at Quebec thought differently about Carleton's brazen escape and ceremoniously greeted him when he reached the capital on November 19. Captain Hamilton rejoiced at the news. He reopened a report he had completed to the admiralty dated November 20 and added the following postscript: "I have the pleasure to acquaint their Lordships that His Excellency Genl. Carleton has just arrived."[110]

A similar celebration took place among the rebels on the night of December 2, when General Montgomery arrived at Point aux Trembles from Montreal.[111] The general's approach was heralded by Captain Ogden, who returned from Montreal just ahead of Montgomery with some supplies for Arnold's hard-pressed corps. The threadbare Kennebec veterans marched down to the shoreline with lanterns and torches to greet their champion. Despite the frigid temperatures and a foot of snow on the ground, Arnold's men were warm with excitement. Montgomery triumphantly arrived aboard the *Gaspe*, Carleton's former flagship, which had been snared by the rebel blockade at Sorel. Arnold's men strained to see their hero as his long boat came into view. With the exception of Arnold, it was probably the first time that any of them ever saw him. Montgomery came ashore and received Arnold and his corps courteously, with as much military pomp as could be mustered on the blustery night. Afterward, Montgomery made a short but eloquent speech applauding their courage in "passing the wilderness" and hoped that their perseverance would continue.[112]

Despite the bitter cold, the men answered his little speech with enthusiastic huzzas. Later that night, Lieutenant Humphrey recorded his impression of Montgomery: "[H]e is a gentle, polite man, tall and slender in his make, bald on the top of his head, resolute, mild, and of a fine temper and an excellent general."[113] Private Morison agreed with Humphrey, adding, "Gen. Montgomery was born to command. His easy and affable condescension. . . creates love and esteem; and exhibits him the gentleman and the soldier. He is tall and very well made. . . ."[114] Montgomery was equally impressed, calling Arnold's corps "an exceedingly fine one, inured to fatigue, and well accustomed to cannon shot. . . . There is a style of discipline among them, much superior to what I have been used to see this campaign."[115]

Montgomery was worried Arnold might be an insubordinate glory seeker like Ethan Allen. Writing to Schuyler on the subject, Montgomery asked, "Should Arnold come into my neighborhood, has he orders to put himself under my command? You know his ambition."[116] His concerns were put to rest after his first meeting with Arnold, who willingly yielded command of his corps to Montgomery. Besides, Washington had ordered the colonel to put his expedition under General Schuyler's command if the two armies should meet in Canada. Concerned about Arnold's reputation for quarreling with fellow officers, Washington cautioned him at Cambridge to "avoid all Contention about Rank."[117]

Arnold, however, was in no mood to argue with Montgomery over command. He was relieved that help had arrived and that an experienced officer was on the scene to deal with Maclean's craftiness. Besides, Arnold and Montgomery liked one another. Arnold's audacity and eagerness balanced Montgomery's meticulous planning and military experience, and the two men quickly developed a close rapport. With Montgomery's arrival, the Arnold Expedition ceased to exist as an independent command, and Benedict Arnold was about to learn how to run an army from an experienced professional.

Looking back over recent events, Arnold wrote Washington, "Had I been Ten days Sooner, Quebec must inevitably have fallen into Our Hands, as there was not a Man there to oppose us."[118] Had Arnold crossed the St. Lawrence on November 4 instead of the 14th, he would have found the city virtually defenseless and the jittery lieutenant governor under pressure from the frightened civilians to surrender. November 5 was the turning point in the city's resolution to fight. It was on that date the *Lizard*, with its contingent of marines and two store ships loaded with military equipment and money, symbolizing the British government's resolution to defend the colony, arrived at Quebec. The situation further improved for the defenders just hours before Arnold crossed the river when feisty Colonel Maclean entered the city with some more troops. Arnold also wrote Schuyler bemoaning his poor timing, stating that "not a minute was lost" in the grueling trek from Fort Western to Quebec, a march "not to be paralleled in history," but that his Kennebec veterans arrived at Quebec too late to take advantage of its helpless situation.[119]

Arnold and his disciplined "famine proof veterans" also proved to be a welcome relief for Montgomery, who had struggled from the outset of his campaign with insubordinate troops and argumentative, sometimes cowardly officers. Arnold called Montgomery "my truly great and good friend," while Montgomery described Arnold as an "active, intelligent and enterprising" officer who had come close to capturing Quebec."[120] Other men might have abandoned a frigid winter campaign against Quebec in favor of celebrating their exploits in warm winter quarters in Montreal. Montgomery and Arnold, however, were of one mind in their determination to push on to Quebec, with Montgomery reporting to have said that he either would eat his Christmas dinner in Quebec or in hell.[121]

Accompanying Montgomery from Montreal were three armed sloops crammed with everything that the captured city could provide for Arnold's needy corps: food, warm clothing, blankets, muskets, and ammunition. But the hardships and discord that marked his campaign from its start became apparent when Montgomery was able to bring with him only 300 troops from the 1st New York regiment and 50 artillerymen from Captain John Lamb's Independent New York artillery company. This disappointing number of men made the 600 survivors of the Arnold Expedition critical to Montgomery's continued success.[122]

More troops eventually joined Montgomery and Arnold. They were 160 Massachusetts troops under the command of Major John Brown, camped at the St. Lawrence River town of Sorel. Ironically, these were the same Massachusetts troops raised and commanded by Arnold early in the war to defend the Lake Champlain region. Their current commander, Major Brown, was also well known to Arnold. He first appeared in this narrative as the young Massachusetts lawyer who journeyed to Montreal to measure local political sentiment prior to the start of the war. Brown subsequently participated in the attack on Fort Ticonderoga, for which he received a commission as a major in the Continental Army and assignment to the Northern army. He proved to be one of Montgomery's best officers, and the general entrusted him with several important assignments, including joint command of the seizure of Fort Chambly.

Brown also was one of Arnold's earliest and most passionate enemies. The major's hatred of Arnold had begun when the colonel stormed into the officer's council chaired by Ethan Allen to finalize their surprise attack on Fort Ticonderoga. Brown decided that Arnold was an arrogant usurper and used his skillful pen to help buoy the military career of the Allen clique (of which he was a part) while working to discredit Arnold. The major must have been shocked to find months later that his old antagonist Arnold was Montgomery's senior lieutenant and closest confidant. Brown was a shrewd person who, by listening to camp gossip, learned that Captain Oliver Hanchett detested Arnold. Brown would later befriend Hanchett, and manipulated him into a plot to discredit their common enemy while boosting Brown's own career.

Montgomery left Point aux Trembles on December 3, leading his little army through rain and sleet to reach Quebec the following day.[123] His total strength, when assembled at Quebec, consisted of about 1,100 men, if the sick, Indians, and men on detached duty (transporting supplies from Montreal for example) were included.

Montgomery was counting on Canadian volunteers to boost his depleted ranks. The Canadians took the rebels more seriously following Montgomery's capture of Montreal. Working with Montgomery to recruit the locals were James Livingston, a merchant and farmer born in New York, who married a Montreal woman and was living near Fort Chambly, and Jeremy Duggan, a former Quebec hair dresser. These two newly appointed rebel officers went into the countryside following the capture of Montreal to enlist men for Montgomery's army. Their mission met with partial success, and they eventually rendezvoused with Montgomery at Quebec with about 200 Canadian recruits.[124]

Montgomery's largest unit was Arnold's corps, which continued to be commanded by the same officers who had participated in the epic trek across Maine. Arnold's second in command, Lieutenant Colonel Christopher Greene, had refused to turn back with Enos on the Dead River. Next in line of command were Majors Timothy Bigelow and Jonathan Meigs. Then there was Captain Daniel Morgan, commanding the corps riflemen. His Virginia company's exploits included shouldering their bateaux across the Terrible Carry. Arnold's remaining company captains included Henry Dearborn, John Topham, Oliver Hanchett, Simon Thayer, and Samuel Ward. The gentlemen volunteers were also present, although Aaron Burr was now an aide-de-camp to General Montgomery. Burr's friend Matthias Ogden continued to serve under Arnold along with the other gentlemen volunteers on the expedition—Matthew Duncan, John McGuire, David Hopkins, and Charles Porterfield. Christian Febiger continued as Arnold's adjutant, along with Dr. Isaac Senter and Chaplain Samuel Spring.

We cannot forget those valiant common soldiers, whose names are too numerous to mention, who followed Arnold across Maine and were now marching with Montgomery to Quebec. Just by counting heads, we can see how important Arnold's Kennebec veterans were to the success of Montgomery's mission. But Arnold's corps also gave Montgomery, for the first time since the start of the Canadian invasion, a body of well-disciplined soldiers led by dedicated officers.

Montgomery wrote his commander and confidant Schuyler after arriving at Quebec, saying that he was "at the head of upwards of eight hundred men." This total did not include the sick and some of the men transporting supplies from Montreal. This command, continued Montgomery, is "a force you will say not very adequate to the business in hand, but we must make the best of it. It is all I could get."[125]

Thus, the American siege of Quebec, begun by Arnold, was renewed by Montgomery.

Beyond the River the Beautiful City of Quebec, Hemmed in by her Lofty Precipices[1] [2]

The men of Benedict Arnold's corps left Point Aux Trembles on the morning of December 3, retracing their steps back to Quebec through a cold rainstorm that periodically changed to sleet.[2]

Despite the miserable weather, the 600 survivors of the expedition were in high spirits because they were returning to Quebec with artillery and a general who had routed the British at St. Johns, Montreal, and Sorel. Marching along the road that paralleled the St. Lawrence, the rebels could see sheets of ice floating in the river, which made it difficult for Montgomery's little flotilla—carrying the army's artillery and baggage—to make its way downriver toward Quebec. A hard frost hit during the night, but the following morning dawned clear with a light wind. The men of the Kennebec corps completed their trek and again looked upon the elusive object of their long and terrible ordeal. About a foot of snow covered the ground when the Americans arrived. They took in the distant city's snow- and ice-coated ramparts and rooftops, which gave Quebec a storybook appearance.

Montgomery immediately ordered his troops to besiege the place, and started by suspending communications between the city and the surrounding countryside. He assigned his New York troops to positions on the Plains of Abraham to prevent anyone from entering or leaving the city through the St. Louis Gate. To their left he placed Arnold's musket companies with orders to occupy the suburbs of St. Jean and St. Roch and to watch the St. John's Gate. Morgan's riflemen completed the closure of the land side of the city by occupying the northeastern suburb of Palais, which sat on flat terrain, just below the city's ramparts and near the lower town. Palais was the most exposed and dangerous section of the American encirclement. Morgan and his riflemen, undaunted by the hazard hiding behind houses, fences, and rocks in Palais, fired "wherever a sentry shew'd his head over the walls."[3]

The American encirclement extended from Wolfe's Cove to the St. Charles River, which virtually isolated the city from the outside world. The St. Lawrence already was chocked with ice, and it was only a matter of days before Quebec would be cut off from any hope of reinforcement from the sea until spring. Satisfied with his deployments, Montgomery established his headquarters at Holland House, the mansion of Major Henry Caldwell located two miles southwest of St. John's Gate that Arnold had occupied during his brief siege of the city. Arnold made his headquarters in a much less impressive tavern in the suburb of St. Roch.

Some of Arnold's men had replaced the clothing they were wearing when departing Cambridge with British army uniforms captured at Montreal. Though a rumor circulated in the city that a Russian army had arrived to help the Americans conquer Quebec, there was no confusing Arnold's men with British soldiers, as anyone outside the city in uniform was a rebel.[4] The story of the Russians coming to Quebec to help the rebels (Carleton sent the person who spread the rumor to prison to await the Russians' arrival) competed with another whopper being circulated by the peasants to explain why Arnold's men were wearing lightweight clothing when they arrived in the Chaudière Valley. The yarn was that the Americans wore skimpy garb because they were impervious to cold weather. Another rumor claimed the rebels were "musket proof," because they were covered with sheet iron. This story began when the Canadian peasants saw that Arnold's men, especially the riflemen, wore linen frocks. The word linen in French—*toile*—changed with the retelling of the story to *tôle* (iron plate). Thus the rumor spread that the *Bostonnais* dressed in bullet-proof armor.[5]

Montgomery and Arnold studied Quebec with their spyglasses from a sheltered location on the frozen Plains of Abraham. Arnold pointed out Quebec's landmarks to his new commander, who had never seen the city before. Probably dressed in a surtout (a long, close-fitting overcoat commonly worn by gentlemen) over his uniform to help protect him from the cold, Montgomery observed the city with Arnold, who was reported to be wearing a capote (a long coat with a hood made from a blanket).

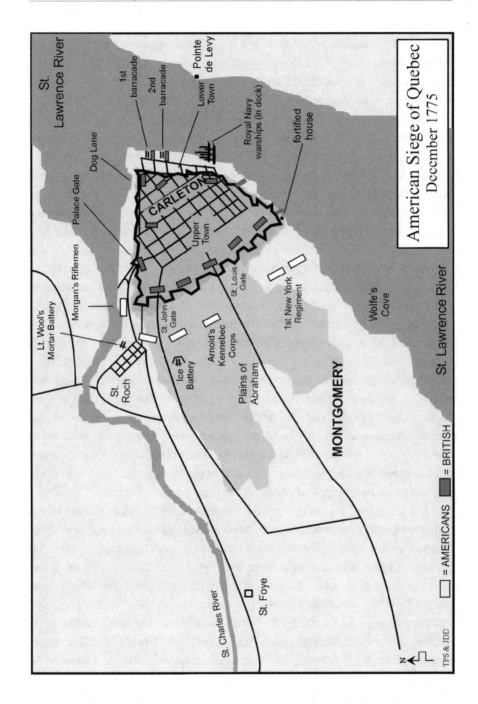

American Siege of Quebec
December 1775

Unseen by Arnold, behind Quebec's walls his old business acquaintances were talking more confidently about defending their homes and warehouses. They recalled Arnold's prewar business trips to Quebec to sell horses and began to deride him as a "horse jockey."[6] Calling someone a "jockey" at the time was the equivalent of calling him a swindler, and a "horse jockey" was a shifty, dishonest horse dealer.[7] Carleton and his officers assailed Montgomery, a former British army officer, as a traitor to his country. But while the British inside Quebec were insulting Arnold and Montgomery, the rebels across the Plains of Abraham were joking how the exalted Governor Carleton had to disguise himself as a woman and paddle with his hands to escape the trap that Montgomery had set for him at Sorel.[8]

Back in uniform at Quebec, Carleton eagerly watched his adversaries through his glass from the city's ramparts. He paid particular attention to their artillery. It looked formidable enough to terrify Quebec's civilian population, but Carleton and the handful of professional soldiers with him breathed a sigh of relief as they caught a glimpse of the rebels wheeling their guns into place outside the city's walls. Despite their formidable appearance, Carleton knew that the rebel cannons were too small to pose a serious threat. This fact also was well known by Montgomery and Arnold. All of the military men on the scene knew that the rebels needed heavy artillery—known as siege guns—to seize Quebec, or at least intimidate it into surrendering. Cannons had become standardized by the time of the American Revolution and classified according to the weight of the ball that they fired.

For example, one of the smallest pieces of artillery at the time was a "three-pounder," meaning that it fired a cannonball that weighed three pounds. A three-pound brass gun, mounted on wheels, weighed over 500 pounds. Larger-size cannons were usually classified as six-, nine-, and 12-pounders. Cannons of these sizes, when mounted on wheels and pulled by horses or oxen, were known as field artillery, and they provided effective support of infantry in battle. A twelve-pounder, mounted on wheels for use in the field, weighed about 3,000 pounds and was the largest piece of field artillery that could conveniently accompany an army.[9]

Besides the heavy weight of the cannons, a variety of supplemental equipment was required to move and operate the guns, including gear to hitch horses or oxen to the cannons (limbers), wagons for carrying extra ammunition, and traveling forges to make repairs in the field. There were larger cannons (heavy artillery) in use at the time that fired balls weighing 18, 24, 36, or even 42 pounds. These smashers or "great guns" were used on large warships, siege trains (heavy artillery and the men and equipment to move them), and permanent fortifications, such as Quebec. Besides firing a larger ball, these big cannons had a longer range than field artillery.

Carleton had the advantage in artillery, with 24- and 32-pounders mounted on Quebec's ramparts that could blast apart the lighter, shorter-range field guns that Montgomery brought from Montreal. Heavy artillery was also key to carrying out a successful siege, where powerful guns could be used to breach the walls of a fortified city like Quebec. Montgomery and Arnold arrived at Quebec with some nine- and 12-pounders that were too weak to smash holes in Quebec's thick walls. Even if Montgomery possessed the artillery and men to attempt a siege, the ground was frozen, making it impossible to dig the necessary trenches to protect the guns from enemy artillery and infantry counterattacks. Montgomery understood the problem long before he reached Quebec. Writing to a friend from Montreal, he eliminated the possibility of laying siege to the city: "from the difficulty of making trenches in a Canadian winter, [and] . . . from the fewness and lightness of our artillery, which is quite unfit to break walls like those of Quebeck."[10]

Lacking siege artillery, Montgomery would have liked Carleton to sally forth from Quebec and fight. "In this idea," Montgomery quixotically wrote from Montreal, "there is a glimmering of hope." Referring to the Battle of the Plains of Abraham, Montgomery continued, "Wolfe's sober and scientifick calculation was against him, until Montcalm [the French general defending Quebec], permitting his courage to get the better of his discretion, gave up the advantages of his fortress, and came out to try his strength on the plain." But Wolfe had a large army with siege artillery that intimidated Montcalm to come out and fight rather than face the ordeal of a protracted siege. Carleton was not likely to repeat Montcalm's mistake, especially since the Americans had with them no large army, siege artillery, or warships.

Commenting on what he called Wolfe's "lucky hit," when Montcalm decided to risk a battle instead of a siege, Montgomery said, "Carleton, who was Wolfe's Quartermaster-General, understood this well, and, it is to be feared, will not follow the Frenchman's example."[11] An alternative was to starve the enemy into surrendering, but this was not a practical solution because Quebec had a large stockpile of food which, if carefully rationed, could last up to six months. Obviously informed on the quantity of provisions inside the city, Montgomery conjectured, "I should have been inclined to a blockade till the first of April, by which time the garrison would probably be much distressed for provisions and [fire] wood."[12] Montgomery did not have six months to starve Quebec's population of 5,000 into capitulating. He had only a few weeks, because Arnold's men, who represented the bulk of his army, planned to leave for home when their enlistments expired at the end of December.

To explain the problem, when the Revolutionary War began, Congress envisioned a citizen army whose members would volunteer to serve for up to one year. Congress opposed a professional army, which they feared could overthrow the civilian government and establish a military dictatorship. Congress' insistence on short-term enlistments at that time wreaked havoc for General Washington, who had to reorganize the Continental Army and train new recruits each year.

The Arnold Expedition formed at Cambridge in September 1775 from men already in the ranks who had agreed to serve until the end of the year. Even as they were marching back to Quebec with Montgomery, Arnold's soldiers talked about the joy of returning home. They believed that they had done their duty and that other citizens should take their place in the American siege lines surrounding the city. The New York troops had the same attitude; they were leaving for home on April 15, 1776, no matter what.[13]

With no sign of replacements or reinforcements, and realizing that Quebec could hold out for months, Montgomery lamented his situation in a letter home:

> [U]nless we do something before the middle of April, the game will
> be up; because, by that time the river may open and let in supplies
> and re-enforcements to the garrison, in spite of anything we can do
> to prevent it; and again, because my troops are not engaged beyond
> that term, and will not be prevailed upon to stay a day longer.[14]

The only practical solution, under the circumstances, was for the rebels to attack the city before the enlistments of Arnold's men expired by scaling Quebec's ramparts with ladders at night and fighting their way through the streets with muskets and axes. Such a surprise attack posed the most dangerous threat to Carleton, who had a large perimeter to defend with a force composed largely of untrained militia and sailors recruited from the merchant ships in the harbor.

Montgomery knew from the start that a surprise attack over the walls was his best chance. Writing on the subject before reaching Quebec, he said,

> Masters of our secret, we may select a particular time and place for attack, and to repel this, the garrison must be prepared at all times and places; a circumstance which will impose upon it incessant watching and labour, by day and by night, which, in its undisciplined state, must breed discontents that may compel Carleton to capitulate, or perhaps make an attempt to drive us off.[15]

Although both sides possessed sketchy information about the other, Carleton was thought to have about twice as many combatants as the rebels. Also to his advantage, he was defending a walled city bristling with heavy artillery. Carleton's weaknesses were the unreliability of four-fifths of his army, which was composed of untrained British and Canadian militia, and his need to be ready at any time for an American surprise attack, which could be concentrated against any sector in his extensive, undermanned fortifications.

Montgomery and Arnold understood all of this as they looked across the frozen ground toward Quebec, the last British stronghold in Canada. An attack over the ramparts was a dangerous last resort, and Montgomery decided to look for an alternative.

Thomas Ainslie, Quebec's collector of customs, was a staunch British patriot who volunteered to defend Quebec at the first signs of trouble. Although he apparently had no military experience, Ainslie received an appointment as a temporary captain in the British militia.[16] He kept a remarkably accurate—although biased—diary in which he described the cat-and-mouse game being played by Carleton and Montgomery. Ainslie's contempt for the Americans is revealed in spirited passages, such as his portrayal of Morgan's Virginians as "skulking riflemen whose intention is to kill any single person walking on the ramparts—this is the American way of making war. . . they are worse than Savages, they will ever be held in contempt with men of courage."[17] As collector of customs, it is probable that Ainslie knew

Arnold, who he accurately described in his journal as "the master of a vessel trading from N: [New] England to this place & from hence to the West Indies with horses."[18]

Ainslie recorded the first move in the contest for control of Quebec when the governor ordered anyone unwilling to help defend the city to leave. Carleton issued the proclamation on November 22, before Montgomery's army reached Quebec. Ainslie reported the event in his diary:

> On the 22d, a proclamation, most acceptable to the Garrison, was issued by the General commanding all persons contumaciously [rebelliously] refusing to enroll their names in the militia lists to assist his Majesties troops in the preservation of the City . . . to quit the town in four days & to withdraw themselves out of the limits of the district of Quebec before the 1st day of December.

Ainslie endorsed the governor's action, declaring that anyone who left the city was a disgrace to their country. "[T]he consciousness of their pusillanimous [cowardly] behaviour must redden their faces many years hence & make their offspring blush," he wrote. "[W]henever Quebec sounds in their ears their shame will appear in their faces."[19] Major Caldwell also approved of Carleton's proclamation, saying that prior to it, "We could guard against open and avowed enemies, but not against those lurking about town."

The rebels received copies of Carleton's proclamation, and they sat around their campfires satirizing and rewriting it for their own amusement. Here is an example of their handiwork:

GOD SAVE THE KING

Whereas I'm chased from place to place,
By rebels void of sense and grace;
Crown Point, Montreal, Chamblee,
By Arnold and Montgomery,

. . . They'll find that what I now say true is;
Before they've counted o'er their beads
or paid the Priest or said their creeds,
As spies or rebels up I'll string em
Till to their senses I can bring 'em;

Each one who wont swear he's a tory,
I swear shall go to Purgatory

. . . Given at St. Louis Castle, in
Quebec, the year of George sixteen,
Of Britain, France and Ireland King,
(Of Rome) the faith's defender being,
And so forth—by me GUY CARLETON,
Kenneled and toothless yet I snarl on.
Witness, Henry T. Crahame,
My Catholic liege Secretary
Thus ends our BULL, and ten to one on't
Some Yankee'll get it and make fun on't.[20]

The governor's proclamation that ordered "all useless, disloyal and treacherous persons" to leave Quebec pleased Caldwell, since it ridded the city of dangerous rebel sympathizers and required those who remained to join the militia. The decree resulted in some unexpected dividends for the rebels, which Montgomery described in a letter to General Schuyler: "The Governour has been so kind as to send out of town many of our friends who refuse to do military duty, among them several very intelligent men, capable of doing me considerable service. One of them, a Mr. Antill [Edward Antill III, a Piscataway, New Jersey, lawyer who immigrated to Quebec], I have appointed chief engineer."[21] Antill, 33, was a 1762 graduate of Kings College (today's Columbia University) with an aptitude for mathematics.[22]

In another move to add men to the defense of the city, the governor placed an embargo on the remaining ships in the harbor, ordering all the seamen in port to come ashore and take up arms. Carleton organized what amounted to 1,800 defenders into four detachments, or brigades as he called them. His first and most important brigade consisted of his best men: 70 soldiers from the 7th Regiment, the handful of men belonging to the Royal Artillery, the Royal Highland Emigrants, marines from the *Lizard* and the *Hunter*, and masters and mates from the ships in the harbor. Colonel Maclean, the most experienced officer on the scene, commanded these 407 men. The second brigade consisted of 330 British militia under the command of Major Caldwell, whom Carleton gave the temporary rank of lieutenant colonel. The city's French-Canadian militia, amounting to 543, made up the third brigade, which Lieutenant

Colonel Noel Voyer, a former French army officer, led. The fourth brigade consisted of all the sailors and ship workers (artificers) in the port, numbering about 520, who were armed and uniformed from the store ships that arrived with the *Lizard*.[23]

A document titled "State of the Garrison of Quebec on the first of December" enumerates the defenders according to their backgrounds:

70	Royal Fuslieers [7th Regiment],
230	Royal Emigrants,
22	Of the Artillery, Fireworkers, &c.
330	British Militia,
543	Canadians [French-Canadian Militia],
400	Seamen,
50	Masters and Mates of Vessels,
35	Marines,
100	Artificers.
1800	Men bearing arms.[24]

Despite his military background, Lieutenant Governor Cramahé did not play an active part in Quebec's defense. He was a loyal and capable bureaucrat who failed to rise to the occasion.[25]

Across the snow-covered Plains of Abraham, Montgomery was conferring with Arnold about their first gambit. The general wanted to exploit the jittery nerves of Quebec's civilians, whom he hoped would pressure Carleton into surrendering. Arnold described how he had tried this tactic unsuccessfully a month earlier, when he paraded his corps within view of the city before sending Ogden toward St. John's Gate to parley with the enemy.

Approaching the city under a flag of truce with generous terms of surrender was worth another try, and Montgomery wrote out a surrender ultimatum designed to appeal to the city's businessmen and homeowners by promising to protect their property from looting. Montgomery began by cajoling his adversary to surrender Quebec in order to save it from destruction. Then he informed Carleton that he was well aware of the situation inside Quebec, and "the motley Crew" defending the place. "I am at the head of troops accustomed to success," Montgomery admonished Carleton, "confident of the Righteousness of the Cause they are engaged in; accustomed to danger and fatigue. . . . [S]hould you persist in an unwarrantable defence the consequences will be on your own Head."[26]

After completing his call for surrender, Montgomery sent a flag of truce to St. John's Gate asking for permission to deliver it to Governor Carleton. A runner was dispatched to the governor's palace requesting instructions. Carleton replied that he would never accept any communication, written or verbal, from the rebels.[27] An undaunted Montgomery gave his ultimatum to an old woman with instructions to deliver it to Carleton. She got into the city with the rebel missive concealed in her clothing and went directly to the palace, stating that she had vital information for the governor. Ushered into Carleton's presence, she found him comfortably seated in his office near a blazing fireplace. However, he leaped to his feet when the old woman tried to hand him the rebels surrender terms. Montgomery's trick infuriated Carleton. He told the woman to put the document on his desk, then summoned a drummer boy to throw it into the blazing fireplace while Montgomery's emissary looked on. He had the old woman escorted to the nearest gate and drummed out of town with a warning never to return. She reported to Montgomery's headquarters and told him what had happened.

The plucky Montgomery tried again, using another woman to smuggle a letter into the city. This time he addressed his letter to the merchants of Quebec. It described a lurid picture of the city in flames and urged the businessmen to take a determined stand against their tyrannical governor. Montgomery also assured the merchants of his intention to protect their property, which he characterized as "having ever by us been deemed sacred."[28] The authorities discovered the scheme before the woman could complete her mission and threw her in jail.

Montgomery refused to give up. He had copies of his surrender terms and his letter to the merchants of Quebec attached to arrows that Arnold's Indians shot over the ramparts. But this connivance failed, because by now Carleton was in tight control of the city and no one would dare suggest that he negotiate with the rebels. Besides, he was waging his own game of psychological warfare that included appealing to the humor of the *habitants* by placing a large wooden horse, surrounded by hay, on Cape Diamond and announcing, "I shall not surrender Quebec until the horse has eaten the hay." The news of "Carleton's horse" spread through the city and people enjoyed visiting Cape Diamond to see if the wooden horse had eaten the hay.[29] Carleton also countered by testing the resolve of the freezing rebel troops besieging Quebec with offers of generous rewards for switching sides "during the present troubles in North America," including 200 acres of land and gold coins.[30]

Montgomery had successfully used mortars to help pound the obstinate garrison at Fort St. Johns into submission, and he now turned these lethal weapons against Quebec. A battery of five mortars was concealed in the suburb of St. Roch, near the Palace Gate.[31] Lieutenant Isaiah Wool, a junior officer in Lamb's New York artillery company, commanded the battery and began hurling bombs into Quebec on December 9.[32] Wool periodically moved his mortars around St. Roch, hiding them among buildings and fences to prevent the British artillery from zeroing in on their position.

Mortars were a marvelous way to create panic among Quebec's civilian population. Unlike cannons, which fire their balls on a straight or elliptical projection, mortars hurl their lethal round projectiles (called bombs) high into the air, up and over the walls of a fort or walled city (like Quebec), to plunge indiscriminately to earth with a spine-chilling whistling sound, exploding into shards of jagged metal. A military dictionary of the day described their appearance and great destructive force:

> Mortars are a kind of short cannon, of a large bore. . . . Their use is to throw hollow shells, filled with powder; which falling on any building, or into the works of a fortification, burst, and their fragments destroy everything within reach. Carcasses are also thrown out of them, which are a sort of shell, with 5 holes, filled with pitch and other combustibles in order to set buildings on fire . . .[33]

The rebels' mortar bombs at first terrified Quebec's inhabitants. However, the people soon calmed as they realized the mortars were unable to do much damage, since the upper town encompassed a large area with widely separated buildings. Most of the rebel bombs fell harmlessly in the snow; total casualties in Quebec from mortar fire reported to be one person wounded and one dog killed.[34] Captain Ainslie provided a nice summary of the situation in his diary:

> Before they gave us a sample of their savoir faire in the bombarding way, the towns people had conceived that every shell wou'd inevitably kill a dozen people . . . but after they saw that the rebel

bombettes as they called them, did not harm, woman and children walked the streets laughing at their former fears.[35]

Meanwhile, the British continued smashing away the buildings and fences of St. Roch in an attempt to silence Lieutenant Wool's mortars. One diarist said the city's guns, intent on destroying the mortars, fired in the direction of any noise they heard coming from St. Roch.[36] But Wool kept moving his mortars, and the only reported casualty in St. Roch was a French prostitute who was killed by British artillery "while administering . . . to one of our lads" in her brothel.[37]

In another maneuver, some of Morgan's riflemen occupied the ruins of a large building, called the Intendant's Palace, situated near the lower town. Climbing into a small cupola on the top of the building, Morgan's marksmen began picking off enemy sentinels inside the city. But this tactic failed, as British artillery killed or chased off the rebel snipers. Captain Ainslie, among those manning the nearby ramparts, said he saw the riflemen carrying off the bodies of some of their comrades in sleighs.[38] Ainslie also commented about the ineffective rebel artillery, boasting that they had the same impact as throwing "peas against a plank."[39]

Captain John Lamb, commander of the Independent New York artillery company, was one of Montgomery's most reliable and ardent supporters. Lamb's was called an independent company because it was raised and funded locally (in the colony of New York) and attached to the Continental Army. Lamb's company, consisting of about 50 men, were the only artillerymen who stayed with Montgomery following the capture of Montreal. With Lamb's help, Montgomery decided to build a gun battery in an advantageous position on the heights, about 800 yards from St. John's Gate.[40] The idea was to get his biggest guns (12-pounders) as close as possible to the walls to give their projectiles the greatest possible destructive force. The rebels hid this new battery among some buildings at a place where they figured the British big guns, which were difficult to maneuver, could not effectively fire back.

The American battery still had to be shielded from possible enemy cannon fire. Traditionally this was done by constructing a protective barrier, called a breastwork, in front of the guns. The earth from the entrenchment-filled gabions (portable defenses) was placed in front of the position facing the enemy. The artillery moved into position when the breastwork was completed. However, the ground at Quebec was frozen, making it impossible to dig out the necessary field works. Captain Lamb is credited with the solution, which was to construct earthworks made of ice. His technique consisted of packing gabions with snow, which were piled up in front of the intended artillery position. Once in position, men poured water over the snow-packed gabions, freezing them instantly into solid blocks of ice.

The rebels' intimidating ice battery was ready at dawn on December 15, bristling with five pieces of field artillery (four 12-pounders and one six-pounder) and one mortar. An American officer wrote home boasting about how they "have thrown up ramparts of snow and water. . . . Who but Yankoos [Yankees] would have thought such a contrivance?"[41] Others had a different opinion of the ice battery, including common soldier Fobes from Arnold's corps, who helped build it. He called it "a heap of nonsense" in his diary, and said that he almost froze to death building the thing in the frigid night.[42]

Montgomery wanted to see if the ice battery would intimidate Carleton into surrendering. Arnold made the attempt, advancing on foot toward the city with a white flag in hand. Captain John Macpherson, one of Montgomery's aides-de-camp, accompanied him, along with a drummer beating the parley. The little troupe reached the walls, where Arnold announced that he had a letter for Carleton. This missive was another surrender demand coupled with a promise of safe passage for Carleton to England. An officer yelled down to them that the governor had ordered that no communiqué was to be accepted from the rebels and ordered them to withdraw immediately.[43]

Captain Ainslie witnessed the incident, and his journal provides some interesting details. Ainslie said that at about 9:00 a.m., he saw a drummer followed by two men dressed in blanket coats approaching the city with a white handkerchief tied to a stick. When they were ordered to leave, one of them (probably Arnold) said, "[T]hen let the General [Carleton] be answerable for all the consequences."[44] Writing later about the incident, an American officer noted that some of men lining Quebec's ramparts were ready to kill Arnold: "Yesterday we sent a flag of truce to them, which they would not receive, and it was with great difficulty the raw sailors [British seamen aboard ships in the harbor pressed into service to defend Quebec] could be prevented on firing on the person who carried it."[45]

Montgomery, incensed by this insult, wrote Carleton another letter the following day, claiming that Arnold and Macpherson were fired upon when they approached the city under a white flag. "Firing upon a flag of truce, hitherto unprecedented, even among savages, prevents my following the ordinary mode of conveying my sentiments," he wrote.[46]

Montgomery's angry letter—of which one early chronicler of the Revolution said "he departed from the common mode of conveying his sentiment; and made use of threats and language that he would otherwise have probably declined"—was a masterpiece of intimidation that, like its predecessors, Carleton probably never read. Montgomery wrote:

> Give me leave to inform you that I am well acquainted with your situation. A great extent of works, in their nature incapable of defence, manned with a motley crew of sailors, most of them our friends . . . a few of the worst troops, that call themselves soldiers . . . Should you persist in an unwarrantable defence, the consequence be upon your own head.[47]

Montgomery decided to end the propaganda war and give Carleton a taste of his ice battery, ordering its cannons to open fire on the morning of December 16. Other isolated American cannons joined in as the rebels poured as much fire into the city as they could muster. The noise and smoke were impressive, but the artillery did little damage. The gunners in Quebec pinpointed the position of Lamb's ice battery and smashed it apart with their 24- and 32-pounders, causing Montgomery to lament, "the enemy have very heavy metal, and I think will dismount our guns very shortly."[48]

The big British guns drove Arnold from his headquarters in St. Roch, and Montgomery had a close call when a cannonball crashed to earth near him as he was alighting from a sleigh. The shell demolished the sleigh and decapitated the horse harnessed to it. The ice battery became dangerous work and was quickly abandoned while the siege continued.

The teenage American rifleman John Joseph Henry explained in his narrative how he managed to kill sentries on Quebec's ramparts with his rifle. Henry said he crept among the deserted and bombed-out buildings near the Palace Gate to the remaining log wall of what had been a blacksmith's shop, "through the crevices of which we could fire, at an angle of 70 degrees, at the sentries above us." Henry said he picked off many sentries from this secret hiding place, the location of which the enemy never discovered. We get another view of the dangerous daily skirmishes taking place from the diary of an unknown artillery officer inside the city, whose journal illustrates the violence of the siege:

> December 18, Still continued to Snow . . . afternoon the Rebels threw some shells into town which did no damage—A Soldier of the Emigrants wounded mortally in the head by a Musket ball [probably the work of one of Morgan's riflemen]. December 20 . . . small snow . . . turned extremely cold & froze very hard. . . . A few of the Enemy appeared at St. Johns Gate & fired some small Arms, but did no mischief.[49]

The British also participated in harassment and skirmishing. Surveyor Pierce's diary entry for December 13 mentions one such incident: "[W]e had two Yorkers [soldiers from the First New York Regiment or Lamb's artillery company] wounded[. O]ne was wounded in his Cheek and the other had his Leg Broken from the enemys Cannon."[50]

On the 16th, Dr. Senter reported that a brave soldier named Morgan died from a grapeshot wound.[51] Private Haskell's diary recorded the death of Mrs. Warner on December 11 "by a shot from the city."[52] When her young husband, exhausted with fatigue and hunger, died in the swamp below Lake Magentic, she had picked up his musket and continued to march toward Quebec.

After weeks of stubborn resistance, Montgomery determined that he had to storm Quebec's ramparts. He convened a council of war with his officers on December 16 to decide upon a plan of action. Fortunately, Montgomery wrote a report to General Wooster (who commanded at Montreal) shortly after the council of war ended in which he described what had transpired. Montgomery opened his letter by saying that, from the outset, he believed his army would have to fight its way into Quebec by scaling its walls with ladders. "I never expected any other advantage from our artillery," Montgomery admitted, "than to amuse the enemy and blind them as to my real intention." Several of his officers advocated attacking the city via the lower town, where there were no walls. But Montgomery overruled them, pointing out that the lower town possessed no strategic value.

Having agreed upon a direct attack on the upper town, Montgomery described the plan formulated at the council—a third of the army would feign an attack on the lower town, where Carleton was anticipating a rebel strike, while the majority of the army would commence the real attack "by escalade" (scaling ramparts) against the upper town near Cape Diamond. Montgomery closed his report to Wooster with a realistic assessment of his situation: "[W]e have not much above eight hundred men fit for duty, exclusive of a few ragamuffin Canadians. We are exceedingly weak, but the enemy are so too, in proportion to the extent of their works; and as they know not where they will be attacked, all must be guarded."[53]

Montgomery also based his strategy on his belief that the conscripted British and French-Canadian militia, representing the bulk of Carleton's army, were sympathetic to the rebels and would offer token resistance, or even help the Americans once the attack began. Montgomery planned to continue to attack if his initial assault failed. "[S]hould we fail in our first attempt," he mentioned in a letter to Schuyler written on December 18, "a second or a third may do the business before relief [British reinforcements] can arrive to the garrison."[54]

Having formulated a plan, Montgomery ordered additional weapons brought up from Montreal and the men trained in the use of scaling ladders. He also wanted to wait for ideal weather conditions to launch his attack—a dark, stormy night that would hide the movement of his troops. In the interim, Montgomery hoped that his artillery would be able to breach Quebec's ramparts in a few strategic places.

Although the officers who attended the council of war kept their battle plan secret, Arnold's enlisted men sensed that a fight was imminent. Stocking, for example, wrote that the bombardment of the city had no other purpose than to "amuse the enemy and conceal our real design . . . to commence an assault."[55]

Inside Quebec, Carleton also sensed that the rebels were preparing to attack and doubled his efforts to protect the city. He ordered that the recent snow drifts piled against the outside walls be leveled to prevent them from being used as ramps to help the enemy get over the ramparts. Men cleared paths to keep the routes open between defensive positions, and loaded all the cannons ringing the city with grapeshot and canister.[56] The defenders distributed rockets designed to light up the night sky and lanterns on long poles that could probe the terrain in front of the walls for "rebel intruders." James Thompson, an engineer, directed the hasty construction of additional barricades in the lower town, while Carleton personally supervised the training of the militia. The governor put the garrison on a 24-hour alert, with everyone sleeping in their clothes with loaded weapons beside them. Expecting the attack to come against the lower town, Carleton and his principal officers moved their sleeping quarters to the Seminary of the Recollets, located near the anticipated scene of action.

While Montgomery continued to prepare his attack, temperatures plummeted. Captain Ainslie recorded the weather conditions during the siege in his journal. His entry for December 11th reads, "[I]t blew a perfect hurricane—it froze so hard that in half an hour the streets & ramparts were cover'd with ice."[57] Sentries, who were expected to patrol outside while on duty, found the frigid weather particularly torturous. In his entry for December 20, Ainslie commented about the difficulty of soldiering under such harsh conditions when he wrote, "Very cold, wind at W. [West]. . . . If this weather shall continue, Mr. Montgomery would find it difficult to eat his Christmas dinner in Quebec. . . . Ones senses are benumbed. No man after having been exposed to the air but ten minutes, could handle his arms [weapon] to do execution [go through the steps necessary to load and fire a gun]."[58] In another interesting reference to the weather, rifleman Henry said that he suffered from frostbite one night, "and for fifteen, and even twenty years afterwards, the intolerable effects of that night's frost were most sensibly felt."[59]

Besides the frigid weather, another new and dangerous peril emerged as the American siege continued into mid-December: *Variola major*. Better known as smallpox, this highly contagious and sometimes fatal disease spread rapidly among the American soldiers besieging Quebec. Historian Elizabeth Fenn explains that Montgomery's troops were prime candidates for the illness. "After long, stressful marches, more than a thousand men had assembled in one place from disparate provinces from Maine to Virginia," writes Fenn. "If their home colonies were diverse, so were the microbes, infections, and medical histories they carried with them, now conjoined on the Plains of Abraham."[60]

Dirty, congested living conditions, fatigue, insufficient and unwholesome food, and poor camp sanitation helped spread diseases like smallpox. Surveyor Pierce's diary entry for December 16 gives us a glimpse into the unhealthy living conditions among the besiegers: "We have Lice Itch [head lice], Jaundice [yellow discoloration of the skin symptomatic of liver dysfunction or infection], Crabs [pubic lice], Bed bugs and an unknown Sight of Fleas."[61] Dr. Senter provided a more clinical breakdown of the afflictions that were raging in the rebel camp. His list included "pleurisy, peripneumonia and other species of pulmonic complaints."[62] While the importance of good nutrition and cleanliness were understood at the time, shortages of healthy foods and problems in enforcing camp sanitation among the headstrong Americans contributed to the spread of disease.

The first known reference to smallpox among the Americans besieging Quebec appeared in the diary of Caleb Haskell, a fifer in Arnold's corps. Writing on December 6, 1775, Haskell said, "The small pox is all around us, and there is great danger of its spreading in the army."[63] By December 23, another of Arnold's soldiers noted in his journal that "the small pox very breaf [widespread] amung [sic] our troops."[64]

While accurate knowledge about the transmission of diseases was still far off, physicians at the time, including Senter, understood the importance of quarantining anyone with smallpox to prevent its spread.[65] Senter had established a general hospital in the convent owned by the Augustine nuns located along the St. Charles River about a mile from the suburb of St. Roch.[66] He isolated his smallpox cases by sending them to a separate building located in a remote area along the banks of the St. Lawrence River near Wolfe's Cove.[67] However, the obstinate American soldiers did not react well to quarantine, and refused to leave their messmates for the grim army hospitals. Pierce, for example, noted in his diary that a soldier named John McGuire ignored an order to go to the hospital after contracting smallpox.[68]

When too many infected men crowded his smallpox ward, Senter sent some cases to the countryside, where they received care in isolated farmhouses. Unknown to doctors at the time, these secluded patients— removed from the legion of deadly bacteria and germs raging in army hospitals—had the best chances of survival. Caleb Haskell contracted smallpox and soon found himself in Dr. Senter's smallpox ward. He was lucky enough to survive, but watched others around him die from the disease. Haskell noticed, however, that the sick men sent to isolated farmhouses tended to have a better chance of recovering.[69]

How many Americans contracted smallpox at Quebec? There are no known records, but the various diaries and letters written during the siege provide clues as to its spread. Captain Ainslie, writing from inside Quebec on December 9, said that spies reported that 200 rebel soldiers had contracted the disease. "The small pox does havock among them, tis a deadly infection in Yanky [sic] veins," Ainslie said. "We have long had that disorder in town."[70] Ainslie's figure of 200 cases among the rebels seems high when we consider that Mongomery's strength, even counting Major Brown's detachment and Livingston's Canadians, totaled about 1,350 men. However, in another reference to the number of sick, Arnold wrote late in December of "about two hundred privates, sick and on command."[71]

Besides smallpox, desertions to the British began to mount as the siege continued. While we have no known statistics on American defections during the siege of Quebec, diarists mention various men going over to the enemy. Food, warm clothing, and comfortable quarters were in short supply in Montgomery's army, and life seemed more attractive inside Quebec than in the frozen, wind-swept rebel positions along the Plains of Abraham. Governor Carleton encouraged desertions by circulating generous printed offers within the American lines and sending agents to promote defections. Helping to encourage desertion was the apparent ease with which a person could slip into Quebec at night through one of the empty suburbs that surrounded the city. Carleton's work was made easier by the fact that, in this early stage of the war, before the Americans declared their independence from Britain (July 4, 1776), the rebels still considered themselves loyal Englishmen and easily could rationalize the resumption of their allegiance to their mother country. Besides, deserters were a valuable source of manpower, and they tended to be welcomed by both sides during the war.

In the melancholy of escalating desertions, spreading smallpox, and stubborn enemy resistance, Montgomery ordered a meeting of Arnold's officers on the night of December 23 to confront "several affairs of consequence."[72] The meeting took place at Menut's Tavern (the Americans called it the Minute Tavern or Mr Menues Tavern in their diaries) in St. Roch, which Arnold was using as his headquarters.[73] The reason for the meeting was that three of Arnold's company commanders (Hanchett, Hubbard, and Goodrich) claimed their men were unwilling to risk their lives in a hazardous attack on the city.[74]

However, the underlying problem was that these three dissident captains did not want to continue to serve under Arnold's command. The shadowy leaders behind this insurrection were Major John Brown and Captain Hanchett, who recruited Hubbard and Goodrich into their little cabal. Brown arrived at Quebec with Montgomery's army with his abhorrence of Arnold intact, and he conspired with Hanchett to disgrace Arnold, whom they both despised.

Captain Hanchett's hatred of Arnold began when he was racing ahead of the army, on Arnold's orders, with 50 picked men toward Sartigan. After laboriously hauling a few bateaux over the Height of Land, Hanchett and his party were resting on the shores of Lake Magentic when Arnold arrived on the scene. The colonel brusquely commandeered Hanchett's bateaux and some of his best men and took off for Sartigan, telling Hanchett to walk to the French settlements with the rest of his picked men. Angered by Arnold's tactless action and perceived grasp for glory, Hanchett's resentment increased when Arnold curtly ordered him to stay behind to guard the baggage while the other officers crossed the river.

In another incident recorded by surveyor Pierce in his diary, Arnold promised to pay Hanchett's company some past-due money, but a shortage of funds made it impossible for the colonel to fulfill his pledge. Outraged by this indignity, Hanchett told Arnold that his company intended to go home, to which Arnold replied. "[T]he men might all go home and be Dam'd."[75] There is another side to the story, one that claims Hanchett was a poltroon. In the words of one historian, "[T]hough Hanchett had come through the wilderness bravely enough, he was not the man to face an armed enemy."[76]

Other men might have responded differently to Hanchett's confrontation over promised back-pay, but Arnold was an assertive individual with little experience in public office or diplomacy. His background was that of a tough businessman and sea captain accustomed to confrontation and intimidation. Major Brown noticed the hostility between Hanchett and Arnold, and stepped into the rift to manipulate Hanchett for his own benefit. Brown's interest was to have Hanchett's company, along with those of his friends Hubbard and Goodrich, transferred to his under-strength detachment. The addition of three companies to his command would qualify Brown for a promotion to colonel. Montgomery understood Brown's motives, as evidenced by a letter he wrote to Schuyler following the querulous meeting with Arnold's officers:

> A field officer [a reference to Brown] is concerned in it, who wishes, I suppose, to have the separate command of those companies, as the above-mentioned Captains have made application for that purpose. This dangerous party threatens the ruin of our affairs.[77]

Some of Arnold's other officers were unhappy for different reasons. For example, Major Bigelow was quite vocal in his criticism of Montgomery's plan to scale Quebec's walls.[78] However, Montgomery— who had his share of trouble with other quarrelsome officers during the siege of St. Johns—heard no grumbling from Arnold. He appreciated Arnold's fidelity and admired his aggressiveness, courage, and intelligence, proclaiming that he "paid particular attention to Colonel Arnold's recommendations."[79]

The meeting with Arnold's officers ended without any resolution, except that Montgomery made it clear that he fully supported Arnold, whom he called "my friend."[80] Dr. Senter, who also admired Arnold, stepped forward at the end of the meeting with an offer to lead one of the contentious companies into battle. This impressed Arnold, but he declined the doctor's bid in an amicable note: "I am much obliged to you for your offer, and glad to see you so spirited, but cannot consent you should take up arms, as you will be wanted in the way of your profession."[81]

Montgomery decided to appeal directly to Arnold's corps to put aside their differences and join him for the benefit of the rebellion. The meeting took place on December 25 in front of Captain Morgan's headquarters in St. Roch. Captain Dearborn attended, and said that the meeting started at 4:00 p.m. when Arnold's Kennebec veterans were "paraded," meaning that they stood in military formation facing Montgomery.[82] Common soldier Greenman described the assemblage similarly, saying "our Detach't [Arnold's corps] was drawed up and form'd a Square."[83] Though several feet of snow covered the ground that day, the weather was mild for the season, with a light breeze blowing from the southwest.[84]

The appearance of the remaining members of the expedition had changed considerably since they paraded on a bright September day at Newburyport. Then they were healthy, full of energy, and excited with the prospects of an easy march across Maine and surprise attack on

Quebec. Now, four months later, they were cold, sick, and dirty. Their numbers had dwindled to half of those who started out from Newburyport. Some had died of sickness and starvation; others had lost their way in the woods, never to be seen again. Whole companies had turned back after losing hope or being prodded to return by faint-hearted officers. The men who remained, though tough, were only human, and thoughts of going home occupied their minds, especially since not all of them had been issued warm clothing. According to rifleman Henry's diary entry for December 12, "The officers and men, still wore nothing else, than the remains of the summer clothing. . . . Many impediments occurred, to delay the transportation of the clothing, which general Montgomery had procured for us at Montreal."[85]

By the time the Kennebec corps mustered on December 25 to listen to Montgomery's speech, some of them were wearing articles of captured British uniforms. Writing from inside Quebec, Captain Ainslie said that he saw rebels crossing the streets in St. Roch "arm'd; some are cloth'd in red."[86] The men supplemented these uniform pieces with blanket coats (capotes), ordinary blankets, and any other warm clothing they could find.

The blanket coat was a particularly distinctive article of clothing. Usually white in color with a cape, Montgomery had seized a number of them when he captured Montreal.[87] Those of Arnold's soldiers who had not been lucky enough to get one of the capotes had instead draped a blanket (or blankets) over their summer clothing and pieces of British uniforms and secured it at the waist with a belt or rope, allowing the arms to extend from the open sides. A collar or hood could be made by draping the blanket high on the shoulders. Everyone was wearing gloves or mittens in the frigid late December weather, as well as some type of warm hat. Some of the men donned red stocking caps, which were part of the booty captured by Montgomery, while others continued to wear their old caps on which they had sewn or painted the words "Liberty or Death" at the start of the campaign. The soldiers kept their ears warm by covering them with pieces of wool cloth draped around their heads and tied below their chins.

Leggings were another distinctive item of clothing worn by Arnold's men.[88] Made of sturdy woolen blanketing or leather, leggings extended from the waist to the ankles and covered the tops of the shoes. They were commonly worn by soldiers on campaign as protection against rough surfaces and sharp objects, especially during the early years of the Revolutionary War when breeches and long stockings were still in fashion (later replaced by more practical trousers and overalls). Leggings came in a variety of hues, but blue, brown, or black are mentioned as the most popular. [89]

By the time of the meeting with Montgomery, Arnold's men carried a wide variety of weapons, including guns, pikes, axes, knives, and swords held or secured to their bodies with belts and straps. This hodgepodge of weapons included the hunting fowlers they brought from home and the larger-caliber military muskets that Montgomery captured from the British at St. Johns, Chambly, and Montreal. However, the elegant long-barreled rifles carried by Morgan's division stood out from the rest of this arsenal of personal weaponry. Brought from frontier farms in Virginia and Pennsylvania, these distinctive weapons were the personal property of the men who cradled them. Their amazing accuracy at long range brought about the demise of any man unwary enough to show his head above Quebec's ramparts.

Some of the men who gathered to hear Montgomery speak wore a sprig of hemlock in the front of their hats so as to distinguish them from the British, a good idea since many of the Americans were wearing articles of captured British clothing. One early historian of the Revolution, Charles Botta, gave a different explanation for the hemlock sprig. His incongruous interpretation was that soldiers who had contracted smallpox were ordered to wear the device: "[T]he smallpox broke out in the camp; this scourge was the terror of the soldiers. It was ordered that those who were attacked with it, should wear of sprig of hemlock upon their hats, that the others might know and avoid them."[90]

General Montgomery stood before Arnold's tough, famine-proof veterans, readying to speak. With their enlistments close to expiring, many of the expedition's men were disinclined to attack Quebec. In the spirit of citizen soldiers (a view promoted by the high-minded Continental Congress), Arnold's gaunt troopers felt they had done their duty and were entitled to return to their homes and families when their enlistments expired. Although the military situation at Quebec was critical, they believed that other patriots should leave their warm homes to take their place on the icy Plains of Abraham. Arnold's veterans also knew that Montgomery had wiry young Aaron Burr training 50 picked men in the use of scaling ladders. Were they expected to follow little Burr and his volunteers over the ramparts? Stocking said that many of his fellow soldiers "appeared unwilling to attempt so daring an enterprize."[91]

Montgomery began to speak to Arnold's assembled corps. Dearborn said he did so "in a very sensible Spirit'd manner—which greatly animated our men."[92] Private Morison recalled that "we were addressed in a handsome manner . . . on the subject of the intended attack."[93] Montgomery told Arnold's veterans that the taking of Quebec would likely lead to a negotiated peace. "The fire of patriotism kindled in our breasts," Stocking wrote in his journal after listening to the general's passionate speech, "and we resolved to follow wherever he should lead."[94]

Unbeknownst to these veterans at the time, an inspiring letter written by General Washington was en route to them. Penned at Cambridge on December 5, the missive contained the commander-in-chief's warmest congratulations to Arnold and his corps for their "glorious work." "My thanks are due, & sincerely offered to you [Col. Arnold], for the Enterprizing & persevering spirit—To your brave followers I likewise present them," wrote Washington.[95] The heroic march of the Arnold Expedition across Maine was the talk of the infant nation, and the capture of Quebec would be their crowning achievement.

Following Montgomery's speech, the plotting against Arnold and the grumbling among the men apparently ceased. When four soldiers in Thayer's company feigned illness to avoid participating in the attack, they were paraded through camp with nooses around their necks and ridiculed into admitting their cowardice.[96] Everyone seemed to be behind Montgomery, who said that he was willing to sacrifice his life "to the honor of his Brother soldiers and country."[97]

It was true that Montgomery had Aaron Burr training 50 men in the proficient use of scaling ladders. The plan was for Burr's forlorn hope (the name given to men engaged in dangerous missions) to go over the walls with their ladders and open one of the gates for the rest of the army.[98] The British knew the rebels possessed scaling ladders that they planned to use at night to ascend Quebec's walls. Although Ainslie mentioned this danger in his diary, he did not take the threat seriously: "December 23d . . . Can these men pretend that there is a possibility of approaching our walls with ladders, sinking to the middle [waist] every step in snow! Where shall we be then? Shall we be looking on cross arm'd [i.e., doing nothing to stop them]?"[99]

Knowing that he could rely on Arnold's troops, Montgomery continued to wait for the right weather conditions to launch his attack. Pacing the ramparts on the night of December 26, Captain Ainslie decided the rebels would not attack that evening. "This is no wall scaling weather," he penned in his diary, "the night was clear & inconceivably cold—it is employment enough to preserve ones nose."[100]

Realizing that the British were watching and waiting for a big attack, Montgomery refined his plans in an effort to confuse Carleton and force him to disperse his few reliable troops by assailing the ramparts at four different places. Three of the strikes, however, were only feints to compel Carleton to scatter his men, while the fourth (and largest) assault, aimed at the wall below St. Diamond, constituted the decisive attack.

A snowstorm on December 27 gave Montgomery the natural concealment he wanted to move his men into position covertly, and he passed word that the attack would take place that night. But he called off the assault at the last minute when "the storm abated—the moon shone—and we retired. . . ."[101]

When the sun rose the following morning, the rebels could see that the British had moved artillery and men to the wall where their main attack was scheduled to take place. Montgomery realized that his plan had been given to Carleton. The details of the assault could have been reported to the governor by one of the secret operatives he had circulating in the American camp. Posing as destitute inhabitants or curious peasants selling food, Carleton's spies were slipping in and out of the rebel blockade with information. In this instance, we know that Carleton's informant was Joshua Wolfe, an escaped British prisoner (he was clerk to Colonel Caldwell, who commanded the British militia inside Quebec).[102] An American deserter identified as "Singleton, a sergeant in the troops that accompanied Montgomery" (i.e., a soldier in the 1st New York Regiment) corroborated Wolfe's intelligence.[103]

Realizing that his plan had been compromised, Montgomery agreed to take the advice of Edward Antill and James Price, the latter a wealthy resident of the town of Three Rivers who had joined the rebels and loaned Montgomery money. Antill and Price had been advising Montgomery to attack Quebec via the lower town from the start of the siege. They emphasized that this part of the city had no walls and that valuable goods filled its warehouses. If the rebels controlled the lower town, they argued,

Quebec's merchants would pressure Carleton to surrender, so as to prevent their businesses and homes from looting and destruction.

Montgomery decided to follow their advice. Now he planned to stage two feints against the upper town while he aimed the real attack at the lower town. Montgomery and Arnold personally would lead the main assault, orchestrated to hit the lower town from two directions: Arnold would advance from the north side of the city (through the suburbs of St. Roch and Palais) with his entire corps while Montgomery would attack from the south (around the base of Cape Diamond) with 300 troops from the 1st New York regiment. While the two feints against the upper town kept Carleton confused as to the location of the real attack, the two columns below would overrun the lower town, combine forces, and fight their way into the upper town.

Montgomery planned the dangerous attack in great detail: Arnold would assault with 500 men—every able-bodied soldier from his Kennebec corps along with 40 Canadian volunteers and Indian auxiliaries, and 40 men from Captain Lamb's artillery company pulling a cannon mounted on a sled.[104] Montgomery's column would also be supported by a single cannon.

Turning to the two feints against the upper town, a detachment of Massachusetts troops, under the command of Captain Jacob Brown (the brother of Major John Brown), would hit the wall near Cape Diamond, while a second force, consisting of 200 recently arrived Canadian recruits led by Colonel Livingston, would head for St. John's Gate.[105]

Livingston's mission was to assault St. John's Gate with "prepared faggots of combustible materials" and, as reported by Dr. Senter in his journal, "draw the attention of the enemy that way, and at the same time attempt the walls a little distance with scaling ladders, &c."[106] Lieutenant Wool's battery of five mortars in St. Roch would create additional chaos by lobbing shells into the city once the attack was underway. Captain Brown was to fire five rockets skyward as the signal that Livingston and he were ready and that Montgomery and Arnold should begin to move toward the enemy from their starting positions.

It was a desperate plan. Montgomery and Arnold knew that Carleton had taken additional measures to defend the lower town. From across the St. Lawrence, American lookouts equipped with spyglasses peered into the lower town to locate Carleton's defenses and observed that wooden barricades and field artillery blocked several streets. They also saw men guarding every strategic point in the lower town, as well as buildings that had been boarded up to prevent the rebels from using them as firing points. In addition, huge slabs of ice cast ashore from the motion of the river littered the narrow road that ran along the shoreline. Still, Montgomery's men were confident that he would take Quebec. Private Stocking summed up American sentiment when he said, "[O]ur heroic General seemed resolved on victory or death, and no difficulties were too great for him to encounter."[107]

The Americans besieging Quebec were now determined to take the city. They believed that Carleton and his crew were part of a deliberate scheme to reduce the American colonists to slavery and trusted that Quebec's unwilling militia would throw down their weapons once Montgomery entered Quebec.

With the final days of December 1775 at hand, Montgomery had to launch his attack soon. Not only did he run the risk of losing Arnold's men, whose enlistments expired on December 31, but the armchair generals in Congress—their various petitions to the British government having failed—were calling for action in Canada. The final blow to peace came when King George III addressed the opening session of Parliament on October 26, 1775, declaring his American colonies to be in open "revolt, hostility, and rebellion." "They meant only to amuse," the king proclaimed, "by vague expressions of attachment to the parent state, and the strongest protestations of loyalty to me, whilst they were preparing for a general revolt. . . ." George III said that he would "put a speedy end to these disorders" including taking advantage of "friendly offers of foreign assistance" (hired armies from the German principalities—the feared Hessians).[108]

Congress believed that the American occupation of Quebec would pressure the king and his government to negotiate an end to the war.[109] At the very least, American control of Canada would give the rebels a valuable bargaining chip. Congress also believed that Canada's inhabitants would rally to the rebel standard once Americans seized Quebec. But despite all the pressure to attack, Montgomery had to wait for a dark night and a raging snowstorm in which to hide his movements, especially as Arnold's Kennebec men crossed a path called Dog Lane.[110]

Dog Lane was the only land approach to the lower town from the northern suburbs of St. Roch and Palais. The path ran along a narrow strip of land squeezed between the shoreline of the St. Charles River and the cliff that marked the edge of the upper town. Quebec's perimeter wall straddled the edge of this cliff, giving British troops a perfect shot at anyone moving along Dog Lane. Arnold and his men needed to get across the narrow path without being seen.

Dog Lane led into Sault-au-Matelot, the only street in this part of the narrow lower town. Sault-au-Matelot (literally translated from French as "sailors leap"), about 100 yards long, was a narrow, winding street crowded with businesses and homes. The rear of the buildings on one side (facing west) butted up against the cliff, while the rear of the buildings across the narrow street faced a narrow beach and the river. There were probably no wharves or docks along this section of the lower town, but boats and ships moored for the winter along the narrow beach. Sault-au-Matelot resembled a gorge—there were no open spaces, intersections, or side streets along its entire length. It ended at the Cote de Montagne, which ran from King's Wharf, up the side of the cliff, and into the upper town. Cote de Montagne was the only road from the lower town to the upper town. A barrier, later called Prescott Gate, had been constructed to defend this strategic road. Once Arnold's men entered Sault-au-Matelot, the only way out was to advance toward Cote de Montagne or to turn back to the suburb of Palais through Dog Lane.

Carleton had erected two wooden barriers across Sault-au-Matelot to bar anyone from using this strategic street to reach the heart of the lower town. The first barrier blocked the entrance to Sault-au-Matelot from Dog Lane. The second barrier was near Rue Petit Champlain. The front of both obstructions faced toward Dog Lane, which was the direction from which the rebels were expected to attack. Behind each barricade were field artillery and infantry who could fire through small openings (called loopholes) in the wooden barricades. A parapet (elevated walkway) near the top of each barricade allowed musketmen to fire down onto the street or repel any enemy attempt to scale the barricades with ladders. The defenders needed to hold just one of the barricades until reinforcements arrived.

The two barricades on Sault-au-Matelot Street were a potential trap: once the Americans entered the street, British reinforcements could rush in behind them and block their escape back to Palais. Even if Arnold made it through Sault-au-Matelot, his Kennebec veterans still had to fight their way up heavily defended Cote de la Montagne in order to reach the upper town.

Like Arnold, Montgomery had few options for maneuvering on the other side of town. Montgomery's New Yorkers had to reach the southern end of the lower town by descending the snow-covered path that led to Wolfe's Cove from the Plains of Abraham. Their difficult route continued along an ice-choked trail that ran along the shoreline of the St. Lawrence River. After going around the base of Cape Diamond, this path led to the southeastern edge of the lower town, called Pres de Ville. The British erected several strong picket fences to block anyone trying to enter the town from this direction. Beyond the fences was a strategic building that Carleton had transformed into a small fort (blockhouse) by reinforcing its doors and covering its windows with wooden boards through which musket and cannon ports were cut. Four small cannons occupied this fortified building, which defended all approaches from Pres de Ville to the center of the lower town. However, if Montgomery made it past the blockhouse, he had a clear run to the center of the lower town and his rendezvous with Arnold.

If this strategy were successful, Carleton and his principal officers would be fooled into thinking that the rebel threat was against the upper town, and deploy their best troops accordingly, while Montgomery and Arnold overran the lower town. However, the success of Montgomery's plan depended on the precise coordination of his attacks and feints. Delays in executing the complicated plan had to be expected due to the deep snow (estimated at six feet with deeper drifts in some places) and huge chunks of ice along the waterfront. Montgomery needed to allow plenty of time for everyone to get into position and figure out how to synchronize the attack of his four widely dispersed detachments. Since Arnold had a more difficult assignment than Montgomery, he received more men—500, as opposed to Montgomery's 300. Per their orders, the soldiers in the attack pinned white pieces of paper to their hats with the words "Liberty or Death" so as to distinguish them from the enemy.[111]

The nights of December 27, 28, and 29 were clear, but during the evening of the 30th a violent northeasterly wind kicked up, accompanied by snow. "It was a tremendous storm," noted Dr. Senter. "[A] heavy darkness pervaded the earth."[112] It was just the kind of weather Montgomery had been hoping for. As the snow continued to fall, word circulated that the attack would start before dawn.[113]

Montgomery held a final council of war that night, after which the officers returned to their units to get ready. Everyone knew the dangers that lay ahead as they made their final preparations. Captain Jacob Cheesman (sometimes spelled Cheeseman), one of Montgomery's aides-de-camp, "dressed himself extremely neat putting five half-joes [slang for a Portuguese coin called a johannes] in his pocket," saying that if he were killed, the coins would be found on his body and used to bury him with decency.[114] Captain Macpherson, Montgomery's other aide, penned a letter to his father with instructions that it should be delivered if he did not survive the attack. "Orders are given for a general storm of Quebec this night," young Macpherson wrote his father. "I assure you that I experience no reluctance in this cause, to venture a life which I consider is only lent to be used when my country demands it."[115]

At 2:00 a.m. on December 31, Captain Brown fired five flares into the sky, the prearranged signal that the attack was on. The miserable weather—a blizzard on a dark night—was perfect for the assault. One New Englander called it "the most Terrible Night I ever saw."[116] Brown's 100 Massachusetts troops hid along the ridges of the Plains of Abraham near Montgomery's starting point, Colonel Livingston's Canadians sheltered themselves from view farther north on the heights facing St. John's Gate, and Arnold's Kennebec veterans were forming up in St. Roch.

On the other side of the ramparts, the violent snowstorm had the British command on high alert. Some said that Carleton could almost smell the rebels preparing to attack—he knew that the enlistments of some of the rebels were expiring and had warned his officers that the rebels would attack "on the first dark night."[117] Carleton was alert, at his command post in the Récollect monastery, fully dressed in his uniform with sword and pistols at the ready.[118] His second in command, Colonel Alan Maclean, was nearby along with Colonel Henry Caldwell, the third in command and commanding officer of the British militia.

Malcolm Fraser of the Royal Highland Emigrants (Maclean's unit), captain of the guards that night, was making his rounds when he saw the five rockets illuminate the night sky. Although everything remained still, Fraser decided that the rockets were some kind of signal from the rebels that an attack was imminent. He ordered reinforcements to man the upper town ramparts while he rushed to sound the alarm. Within moments, drums beat and church bells rang as the entire garrison turned out and peered into the blizzard, searching for menacing movements from the rebel camp. The defenders thrust lanterns on poles out over the tops of the walls and threw flaming fire balls over the battlements to light up the area.

Everything remained quiet until 4:00 a.m., when two additional rockets momentarily lit the sky; unknown to the British, these rockets were the second prearranged signal from Brown to inform the others he was launching his attack. Moments later, rebel artillery began firing from St. Roch (Wool's battery) and the distinctive sound of musket fire could be heard coming from the vicinity of Cape Diamond and St. John's Gate. Captain Ainslie described these opening events:

> 31st [December] It snow'd all the night, it was very dark, the wind was strong at N E. . . . Capt: Fraser order'd the Guards and Pickets on the ramparts to stand to their arms.

> Two Rockets sent by the enemy from the foot of Cape Diamond were immediately followed by a heavy & hot fire from a body of men posted behind a rising ground within eighty yards of the wall, at Cape Diamond, the flashes from their muskets made their heads visible—their bodies were cover'd: we briskly return'd the fire directed by theirs—at this moment a body of men suppos'd to be Canadians appear'd in St Johns surburs—& the enemy [Wool's artillery] threw shells into town from St Roc [St. Roch].[119]

Montgomery watched the first rockets illuminate the sky with his men at the southern edge of the Plains of Abraham. Arnold viewed them as well, and began his advance through the bombed-out suburb of St. Roch toward Palais and Dog Lane. From the south came General Montgomery with his battle-hardened New York troops, veterans of the 45-day siege of St. Johns. From the north came Colonel Arnold with every able-bodied man who remained from the Arnold Expedition. There were 429 of them, each of whom had endured unspeakable hardships to arrive at this culminating moment of their long campaign.

Arnold's Kennebec men slowly made their way through Palais. Visibility was almost zero, as gale-force winds pelted snow and hail into the men's faces. Arnold personally led a forlorn hope of 25 men, who staggered through Palais and onto Dog Lane. They now were close to the water, and deep snow and large ice chunks covered the narrow path. Lamb's artillery company was just behind Arnold's forlorn hope, pulling a brass six-pounder on a sled. Morgan's Virginia rifle company was next in line, accompanied by Lieutenant Colonel Greene. The attacking

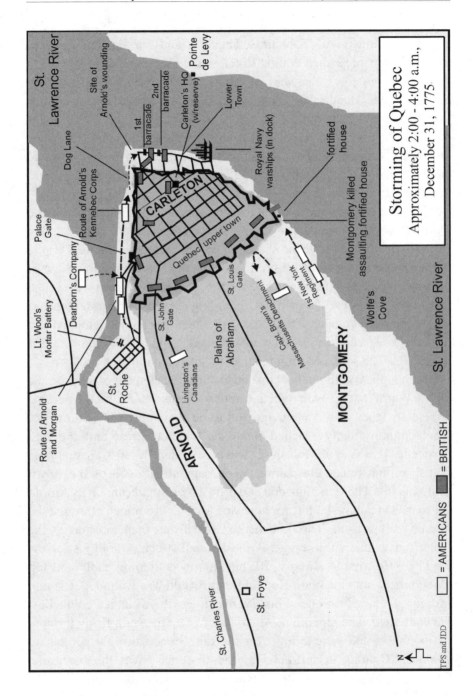

Storming of Quebec
Approximately 2:00 - 4:00 a.m.,
December 31, 1775

column continued with Topham's, Thayer's, and Ward's New England musket companies, then Major Bigelow's mixed company of musket men, Canadian volunteers, and Indians (including Natanis), followed by Smith's and Hendrick's Pennsylvania rifle companies. Captains Goodrich's and Hubbard's companies brought up the rear, with Major Meigs as their senior officer.[120] Dearborn's company was missing—they had been posted across the St. Charles River to intercept anyone trying to enter Quebec from that quarter, and were delayed ferrying themselves across the river to St. Roch.

Dog Lane was so narrow that the attackers had to march in single file along its length. A handful of troops avoided this bottleneck by moving out onto the thin ice near the shoreline, a very dangerous tactic. Despite the terrible weather, sentries on the cliff above spotted the long line of men moving on Dog Lane and opened fire. A number of men were killed or wounded crossing the gauntlet, including Captain Hubbard. Hubbard was leading his company along the path when he suddenly stopped and leaned against a building. "Are you wounded, Captain?" asked one of his men. "Yes," he said, ordering his men to "march on, march on!"[121]

Although Arnold realized that he had lost the element of surprise, he did not turn back, even when Captain Lamb's field piece became hopelessly stuck in the snow and had to be abandoned. The van of the rebel column finally reached Sault au Matelot Street and the first barricade. It was a ten-foot-high fence defended by 30 Canadian and British militia under the command of Captain McLeod of the Royal Emigrants.[122] These men loaded and primed two small cannon as Arnold approached leading the forlorn hope and Morgan's company through the blinding snowstorm. The defenders started firing their muskets as the Americans came within range. A musket ball struck Arnold just below the knee. He tried to shrug it off, but soon was limping badly and felt blood oozing into his boot. Noticing that Arnold was wounded, Captain Morgan screamed for one of his riflemen to get the wounded colonel off the battlefield. The remaining Americans rushed the wall, firing through its loopholes and scrambling over the top. Some said that gentleman volunteer Charles Porterfield was the first man over the barricade. Captain Lamb and his artillerymen, armed with muskets and swords, joined the melee.[123] The fighting was fierce but brief, lasting only a few minutes before most of the defenders surrendered and the others ran to safety.

After taking the first barricade, Morgan "raised his voice, always terrible in the hour of battle," ordered "his riflemen to the front," and began running toward the second barricade without waiting for Lieutenant Colonel Greene or any of the other senior officers to come up.[124] "[Th]e people [enemy troops] came running," wrote Morgan, ". . . in whole platoons, giving themselves up as prisoners" in the street as he and a handful of men raced forward.[125] Writing about the attack years later, Morgan explained that he reached the second barricade and found it abandoned. Passing through a sally port (door) in the barrier, Morgan claimed he found himself standing in the heart of the lower town with no one around. He ran back to gather men to secure the second barricade at the same time Arnold was being helped to Dr. Senter's hospital, a mile behind St. Roch, by one of Morgan's riflemen and Chaplain Spring.

Montgomery, meanwhile, was approaching from the other end of the lower town. Snow drifts slowed the advance of his column, whose members slipped on the steep, icy trails while trying to maneuver the clumsy scaling ladders they had brought along. When they reached the shoreline, Montgomery's men had to march two miles along a narrow, ice-clogged trail wedged between the St. Lawrence River and Cape Diamond. Moving no more than three or four abreast, Montgomery's detachment reached the first of two sturdy picket fences that blocked their approach into the lower town. The pioneers quietly made an opening in the fence, allowing the advance party to slip through and silently advance about 100 feet to the second fence. The general, who stood by as his pioneers sawed away at the second fence, became uneasy with their slow progress. Taking an axe from one of his soldiers, Montgomery hacked away at the sturdy barrier, pushing the splintered wood aside with his bare hands. The men behind him quickly enlarged the opening with their axes and followed their commander through the gap and into Pres de Ville.

Macpherson, Chessman, Burr, Desmarais (a Canadian guide), and some soldiers from the 1st New York crawled through the opening. Ahead of them, through the blinding snowstorm, they could see the outline of a house. It sat about 50 yards to their front, blocking their advance. The home belonged to a businessman named Simon Fraser. Montgomery knew that Carleton had fortified at least one house in this section of town, but had no information as to its exact location. There were no signs of life from the building, and the only sounds they could hear were the gale-force winds, the ringing of the city's church bells, and some distant gunfire.

About 7:00 a.m., Montgomery and his advance party cautiously approached the silent building, which he assumed to be the fortified house.[126] One account has the general saying to Burr, "We shall be in the fort in two minutes."[127] Montgomery moved closer, as if suspicious of the deathlike calm surrounding him, and stopped for a moment. Then he drew his sword, waved it above his head, and shouted, "Push on, brave boys, Quebec is ours."[128]

Having made his decision, Montgomery starting running toward the lonely building. Macpherson was just behind him, along with Captain Chesseman and some troops. Unknown to the attackers, 30 heavily armed men inside Fraser's fortified house were observing them. The bulk were jittery French Canadians under the command of two inexperienced militia officers (Captain Chabot and Lieutenant Alexander Picard), a handful of sailors commanded by a ship's master named Captain Barnsfare (or Bairnsfeather), and a volunteer named John Coffin. Coffin was a loyalist who ironically had come to Quebec from war-ravaged Boston earlier in 1775 seeking a peaceful place to live with his family.[129] He and Barnsfare were in charge of the fortified house, and although they lacked military experience, they remained resolute and calm.[130] Both had been on alert all night and watched the enemy approaching. As the rebels moved closer, the men inside the house readied their arsenal of weapons, which included four small cannon loaded with grapeshot.

Nervous but determined, the men inside the house waited until the enemy was within close range, when Captain Barnsfare yelled, "Fire!" A loud explosion erupted from the bowels of the house as a charge of grape screamed through the air, attended by a shower of musketry. Captain Cheesman caught shards through his midsection and fell to the ground. He tried to get up while motioning with his hand for his men to push forward, but fell back to the ground a corpse.[131]

Montgomery was nearby, sprawled in the snow; killed instantly by grape shot that had torn open his head. His young aide Macpherson lay dead next to him. The well-timed British salvo also killed Desmarais and nine soldiers from the 1st New York.[132] But the other attackers escaped, including Captain Burr, who claimed he was within ten feet of Montgomery when the shooting started.[133] Burr and the others were joined by some New Yorkers who arrived on the scene from the second fence and immediately began exchanging shots with the men inside the fortified house.

A determined American attack might have sent the bulk of the blockhouse's jittery occupants scurrying out the back door for safety. But at this moment Colonel Donald Campbell came down the street from the splintered fence and surveyed the gruesome scene. He was Montgomery's quartermaster officer, unqualified for the challenge thrust upon him by Montgomery's death.[134] Some of the New Yorkers were advancing, but instead of inspiring them and ordering additional troops forward, "and pressing on the victory half won," Campbell lost his nerve and ordered a withdrawal.[135] As the New Yorkers retreated, Burr struggled to lift the body of his dead commander and carry him away. Montgomery was a big man, but some eyewitnesses reported seeing the small captain carry the heavy, blood-soaked corpse a few feet before giving up the effort and scurrying off with the rest.

There are stories that the men inside Fraser's house had been half-drunk and terrified during the encounter. One version claims that the militia and sailors in the house were "kept from running by a ranting Loyalist officer [Coffin?] who was threatening to bayonet the first coward to try to get past him."[136] Another popular legend says that the frightened defenders in the house threw down their weapons and were preparing to flee the fortified house when a drunken sailor among them decided to fire one of the primed and loaded cannons before running off.[137]

Such stories are untrue, as evidenced by a letter that Colonel Maclean wrote after the battle, in which he congratulated Coffin and Barnsfare for their courage and "great coolness with which you allowed the rebels to approach."[138] Not only did the defenders in the fortified house stand their ground, but some of them came out later to examine the American bodies lying in the snow. They found one rebel soldier desperately wounded and asked him whether his commanding officer had been killed. The mortally wounded trooper, aware that he was lying next to Montgomery's body, provided his enemies with an evasive answer. He died soon after, without giving the British the satisfaction of knowing they had killed the gallant Montgomery.[139]

Unaware of the terrible events that had just transpired across town, Morgan raced back toward the second barrier with some of his riflemen. He approached only to find that it was now well manned, including the two cannons mounted on a high platform behind the sturdy barricade. Morgan, who was no fool, decided to back off and wait until more men and scaling ladders arrived from the first barricade, where his comrades were hastily arranging for guards for their prisoners and providing for the wounded. Captain Dearborn, who came up late with his company, said that he passed a lot of wounded Americans ("we met the wounded men very thick," were his exact words) coming from the fight at the first barricade—including Arnold, who was hobbling along, supported by two men.[140] Dearborn might also have passed Lamb's cannon, which was hopelessly stuck in the snow.

Every rebel moving—in either direction—along Dog Lane was now under intense enemy fire from small arms and artillery on the bluff above. Colonel Arnold safely limped through the gauntlet; Dr. Senter reported his arrival at the hospital a mile beyond St. Roch: "Colonel Arnold was brought in, supported by two men, wounded in the leg, with a piece of musket ball." Senter explained that the musket ball apparently first struck some heavy object, causing it to shatter into several pieces before it entered the colonel's leg. Senter extracted the splintered pieces of the bullet, and put Arnold, nearly delirious from pain and blood loss, in bed.[141] Meanwhile, Morgan was losing precious time waiting for reinforcements to attack the second barricade, while high above him in the upper town Governor Carleton and his senior officers were quickly piecing together the American assault.

Since his return to Quebec, Carleton had been working hard preparing for this climactic moment. According to one account, he was ready for a fight: "[H]e was a veteran, loved his King . . . and hated traitors. Such a man was not to be easily frightened into a tame and timid surrender of a garrison which he had the honour of commanding."[142] Carleton had 1,800 men under arms when the Americans attacked. The British and French-Canadian militia, representing almost half of Quebec's defenders, were considered Carleton's worst troops. They were perceived to be made up of inexperienced civilians forced into military service. In addition, some of these conscripts were thought sympathetic toward the rebels. Once the fighting started, however, most of Quebec's militia proved to be determined fighters. A possible explanation for their fighting abilities was the fact that some were French and Indian War veterans.

When the shooting started at the upper town near Cape Diamond, Maclean ordered Caldwell to find out what was happening. Caldwell, a seasoned veteran of the French and Indian War, rushed to the scene with some militia. He discovered the enemy firing at a safe distance and decided that "nothing serious [was] intended."[143]

The experienced colonel looked in on the situation at the St. Louis Gate and determined that it was only a noisy demonstration. Livingston's untested Canadians were unconvincing in their attack, many of them running off as soon as the shooting started. There was a British reserve detachment near St. John's Gate composed of 30 soldiers—a squad of regulars belonging to the 7th Regiment and men from the Royal Highland Emigrants. With the situation at the gate under control, Caldwell ordered the 30 reliable men in reserve to report to headquarters and await further orders. Arriving there behind the 30 troopers, Caldwell listened to the reports coming in from other sectors of the city. After taking everything they knew into account, Carleton, Maclean, and Caldwell correctly decided that Montgomery's main attack was aimed at the lower town.

Lieutenant Colonel Noel Voyer (commander of the Canadian militia) was in charge at the lower town with a mixed force of militia and civilian sailors. Without hesitation, the governor ordered Caldwell to lead reinforcements to Voyer. Caldwell took the 30 dependable soldiers standing by at headquarters and commandeered a picket (sentry post) of additional men from the Royal Highland Emigrants stationed near the Hotel Dieu in the upper town under the command of John Nairne, a former British army captain. Caldwell added 50 sailors who were stationed near rue de la Montagne under the command of Matthew Anderson, a retired Royal Navy lieutenant, as he dashed toward the lower town.[144]

With this force, estimated at 200 men, Caldwell reached the second barricade, where he added his reinforcements to the unsteady Canadian militia who manned the place. Other troops arrived, giving Caldwell about 400 men with which to defend the second barricade. But instead of putting his best troops on the barricade, he shrewdly lined them up with fixed bayonets on the ground about 100 feet behind the barrier, where they could fire up at any rebel who managed to scale the wall. Other defenders were ordered to climb into the upper stories of the houses lining both sides of the barricade and position themselves to fire down at

the rebels as they approached. The two cannons on the platform behind
the barricade were primed and loaded with grapeshot. Rifleman Henry's
journal includes an eyewitness description of the second barricade:

> [T]he barrier . . . was about twelve or more feet high and so strongly
> constructed that nothing but artillery could effectuate its
> destruction. There was a construction fifteen or twenty yards within
> [behind] the barrier, upon a rising ground, the cannon of which
> much overtopped the height of the barrier; hence we were assailed
> with grape shot in abundance.
>
> Against, within the barrier, and close in to it, were two ranges of
> musketeers, armed with musket and bayonet, ready to receive those
> who might venture the dangerous leap.[145]

Unknowingly, Morgan had lost his best opportunity to take the
second barricade.[146] When he finally gathered enough men to overcome
what he assumed would be light resistance and secure the second
barricade, the British were ready for him. Morgan's riflemen led the
assault with scaling ladders at the ready, yelling, "Quebec is ours!"
Running close behind were hundreds of Arnold's other "famine proof"
veterans commanded by Greene, Bigelow, and Meigs. Additional
Kennebec men advanced into the dock area and worked their way toward
the barricade while the blizzard continued unabated. The riflemen met
only sporadic resistance as they threw their scaling ladders against the
wall and clambered up. They reached the top of the barricade and seemed
to be on the verge of success when Caldwell ordered the line of soldiers
he had positioned on the ground behind the barricade to open fire. The
well-aimed volley struck with devastating results.

The blast of gunfire stunned Morgan, who toppled backward off the
ladder into the snow-covered ground below. He was unhurt, but it was a
close call: one enemy musket ball pierced his hat and another ripped
through his coat. Others were not as lucky, and the ground around the
barricade soon became littered with dead and wounded Americans.
Moments later, Morgan spotted a party of enemy troops come through
the sally port in the barricade. They were led by Lieutenant Matthew
Anderson, who summoned the pugnacious Morgan to surrender.
Morgan's response was to shoot his antagonist through the head, and the

rest of the British retreated behind the barricade, dragging their dead commander's body with them.[147]

The fighting paused as both sides caught their breath and prepared to continue the contest for the barricade. By now Canadian militiamen were firing at the rebels from second-story windows of buildings behind the barricade. The Americans broke into the buildings on their side of the barrier and, climbing to the upper stories, commenced firing down at the British behind the barricade as Morgan renewed the assault with scaling ladders. At one point, a party of British clambered up a ladder to an upper-story gable window in the back of a building on Sault au Matelot Street as some Americans entered the same building through the front door. Fierce hand-to-hand fighting ensued inside the house, before the more numerous and better-armed British swept the rebels back into the street.

Captain Hendricks was inside a building taking aim with his rifle through a window when an enemy musket ball struck him in the chest. He staggered across the room, fell onto a bed, and died. Lieutenant Humphrey (a young officer in Morgan's company) was shot dead in the street. Captain Lamb took part of a blast of grapeshot in the face and was carried into a building, where he was left for dead.[148] Lieutenant Steele, who commanded the scouting party from Fort Western, was hit in the hand and lost three fingers.

Despite heavy losses, Arnold's men fought on, presuming that Montgomery would arrive at any moment from the other side of town and attack the second barricade from behind. Morgan and the others were considering holding their position and sending a scout off to see what had happened to Montgomery when enemy troops suddenly appeared in their rear. The British sortie, which originated from Palace Gate, consisted of 120 men from the Royal Highland Emigrants led by a Captain McDougal (an officer in that regiment) and George Laws, a half-pay British lieutenant. Also included were Captain Hamilton of the *Lizard* with about 60 sailors, who, according to one eyewitness, "behaved as they do on all occasions, like British Tars."[149]

Accompanied by two light field pieces, these men counter-attacked on Carleton's orders and quickly overran the suburb of Palais, where they captured wounded rebels heading for the hospital. Advancing farther, they encountered Dearborn's company, bewildered and lost in the storm. Shooting started, but it was impossible to tell friend from foe in the blinding snowstorm. Dearborn said he made out the outline of some men through the falling snow and was about to hail them, when one of them spoke up, asking "who he was." Dearborn replied in a loud voice, "A friend," to which he was asked who he was a friend to. "I answer'd to liberty," Dearborn replied, and received the response, "Then God-damn you," followed by a volley of musket fire.[150] Dearborn's men were surrounded and forced to surrender.

The British counter-attack followed the tracks of Arnold's corps in the snow and arrived at the first barrier on Sault au Matelot, which they retook, capturing more rebels. After securing the first barrier, Captain McDougal remained with a detachment to defend it and guard the prisoners while Laws and Hamilton continued with the rest of their men down the street toward the fighting at the second barrier. Morgan, Greene, Bigelow, Meigs, and the others saw this new threat coming toward them from the rear that "most fairly and handsomely cooped us up."[151]

Some of the Kennebec men tried to fight their way out, others jumped into the buildings along the street or ran toward the river in hopes of escaping across the treacherous ice. They also ran among the ice-bound ships wintering along the waterfront, stumbling in the blinding storm over the cables and lines that secured these vessels to the wharves. The 40 or so Canadians and Indians who took part in the attack tried to make their escape across the ice. They all got away except Natanis, who had been shot through the wrist by a musket ball, and another Indian who was captured by the British.[152]

The rebels who continued to fight at the second barricade, including Morgan, were hopelessly surrounded. One by one they surrendered, some throwing their weapons out into the street through open doors and windows as a sign of submission. Among those who surrendered was John Hall, the former British soldier who spoke French. As the rebels gave up, they were muscled through the sally port in the barricade and assembled on the British side of the fence. A few of the Kennebec men tried hiding in cupboards and attics in the buildings along the Sault au Matelot but they were found in a house to house search. Morgan was probably the last man to surrender. With several of his officers dead or wounded around him, he finally gave his sword to a priest and surrendered at about 9:00 a.m. Codman has the best account of his surrender:

Morgan, crying like a child with vexation and anger, backed against a wall and, sword in hand, dared any one of the enemy to come and take the weapon. In spite of the threats of his enemies and the entreaties of his own men not to sacrifice his life uselessly, he persisted in his determination. None took up his gage. At length, noticing a priest among the crowd, he delivered his sword to him, saying, "Then I give my sword to you; but not a scoundrel of these cowards shall take it out of my hands!"[153]

Carleton made one further stroke against the rebels by sending a detachment out of Palace Gate to St. Roch to silence Lieutenant Wool's mortars and round up any rebel stragglers. Dr. Senter was treating the wounded in the hospital, about a mile west of St. Roch, when he was warned of the approaching enemy and told to make preparations to evacuate the wounded into the countryside. However, Wool stood his ground in a defiant act of bravery. According to Senter, this young officer "much distinguished himself on this occasion" by surprising the enemy with well-directed artillery fire that sent them scurrying back toward Palace Gate.[154]

The British, however, might launch a second attack toward the hospital at any moment. The wounded Colonel Arnold ordered everyone to stay at the hospital. In a now-famous reference to Arnold's courage, Dr. Senter wrote, "[H]e ordered his pistols loaded, with a sword on his bed, &c. adding that he was determined to kill as many as possible if they came into the room." "We were now all soldiers," Senter observed, and the wounded, most of whom were lying on the ground on straw mattresses, were issued weapons and expected to fight.[155] The situation remained confusing as the morning of December 31 wore on.

Although unable to move from his bed, Arnold was the senior officer present. He was told that Montgomery's assault had failed and that his friend the general had been killed. But there was no news from Greene, Morgan, or any of the other Kennebec veterans, and Arnold hoped that they were in control of the lower town. The fierce snowstorm continued throughout the day, making it impossible to hear any gunfire that might be coming from the city.

By the late afternoon there was still no news from the Kennebec column, and Arnold worried for its safety. "I am exceedingly apprehensive," he wrote General Wooster later that afternoon. "[T]hey will either carry the lower town, be made prisoners, or cut to pieces. I thought it proper to send an express to let you know the critical situation we are in."[156]

One of Arnold's gentleman volunteers, Matthew Duncan, left to reconnoiter but failed to return.[157] Arnold's information remained sketchy until January 2, when Major Meigs, who exited the city on parole, appeared and provided Arnold with an accurate account of the fighting. The major strongly condemned Montgomery's New Yorkers for not "advancing like men" and blamed them for the defeat.[158] Meigs also confirmed the unthinkable: every officer and enlisted man from the Arnold Expedition who had attacked Quebec was either dead or a prisoner of war.

Chapter 10

The Very Flower of the Colonial Youth[1]

𝔄 **snowstorm pelted** Quebec during the early morning of December 31. It fell throughout the day, limiting visibility and muffling sounds. The weather finally cleared during the night. The British ventured out the following morning, New Year's Day 1776, to inspect the battlefield and retrieve the dead.

At first, they saw nothing unusual in the freshly fallen snow. Then someone noticed a frozen arm protruding through the flurries in the Pres de Ville. They shoveled away the snow and uncovered the body of a rebel soldier. Additional probing and digging turned up a total of 13 frozen corpses. A similarly grim scene occurred on the other side of town, where additional bodies were found. Some civilians came out to watch the gruesome scene as the British removed piles of frozen corpses, their limbs distorted in various positions, in horse-drawn sleighs.

On the following day, Governor Carleton toured the lower town to inspect the sites of the British victory. He was proving to be a humane jailer, and granted Major Meigs permission to visit the American camp to retrieve some clothes for himself and his fellow officers.[2] The major gave Carleton his word of honor that he would quickly return to captivity. Meigs also was under oath as a gentleman not to reveal information about Quebec's defenses, but he felt that he could divulge that the governor had segregated the officers from the enlisted men, as was the custom, and that both groups were confined in the upper town. The officers were quartered in the seminary while the enlisted men were kept in the Recollects building that formerly housed a monastery and Jesuit college. It was heartbreaking that, after their terrible ordeal in the Maine wilderness and perilous siege, Meigs and the others found themselves prisoners in the city that they had come to conquer.

Despite his painful wound, Arnold was numb as Meigs informed him that he believed every man belonging to the colonel's celebrated corps had been killed or captured in the attack. According to the British, 426 rebels were killed or captured in the fight.[3] Of this number, 60 were reported to have died in the battle, including three of Arnold's best officers: Captain Henricks, shot dead while he was taking aim with his rifle from an upper-story window in the Sault-au-Matelot; Lieutenant Humphreys, a promising young lieutenant in Morgan's rifle company, who died trying to scale the second barricade; and Lieutenant Samuel Cooper, from Handchett's Connecticut company, killed trying to retake the first barricade. Meigs told Arnold that of the 366 Americans captured, 100 were wounded, including Captain Jonas Hubbard, one of the expedition's company officers, who was not expected to live.[4]

Those captured unscathed, besides Meigs, included the Kennebec corps senior officers; Lieutenant Colonel Greene, Major Bigelow, Adjutant Febiger, Captain Morgan, and the commanders of the New England musket companies; Thayer, Topham, Hubbard, Dearborn, Ward, Hanchett, and Goodrich. In addition, 15 of Arnold's lieutenants had been taken prisoner, including Archibald Steele, who led Smith's Pennsylvania rifle company in the absence of its commander, Captain Matthew Smith. Steele had three of his fingers shot off during the fighting. Eleazer Oswald also was a prisoner. He was part of Arnold's courageous selected party of 25 volunteers who led the dawn attack against the Sault-au-Matelot. Even the corps quartermaster, Benjamin Catlin, had fought bravely and yielded with the others. Captain Ainslie, who saw them shortly after they surrendered, called them "the Flower of the rebel army." He noted how they had all been taken prisoner with slips of paper pinned to their hats reading "Liberty or Death."[5]

Sitting at Arnold's bedside, Meigs gave a detailed account of what occurred after the wounded colonel left the field. Meigs recalled that the fighting at the first barricade began at about 6:00 a.m. and that the surrender of the last man, reported to be Captain Morgan, took place three hours later. He described how Arnold's desperate men broke into the buildings along the Sault-au-Matelot during the fighting looking for safe, dry places to remove the wet powder and ball from their weapons and reload them with dry charges. After finishing his unhappy story,

Meigs removed a folded piece of cloth from his pocket, opened it, and showed the contents to Arnold. In his cradled hands he held out a pair of gentlemen's knee buckles that belonged to General Montgomery. It was reported that the general was hit by a bullet to his head and had died instantly. In his hands Meigs also held a gold broach that had been found on Captain Macpherson's body. A chivalrous British officer gave the relics to Meigs, who said he highly valued them "for the sake of their late worthy owners."[6]

At the end of their conversation, Arnold handed Meigs a generous amount of money from his personal funds, telling him to use it to buy whatever he could in the city to ease the distress of his imprisoned men. In fact, Arnold had been using his own money and credit throughout the campaign to help keep his troops supplied with food and clothing. Meigs thanked the colonel for his gift and left the room to gather up whatever clothing and personal articles belonging to his fellow officers he could find. He then left the gloomy American camp and silently returned to captivity behind Quebec's walls.

Arnold had a force of about 800 in early January to continue the siege of Quebec. It consisted of five companies from the 1st New York regiment, a small Massachusetts detachment commanded by Major Brown, and the Canadian partisans led by Colonel Livingston. Arnold determined to continue the blockade, telling his sister Hannah, "I have no thoughts of leaving this proud town, until I first enter it in triumph."[7]

Arnold later discovered that a handful of his Kennebec men were still part of his command. They included Lieutenant Isaac Hull and volunteer David Hopkins, both of whom had escaped the British counterattack. Dr. Senter never took part in the battle; he had been ordered to stay at the hospital to care for the wounded. Pierce (the expedition's surveyor) was also among the living. It was rumored that he returned to camp early in the assault with a case of "cannon fever" (cowardice). Captain Smith, who commanded one of the Pennsylvania rifle companies, had never left camp. Private Henry would only say years later that Smith was "absent for particular causes," the implication being he was too drunk to lead his company on the morning of the battle.[8] Another original member of the expedition who survived the attack was feisty Aaron Burr.[9]

Matthias Ogden, Burr's friend and fellow gentleman volunteer, also lived. He was wounded in the shoulder early in the attack and managed to limp back to the hospital. Besides these men, any other Arnold

Expedition veteran still alive either was locked up in a British prison or lying prostrate in Dr. Senter's hospital with smallpox, typhoid, influenza, dysentery, pneumonia, or trench fever.

News of the American defeat at Quebec soon began reaching the outside world. Colonel Campbell authored one of the first reports within hours of his shabby retreat from the fortified house following Montgomery's death. Aware that some accused him of cowardice, Campbell blamed Arnold's Kennebec corps for his flight, claiming that their expiring enlistments had forced Montgomery to execute a desperate attack on Quebec. Unaware of what Campbell had written, Arnold composed his own matter-of-fact report of the attack to General Wooster, who commanded the rebel garrison at Montreal. He begged the general to send reinforcements and to forward to General Washington and Congress the news of the futile American attack on Quebec and Montgomery's death.

The members of the Continental Congress had no inkling in early January 1776 of the disaster that had befallen their army in Canada. In fact, they were in a confident mood as they awaited the expected news that the brilliant young General Montgomery and the fearless Colonel Arnold had captured Quebec. Congress voted promotions for both officers, Montgomery from brigadier to major general and Arnold from colonel to brigadier general. The delegates were especially thrilled with accounts of Arnold's courageous march across Maine. "Arnold's Expedition," delegate William Hooper wrote home on January 2, "has been marked with such scenes of misery that it requires a stretch of faith to believe that human nature was equal to them."[10]

Representative Joseph Hewes penned an account of the expedition for a friend in which he compared Arnold's march to Hannibal's: "that extraordinary March is thought to equal Hanibals over the Alps."[11] Samuel Ward, from Rhode Island, equated Arnold's achievement to that of the ancient Greek warrior Xenophon, who led his army to safety through hostile enemy territory: "Arnold's March is considered as the greatest Action done this War. Some say it equals Xenophons Retreat from Persia . . . nothing greater has been done since the Days of Alexander."[12]

On the morning of January 17, Charles Thomson, the secretary to Congress, interrupted the members' tedious debate over foreign trade to deliver dispatches that had just arrived by courier from Quebec. While

Thomson read the reports, the faces of the delegates turned ashen as they started to comprehend the enormity of the disaster. Particularly alarmed by the tragic news was Samuel Ward, whose son, Samuel Jr., and son-in-law, Christopher Greene, were officers in Arnold's corps. Congress previously had voted to raise eight regiments for service in Canada, and the news of the defeat at Quebec caused the process to accelerate. New Hampshire received instructions to race to reinforce Arnold in Quebec, and General John Thomas received an appointment as Montgomery's successor.[13]

Back at Quebec, Arnold attempted to maintain the semblance of a siege while he awaited reinforcements. Fortunately, Carleton was content to remain behind Quebec's walls, sallying out only to gather firewood from the derelict buildings in the suburbs while Arnold continued to send emissaries to parley. His missives all received the same reply: "[N]o flag will be received, unless it comes to implore the mercy of the King."[14]

Carleton proved more aggressive in trying to increase the size of his garrison by encouraging his prisoners to join Colonel Maclean's Royal Highland Emigrants. The governor focused his recruiting efforts on his English- and Irish-born captives who were particularly vulnerable to threats of being shipped back to England to be tried and hanged as traitors. Enlistment efforts started soon after the failed rebel attack when Maclean began interviewing each prisoner, asking them where they were born. He told those who confessed to British or Irish birth that they must serve his majesty in the Royal Highland Emigrants or face the prospect of being returned to England in chains. To sweeten the offer, Maclean offered land bounties and cash to those prisoners who agreed to fight for their mother country. His bribes and threats worked, and 78 men from the Arnold Expedition joined the Highland Emigrants. After taking an oath of allegiance to serve the king, they were issued uniforms and weapons and absorbed into the regiment.

The Kennebec corps officers need not have worried that so many of their men deserted to the enemy, because those who joined the British ranks ran for freedom at the first opportunity. The story of two of them, Edward Cavenaugh and Timothy Conner from Smith's rifle company, is typical of the outcome of Maclean's machinations. The two riflemen decided that their oath of fidelity to King George III was not binding, and that they would escape at the first opportunity. Their chance came toward the end of January, when they were on guard duty at the Palace Gate on a moonless night. The gate was locked and the surrounding walls were 40 feet high, but there were deep snow drifts that they hoped would cushion their fall. Deciding to take their chances, they threw their muskets over the parapet then leaped from the top of the wall into the snow bank. Both men survived the perilous jump, grabbed their muskets, and started racing toward the rebel lines. As they ran, the other sentries spotted them and started shooting. Soon cannons opened fire, hurling shells at the two as they raced through the wrecked suburb of St. Roch. Despite the gunfire, Cavenaugh and Conner made it to freedom and rejoined the rebel army with their fine British muskets and warm uniforms.

After a few similar episodes, all the remaining prisoners who had enlisted in Maclean's regiment were rounded up and stripped of their weapons and clothing. They then were returned to confinement, where their old messmates cheered their return, much to the frustration of a British officer, who wrote in his diary, "[A]s we cannot read their hearts, prudence says keep them close."[15]

Closely guarding the Arnold Expedition prisoners was prudent, as they were desperate, well-organized, and resourceful men. The 37 American officers being held captive at the time attempted various escape plots, including bribing guards, chipping away at doors, and making ropes from bed sheets. But their intrigues were modest in comparison to the massive prison break organized by the 300-plus enlisted men whose scheme included the capture of Quebec. These men hatched their plan when they were transferred from the Rocollects complex to a smaller building in the upper town called the Dauphin Redoubt. Although they were confined to a small section of the building, the structure was old and dilapidated, close to St. John's Gate, and they were being guarded by apathetic militiamen. The situation was ripe for mayhem, and the quick-witted men of Arnold's Kennebec Corps went to work at night picking every lock in the building and making knives, swords, and pikes from discarded pieces of metal and wood.

A council of captives organized a carefully orchestrated prison break for the morning of April 1. A prisoner named John Martin volunteered to escape and inform Arnold of their plan. Martin dressed entirely in white clothing, including gloves and a hood made for him by the other prisoners. Under cover of night, he slipped out of the jail and, undetected in his camouflage gear, cautiously made his way to the ramparts surrounding the city, where he successfully made the leap to freedom. Watching from a trapdoor in the roof of the Dauphin Redoubt, the prisoners saw a flag flying from the American lines that the wind seemed to have twisted into a knot. It was a prearranged signal from Martin that Arnold had agreed to attack the city as soon as the prisoners seized St. John's Gate.

The ringleaders of the breakout, whom their fellow prisoners chose to be officers, selected an old cellar door in the Redoubt for their escape. Unfortunately, John Hall, the British spy, was among the prisoners. He realized that he had to alert the garrison to the dangerous plot without jeopardizing his own life. His chance came on the evening of March 31, just hours before the breakout was to occur, when the provost marshal (the commander of the military police) was in the prison with an armed guard following a report of strange noises coming from the cellar of the building. The timid-looking prisoners insisted that nothing was wrong when Hall stepped forward, claiming he had knowledge of the incident. Armed guards immediately surrounded him and ushered him away. A short time later, all hell broke loose in the Redoubt when a detachment of veteran soldiers arrived and locked all the prisoners in manacles and leg irons. The troopers knew exactly where the prisoners had hidden their weapons and confiscated the lot. They also collared the plot's ringleaders, who they hustled away for interrogation. The prisoners never saw Hall again, but his former comrades never forgot him. Private Abner Stocking called him a "vile traitor" and remembered that Hall claimed he was a deserter from the British army back at Cambridge.[16] Rifleman John Joseph Henry said that when the leaders of the plot were taken to Governor Carleton, "they found that the wretch [Hall] had evidenced all our proceedings minutely."[17]

Following the failed escape, Colonel Maclean ordered all of Arnold's enlisted men paraded in the prison yard in chains. The colonel inspected them, accompanied by other officers of the garrison. As Maclean walked along the ranks of shackled men, he stopped in front of a particular prisoner, saying, "This is General such-a-one—that is Colonel such-a-one," and in this manner pointed out the ringleaders of the failed plot.[18]

The American officers drew similar contempt from their captors. The British were astonished at their prisoners' undistinguished backgrounds. Major Cadwell commented on them in a letter. "You can have no conception of what kind of men composed the officers. Of those we took, one major was a blacksmith [Timothy Bigelow], another a hatter [Return Jonathan Meigs]; of their captains, there was a butcher, a tanner, a shoemaker, a tavern-keeper, etc., yet they all pretended to be gentlemen," he wrote.

As the months passed, the captives inside Quebec received some indications that American reinforcements had arrived outside the city. Unknown to the Kennebec men, Arnold had been assigned to defend Montreal, while the more experienced and senior General Thomas took charge at Quebec. Cannon fire from new American batteries could be heard in the distance, and there were several false alarms that the city was under attack.

The increased rebel activity provided the prisoners with hope that they would be liberated. However, their situation changed dramatically on the evening of May 5, when rumbling sounds could be heard at Quebec from downriver. The sounds grew louder during the night and were identified as cannon fire. At about 6:00 a.m. on the following morning, a Royal Navy frigate approached the besieged city. Other British ships soon arrived with reinforcements—the Americans had lost the race to take Quebec.

From their fourth-story prison widows in the seminary building, the Arnold Expedition officers glumly watched the spectacle unfolding below them. Captain Dearborn wrote, "[W]e now gave over all hopes of being retaken [by the American besiegers] and Consequently of seeing our families again until we had first taken a Voyage to England and there Tried for rebels, as we have often been told by the officers of the Garrison."[19] Listening to the cheers and triumphant strains of martial music coming from the waterfront, Lieutenant Colonel Greene turned to his comrades and swore that if he ever got out of prison he would continue to fight and "never again be taken prisoner alive."[20] Sadly, Greene kept his promise; when a party of British loyalists cornered him later in the war, he fought them rather than surrender, and his attackers hacked him to death.

About noon, Governor Carleton ventured out from his winter hibernation to find that the rebels had departed. They were retreating rapidly toward Montreal, leaving behind tons of valuable equipment and hundreds of sick soldiers who were too weak to travel.

The lifting of the siege of Quebec brought some relief for the Kennebec corps prisoners, as Carleton began discussing exchanging them for British soldiers captured by Montgomery the previous year. In a show of good will, Carleton agreed to parole his captives and allow them to return home, provided they signed an oath not to take up arms against the king until such time as they were exchanged.[21] The governor was feeling beneficent since his army was reclaiming Canada despite thousands of American troops sent north to oppose him. Among the reinforcements who arrived in Canada in 1776 was a young captain named James Wilkinson, whose later deeds included allegedly conspiring with Aaron Burr to create a new empire in the American west. Wilkinson is interesting to this narrative because some historians say that he was on the Arnold Expedition when he first befriended Burr.[22] This is incorrect. Wilkinson arrived at St. Johns, Canada, on May 22, 1776, leading a company from Colonel James Reed's 2nd Continental regiment sent from New York City. He met Burr later in the war.

The paroled Arnold Expedition survivors sailed into New York harbor on September 12 aboard British transports. About 350 of the original 1,150 members of the corps were allowed to go ashore at American-held Elizabethtown Point, New Jersey, on September 24. John Joseph Henry recalled the event, saying that all the returning men were filled with emotion. Captain Morgan reportedly leapt from the boat that was rowing him ashore, fell upon the ground with arms outspread, and cried, "Oh my country!"

The survivors of the Arnold Expedition returned home to find that many changes had taken place since their ascent into the Maine wilderness. One of the most noticeable was that the colonists were no longer fighting for a "redress of grievances," but for independence from Great Britain. Another sharp difference was that the seat of the war had shifted from Boston to New York City. Another change, this one more subtle, was the decrease in the number of men volunteering to serve in the Continental Army.

In April 1775, thousands of patriotic Americans flocked to Cambridge to join the rebel cause. The men who volunteered for the Arnold Expedition came from this legion of dedicated, public-spirited citizens who were willing to make personal sacrifices to preserve their liberties for themselves and their children. But a couple of bloody battles, and the realization that the war was not going to end quickly, had sobered the martial spirit of many patriots. Routed and disheartened on every battle front, including Canada, where the rebels had retreated back to Fort Ticonderoga, many Americans were reluctant to enlist, and those serving in the army talked only of returning home. Many of Arnold's veterans, however, wanted to get back into the war. Their eagerness was rooted in the fact that they were all volunteers who had been selected to go on the Quebec expedition from a multitude of eligible applicants. Even after their march began, the faint-hearted and sickly returned to Cambridge with Lieutenant Colonel Enos. Those men who completed the trek to Quebec and managed to make it back alive were relics of the American patriot virtue of self-sacrifice that reigned during the opening months of the war. General Washington desperately needed such men, who were not only devoted patriots, but experienced, disciplined soldiers.

Daniel Morgan was among the first of the Arnold Expedition men to be exchanged. In fact, he was secretly appointed colonel of the new 11th Virginia rifle regiment even before he was released from his parole. His early exchange was based partially on a letter that General Arnold wrote the commander-in-chief on November 6, 1776, from Fort Ticonderoga, in which he recommended Morgan as an officer distinguished for his "Bravery and Attachment to the Public Cause." Morgan went on to become an outstanding general who made significant contributions to the winning of American independence, including his command of the American forces at the 1780 Battle of Cowpens, which historians cite as the best-fought battle of the Revolutionary War. Many other officers from the Kennebec corps returned to the war, including Christopher Greene, Henry Dearborn, Christian Febiger, Eleazer Oswald, Samuel Ward, Return Jonathan Meigs, and Timothy Bigelow. Their contributions, plus those of the enlisted men who returned to the army, are unfortunately beyond the scope of this book.

Perhaps the most important result of the Arnold Expedition, and the 1775 Canadian campaign at large, was that it validated Washington's demand for a professional army. From the start of the war, he had been patiently lobbying Congress for what he called a "respectable army" of long-term professional soldiers. More than any other event, the death of General Montgomery probably shocked the members of Congress into understanding the shortcomings of their high-principled, but impractical, policy of a citizen army composed of one-year enlistees.

Writing to Washington on the subject from Philadelphia on September 24, John Hancock said, "The untimely Death of General Montgomery alone, independent of other Arguments, is a striking Proof of the Danger and Impropriety of sending Troops into the Field, under any Restriction as to the Time of their Service."[23]

As a result of Montgomery's hasty attack on Quebec and other events, the Continental Army began recruiting men in 1777 who agreed to serve for three years or for the duration of the war. This policy was instrumental in creating trained, experienced regiments of "Continentals," who constituted the heart of the American army for the balance of the war.

* * *

Although the Arnold Expedition failed to achieve its mission, and its commander, Benedict Arnold, later betrayed his country, the campaign proved to be a vital training ground for future American combat officers. The survivors of the expedition returned home with valuable martial experience and went on to make vital contributions to winning American independence and building the new nation.

Despite its failure, the Arnold Expedition was a spectacular effort by brave men whose perseverance and dedication represents a proud episode in American military history. Although Benedict Arnold's horrendous treason remains the defining act of his life, his resourcefulness and valor as an American officer enabled him to motivate his troops to perform incredible feats of bravery and endurance on behalf of the rebel cause. We all may learn from their courage, determination, and patriotism.

A modern view of the City of Quebec from Point Levi. *Amy Lawrence*

Restoration of Fort Western. *Amy Lawrence*

Appendix

Following the Trail of the Arnold Expedition

hat can you see if you travel to Maine to trace the route of the Arnold Expedition? The lower Kennebec River is beautiful and worth following north to Pittston, where Reuben Colburn's preserved house is one of the few places to view some artifacts from the campaign and learn about the expedition. The house, however, is only open on weekends. Farther up the Kennebec is Augusta, the state capital. A reconstructed Fort Western sits on its original site downtown and is worth visiting, although the focus of its interpretation is the fort's role in the French and Indian War. Farther up the Kennebec is the site of Fort Halifax, now located in the town of Winslow. A reproduction of a blockhouse and a faded sign mark the site.

Though the small towns along the route farther upriver likely take pride in their association with the expedition—I am sure that the schoolchildren in Skowhegan Falls and Norridgewock are aware of their region's association with the Arnold Expedition—I have not found anything in these towns to mark the passage of more than 1,000 men on what was one of the greatest events in American military history. There is one stretch of beautiful road that parallels the Kennebec River south of Skowhegan where you can look out and see spectacular views of the river. Beyond Skowhegan Falls (there is a hydroelectric dam just above the falls) you are rewarded with lovely scenery as the land becomes more rugged and mountains appear in the distance.

Continue north along the Kennebec to the modern town of Bingham, where manmade Lake Wyman, created by damming the river, begins. About five miles north of where the lake starts was the entrance to the Great Carry (now underwater). There is a rough road from the western shoreline of the modern lake to the three ponds that were landmarks on the Great Carry. The land along the shoreline of the three ponds is mostly privately owned; access to the area is difficult and many private roads are gated and locked.

The Appalachian Trail traverses between Middle and West Carry Pond and provides some good hiking and views. There is little to see for a distance beyond the ponds, as the Dead River has been dammed to create Flagstaff Lake. The exception is the view of the 14-mile-long Bigelow Mountain Range, which probably looks exactly the same as when the members of the Arnold Expedition first saw them over 200 years ago. The range, which runs east to west, consists of five peaks (Little Bigelow Mountain, Myron Avery Peak, West Peak, The Horns, and Cranberry Peak) that collectively are called the Bigelow Mountains or simply the "Bigelows."

A good place to begin hikes into the Bigelows is the modern town of Stratton. The Appalachian Trail traverses the summit of all five peaks, the tallest of which is West Peak at 4,150 feet above sea level. My friend Duluth (Dude) Wing lives in the region. He told me the Abenakis Indians called the Bigelows *Tiaouiadicht*. "We don't know what the word meant," Dude explained, "but it surely was something majestic. Later, farmers in the Dead River valley used the Bigelows to forecast the weather: if her peaks were capped in fog, you did not mow the hay, and if they were blue, it surely would storm."

Beyond the Bigelow range, the next Arnold Expedition sites are near the village of Eustis, located close to the northern end of man-made Flagstaff Lake. Here the Dead River returns to its natural beauty and can be followed by road to the Chain of Ponds. This is magnificent country, and the spectacular scenery continues into Canada.

At the border, Lake Magentic is visible in the distance. As you drive toward Lake Magentic you can look back to see the Height of Land. The Arnold River passes through this region, and although much of the swampland from the Canadian border to the southern shore of Lake Magentic has been drained, enough of the old terrain remains to provide a feel for what this land looked like when Arnold and his men crossed it. In Canada, the land along the Chaudière River has changed dramatically since Arnold's time. The forests have all been cut down and replaced with open plains covered with dairy farms. The big treat is Quebec City. The wall surrounding the city is largely intact, and historic plaques mark many of the places connected with Montgomery's 1775 assault, including the site of the fortified house, the Sault au Matelot, and Montgomery's original grave. Numerous historic buildings, museums, and exhibits describe the city's rich heritage, including its role in the American Revolution.

A long history of private land ownership in Maine, the damming of the Kennebec and Dead rivers, a lack of money, and a desire to keep the remnants of the trail unmarked to discourage people from scrounging for artifacts have contributed to the difficulty of marking and preserving the route of the Arnold Expedition. As a result, if you are planning a field trip to retrace Arnold's steps, be sure to pack your imagination.

Notes

Introduction

1. Major General Philip Schuyler to John Hancock, Nov. 22. 1775, in William Bell Clark, ed., *Naval Documents of the American Revolution* 10 vols. to date (Washington, D.C.: U.S. Government Printing Office, 1964-), 2:1,100.

2. Carleton had four regiments in Canada in September 1774. They were the 10th, 52nd, 7th, and 26th. At General Gage's urging, he sent two of them (the 10th and 52nd) in late 1774 to reinforce the British garrison at Boston, leaving him with only two under-strength regiments with which to defend Canada. Carleton believed at the time that he could easily raise additional regiments from among the French Canadians. See George F.G. Stanley, *Canada Invaded 1775-1776* (Toronto: A.M. Hakkert, Ltd, 1973), 10. The full story of Carleton's poor judgment in agreeing to release two of his four regiments to Gage is explained in George Athan Billias, ed., *George Washington's Opponents* (New York: William Marrow and Company, Inc., 1969), 108-110.

3. This population estimate is from the Statistics Canada website. It includes the estimated population of Cape Breton, St. John's Island (now Prince Edward Island), and Newfoundland. It did not include blacks or Indians.

4. Despite the fact that the Indian population east of the Mississippi River had been drastically reduced in the years prior to the American Revolution, these natives still represented a major threat to the rebels. It is estimated that there were still 150,000 Indians living in the area east of the Mississippi in 1775, most of whom sided with the British. While the Indians living in New England had been drastically reduced, mainly by disease, Carleton could still rely on about 2,000 warriors left from the once-formidable Six Nations of the Iroquois living in upper New York. British agents could recruit as many as 12,000 Indian fighters from the tribes living in the Susquehanna and Ohio River Valleys. See Gordon S. Wood, *The American Revolution* (New York: The Modern Library, 2002), 9-10. This book is recommended reading for anyone interested in a general history of the Revolutionary War.

5. An eloquent commentary about North America's network of waterways appeared in the *Federalist Papers* (1787-1788). Using the pen name *Publius*, Federalist No. 2 (authored by John Jay) argued that America "was not composed of detached and distant territories." Jay said: "Providence has in a particular manner blessed it [America] with a variety of soils and productions, and watered it with innumerable streams, for the delight and accommodation of its inhabitants. A succession of navigable waters forms a kind of chain round its borders, as if to bind it together; while the most noble rivers in the world, running at convenient distances, present them with highways for the easy communication of friendly aides, and the mutual transportation and exchange of their various commodities." See Jacob E. Cooke, ed., *The Federalist* (Middletown, Connecticut: Wesleyan University Press, 1961), 9.

6. The distance from Albany to Lake George at the time depended on the method of transportation (water or land route) used. The figure of "65 mile land carriage" was used in a report from Gen. Schuyler to Congress dated Albany, July 11, 1775. See Peter Force, ed., *American Archives* (Fourth Series), 6 vols. (Washington, D.C.: M. St. Clair Clarke and Peter Force, 1843), 2:1, 645-646.

For those readers unfamiliar with this reference source, Peter Force was a successful printer and collector of historical documents. He lobbied Congress in the 1830s to fund a documentary history of the United States, from the time of its earliest exploration up to the ratification of the Constitution. Congress agreed to finance the project, which Force prodigally titled *American Archives: Consisting of A Collection of Authentick Records, State Papers, Debates, and Letters and Other Notices of Publick Affairs, The Whole Forming A Documentary History of The Origins and Progress of The North American Colonies; of the Causes and Accomplishments of The American Revolution; and of The Constitution of Government For the United States, To The Final Ratification Thereof.* Force divided his massive undertaking into six series that would cover different periods of American history. Luckily for Revolutionary War historians, he started his massive project with his Fourth Series, which dealt with events from 1774-1776. Force completed this series consisting of six large volumes, as well as part of the Fifth Series (three volumes), which deals with events that took place in late 1776. Congress lost interest in the project and cut off funding before Force could publish any additional volumes in his projected series. Congress' decision was shortsighted—Force's books proved to be a valuable reference source. Many of the documents available to him were subsequently misplaced, burned, or squirreled away in numerous institutions and private collections. Fortunately, however, anyone working on the early Revolutionary War period has the benefit of Force's outstanding work.

7. Francis Parkman, *Count Frontenac and New France Under Louis XIV* (Boston: Little, Brown and Company, 1896), 310.

8. Benson J. Lossing, *The Pictorial Field-Book of The Revolution* 2 vols. (New York: Harper & Brothers, 1860), 1:605.

9. James Kirby Martin, *Benedict Arnold Revolutionary Hero* (New York: New York University Press, 1997), 423.

10. Anyone sympathetic to Arnold does not understand the dismal circumstances of the infant United States at the time of his treason. Arnold planned to carry out his scheme in 1780 when the new nation was bankrupt and its armies had suffered two recent staggering military defeats in South Carolina: the surrender of Charleston and the Battle of Camden. Referring to these American losses, historian John Ferling called Arnold's scheme to deliver West Point to the British "a treasonous act so monstrous that it may have provoked even more widespread despair than that aroused by the military defeats in the South." See John Ferling, *A Leap in the Dark* (New York: Oxford University Press, 2003), 227. The foundation of the American patriot cause would have assuredly been rocked to its very foundation had Arnold's plan succeeded.

Historians have speculated for more than 200 years on what would have happened to the American patriotic cause had Arnold been successful. In his 1788 history of the American Revolution, William Gordon considered the issue:

> Had the execution of that been completed, the forces under his [Arnold's] command must probably have either laid down their arms or have been cut to pieces. Their loss and the immediate possession of West Point, and all its neighboring dependencies, must have exposed the remainder of Washington's army to the joint exertion of the British forces, by land and water, that nothing but final ruin could have been the result with respect to the Americans. Such a stroke could scarcely have been received. Independent of the loss of artillery and stores, such a destruction of their disciplined force, and many of their best officers must have been fatal.

See William Gordon, *The History of the Rise, Progress and Establishment of the Independence of the United States of America* 4 vols. (London: 1788), 3: 485-486.

11. Lossing, *The Pictorial Field-Book of the Revolution*, 1: 605.

12. Mrs. Mercy Otis Warren, *History of the Rise, Progress and Termination of the American Revolution* 3 vols. (Boston: Printed by Manning and Loring for E. Larkin, 1805), 1:260.

13. Eric Froner, ed., *Thomas Paine Collected Writings* (New York: Literary Classics of the United States, Inc., 1995), 251-252.

14. David Ramsay, *The History of the American Revolution*, 2 vols. (Trenton, New Jersey: James J. Wilson, 1811), 2: 252. This is a reprint of the 1789 edition.

15. Hannah Adams, *A Summary History of New England, From the First Settlement at Plymouth, to the Acceptance of the Federal Constitution. Comprehending a General Sketch of the American War* (Dedham, Massachusetts: H. Mann and J.H. Adams, 1799), 437-438.

Although Mrs. Mercy Otis Warren is frequently credited with being the first American woman to publish a non-fiction book, that distinction belongs to Ms. Adams, who published a one-volume history of New England six years prior to the release of Ms. Warren's three-volume history of the American Revolution.

Another contemporary historian who used Arnold's need for money to explain his treason is William Gordon, who wrote in 1788, "General Arnold, who had the command of that post [West Point], was brave but mercenary, fond of parade and extremely desirous of acquiring money to defray the expenses of it. When he entered Philadelphia after the evacuation [the British army quit the city in June 1778], he made Governor Penn's, the best house in it, his head quarters. This he furnished in a very costly manner, and lived in a style beyond his income. He continued his extravagant course of living; was unsuccessful in trade and privateering; [outfitting warships to capture enemy merchant ships] his funds were exhausted, and his creditors importunate, while his lust for high life was not in the least assuaged. . . . Disgusted at the treatment he had met with, embarrassed in his circumstances, and having a growing expensive family, he turned his thoughts towards bettering his fortune by new means." See Gordon, *The History of the Rise, Progress . . . of the United States*, 3: 481.

Mason Locke Weems (1759-1825), in his popular *The Life of George Washington*, also explained Arnold's treason as a money issue: "I allude to the affair of Arnold's treason. That which makes rogues of thousands, I mean Extravagance, was the ruin of this great soldier. Though extremely brave, he was of that vulgar sort, who having no taste for the pleasures of the mind, think of nothing but high living, dress, and show. To rent large houses in Philadelphia— to entertain French Ambassadors—to give balls and concerts, and grand dinners and suppers, required more money than he could honestly command. And, alas! such is the stuff whereof spendthrifts are made, that to fatten his Prodigality Arnold consented to starve his Honesty." See Mason Locke Weems, *The Life of George Washington* (Philadelphia: Matthew Carey, 1809), 102. Weems's fictionalized biography of Washington first appeared in 1800 and went through 25 editions. It was one of the most popular books in eighteenth century America.

Charles Stedman's 1794 *History of the Revolution* also explains Arnold's treason as a way to get money. See Charles Stedman, *The History of the Origin,*

Progress, and Termination of the American War 2 vols. (London: 1794), 2: 247-248.

Chapter One

1. John Codman, 2nd, *Arnold's Expedition to Quebec* (New York: The Macmillan Company, 1901), 17.

2. Lossing, *Pictorial Field-Book*, I: 605.

3. Charles Coleman Sellers, *Benedict Arnold The Proud Warrior* (New York: Minton, Balch & Company, 1930), 15.

4. *Ibid.*, 9.

5. Arnold's first-born son, Benedict, died on the island of Jamaica at age 27; Richard died in 1847 and Henry died on December 8, 1826.

6. This house was included in Arnold's claim to the British government for compensation of his losses when he joined the British side: "A Large and handsome new House with Store House, Coach House, Stables, Wharfs, large and fine fruit Garden containing between 2 & 3 acres in New Haven, Colony of Connecticut." See J.G. Taylor, *Some New Light on the Later Life and Last Resting Place of Benedict Arnold and of His Wife Margaret Shippen* (London: George White, 1931), 54.

7. John Greenwood, *A Young Patriot in the American Revolution, 1775-1783* (Westvaco, 1981), 41.

8. The 1st Company Governor's Foot Guard was established in Hartford (the capital of Connecticut) in 1771 for the purpose of providing an escort for Connecticut's governor and assembly. The company was known as the Governor's Guard until 1775 when the second company formed in New Haven, causing the Hartford unit to be renamed the 1st Company Governor's Guard. An additional change became necessary in 1778 when a mounted detachment organized as the Horse Guard. The original company, composed of infantrymen, became the 1st Company Governor's Foot Guard. Both the Hartford and New Haven companies exist today as honorary military organizations.

9. Force, ed., *American Archives* (Fourth Series): 2:383-384.

10. The story of Arnold's departure from New Haven appears in E.E. Atwater, *History of the City of New Haven* (New York: 1887), 42, 650.

11. *Extract of a Letter From A Gentleman in Pittsfield to an Officer at Cambridge, Dated May 4, 1775* in Force, ed., *American Archives* (Fourth Series) 2: 507. According to this source, the Connecticut plan was organized "*last Saturday by the Governour and Council.*" This corresponds to Saturday, April

29, 1775. See calendar in Mark Boatner, *Encyclopedia of the American Revolution* (New York: David McKay Company, Inc., 1976), 156.

12. Michael A. Bellesiles, *Revolutionary Outlaws, Ethan Allen and the Struggle for Independence on the Early American Frontier* (Charlottesville: University Press of Virginia, 1993), 116.

13. Force, ed., *American Archives* (Fourth Series), 2: 450.

14. *Ibid.,* Fourth Series: 2:751. Arnold's orders were dated May 3, 1775, and signed by Dr. Benjamin Church Jr., who General Washington later discovered to be a British spy. For information about Dr. Church's subversive activities see Ralph E. Weber, ed., *Masked Dispatches: Cryptograms and Cryptology in American History, 1775-1900* (National Security Agency, 1993), 25-40.

15. Force, ed., *American Archives* (Fourth Series): 2:750. The minutes of the May 2, 1775, meeting of the Massachusetts Committee of Safety record its actions concerning its decision to organize a military campaign under Arnold:

> Doctor Warren, Colonel Palmer, and Colonel Gardner were appointed a Sub-Committee to confer with General Ward, relative to the proposal made by Colonel Arnold, of Connecticut, for an attempt upon Ticonderoga. . . . Voted, That the Massachusetts Congress be desired to give an order upon the Treasurer for the immediate payment of one hundred Pounds, in cash; and also order two hundred pounds of Gunpowder, two hundred weight of Lead Bass, and one thousand Flints, and also ten Horses, to be delivered unto Captain Benedict Arnold, for the use of this Colony, upon a certain service approved of by the Council of War. . . . Voted, That Colonel Arnold, appointed to a secret service, be desired to appoint two Field-Officers, Captains, &c., ...

16. Oswald's occupation in pre-war New Haven is confusing. He was trained as a printer, a profession he pursued following the war, but he is frequently described as being a distiller during the time he lived in New Haven. For examples of Oswald depiction as a distiller see Martin, *Benedict Arnold Revolutionary Hero,* 65, and Willard Wallace, *Traitorous Hero, The Life and Fortunes of Benedict Arnold* (New York: Harper & Brothers, 1954), 43. It was common for men to have two professions at the time, and perhaps Oswald was both a printer and distiller in pre-war New Haven.

17. Joseph Towne Wheeler, *The Maryland Press, 1777-1790* (Baltimore: The Maryland Historical Society, 1938), 19. Oswald later became a printer in Baltimore.

18. French, *The First Year of the American Revolution* (Boston and New York: Houghton Mifflin Company, 1934), 148.

19. Allen French, *The Taking of Ticonderoga in 1775: the British Story* (Cambridge: Harvard University Press, 1928), 79-80. In his book, French presents the various sources regarding the number of men who assembled at Shoreham for the attack on Fort Ticonderoga. The number varies from a low of 150 (according to Benedict Arnold's count) to a high of 270 (as stated in the *History of Shoreham* and the *Gazetteer of Vermont*).

20. Report of Lieutenant Jocelyn Feltham in French, *The Taking of Ticonderoga in 1775*, 45.

21. Force, ed., *American Archives* (Fourth Series): 2:556.

22. *Ibid.*, 558-559.

23. *Ibid.*, 557.

24. Sheldon Cohen, ed., *Canada Preserved, The Journal of Captain Thomas Ainslie* (Canada: The Copp Clark Publishing Company, 1968), 18. Ainslie said that Arnold robbed the mail at St. Johns.

25. Benedict Arnold to the Massachusetts Committee of Safety dated Crown Point, May 29, 1775, in Force, ed., *American Archives* (Fourth Series): 2: 735.

26. *Ibid.*, 1087.

27. *Ibid.*, 1087. This incident appeared in an anonymously written defense of Arnold's activities in the Lake Champlain region. Calling himself *Veritas* (Latin for truth), the author likely was Arnold.

28. For Congress' use of the phrase "to take into consideration the state of America," see Worthington C. Ford, et. al., eds., *Journals of the Continental Congress* 1774-1789 34 vols. (Washington, D.C.: Government Printing Office, 1904-1934), 2: 75.

29. *Ibid.*, 2:73-4.

30. For a description of the election of Washington as commander-in-chief of the Continental Army see Douglas Southall Freeman, *George Washington—A Biography* 7 vols. (New York: Charles Scribner's Sons, 1951-57), 3: 434-437.

31. Ford, et al., eds., *Journals of the Continental Congress*, 2: 92.

32. Allen mentioned Brown in his May 11, 1775, report to the Massachusetts Congress as "John Brown, Esq., Attorney at Law, who was also an able counsellor, and was personally in the attack." See Force, ed., *American Archives* (Fourth Series): 2:556.

33. *Ibid.*, 1,088.

34. *Ibid.*, 1,646-1,647.

35. An August 20, 1775, letter from Silas Deane to Philip Schuyler included the comment, "You once wrote to Me in his [Arnold] favor for the Office of

Adjutt. [adjutant] Genl. in Your Department. If the post is not filled wish You to remember him as I think he has deserved much & received little. . . ." See Paul H. Smith, ed., *Letters of Delegates to Congress 1774-1789* 26 vols. (Washington, D.C.: United States Government Printing Office, 1976-2000), 1: 704.

36. Wallace, *Traitorous Hero*, 55.

37. Robert R. Livingston (1746-1813) was one of the political leaders of the American Revolution. He is frequently identified by historians and genealogists as Chancellor Livingston to avoid confusion with his father, whose name was Robert R. Livingston Jr. (1688-1775), and grandfather Robert R. Livingston (1654-1728). Chancellor Livingston's career included serving as a New York delegate to the Continental Congress, during which time he was appointed to the committee responsible for drafting the Declaration of Independence. He subsequently served as the first United States minister of foreign affairs (today's secretary of state) and chancellor (the presiding judge) of the state of New York. It was in this office that Livingston had the honor of giving the oath of office to George Washington as first president of the United States. The chancellor concluded his public career as American minister to France (1801-1804) during Thomas Jefferson's first presidential administration. During his tenure in France, Livingston negotiated the Louisiana Purchase and entered into a partnership with Robert Fulton, an American painter living in Paris at the time, who shared the chancellor's fascination with steam navigation. Although officially named the *North River*, Fulton's first steamboat is best known as the *Clermont,* which was the name of Chancellor Livingston's ancestral home on the Hudson River.

38. Smith, ed*., Letters of Delegates to Congress,* 1: 15. Arnold's name is mentioned only once in a long letter, dated August 31-September 5, 1774, that Deane wrote to his wife. The pertinent text reads: "I am well provided for at a Widow Lady's one Mrs. House [sic.]. Mr. [Christopher] Gadsden, & Son from Charlestown S. Carolina, S. Webb [Samuel B. Webb, Deane's stepson who later served as an aide-de-camp to General Washington and commanded a regiment in the Revolution], young Mr. Dyer [the son of Colonel Eliphalet Dyer, a Connecticut delegate to Congress], Mr. [Benedict] Arnold & self are the Lodgers. . . ."

Chapter Two

1. Codman, *Arnold's Expedition to Quebec*, 23.

2. Worthington Chauncey Ford, et. al., eds., *Journals of the Continental Congress* 34 vols. (Washington, D.C.: Government Printing Office, 1904-37), 2: 95.

3. Although Schuyler's separate command was officially called the New York Department, it was more commonly referred to as the Northern Department. See Robert K. Wright Jr., *The Continental Army* (Washington, D.C.: Center of Military History, United States Army, 1989), 41. There seems to be confusion regarding Schuyler's military career. He was not a British officer during The French and Indian War, and he was not appointed to his post as commander of the Northern Department by Washington. See, for example, Thomas A. Desjardin's *Through a Howling Wilderness* (New York, St. Martin's Press, 2006), 11.

The term Grand Army or main army was used during the Revolutionary War to identify all the troops under Washington's immediate command, be they Continental regiments, state troops, or militia. Congress used the term Grand Army to identify the main army as early as June 16, 1775, when it resolved, "That there be one quarter master general for the grand army, and a deputy, under him, for the separate army." See Ford, et. al., eds., *Journals of the Continental Congress*, 2: 94.

4. Don R. Gerlach, *Proud Patriot, Philip Schuyler and the War of Independence 1775-1783* (Syracuse, New York: Syracuse University Press, 1987), 18.

5. W.W. Abbot et. al., eds., *Papers of Washington, Revolutionary War Series*, 1:188.

6. Justin H. Smith, *Our Struggle For the Fourteenth Colony, Canada and the American Revolution* 2 vols. (New York: G.P. Putnam's Sons, 1907), 1:497, and Francis Parkman, *A Half-Century of Conflict* 2 vols. (Boston: Little, Brown, and Company, 1892), 1: 3-4.

7. Smith, *Our Struggle For the Fourteenth Colony*, 1:497, and Parkman, *A Half-Century of Conflict*, 1:3.

8. Justin H. Smith, *Arnold's March From Cambridge to Quebec* (New York: G.P. Putnam's Sons, 1903), 20. Smith's book is only a partial history of the Arnold Expedition. It ends with the arrival of the detachment to the south shore of the St. Lawrence River.

9. Captain John Montresor (1736-1799) was a fascinating figure in American history. He was born in Gibraltar, the son of James Montresor, who was the chief engineer at that British outpost.

10. Montresor's Journal in Kenneth Roberts, ed., *March to Quebec, Journals of the Members of Arnold's Expedition including the Lost Journal of John Pierce* (Garden City, New York: Doubleday & Company, Inc., 1940), 21.

11. G.D. Scull, ed., "Journals of Capt. John Montresor 1757-1778," in the *Collections of the New York Historical Society for the Year 1881* (New York: The New York Historical Society, 1882), 119.

12. *Ibid.*, 125.

13. For information about the history of shipbuilding in Maine see William Hutchinson Rowe, *The Maritime History of Maine* (Gardiner, Maine: The Harpswell Press, 1989).

14. Francis Parkman, *France and England in North America* (New York: Literary Classics of the United States, Inc., 1983), 347.

15. See *The Committee of both Houses appointed to confer with the Indian Chief of the Tribe of St. Francois, in Canada, now in this Town* [Cambridge]. . ., August 17, 1775, in Force, ed., *American Archives* (Fourth Series): 3: 339.

16. W.W. Abbot et al., eds., *Papers of Washington, Revolutionary War Series*, 1: 306-7, n. 1. Colburn is referred to in a letter Washington's military secretary (Joseph Reed) wrote to James Otis Sr., president of the Massachusetts council: "The Bearer is accompanied by an Indian Chief of the Tribe of St. Frances in Canada who has come down upon a friendly Errand. . . . The Person at whose Instance His Visit is made [Colburn] can give a more Circumstantial Account of him and his Business than the Limits of a Letter will admit."

17. Smith, *Arnold's March From Cambridge to Quebec*, 296. The evidence that Colburn made three round-trips from Gardinerston to Cambridge is a bill from him that reads, "To My Self Going on Express from Cannibeck [the Kennebec River region of Maine] to Cambridge 3 times. . . ."

18. Parkman, *A Half-Century of Conflict*, 1: 32-33.

19. Captain George Smith, *An* [sic] *Universal Military Dictionary* (London: Printed for J. Millan, 1779), 86-7. Although published in 1779, Smith's dictionary was probably stating long-standing practices.

20. W.W. Abbot et al., eds., *Papers of Washington, Revolutionary War Series*, 1: 336-37.

21. *Ibid.*, 1: 206.

22. *Ibid.*, 1: 332.

23. Horatio Gates acknowledged receipt of Arnold's plan on behalf of Washington in a letter dated August 25, 1775. Gates' letter reads as follows:

> To Col. Arnold at Watertown, Sir, I am confident you told me last night that you did not intent to leave Cambridge until the express sent by your friend [Oswald] returned from General Schuyler. Lest I should be mistaken, I am directed by his Excellency, General Washington, to request you to wait the return of that express. I have

laid your plans before the General who will converse with you upon it when you next meet Your answer by the bearer will oblige, sir.

See *Historical Magazine* Vol. 1., No. 12 (December 1857): 372.

24. W.W. Abbot et al., eds., *Papers of Washington, Revolutionary War Series*, 1: 332-333.

25. *Ibid.*, 1: 368.

26. *Ibid.*, 1: 406. The draft of Washington's August 20, 1775, letter to General Schuyler mentioned sending "12, or 1500 Men" on the expedition. Washington changed the number to "1000 or 1200 men." See *Ibid.*, 1:334 footnote. This change is further evidence that the Arnold Expedition left Cambridge with between 1,000 and 1,200 men. Arnold recruited some additional soldiers, guides (river men), and Indians en route, which accounts for the confusion regarding the size of his corps.

27. *Ibid.*, 1: 436.

28. Smith, ed., *Letters of Delegates to Congress*, 1: 685.

29. W.W. Abbot et al., eds., *Papers of Washington, Revolutionary War Series*, 1: 436.

30. Gerlach, *Proud Patriot, Philip Schuyler and the War of Independence*, 37.

31. W.W. Abbot et al., eds., *Papers of Washington, Revolutionary War Series*, 1:409 footnote.

32. *Ibid.*, 2: 95.

33. E. James Ferguson, *The Power of the Purse* (Chapel Hill, North Carolina: The University of North Carolina Press for the Institute of Early American History and Culture, 1961), 8-9.

34. *Ibid.*, 26.

35. W.W. Abbot et al., eds., *Papers of Washington, Revolutionary War Series*, 1:446.

36. *Ibid.*, n. 1. This footnote reads, "On 13 Sept. Washington signed warrants of L 1,000, L752.2 shillings and L 2,590.16 shillings for Arnold."

37. Roberts, ed., *March to Quebec*, 94-5.

38. W.W. Abbot et al., eds., *Papers of Washington, Revolutionary War Series*, 2: 95.

39. Smith, *An Universal Military Dictionary*, 66.

40. Robert E. Wright, letter to author.

41. W.W. Abbot et al., eds., *Papers of Washington, Revolutionary War Series*, 1: 404-5.

42. *Ibid.*, 1: 405 footnote 1. Reed's letter to Tracy is dated September 7, 1775. Here is its significant text:

> *Colo.*[John] Glover has just informed the General that there are 5 Vessells at Beverly & two at Newbury which were fitted out for another Purpose, but will answer their Present equally well—as they are completely equipp'd with Platforms, Wood, Water &c.—It will be a saving both in Time & Expence to make Use of these, You will therefore be pleased in your Transaction of this Matter to consider these seven Vessells as a Part of the Transports, & only extend your Care to the Remainder. . . .

Joseph Reed was a talented Philadelphia lawyer recruited by Washington at the start of the war to serve as his military secretary. As commander-in-chief of the army, Congress authorized Washington to select a personal staff consisting of three aides-de-camp and a military secretary. The military secretary's customary function was to prepare letters and orders for the commander's review and signature.

43. *Ibid.*, 1: 409, contains an accurate and complete text of Colburn's contract. The original contract is in the handwriting of General Horatio Gates, who was the adjutant general (chief administrator) of the Continental Army. Titled "Instructions to Reuben Colburn," the contract contains many important details about the outfitting of the expedition.

44. The term "Indian corn" implied corn that was ground into meal.

45. Smith, *An Universal Military Dictionary*, 66.

46. The fact that Farnsworth and Colburn left Cambridge shortly after receiving their orders from Washington is evidenced by a revealing letter written by Nathaniel Tracy dated "Newbury Port Sept. 6. 1775," only three days after Colburn received his contract to build the 200 boats. Tracy addressed his letter to Joseph Trumbull, who was the commissary general of the Continental Army. It read in part, "Inclosed you have a Bill, of what Articles I have deliver'd to Mr. Reuben Colburn—I procured a Vessell to carry his Goods, & she is now ready to embrace the first fair wind—Colburn and Farmsworth [Farnsworth] set out early yesterday Morning."

Tracy's letter also shows that some provisions for the expedition were purchased in Massachusetts:

> Farmsworth purchased the 160 Bbls Flour at the Eastward. . . . Mr. Colburn forgot to mention before he left head Quarters, that 60 wood Axes, wou'd be necessary to be sent down; if you have not 'em all at Cambridge, I cam procure a few here—pray advise me by

the Bearer, what Quantity of Park &c. will be sent here to go in the
Vessells, that I may know what Ballast to procure.

Manuscript Letter, Joseph Trumbull Papers, Connecticut Historical Society.

47. W.W. Abbot et al., eds., *Papers of Washington, Revolutionary War
Series*, 1:415. The General Orders for September 5, 1775, specified that Arnold
was to be assisted by the adjutant general (the chief administrator of the army—
Horatio Gates at the time) in the selection of the officers and common soldiers
for the expedition. However, I believe that Gates did not participate in the
selection of the men but rather was on hand to record their names, issue any
necessary orders, and otherwise assist Arnold in the organization of his
independent corps.

48. Charles Martyn, *The Life of Artemas Ward* (New York: privately
published, 1921), 169-170. Ward was a popular New England militia officer and
second in command of the Continental Army during this early period of the war.
The pertinent text reads: "On September 2 there called at Ward's headquarters a
man who later passed through glory into perpetual infamy—Benedict Arnold,
then bearing a commission as colonel and about to start on his expedition
through the wilderness to Quebec. He came to Roxbury with a letter from
Washington's headquarters requesting the 'advice and assistance' of Ward and
his brigadiers "in promoting this important service. . . . The men were 'taken off
the roll of duty' on September 8, and on that date and the ninth were encamped in
separate quarters at Cambridge while preparations were completing for their
departure the following week."

49. Henry Childs Merwin, *Aaron Burr* (Boston: Small, Maynard &
Company, 1899), 18.

50. The phrase appears in a May 1776 letter written by a gentleman
volunteer named John Howard. See Holly A. Mayer, *Belonging to the Army:
Camp Followers and Community During the American Revolution* (University
of South Carolina Press, 1996).

51. Wright, *The Continental Army*, 36.

52. *Ibid*.

53. Samuel Spring, a Congregational clergyman, remained with the
Continental Army until the end of 1776. In August 1777 he became pastor of a
church in Newburyport, Massachusetts.

54. Although Arnold's two infantry battalions possessed the correct number
of men and organization of a regiment, they were not referred to as such, because
Washington had no authority from Congress to create any regiments.

55. Smith, ed., *Letters of Delegates to Congress*, 3: 128 footnote 2. Samuel Ward won election to both the First and Second Continental Congress. He died from smallpox in Philadelphia in March 1776.

56. Richard K. Showman et al., eds., *The Papers of General Nathanael Greene* 12 vols. to date (Chapel Hill: The University of North Carolina Press, 1976-), 8: 305 note.

57. Major Meigs' first wife, Joanna Winborn, died in 1773. He had five children from this marriage. In 1774 he married his second wife, Grace Starr, who gave birth to their first child, Elizabeth, while Meigs was on the Arnold Expedition.

58. John A. Garraty and Mark C. Carnes, *American National Biography* 24 vols. (New York: 1999, Oxford University Press), 6: 299-300.

59. Lloyd A. Brown and Howard H. Peckham, *Revolutionary War Journals of Henry Dearborn 1775-1783* (Chicago: The Caxton Club, 1939), 37.

60. Rifled long guns were used at the time all along the American frontier. As an example, in 1775, a newly arrived immigrant from England wrote home from South Carolina with an account of rifles: "I am just returned from the Back parts where I seed eight thousand men in arms [an exaggeration], all with riffled Barrel guns which they can hit the bigness of a Dollar betwixt two and three hundred yards distance...and all their Cry is 'Liberty or Death.'" See Edward J. Cashin, *William Bartram and the American Revolution on the Southern Frontier* (Columbia, South Carolina: University of South Carolina Press, 2000), 211.

61. Smith, ed., *Letters of Delegates*, 1: 497.

62. Ford, et. al., eds., *Journals of the Continental Congress*, 2:89. Congress authorized the raising of riflemen for the Continental service in the following manner:

> Resolved, That six companies of expert riflemen, be immediately raised in Pennsylvania, two in Maryland, and two in Virginia; that each company consist of a captain, three lieutenants, four sergeants, four corporals, a drummer or trumpeter, and sixty-eight privates.
>
> That each company, as soon as compleated, shall march and join the army near Boston, to be there employed as light infantry, under the command of the chief Officer in that army. . . .
>
> That the form of the enlistment be in the following words: "I [insert name] have, this day, voluntarily enlisted myself, as a soldier, in the American Continental Army, for one year, unless sooner discharged: And I do bind myself to conform, in all instances, to such rules and regulations, as are, or shall be, established for the government of the said Army.

Hugh Stephenson (died 1776) from Berkeley County (now West Virginia) and Daniel Morgan (1735-1802) from Frederick County commanded the Virginia rifle companies. Michael Cresap (1742-1775) and Thomas Price (1732-1795) raised the two Maryland companies in Frederick County. The rifle company that Morgan raised in 1775 should not be confused with another outfit raised by Morgan in 1777 known as Morgan's Rifle Corps. The latter was organized on a temporary basis.

63. Don Higginbotham, *Daniel Morgan* (Chapel Hill, North Carolina: The University of North Carolina Press, 1961), 5.

64. James Graham, *The Life of General Daniel Morgan* (New York: Derby & Jackson, 1859), 54.

65. Don Higginbotham, *Daniel Morgan*, 25.

66. George Morison, "Journal of the Expedition to Quebec" in Roberts, ed., *March to Quebec*, 507.

67. W.W. Abbot et al., eds., *Papers of Washington, Revolutionary War Series,* 1: 445-446.

68. Matthew Smith was one of the leaders in the senseless killing of Indians on the Pennsylvania frontier between 1763 and 1765. Calling themselves the Paxton Boys, Smith and his fellow renegades were angry with the Quaker-dominated, pacifist-minded Pennsylvania Assembly that refused to provide troops to defend their frontier settlements against hostile Indians. The Paxton Boys massacred a band of defenseless Indians living near Lancaster before marching to Philadelphia, where they demanded protection for their western settlements.

69. John Jospeh Henry, *An Accurate and Interesting Account of the Hardships and Sufferings of that Band of Heroes, Who Traversed in the Wilderness In the Campaign Against Quebec in 1775* (Lancaster, Pennsylvania: William Greer, 1812), 15. Although considered one of the most important private soldier's narratives from the Revolutionary War, it is of questionable accuracy because Henry dictated it to his daughter, Anne Mary, 40 years later, shortly before his death in 1811. For a biography of Henry and additional information about his narrative, see the "Memoir of John Joseph Henry, by His Grandson," in the 1877 reprint published by Joel Munsell Co., Albany, New York.

70. Silas Deane to Elizabeth Deane, Philadelphia, June 3, 1775, in Smith, ed., *Letters of Delegates*, 1: 437.

71. Henry, *An Accurate and Interesting Account . . . in the Campaign Against Quebec in 1775*, 15.

72. Riflemen generally wore shoes and not boots. Farmers wore heavy boots in colonial America as a practical necessity. Lighter and better quality boots were worn for riding. Everyone else wore shoes.

73. Martin, *Benedict Arnold*, 463-464 footnote 28. The British spy is identified as Benjamin Thompson, a New Hampshire militia major who was a British sympathizer reporting directly to General Gage. For additional information about Major Thompson's spy activities, see Sanborn C. Brown, *Benjamin Thompson, Count Rumford* (Cambridge, Massachusetts: The MIT Press, 1979), 42-46.

74. General Artemas Ward commanded the New England Army of Observation prior to Washington's arrival. Ward and his fellow New England officers, including Israel Putnam from Connecticut, are frequently ignored by historians, many of whom consider them bumbling incompetents. This is an over-simplification of a complicated and difficult situation. Ward and Putnam had their talents. The fact that apparently more than 1,000 coats and work frocks, which took months to make, were available in early September is an example of Ward's enterprise and planning.

75. While the terms axe and hatchet were used interchangeably in America during most of the eighteenth century, there were significant differences between them. An axe is a large tool requiring both hands and used to fell trees and cut wood. A hatchet is a smaller version of the axe adopted for one-handed use. The hatchet, also called a belt axe, was used as a personal weapon and was popular among the Americans early in the war. The Americans adopted the more effective bayonet in lieu of the hatchet as their second weapon (the musket being their primary weapon) as the war progressed. However, riflemen continued to carry hatchets because their fragile rifles could not hold a bayonet. Some special military units such as light infantry used the hatchet as a distinctive personal weapon. Tomahawk was another word used to describe an axe or hatchet.

76. Sheldon S. Cohen, ed., *Canada Preserved, The Journal of Captain Thomas Ainslie* (Canada: The Copp Clark Publishing Company, 1968), 72.

77. No history of the Arnold Expedition would be complete without mentioning the novel *Arundel*. It is a fictional version of the expedition written by Kenneth Roberts and first published in 1930. Arundel was a town in Maine that was home to several of the principal characters in the story. The modern name of Arundel is Kennebunkport, the popular seaside summer resort community. However, the name Arundel was adopted by a town just north of Kennebunkport.

78. Smith, *Arnold's March From Cambridge to Quebec*, 279 footnote 5, and manuscript document, Revolutionary War pension claim of David Hopkins, Continental Maryland Troops, S. 34925.

79. Heitman, *Historical Register of Officers of the Continental Army* (Washington, D.C., The Rare Book Shop Publishing Company, Inc.: 1914), 448.

80. For a list of the home town of Arnold's officers see Force, ed., *American Archives* (Fourth Series): 4:709.

Chapter Three

1. Codman, Arnold's Expedition to Quebec, 39.

2. See instructions to Colonel Benedict Arnold in W.W. Abbot et al., eds., *Papers of Washington, Revolutionary War Series*, 1:458. His instructions also stated: "Whatever King's Stores you shall be so fortunate as to possess. . .are to be secured for the Continental [army] use." Washington was specific on this point because he believed that Quebec held the largest stock of British ammunition in North America. See Chester G. Hearn, *George Washington's Schooners-The First American Navy* (Annapolis, Maryland: Naval Institute Press, 1995), 27.

3. A number of histories of the Arnold Expedition state that the entire corps paraded at Cambridge prior to its departure for Maine. See, for example, James A. Houston, *Logistics of Liberty, American Services of Supply in the Revolutionary War and After* (Newark, Delaware: University of Delaware Press, 1991), 44, which states, "the detachment paraded on the common at Cambridge on 11 September under the supervision of Colonel Arnold and the adjutant general" (General Horatio Gates). Such a large assembly of troops would typically have been included in the General Orders of the army. However, there are no such instructions included in the General Orders for September 9 or 10. The General Orders for September 8 mention an interesting reference to the Arnold Expedition: "The Detachment going under the Command of Col. Arnold, to be forthwith taken off the Roll of duty, and to march this evening to Cambridge Common; where Tents, and every thing necessary, is provided for their reception—The rifle Company at Roxbury, and those from Prospect-hill [two places surrounding Boston], to march early to morrow Morning to join the above detachment." See W.W. Abbot et al., eds., *Papers of Washington, Revolutionary War Series*, 1: 432. This order does not state or imply that Arnold's complete expedition was to be paraded prior to its departure. It is possible that Arnold assembled his army at Cambridge on September 6, after selecting his officers and common soldiers from among the numerous volunteers. If he did parade his troops on the 6th, after selecting the men who would "go upon Command with Col. Arnold of Connecticut," it must have attracted the attention of every British spy and sympathizer in town. *Ibid.*, 1: 415.

4. Isaac Senter, 'The Journal of Dr. Isaac Senter, Physician and Surgeon to the Troops Detached From the American Army Encamped at Cambridge, Mass., on a Secret Expedition Against Quebec," *Bulletin of the Historical Society of Pennsylvania*, Vol. 1, No. 5 (1846): 2. There is an interesting note concerning Senter's journal that appeared in an 1867 book about the Arnold Expedition: "This Journal was carried to Philadelphia, where it was lost sight of for many years and finally came into the hands of Dr. Lewis Roper, of that city, whose perception of its importance induced him to communicate it to the Pennsylvania Historical Society." See Edwin Martin Stone, ed., *The Invasion of Canada in 1775: Including the Journal of Captain Simeon Thayer, Describing the Perils and Sufferings of the Army Under Colonel Benedict Arnold. . .* (Providence, Rhode Island: Knowles, Anthony & Co, 1867), preface v. This accounts for the publication of Senter's journal by the Historical Society of Pennsylvania in 1846. The journal was reprinted by the New York Times/Arno Press in 1969.

5. Apparently Washington obtained the money to pay the men by signing warrants for various sums on September 13, 1775. See W.W. Abbot et al., eds., *Papers of Washington, Revolutionary War Series*, 1: 446 footnote.

6. George Washington to Joseph Reed, November 28, 1775, in *Ibid.*, 2: 449.

7. "Journal of Abner Stocking As Kept by Himself During His Long and Tedious March Through the Wilderness to Quebec, Until His Return to His Native Place" in Roberts, ed., *March to Quebec*, 545. According to Roberts, much of Stocking's journal was copied from others, and although he was in Captain Hanchett's company (part of Meigs' third division), much of his journal is written as if he had been with the riflemen in Morgan's first division. See *Ibid.*, 543.

8. In 1764, part of the town of Newbury broke away and incorporated itself as Newburyport. See John J. Currier, *History of Newburyport, Mass. 1764-1905* (Newburyport, Massachusetts, 1906), 387.

9. Major Return J. Meigs, *Journal of the Expedition Against Quebec, Under Command of Col. Benedict Arnold* (New York: Privately Printed, 1864), 8.

10. Senter, *The Journal of Dr. Isaac Senter*, 11-12.

11. Force, ed., *American Archives* (Fourth Series): 3:1058. The title of Arnold's journal is "A Journal of an intended Tour from Cambridge to Quebeck, via Kennebeck with a detachment of two Regiments of Musketeers and three Companies of Riflers, consisting of about eleven hundred effective men, commanded by Benedict Arnold." The terms regiment and battalion were frequently interchanged at the time. As previously mentioned, Arnold's musketmen were organized into two provisional battalions. Eleazer Oswald wrote the first part of Arnold's journal. The first entry made by Oswald was on

September 15, 1775. He continued to keep Arnold's journal until October 13, 1775.

12. For example, John Knox wrote from Quebec City in March 1760, "Ginger being esteemed a most specific corrective in scorbutic cases, a quantity of that spice is issued out to the troops, for which, as is mentioned in the order, 'they will pay the government price.'" See Brian Connell, ed., *The Siege of Quebec and the Campaigns in North America, 1757-1760* (Edinburgh, U.K., 1976), 240. This is a reprint of the 1969 first edition.

13. "A Journal of an intended Tour Commanded by Benedict Arnold" in Force, ed., *American Archives* (Fourth Series): 3:1058. Oswald signed his name at the end of the journal as "Eleazer Oswald, Sec'y pro tem." The term "pro tem" is a Latin phrase that best translates to "for the time being."

14. Senter, *Journal of Dr. Isaac Senter*, 13; Meigs, *Journal of the Expedition Against Quebec*, 12.

15. Justin Winsor, ed., *Arnold's Expedition Against Quebec 1775-1776, The Diary of Ebenezer Wild* (Cambridge, Massachusetts: John Wilson and Son, 1886), 5. Another reference to the parade appears in William Humphrey's diary for the date, which reads in part, "This day we paraded our men. . . ." See Shipton and Swain, eds., "Humphrey Journal" in *Rhode Islanders Record the Revolution*, 12.

16. Henry, *An Accurate and Interesting Account . . . In the Campaign Against Quebec in 1775*, 16. Henry studied law following his military service and eventually was appointed a judge and president of the second judicial district in Pennsylvania.

17. Gore Vidal, *Burr: A Novel* (New York: Random House; First Vintage International Edition, 2000), 43.

18. "Journal of John Pierce" in Roberts, ed., *March to Quebec*, 698.

19. W.W. Abbot et al., eds., *The Papers of Washington, Revolutionary War Series*, 1: 158.

20. George C. Neumann and Frank J. Kravic, *Collector's Illustrated Encyclopedia of the American Revolution* (Texarkana, Texas: Scurlock Publishing Company, Inc., 1997), 248; George C. Neumann, *Battle Weapons of the American Revolution* (Texarkana, Texas: Scurlock Publishing Company, Inc. 1998).

21. Major General Charles Lee wrote a plan for the organization of a regiment in the Continental Army and sent it to Congressman Silas Deane. Lee's plan was likely prepared after he arrived at Cambridge with recommendations from Washington. His regimental scheme included a standard (flag) for each company in the regiment and "one Regimentary [regimental] or Great Colour, by which the four Standards of the four Companies are to regulate their advances,

their retreats, their Conversions and all their Movements. . . . In the Colour and the standards must be embroider'd the word liberty." See Worthington Chauncey Ford, ed., *Correspondence and Journals of Samuel Blachley Webb* 2 vols. (New York, 1893), 1: 85, and Edward W. Richardson, *Standards and Colors of the American Revolution* (University of Pennsylvania Press, 1982), 75, 90, 95.

22. Nancy Druckman, *American Flags, Designs for a Young Nation* (New York: Harry N. Abrams, Inc., 2003), 12.

23. "Stocking Journal" in Roberts, ed., *March to Quebec*, 546.

24. Marquis de Chastellux, *Travels in North-America, In The Years 1780, 1781, and 1782* 2 vols. (London: Printed for G.G.J. And J. Robinson, 1787), 2: 241, 249.

25. Charles Royster, *A Revolutionary People at War* (Chapel Hill, North Carolina, University of North Carolina Press, 1979), 24; Martin, *Benedict Arnold, Revolutionary Hero*, 119. Martin points out that none of Arnold's officers mention the visit to Whitefield's tomb, and the validity of this story is suspect.

26. "Fobes Narrative" in Roberts, ed., *March to Quebec*, 581.

27. W.W. Abbot et al., eds., *Papers of Washington, Revolutionary War Series*, 1:457.

28. Nathaniel Tracy to Joseph Trumbull dated *Newbury Port, Sept 6. 1775.* Manuscript letter, Joseph Trumbull Papers, Connecticut Historical Society.

29. Bray & Bushnell, eds., *Diary of a Common Soldier in the American Revolution, 1775-1783—An Annotated Edition of the Military Journal of Jeremiah Greenman* (DeKalb, Illinois: Northern Illinois University Press, 1978), 13. Greenman's diary is difficult to read because of its poor spelling and grammar. The subject entry reads, "T [Tuesday, September] 19. Early this morn. waid anchor with the wind at: SE[.] A [fresh?] gale[,] our Colours fliing [flying] Drums beating[,] fifes a plaing [playing.] the hils [hills] and warfs a Cover [with people?] bidding their friends fair well." Greenman hailed from Rhode Island and served as a private in Captain Samuel Ward's company.

30. On September 8, 1775, while the British were working to destroy the Arnold Expedition, General Washington was still organizing it per his General Orders for that date, which read in part: "The Detachment going under the Command of Col. Arnold to be forthwith taken off the Roll of duty, and to march this evening to Cambridge Common; where Tents, and every thing necessary, is provided for their reception. . . . Such Officers & men as are taken from Genl Green's brigade, for the above detachment, are to attend the Muster of their respective regiments to morrow morning at seven 'Oclock, upon Prospect hill, when the Muster is finished, they are forthwith to rejoin the Detachment at

Cambridge." See W.W. Abbot et al., eds., *Papers of Washington, Revolutionary War Series*, 1:432.

31. Clark, ed., *Naval Documents of the American Revolution*, 2: 47. In 1775 Nova Scotia included the modern Canadian province of New Brunswick. The French called this area Acadia. The British government established the new colony of New Brunswick as a refuge for loyalists at the end of the American Revolution.

32. Weber, ed., *Masked Dispatches*, 25-40.

33. Brown, *Benjamin Thompson, Count Rumford*, 41-46. Using lemon juice in place of ink is the easiest way to write invisibly. The secret writing becomes visible when the piece of paper is held up to a light source (candle) or bright daylight. However, writing in lemon juice is also easy to detect. Any good spy in the Revolutionary War would have used more complex liquids, and a 1761 military text book provides the formula for such an ink:

> Secret Correspondence is carried on either by Cyphers, or certain Compositions used in Place of Ink. One of the best of these compositions is made of distilled Vinegar, in which is boiled Silver Litharge,[lead monoxide also called massicot] about an Ounce of Litharge to an English Pint of Vinegar. When settled, decant off the Vinegar and the Grounds, and it is clear as Rock Water. This may be made Use of to write between the Lines of a Letter on any different Subject, on Paper which serves to wrap up any thing, on the blank Leaves which are commonly at the Beginning or End of Books, or on the Margins of the Leaves of a Book. When dry, it is not possible to perceive the least Impression on the Characters traced with this Liquor. In order to make them appear, you must make use of Water, in which has been dissolved quick Lime mixed with Orpiment [a mineral also called yellow arsenic sulfide or king's yellow]. This Water, when decanted, is as clear as the other. They Way to use it, is to rub it gently on a Leaf of clean Paper which you apply to what has been wrote with the first Composition. This second Composition is so penetrating, that when applied to the Writing, if you fix several Leaves of Paper above it, the Writing will immediately distinctly appear through the Whole.

See *Essay on the Art of War In Which The General Principles of All the Operations of War in the Field Are Fully Explained* (London: Printed for A. Millar, 1761), 207-208.

34. Scull, ed., "Journals of Capt. John Montresor," 135.

35. Clark, ed., *Naval Documents of the American Revolution*, 2: 220. In a September 20, 1775, intelligence report to London, General Gage reported that

the Arnold Expedition was marching to Quebec but was more concerned about defending the Royal Naval base at Halifax, Nova Scotia, which he believed might still be their objective:

> A body of about 1200 Men was detached some Days ago from the Rebel Army as we learn towards Canada, by way of the Chaudiere. They marched to Newbury where they embarked in Sloops and Schooners and as they gave out [told] were to proceed up the Kennebec as high as Fort Halifax. It is impossible without a Defection of the Canadians that they can succeed in any attempt against that Province; and Admiral Graves assures me, that there is a Frigate with two armed Schooners besides some armed Transports in the Bay of Fundy, and the Somerset of Sixty Guns at Halifax, should they attempt Nova-Scotia.

See *Ibid.*, 2: 161.

36. *Ibid.*, 2: 487.

37. Force, ed., *American Archives* (Fourth Series): 3:1680.

38. Clark, ed., *Naval Documents of the American Revolution*, 2: 417. Despite the opinion of his officers, Graves could have attempted to reinforce Quebec because ships were known to have docked safety there as late as the end of November. See Robert McConnell Hatch, *Thrust For Canada, The American Attempt on Quebec in 1775-1776* (Boston: Houghton Mifflin Company, 1979), 61; Smith, *Our Struggle For the Fourteenth Colony*, 2:15.

39. For a detailed list of Grave's fleet see Clark, ed., *Naval Documents of the American Revolution*, 2: 373- 374.

40. Captain W.M. James, R.N., *The British Navy in Adversity, A Study of the War of American Independence* (London: Longmans, Green and Co., Ltd, 1926), 27. For a biography of Graves see Richard L. Blanco, ed., *The American Revolution 1775-1783, An Encyclopedia*, 2 vols. (New York: Garland Publishing, Inc., 1993), 1: 675-77.

There are two encyclopedia sources for the American Revolution. Besides the above-mentioned reference work there is Mark M. Boatner III, *Encyclopedia of the American Revolution* (New York: David McKay Company, Inc., 1974). Boatner's work, first published in 1966, is considered by many Revolutionary War enthusiasts to be a primer on the subject. Apparently working alone, Boatner created a seemly impressive reference work on the Revolutionary War. However, his encyclopedia is flawed, and Blanco's later two-volume series (written by a team of historians) is more reliable. A pertinent example in Boatner's *Encyclopedia* is his information concerning the early military careers of General James Wilkinson (commander-in-chief of the U.S. Army during

Jefferson's administration and believed to be a spy for the Spanish government): "9 Sept. '75- March '76, he and Aaron Burr took part in Arnold's March to Quebec (An interesting collection of scoundrels, but their performance in this expedition was creditable). Wilkinson remained with Arnold until Dec. '76." This is incorrect. Wilkinson was not on the 1775 Arnold Expedition and did not even arrive in Canada until 1776.

41. James, *The British Navy in Adversity*, 28.

42. *Ibid.*, 32.

43. Brown and Peckham, eds., *Revolutionary War Journals of Henry Dearborn*, 38.

44. Meigs, *Journal of the Expedition Against Quebec*, 8.

45. Senter, *Journal of Dr. Isaac Senter*, 6.

46. Meigs, *Journal of the Expedition Against Quebec*, 9-10.

47. W.W. Abbot et al., eds., *Papers of Washington, Revolutionary War Series*, 1: 21-22.

48. *Ibid.*, 1: 91.

49. *Ibid.*, 2: 27-28. The delegates to Congress had some informal news of the existence of the Arnold Expedition prior to Washington's September 21, 1775, letter on the subject. Delegate Richard Smith, for example, wrote in his diary on September 20: "An Expedition is on Foot against the Kings Forces in Canada via Kennebec under Col. Arnold from Washingtons Camp at Cambridge." See Smith, ed., *Letters of Delegates to Congress*, 2: 38. On the same date (September 20) delegate Thomas Lynch wrote General Schuyler: "Colo. Arnold is on his Way to Canada by way the Genl [Washington] mentioned to you and will I hope make a powerful diversion in Your Favour." See *Ibid.*, 2: 36.

50. Dale Potter Clark, "How Our Old Homes Began" *Readfield* [Maine] *Historical Society Newsletter* (Fall/Winter 2000-2001): 3.

51. Meigs, *Journal of the Expedition Against Quebec*, 9.

52. "Pierce Journal" in Roberts, ed., *March to Quebec*, 654.

53. Each company on the Arnold Expedition contained about 90 officers and enlisted men. McCobb's company seemed to be the exception. It had the usual compliment of officers but only 44 common soldiers. See W.W. Abbot et al., eds., *Papers of Washington, Revolutionary War Series*, 2: 338 footnote, and Smith, *Arnold's March From Cambridge to Quebec*, 70, 279 footnote.

54. "Pierce Journal" in Roberts, ed., *March to Quebec*, 654.

55. *Ibid.*, Mr. Lewis Flagg from the Maine Department of Marine Resources explained that 11 species of migratory fish can be found today in the Kennebec River: Atlantic salmon, striped bass, rainbow smelt, sea-run brook trout, sea lamprey, Atlantic sturgeon, shortnose sturgeon, alewife, blueback herring,

American shad, and American ell. Mr. Flagg believes that all of these species, at various life stages, were in the river when the Arnold Expedition passed through in the fall of 1775.

The construction of the dam at Augusta in 1837 dealt a harsh blow to the migratory fish in the Kennebec, especially Atlantic salmon and alewives, since virtually all their spawning habitat lay above the Augusta dam. Some of the other types of fish continued to be plentiful (although there was a significant reduction in numbers overall) because much of their spawning habitat existed in the estuaries below the dam. The increasing industrial pollution of the lower river between 1900 and 1976 further diminished the stocks due to water quality deterioration. Since the removal of the Augusta dam in 1999 and water pollution abatement since 1976, alewives, shad, blueback herring, rainbow smelt, striped bass, Atlantic sturgeon, and shortnose sturgeon have made an impressive recovery and migrate upriver as far as Waterville. E-mail to the author.

56. "A Journal of an intended Tour by Benedict Arnold" in Force, ed., *American Archives* (Fourth Series): 3:1059.

57. Brown and Peckham, eds., *Revolutionary War Journals of Henry Dearborn*, 39.

58. "Pierce Journal," in Roberts, ed., *March to Quebec*, 655.

59. *Ibid.* When Dr. Gardiner sided with the British in the Revolutionary War, the local American patriots changed the name of the region to Pittston. The modern towns of Pittston, Farmingdale, Chelsea, Gardiner, West Gardiner, and Randolph were subsequently created from this large parcel of land.

60 "Pierce Journal" in Roberts, ed., *March to Quebec*, 655.

61. *Ibid.*

62. W.W. Abbot et al., eds., *Papers of Washington, Revolutionary War Series*, 1: 409. Arnold may have been angry with Colburn to find that his fleet of newly constructed bateaux were lying on shore instead of floating in the river. The boats were made from newly cut "green" wood that would shrink as the moisture in the wood evaporated. This natural shrinking process would open the seams between the caulked beams of the bateaux, causing them to leak. It would have been better to leave the freshly made bateaux in the water to retard the shrinking process. Perhaps Colburn was proud of his achievement and wanted to display his finished boats lined up on shore.

63. *Ibid.*, 1:409-410 footnote.

64. Smith, *Arnold's March From Cambridge to Quebec*, 297; *The Debates and Proceedings of the Congress of the United States* (Washington, D.C.: Gales and Seaton, 1856), year 1824, vol. 2: 353. The record for March 15, 1824, reads in part: "The report of the Committee on Claims, unfavorable to the petition of Reuben Colburn, was taken up for consideration. This petition prays

compensation for 220 bateaux, built in 1775, for the use of the troops of Colonel Arnold, then about to march into Canada; and for sundry other services rendered. He states that he delivered over his accounts and vouchers for said disbursement and services. . . ."

65. W.W. Abbot et al., eds., *Papers of Washington, Revolutionary War Series*, 1:409-410.

66. Smith, *Arnold's March From Cambridge to Quebec*, 80-81.

67. W.W. Abbot et al., eds., *Papers of Washington, Revolutionary War Series*, 2: 182. There is no known copy of Goodwin's map. Stephen Moylan, who was one of Washington's aides-de-camp, responded to Goodwin's letter on November 4, 1775, "I am Commanded by his Excellency to acknowledge the receipt of your favor of the 17th Ulto—he is pleased that you had Supplied Colonel Arnold with the plans for his Route to Quebec. If it shou'd hereafter be found necessary to Lay out the road you mention, His Excellency wont be unmindful of your Offers of Service for that purpose." See *Ibid.*, 183, footnote.

68. Senter, *Journal of Dr. Isaac Senter*, 7.

69. This is also the origin of the Italian word biscotti. *Bis* means twice and *cotto* is the word for baked or cooked. Biscotti is made in this manner; it is twice-cooked bread.

70. "Letters written while on an Expedition across the State of Maine with a journal of a tour from the St. Lawrence to the Kennebec suppose to have been made by Col. Montresor," *Collections of the Maine Historical Society*, 1831, reprint (Portland: Bailey & Noyes, 1865), 451.

71. Schuyler to Washington dated Ticonderoga, August 31, 1775, in W.W. Abbot, et al. eds., *Papers of Washington, Revolutionary War Series*, 1: 393-94.

72. *Ibid.*, 436-437.

73. Smith, *Our Struggle For the Fourteenth Colony*, 1: 426. Jacques de Chambly built the first wooden fort on the site in 1665 to fend off Iroquois war parties on their way to raid Montreal. Two additional wooden forts were built on this location before a stone fort was raised in 1709 in response to fears of a British attack against Montreal. The French surrendered the fort to the British in 1760 during the French and Indian War. Fort Chambly was restored by Parks Canada according to a 1750 French plan.

74. W.W. Abbot, et al. eds., *Papers of Washington, Revolutionary War Series*, 1: 393-4.

75. Unsigned manuscript letter, *The Philip J. Schuyler Papers*, New York Public Library, Box 41.

76. "Morison Journal" in Roberts, ed., *March to Quebec*, 511.

77. This calculation is based on a study made by Mr. Duluth E. Wing from Eustis, Maine. All additional references to distances are based on Mr. Wing's

measurements. The confusion over the distance that the Arnold Expedition traveled is because a large man-made lake, Lake Flagstaff, was created when the Dead River was dammed in 1950. This large lake flooded a portion of Arnold's route along the meandering Dead River. Another man-made lake, called Lake Wyman, covers a portion of Arnold's route along the upper Kennebec River. In addition, the expedition made detours and got lost when the upper Dead River and the Chain of Ponds regions were flooded following a severe storm.

Another consideration in trying to determine the exact distance the Arnold Expedition traveled is that they had to make numerous round trips to portage their boats and baggage around obstacles. For example, diarist Caleb Haskell estimated that he traveled 320 miles from Fort Western to Quebec City. See "Haskell's Diary" in Roberts, ed., *March to Quebec*, 499. Historian Christopher Ward states that the expedition traveled 350 miles from Fort Western to Quebec. See Christopher Ward, *The War of the Revolution* 2 vols (New York: The Macmillan Company, 1952), 1:180. Commenting further on the distance actually traveled, Mr. Wing said: "My calculations of the distances that the Arnold Expedition traveled are based on measuring water routes which include the meandering Dead River. However I think the poor soldiers who walked traveled at least 25% further than the men on the bateaux." Letter to the author, March 6, 2004.

Chapter Four

1. Codman, *Arnold's Expedition to Quebec*, 54.

2. There is no known evidence that men with artillery experience were selected to go on the Arnold Expedition. Such men would have been useful if Arnold had succeeded in capturing any British artillery when he got to Canada.

3. W.W. Abbot et al., eds., *Papers of Washington, Revolutionary War Series*, 2: 448.

4. *Ibid.*, 1: 221-222.

5. The origin of the term guerilla warfare is the Spanish word for war, which is *guerra*. The Spanish used hit-and-run tactics, ambushes, and raids into enemy territory to fight the French army that invaded their country during the Napoleonic Wars of the early nineteenth century. Partisan warfare by the colonists in the Revolutionary War was regional, and developed out of necessity when the British defeated regular American armies. As an example, the Americans turned to partisan warfare in the south following the capture of Charleston, South Carolina, in 1780. Partisan techniques were also employed by

necessity in New Jersey in late 1776 when the British invaded that state, forcing Washington's main army to retreat to Pennsylvania.

In a deep attack, a force penetrates far into enemy territory to seize a transportation hub or some other key position. The move is meant to throw the enemy into disarray and disrupt his freedom of action. In modern warfare, airborne (parachute or helicopter) forces are frequently used to hold the objective until stronger ground forces can link up with them. Modern examples of deep attacks include the allies' attempt in World War II to get across the Rhine River by seizing Arnhem and airborne drops behind the beaches in Normandy on D-Day. In the 1775 Canadian campaign, Arnold's column was the deep attack, and Montgomery's army was the link up.

6. J. A. Houlding, *Fit For Service; The Training of the British Army 1715-1795* (Oxford, England: Clarendon Press, 1981), 183.

7. W. W. Abbot et al., eds., *Papers of Washington, Revolutionary War Series*, 2: 346-347. Washington wrote his letter of advice, which included his recommended reading list to the newly appointed Colonel William Woodford. His letter is dated November 10, 1775.

8. Roger Stevenson, Esq., *Military Instructions for Officers Detached in the Field* (R. Aitken, Philadelphia, 1775), 160-161. This textbook was originally published in London in 1770.

9. *Ibid.*, 173.

10. The number of men on this surveying party is from the "Pierce Journal" in Roberts, ed., *March to Quebec*, 656.

11. Stevenson, *Military Instructions for Officers Detached in the Field*, 80-81.

12. There is a great story about how Rufus Putnam became an engineer in the Continental Army. Putnam served as a colonial auxiliary during the French and Indian War, during which he learned some rudiments of engineering from the British engineers. He joined the American army at the start of the Revolutionary War and served as a line officer in the Massachusetts regiment. The Americans were desperate for engineers following the Battle of Bunker Hill (June 17, 1775) and Putnam explained in his memoirs what happened next:

> Some of my acquaintence [sic] mentioned me as having ben [sic] imployed in that line [engineering]in the Late war against Canada. I informed the General that I had never read a word on the Subject of Fortification, that it was true that I had been imployed on Some under British Engineers, but pretended to no knowledge of Laying works. But there was no excuse that would do, undertake I must—Oh! What a Sittuation were we in. No Lines to cover us,

better then a board fence in case the enemy advanced upon us & this we had reason to expect—Necessity therefore was upon me, undertake I must.

See Rowena Buell, *The Memoirs of Rufus Putnam* (Boston and New York: Houghton, Mifflin and Company, 1903), 54-55. In April 1776, Washington and Congress sent Silas Deane to France. Part of his assignment was to recruit skilled engineers, who began arriving in America the following year.

13. "Pierce Journal" in Roberts, ed., *March to Quebec*, 666.

14. *Ibid.*, 665.

15. Washington read about Morgan's demand for an independent command in Arnold's report dated Fort Western, September 25, 1775. The general wrote Morgan a scathing reply on October 4, 1775, which reads in part:

I write you in Consequence of Information I have received that you & the Captains of the Rifle Companies on the Detachment agt [against] Quebeck claim an Exemption from the Command of all the Field Officers e[x]cept Col. Arnold. I understand this Claim is founded upon some Expression [of] mine, but if you understood me in this Way, you are much mistaken in my meaning. My Intention is and ever was that every Officer should Command according to his Rank—to do otherwise would Subvert all military Order & Authority which I am Sure you could not wish or expect—Now the Mistake is rectified I trust you will exert yourself to Support my Intentions, every remembering that by the Same Rule that You claim an independent Command & break in upon military Authority others will do the same by you: And of Consequence the Expedition must terminate in Shame & Disgrace to yourselves and the Reproach and Detriment of your Country.

See W.W. Abbot et al., eds., *Papers of Washington, Revolutionary War Series*, 2: 93. Morgan's conduct probably did not surprise Washington, who found the riflemen unmanageable while they were in Cambridge. As previously noted, Washington used the Quebec expedition as a means of getting rid of some of the riflemen who defied military discipline.

16. Manuscript letter. Aaron Burr to Sally Burr Reeve, September 24, 1775, The Papers of Aaron Burr, The New-York Historical Society, microfilm Correspondence, reel 1.

17. Force, ed., *American Archives* (Fourth Series): 3:339, reports a conference with Chief Swashan at Cambridge on August 17, 1775.

18. Writing to Washington on September 25, 1775, from Fort Western, Arnold said: "The Indians with Higgins set out by Land, and are not yet arrived."

See W.W. Abbot, et al. eds., *Papers of Washington, Revolutionary War Series*, 2: 41. In another apparent reference to these Indians, Arnold wrote to Lieutenant Colonel Enos on September 29, just before he departed from Fort Western: "When the Indians arrive, hurry them on as fast as possible." See "Arnold's Letters" in Roberts, ed., *March to Quebec*, 69.

19. Nineteenth century historian Francis Parkman eloquently described the Abenakis' lifestyle:

> Inland Acadia was all forest, and vast tracts of it are a primeval forest still. Here roamed the Abenakis with their kindred tribes, a race wild as their haunts. In habits there were all much alike. Their villages were on the waters of the Androscoggin, the Saco, the Kennebec, the Penobscot, the St. Croix, and the St. John; here in spring they planted their corn, beams, and pumpkins, and then, leaving them to grow, went down to the sea in their birch canoes. They returned towards the end of summer, gathered their harvest, and went again to the sea, where they lived in abundance on ducks, geese, and other water-fowl. During winter, most of the women, children, and old men remained in the villages; while the hunters ranged the forest in chase of moose, deer, caribou, beavers, and bears.
>
> Their summer stay at the seashore was perhaps the most pleasant, and certainly the most picturesque, part of their lives. Bivouacked by some of the innumerable coves and inlets that indent these coasts, they passed their days in that alternation of indolence and action which is a second nature to the Indian. Here in wet weather, while the torpid water was dimpled with rain-drops, and the upturned canoes lay idle in the pebbles, the listless warrior smoked his pipe under his roof of bark, or launched his slender craft at the dawn of the July day, when shores and islands were painted in shadow against the rosy east, and forests dusky and cool, lay waiting for the sunrise.
>
> The woman gathered raspberries or whortleberries in the open places of the woods, or clams and oysters in the sands and shallows, adding their shells as contribution to the shell-heaps that have accumulated for ages along these shores. The men fished, speared porpoises, or shot seals.

See Parkman, *Count Frontenac and New France*, 338-339.

20. "Maine Indians in the Revolution" in *Sprague's Journal of Maine History*, vol. 6, no. 3 (Jan. 1919): 108; *African American and American Indian*

Patriots of the Revolutionary War (Washington, D.C.: National Society Daughters of the American Revolution), 3.

21. See *Ibid.* for the names and information about the five Penobscot Indians on the expedition. Also see James Phinney Baxter, ed., *Documentary History of the State of Maine* (Portland: Lefavor-Tower Company, 1910), 2nd series, vol. 14: 362-363. This source is a letter written by James Bowdoin, dated Boston, July 30, 1776, which reads in part: "With regard to the Penobscots, They appear well disposed. They said that when Gen. Washington sent his Army to Canada, five of their People went with them & were at ye Siege of Quebec . . . that they had been promised, an allowance should be made to those who went with Col. Arnold; the Support of whose families in their absence had been a great burthen to them: and that they had no recompense for these services."

22. Arnold to Washington, Fort Western, September 25, 1775, Manuscript document, *Benedict Arnold's Letter Book* (1775) *and Journal of Lt. John Montresor*, Maine Historical Society Collection, reference Coll. 1765. (Hereafter cited as Arnold's Letter Book, Maine Historical Society.) Aaron Burr presented this relic of the Arnold Expedition to the Maine Historical Society in 1831 as evidenced by a hand-written note enclosed with the letter book signed W.W. (apparently Williams Willis, the recording secretary of the Maine Historical Society at the time): "Original letters of Col. Benedict Arnold written on his expedition to Quebec in 1775. Together with a Journal of Col. [sic] Montresor containing a narrative of an exploring expedition by him about the year 1759. Procured and presented to the Historical Society by Col. Aaron Burr. 1831."

All of Arnold's possessions, including his real estate, personal letters, and library, were confiscated by the Americans following his treason and sold at auction. I believe his letter book from the Arnold Expedition was among his possessions and that Burr purchased it and gave it to the Maine Historical Society in 1831.

23. *Ibid.*

24. Brown and Peckham, eds., *Revolutionary War Journals of Henry Dearborn*, 40.

25. Meigs, *Journal of an Expedition Against Quebec*, 12.

26. *Ibid.*

27. Arnold to Enos, September 29, 1775, in *Arnold's Letter Book,* Maine Historical Society.

28. "Col. Arnold's Journal of His Expedition to Canada" (hereafter cited as Arnold's Journal) in Roberts, ed., *March to Quebec*, 45.

Historian Willard Sterne Randall gives a fantastic account of Arnold's almost-naked departure from Fort Western:

After the last troops had pulled out of sight, Arnold and his aide, Oswald went down to the river's edge and stepped into a long birchbark canoe crammed with bearskin-covered bundles of supplies and paddled by hired Abenaki guides. Waiting for them in the bow of a second canoe was Aaron Burr in his new ranger's uniform with the rabbit-trimmed hat. Steadying the boat, her long black hair spreading down the back of her hunting shirt, crouched the beautiful princess of the Swan Island Abenakis, Jacatacqua, part Indian, part French, wholly in love with Burr. Between them sat her hound dog. As two Abenakis steadied the lead canoe, Arnold, clad only in a breechclout [also spelled breechcloth], climbed in and knelt down. Quickly, silently, the canoes nosed out into the main channel. . . .

Randall, *Benedict Arnold Patriot and Traitor*, 166. There is an interesting account of the Jacatacqua legend in Desjardin's *Through a Howling Wilderness*, 200-202. He attributes the story to an aged Henry Dearborn, who related the tale to a newspaper reporter.

29. *Arnold's Letter Book*, Maine Historical Society.

30. "Morison Journal" in Roberts, ed., *March to Quebec*, 511.

31. "Montresor Journal," *Ibid.*, 17-18.

32. *Ibid.*, 18-23. According to Montresor's journal, he left Fort Halifax on the evening of July 9, 1761, and reached Lake Megantic in Canada on July 20.

33. Force, ed., *American Archives* (Fourth Series): 3:961-962.

34. "Morison Journal" in Roberts, ed., *March to Quebec*, 518.

35. *Ibid.*, 37.

36. Brown and Peckham, eds., *Revolutionary War Journals of Henry Dearborn*, 42.

37. Nathaniel N. Shipton and David Swain, eds., *Rhode Islanders Record the Revolution: The Journals of William Humphrey and Zuriel Waterman* (Providence: Rhode Island Publications Society, 1984), 14 (hereafter "Humphrey Journal" in *Rhode Islanders Record the Revolution*).

38. Shipton and Swain, eds., "Humphrey Journal" in *Rhode Islanders Record the Revolution*, 14.

39. "Morison Journal" in Roberts, ed., *March to Quebec*, 511-12.

40. Smith, *Arnold's March From Cambridge to Quebec*, 79.

41. James A. Huston, *Logistics of Liberty, American Services of Supply in the Revolutionary War and After* (Newark, Delaware: University of Delaware Press, 1991), 49.

42. James A. Huston, "The Logistics of Arnold's March to Quebec" in *Military Affairs,* vol. 32, issue 3 (Dec., 1968): 123.

43. An article in the *Wall Street Journal* about the resurgence of the lost art of building birch bark canoes in the traditional Indian manner began, "Even for a skilled craftsman, building a bark canoe can involve more than 400 hours of meticulous labor. Harvesting the canoe's outer skin means searching the backwoods for a birch roughly 18 inches in diameter and with a long expense of clear bark. After soaking, the bark is sewn into the rough shape of a canoe and its interior is lined with thin planks made from cedar logs that are hand-split and planed to the proper thickness." The article went on to describe the time-consuming and tedious process of building a birch bark canoe. Indian canoes were impractical for use by the Arnold Expedition just based on the time it took to build them. See "Maine Indian Tribe Dips Back In to Craft of Birch-Bark Canoes," *The Wall Street Journal,* Vol. CCLII, No. 43 (August 29, 2003): 1 (front page), 5.

44. Manuscript letter, Aaron Burr to Timothy Edwards, November 22, 1775, Burr Papers, New York Historical Society, reference CtFaiHi: 2,876.

45. Samuel H. Wandell and Meade Minnigerode, *Aaron Burr, A Biography Compiled from Rare, and in Many Cases Unpublished, Sources* 2 vols. (New York: G.P. Putnam's Sons, 1925), 1: 46.

46. Parkman, *A Half Century of Conflict*, 1: 34.

47. Justin Smith says that Morgan's division left Norridgewock Falls on October 3, 1775. See Smith, *Arnold's March From Cambridge to Quebec*, 347 footnote 20.

48. Brown and Peckham, eds., *Revolutionary War Journals of Henry Dearborn*, 43.

49. "Ephraim Squier Journal" in Roberts, ed., *March to Quebec*, 621.

50. Senter, *Journal of Dr. Isaac Senter*, 10.

51. Shipton and Swain, eds., "Humphrey Journal" in *Rhode Islanders Record the Revolution*, 16.

52. "Stocking Journal" in Roberts, ed., *March to Quebec*, 549.

53. Senter, *Journal of Dr. Isaac Senter*, 10.

54. Common soldiers' tents are described in an eighteenth century military dictionary as follows: "The tents of private men are 6-1/2 feet square and 5 feet high, and hold 5 soldiers each." See Smith, *An Universal Military Dictionary*, 243.

55. Samuel Johnson's Dictionary (1755) defines a waiter as "an attendant; one who attends to the attention of others." The Oxford English Dictionary denotes the word as "A man (rarely a woman) of lower rank employed as a household servant." It also describes the word waiter as "a soldier, etc. employed as a domestic servant to an officer." See James A. H. Murray et al., eds, *Oxford English Dictionary*, 19: 823.

56. "Pierce Journal" in Roberts, ed., *March to Quebec*, 697; "Stocking Journal" in *Ibid.*, 555.

57. Brown and Peckham, eds., *Revolutionary War Journals of Henry Dearborn*, 48.

58. *Ibid.*, 67.

59. "Stocking Journal" in Roberts, ed., *March to Quebec*, 559.

60. It is estimated that about one-fifth of the population of the 13 colonies were slaves at the outbreak of the Revolutionary War. The usual numbers cite a total population in America of 2.5 million, out of whom 500,000 were slaves. Daniel Morgan's home colony of Virginia had the most slaves, estimated at 200,000, or 40 percent of the colony's population. Although slavery is most associated with the South, there were also large numbers of slaves in the northern colonies. The statistics are 14 percent for New York, eight percent for New Jersey, and six percent for Rhode Island. See Wood, *The American Revolution, A History*, 56-57.

61. Shipton and Swain, eds., "Humphrey Journal" in *Rhode Islanders Record the Revolution*, 14.

62. W.W. Abbot et al., eds., *Papers of Washington, Revolutionary War Series*, 2: 220.

Chapter Five

1. Codman, *Arnold's Expedition to Quebec*, 58.

2. For the arrival times of the army at the Great Carry, see Smith, *Arnold's March*, 338, footnote 16. As the lead division, the riflemen were ordered by Arnold to start clearing a trail when they reached the Great Carry. Captain Dearborn states this in his September 25 journal entry written at Fort Western. He wrote that the riflemen left the outpost "with orders to proceed up the River as far as the great Carrying place, there to Clear a Road a Cross the Carrying place, while the other divisions were getting up." See Brown and Peckham, eds., *Revolutionary War Journals of Henry Dearborn*, 40-41. Oswald's journal confirms the rifleman's mission. See "Col. Arnold's Journal" in Roberts, ed., *March to Quebec*, 44b (addendum).

The person in charge of the pioneers on the Arnold Expedition is identified by Dearborn as "Capt. Ayres." He was probably a civilian who was given a temporary commission (brevetted) as a captain and put in charge of soldiers who acted under his command. Meigs mentions that he furnished a number of soldiers from his division to act as pioneers "under command of Mr. Ayres." See Meigs, *Journal of the Expedition Against Quebec*, 16. Dearborn said that Ayres accompanied him as far as Lake Magentic, after which there is nothing further mentioned about him in any of the known journals, orders, or correspondence.

3. "Col Arnold Journal" in Roberts, ed., *March to Quebec*, 49.

4. "Morison Journal" in Roberts, ed., *March to Quebec*, 513.

5. W.W. Abbot et al., eds., *The Papers of George Washington, Revolutionary War Series*, 2: 95-96n. Washington mentioned Captain Gamble's letter in a report he sent to General Schuyler dated October 4, 1775, at Cambridge. Washington's report included an update on the known progress of the Arnold Expedition. The commander-in-chief said he was anxious to keep Schuyler informed of Arnold's situation because "Col. Arnold's Expedition is so connected with your operation."

6. "Morison Journal" in Roberts, ed., *March to Quebec*, 513-514.

7. Private Greenman from Ward's Rhode Island company (part of Meigs' third division) reported finding an Indian sugar-making camp near the Great Carry. Surprisingly, none of the other diarists mention this discovery, suggesting that Ward's company traveled cross-country to reach the entrance to the Great Carry. Greenman's diary entry recording this event reads, "T [Tuesday] 10 [October 10, 1775] this mor found a place ware thare was troves [troughs] made of burch bark and two old wigwams and a Number of small bowls wich we supposed thay cuked [cooked] thair mapel juse in to make Sugar of [.] we brought a number of ye bowls a[way] with us: this day got forw[ard] 12 miles up to the great carring place & got sum of our provision part way a crost." See Bray & Bushnell, eds., *Military Journal of Jeremiah Greenman*, 15.

8. Lieutenant Gray is mentioned arriving at Fort Western on September 25 with a letter from Colonel Reed and copies of a printed proclamation, prepared in Cambridge, with instructions for Arnold to circulate it among the Canadians when he got there. See Oswald's addendum to "Col. Arnold's Journal" in Roberts, ed., *March to Quebec*, 44b. The entry reads, "about three o'clock, P.M., Lieutenant Gray arrived, with a number of manifestoes and a letter from Colonel Reed." Apparently Gray was sent from headquarters with Reed's letter and copies of the proclamation. He returned to Cambridge with Arnold's letter dated September 25 with a postscript added on the 27th. For the date of Arnold's letter see W.W. Abbot et al., eds., *Papers of Washington, Revolutionary War Series*, 2: 42.

9. Schuyler to Washington, September 20, 1775, in *Ibid.*, 2: 17-21. Washington replied to Schuyler's letter on October 4, which implies that Schuyler's letter arrived at headquarters sometime in early October. Schuyler's September 20 letter was probably the latest reliable information available to Reed when he wrote to Arnold on October 4.

10. Force, ed., *American Archives* (Fourth Series): 3:947.

11. "Pierce Journal" in Roberts, ed., *March to Quebec*, 657. The term "running tea" was probably a soldier's slang for alcohol, perhaps mixed with tea. For example, one usage of the word "running" listed in the Oxford English Dictionary is "the flow of liquor during the process of wine-making, brewing, or distillation; the liquor obtained at a specified stage of the process."

12. John A. Garraty and Mark C. Carnes, general editors, *American National Biography* (New York and Oxford: Oxford University Press, 1999), vol. 7: 785.

13. Brown and Peckham, eds., *Revolutionary War Journals of Henry Dearborn*, 45. Dearborn identified the surgeon's mate left at the hospital as "Dr. Erving." However, his correct name was Matthew Irvine.

14. Senter, *Journal of Dr. Isaac Senter*, 11.

15. "Arnold's Letter Book," Maine Historical Society.

16. Arnold wrote Colonel Farnsworth on October 14 from the portage between East Carry and Middle Carry Pond, "We have now about twenty five day's allowance. Hope before that is gone, to be in Quebec." See Roberts, ed., "Arnold's Letters," *March to Quebec*, 73. On the following day, Arnold wrote Lieutenant Colonel Enos, "The three first divisions have twenty five days provision, which will carry them to Chaudiere Pond and back. . . ." See *Ibid.*, 74.

17. Senter, *Journal of Dr. Isaac Senter*, 13.

18. In his journal entry for October 11, Arnold said that his men caught a type of fish called salmon trout. The passage reads, "Over the first Pond [East Carry Pond] . . . here our People caught of prodigious number of fine Salmon Trout, nothing being more common than a man's taking 8 or 10 Doz. in one hours time." See "Col. Arnold's Journal" in Roberts, ed., *March to Quebec*, 49. Arnold was probably referring to brook trout, which abounded in this pond.

19. Meigs, *Journal of the Expedition Against Quebec*, 15.

20. "Col. Arnold's Journal" in Roberts, ed., *March to Quebec*, 50.

21. Brown and Peckham, eds., *Revolutionary War Journals of Henry Dearborn*, 46.

22. Senter, *Journal of Dr. Isaac Senter*, 13.

23. "Arnold's Letter Book," Maine Historical Society.

24. Showman et al., eds., *Papers of General Nathanael Greene*, 1: 147. In a letter dated November 5, 1775, at Prospect Hill, Massachusetts, to Governor Nicholas Cooke of Rhode Island, General Greene said that a letter from Colonel Arnold, dated October 13, had arrived that day. Greene's optimistic comments read:

By letters from Colo Arnold this Day Dated the 13th of last month we expect he is in Possession of Quebec for he expected to be there in Ten Days from the Date of his Letter. We are informed by a Gentleman who left Canada about Six Weeks ago that there was not 20 soldiers in Quebec and that Governor Charlton [Carleton] was at Moreal [Montreal]. The City of Quebeck quite defenseless, there being only two Guns mounted on Carriages in the City. Colo Arnold writes his party are in high spirits and have gone through incredible fatigue with out a murmur. In all probability Canada is wholely reduced by this, as Carltons party are small and the French noblesse Lukewarm, but on the other hand Our Army is large and strongly reinforc'd by Canadians, who are rising in the Cause of Liberty.

Chapter Six

1. Senter, *Journal of Isaac Senter*, 26. The quote is from Senter's diary entry for October 24, 1775, when he was traveling on the Dead River.
2. "Arnold's Letter Book," Maine Historical Society. Arnold's letter is dated October 13, 1775, at "Second Portage from Kennebec to the Dead River."
3. W.W. Abbot et al., eds., *Papers of Washington, Revolutionary War Series*, 2: 155.
4. "Arnold's Letter Book," Maine Historical Society.
5. "Maine Indians in the Revolution," in *Sprague's Journal*, vol. six, no. 3 (Jan. 1919): 108.
6. Hall is listed as a member of Hubbard's company in Roberts, ed., *March to Quebec*, 36.
7. W.W. Abbot et al., eds., *Papers of Washington, Revolutionary War Series*, 2: 17.
8. *Ibid.*, 2: 19.
9. Hal T. Shelton, *General Richard Montgomery and the American Revolution* (New York: New York University Press, 1994), 106.
10. George Washington to Joseph Reed, November 28, 1775, in W.W. Abbot et al., eds., *Papers of Washington, Revolutionary War Series*, 2: 449-50.
11. Fort Chamby lay on the Richelieu River between St. Johns and Montreal. It was commanded by Major Joseph Stopford of the 7th Regiment with 81 officers and men from his own regiment and a handful of artillerists. Montgomery launched his attack on the fort on the night of October 13, when 300 Canadians led by James Livingston and Jeremiah Duggan slipped past St. Johns through the woods and advanced farther north on the Richelieu to the fort. They were accompanied by two bateaux, each carrying a nine-pound piece of artillery. Fifty Americans led by John Brown joined the detachment. Although

Fort Chamby was well supplied with three mortars and 124 barrels of gunpowder, Stopford surrendered his post after two days, and only minor damage from the two small-caliber American field pieces. The rebels, almost out of ammunition, were elated to find that Stopford failed to destroy the gunpowder in the fort prior to surrendering his post.

12. W.W. Abbot et al., eds., *Papers of Washington, Revolutionary War Series*, 2: 120.

13. "Stocking Journal" in Roberts, ed., *March to Quebec*, 590.

14. The Bigelow Mountain range is about seventeen miles long and parallels the course of the Dead River. The easternmost peak in the range is named Little Bigelow Mountain. One of the mountains in the Bigelows, West Peak, is the sixth tallest mountain in Maine, standing 4,150 feet above sea level. By comparison, Mount Katadin, at 5,268 feet, is the tallest mountain in Maine. A twelve-foot cairn was built on top of Mount Katadin to make it 5,280 feet— exactly one mile above sea level.

15. Stocking Journal in Roberts, ed*., March to Quebec*, 551.

16. Brown and Peckham, eds., *Revolutionary War Journals of Henry Dearborn*, 46.

17. Shipton and Swain, eds., "Humphrey Journal" in *Rhode Islanders Record the Revolution*, 18.

18. Arnold to Farnsworth, October 14, 1775, at "Second Carrying-Place," in "Arnold's Letter Book," Maine Historical Society.

19. For Arnold's weakness as an administrator see, for example, Allen MacLean, "Arnold's Strength At Quebec" in *Military Collector & Historian* Vol. XXIX, No. 3 (fall 1977): 139.

20. "Stocking Journal" in Roberts, ed., *March to Quebec*, 552.

21. "Montresor Journal" in *Ibid.*, 20.

22. Henry, *An Accurate and Interesting Account . . . In the Campaign Against Quebec*, 55.

23. The Arnold Expedition followed the Chain of Ponds on a northwesterly route for about 12 miles, as far as Moosehorn Pond (known today as Arnold Pond—see Smith, *Arnold's March From Cambridge to Quebec*, 486, footnote), where they started overland across the mountains. The Chain of Ponds takes a sudden change in direction beyond Moosehorn Pond and continues in a southerly direction for another 10 miles. The farthest or uppermost pond is a small pond near the Canadian border called Little Northwest Pond.

24. Arnold to Enos, October 24, 1775, at "Dead River, 30 miles fron Chaudiere Pond," in "Arnold's Letter Book," Maine Historical Society.

25. "Morison Journal" in Roberts, ed., *March to Quebec*, 517.

26. Ward, *The War of the Revolution*, 1: 373.

27. "Humphrey Journal" in Shipton and Swain, eds., *Rhode Islanders Record the Revolution*, 20.

28. Senter, *Journal of Isaac Senter*, 26-27.

29. Mary C. McAuliffe, "Timothy Bigelow the Patriot of Worcester," Master of Education Thesis, State Teacher's College at Hyannis, 1941, no page number shown. A copy of this thesis is in the library of Bridgewater State College, Massachusetts. Bigelow married Anna Andrews on July 1, 1762. By 1775, when Bigelow left for the Arnold Expedition, they had five children. A sixth child named Clarissa was born in 1781.

30. Shipton and Swain, eds., "Humphrey Journal," in *Rhode Islanders Record the Revolution*, 20-21.

31. Senter, *Journal of Dr. Isaac Senter*, 27.

32. *Ibid.*, 17.

33. *Ibid.*, 16.

34. *Ibid.*, 16-17.

35. Edwin Martin Stone, ed., *The Invasion of Canada in 1775: Including the Journal of Captain Simeon Thayer Describing the Perils and Sufferings of the Army Under Colonel Benedict Arnold, In its March Through the Wilderness to Quebec* (Providence: Knowles, Anthony & Co., 1867), 10-11.

36. Simpton and Swain, eds., "Humphrey Journal" in *Rhode Islanders Record the Revolution*, 20; Smith, *Arnold's March From Cambridge to Quebec*, 389.

37. Stone, ed., "Thayer Journal," 11.

38. Brown and Peckham, eds., *Revolutionary War Journals of Henry Dearborn*, 50.

39. Frank Squier, ed., "Diary of Ephraim Squier," *Magazine of American History*, No. 2, part 2 (1878): 687.

40. *Ibid.*, 688. The General Orders for the army for November 25, 1775, included the following, "The Commissioned, Non Commission'd Officers & Soldiers, lately arrived in Camp from Kenebeck river, are to join their respective Corps." See W.W. Abbot et al., eds., *Papers of Washington, Revolutionary War Series*, 2: 425.

41. Force, ed., *American Archives* (Fourth Series): 3:1709.

42. W.W. Abbot, et al., eds., *Papers of Washington, Revolutionary War Series*, 2: 338.

43. Force, ed., *American Archives* (Fourth Series): 3:1709-1710.

44. "Stocking Journal" in Roberts, ed., *March to Quebec*, 552.

45. Force, ed., *American Archives* (Fourth Series): 3:1710. Washington mentioned Enos' court martial verdict in a December 5, 1775, letter to Arnold. The general said: "You could not be more Surprised than I was, at Enos return

with the Division under his Command [.] I immediately put him under Arrest & had him tried for Qui [quitting] the Detachmt [sic] without your Orders—He is acquitted on the Scor [score] of provision [having no food to continue into Canada]." See W.W. Abbot et al., eds., *Papers of Washington, Revolutionary War Series*, 2: 494.

46. W.W. Abbot et al., eds., *Papers of Washington, Revolutionary War Series*, 2: 399.

47. *Ibid.*, 2: 409.

48. *Ibid.*, 2: 452.

Chapter Seven

1. Codman, *Arnold's Expedition to Quebec*, 104.

2. "Montresor Journal" in Roberts, ed., *March to Quebec*, 22.

3. "Arnold's Journal" in *Ibid.*, 56-7.

4. Nehemiah Getchell was hired as a guide for the expedition at Fort Western, along with his three brothers: John, Dennis, and Jeremiah.

5. "Arnold's Journal" in Roberts, ed., *March to Quebec*, 50.

6. "Pierce Journal" in Roberts, ed., *March to Quebec*, 665.

7. "Monstresor Journal" in *Ibid.*, 21.

8. "Morison Journal" in *Ibid.*, 522. Private Morison wrote that after crossing several lakes (the Chain of Ponds): "to what we denominated the Terrible Carrying Place; a dismal portage indeed . . . intersected with a considerable ridge covered with fallen trees; stones and brush."

9. "Montresor Journal" in *Ibid.*, 22.

10. Arnold to Colonels Green and Enos and the captains in the rear of the detachment, October 27, 1775, at "2-1/2 miles on the Great Carrying-Place," in "Arnold's Letter Book," Maine Historical Society.

11. "Arnold's Journal" in Roberts, ed., *March to Quebec*, 58.

12. Arnold to Washington, October 27, 1775, at Chaudiere Pond, in "Arnold's Letter Book," Maine Historical Society.

13. W.W. Abbot et al., eds., *Papers of Washington, Revolutionary War Series*, 2: 244-45. The complete passage in Arnold's letter reads:

Chaudier Pond 27th Oct. 1775, . . . Our March has been attended with am amazing Deal of Fatigue, which the Officers & Men have borne with Cheerfulness. I have been much deceived in every Account of our route, which is longer, and his been attended with a Thousand Difficulties I never apprehended, but if crowned with Success, and conductive to the Public Good, I shall think it but trifling.

14. "Monstresor Journal" in Roberts, ed., *March to Quebec*, 23.

15. This is the route followed by today's Quebec road 161, the major roadway through the area.

16. "Arnold's Journal" in Roberts, ed., *March to Quebec*, 59.

17. "Morison Journal" in *Ibid.*, 522-523.

18. Smith, *Arnold's March From Cambridge to Quebec*, 213.

19. "Morison Journal" in Roberts, ed., *March to Quebec*, 522.

20. *Ibid.*, 523.

21. Shipton and Swain, eds., "Humphrey Journal," in *Rhode Islanders Record the Revolution*, 22.

22. "Arnold to the Field Officers & captains in the Detachment viz to be sent on, that the whole may see it," October 27, 1775, in "Arnold's Letter Book," Maine Historical Society.

23. "Stocking Journal" in Roberts, ed., *March to Quebec*, 553.

24. McAuliffe, "Timothy Bigelow," Masters Thesis, no page number shown.

25. Meigs, *Journal of the Expedition Against Quebec*, 19.

26. Henry, *An Accurate and Interesting Account . . .In the Campaign Against Quebec*, 63.

27. Brown and Peckham, eds., *Journals of Henry Dearborn*, 51.

28. Andrew A. Melvin, ed., *The Journal of James Melvin Private Soldier in Arnold's Expedition Against Quebec in the Year 1775* (Portland, Maine: Hubbard W. Bryant, 1902), 50.

29. Henry, *An Accurate and Interesting Account . . . In the Campaign Against Quebec*, 65.

30. "Stocking Journal" in Roberts, ed., *March to Quebec*, 554-555.

31. Shipton & Swain, eds., Humphrey Journal *in Rhode Islanders Record the Revolution*, 22.

32. "Stocking Journal" in Roberts, ed., *March to Quebec*, 554.

33. Senter, *Journal of Dr. Isaac Senter*, 21.

34. *Ibid.*

35. "Stocking Journal" in Roberts, ed., *March to Quebec*, 553.

36. Senter, *Journal of Isaac Senter*, 32.

37. "Stocking Journal" in Roberts, ed., *March to Quebec*, 555.

38. Rev. Horace E. Hayden, "A Lost Chapter of Arnold's Expedition to Canada, 1775," in Roberts, ed., *March to Quebec*, 635; Brown and Peckham, eds., *Revolutionary War Journals of Henry Dearborn*, 53.

39. Henry, *An Accurate and Interesting Account . . . In the Campaign Against Quebec*, 70-71.

40. Allen, "Account of Arnold's Expedition," in Maine Historical Society Collections, 514.

41. Senter, *Journal of Dr. Isaac Senter*, 20.

42. *Ibid.*, 22.

43. "Stocking Journal" in Roberts, ed., *March to Quebec*, 556.

44. Bernard Bailyn, *The Ideological Origins of the American Revolution* (Cambridge, Massachusetts, The Belknap Press of Harvard University Press, 1967), ix.

45. Royster, *A Revolutionary People at War*, 6.

46. Smith, ed., *Letters of Delegates to Congress*, 2: 285.

47. W.W. Abbot et al., eds., *The Papers of Washington, Revolutionary War Series*, 2: 326-327.

48. Pierce Journal in Roberts, ed., *March to Quebec*, 688.

Chapter Eight

1. Codman, *Arnold's Expedition to Quebec*, 119.

2. Senter, *Journal of Dr. Isaac Senter*, 22-23.

3. "Morison Journal" in Roberts, ed., *March to Quebec,* 526.

4. Brown and Peckham, eds., *Revolutionary War Journals of Henry Dearborn*, 53.

5. Smith, *Arnold's March From Cambridge to Quebec*, 241.

6. "Morison Journal" in Roberts, *March to Quebec*, 531.

7. Meigs, *Journal of the Expedition Against Quebec*, 20.

8. McClellan is identified in Heitman, *Historical Register of Officers of the Continental Army*, 365. Heitman says he enlisted on June 25, 1775, and died November 3, 1775, on the march to Quebec.

9. Henry, *An Accurate and Interesting Account . . . in the Campaign Against Quebec*, 69.

10. "Stocking Journal" in Roberts, ed., *March to Quebec*, 556.

11. Henry, *An Accurate and Interesting Account . . . in the Campaign Against Quebec*, 72-73.

12. Milton Lomask, *Aaron Burr, The Years From Princeton to Vice President 1756-1805* (New York: Farrar-Straus-Giroux, 1979), 22.

13. Ward, *The War of the Revolution*, 1: 166.

14. Martin, *Benedict Arnold Revolutionary Hero*, 139. There are two other creditable estimates of the number of men who died from various causes during the march from Fort Western to Quebec. Both are similar to Martin's calculation. They are historian Don Higginbotham, who says that 60 men died en route (see

Higginbotham, *Daniel Morgan*, 36 footnotes), and diarist George Morison, who claimed, "[W]e. . .lost in the wilds between 70 and 80." See "Morison Journal" in Roberts, ed., *March to Quebec*, 534.

15. "Forbes Narrative" in Roberts, *March to Quebec*, 608.

16. "Arnold's Letters" in *Ibid.*, 81.

17. Shipton and Swain, eds., "William Humphrey's Journal" in *Rhode Islanders Record the Revolution*, 23.

18. "Morison Journal" in Roberts, ed., *March to Quebec*, 531.

19. Brown and Peckham, eds., *Revolutionary War Journals of Henry Dearborn*, 55.

20. "Pierce Journal" in Roberts, ed., *March to Quebec*, 670.

21. *Ibid.*

22. Smith, *Arnold's March From Cambridge to Quebec*, 241.

23. Isaac N. Arnold, *The Life of Benedict Arnold* (Chicago: Jansen, McClurg & Company, 1880), 48.

24. Force, ed., *American Archives* (Fourth Series): 3:947.

25. *Ibid.*, 1327; "Arnold's Letter Book," Maine Historical Society. Arnold's courier is identified only as Robbisho. See Smith, *Arnold's March From Cambridge to Quebec*, 245. The name could have been a misspelling of the French Canadian surname Robichaux. According to Dr. Senter's journal entry for November 5, he was captured by the British. Senter's entry reads, "The colonel had an express arrived this day, informing of Mr. Robbisho's being taken prisoner, an express sent by colonel [sic] from Sartigan." See Senter, *Journal of Isaac Senter*, 39. Roberts published Arnold's letter identifying a Captain Gregory as its probable recipient. See Roberts, ed., *March to Quebec*, 80. However, I believe this letter from Arnold was intended for John Mercier, who was the colonel's most important contact in Quebec. Arnold also said to his anonymous recipient, "I have several times on my march wrote you by the Indians," which is further evidence that this letter was intended for Mercier.

26. Arnold described John Mercier's apprehension and imprisonment in a letter dated June 12, 1778, at Camp Valley Forge. Arnold wrote the letter to Major General Schuyler "or in his absence" to William Duer, both of whom were members of the Continental Congress at the time:

> The Bearer Mr. John Mercier, was a Merchant in Quebec when I went into Canada knowing him to be a friend of the United States, I wrote him requesting he would send some person of my acquaintance, to meet me on the Chaudiere, to give me particular information of the Strength of the Enemy &c. Unfortunately my letter was intercepted, and covey'd to the Governor of Quebec who ordered Mr. Mercier confin'd on board a Man of War where he

remained some weeks, and when Quebec was invested, was set on shore opposite the City and joined our army, but which meant he has lost for the present not only a considerable place under government, but a very large property in w'houses, stores & merchandise left in Quebec part of which will be finally lost, if not the whole: I beg you will be so kind, to make use of my name in recommending him to Congress, as a Gentlemen who has suffered greatly in the Cause of his Country, and who wishes to be employed in some Office in which he can be of Service to his Country, as in Some measure retrieve his Losses; he has been bred a Merchant, and has a knowledge of the French Tongue.

Any Service you are good enough to render him will be gratefully acknowledged by

Your most Obedient

Humble Servant

B. Arnold.

Manuscript letter, John Reed Collection, Valley Forge National Historical Park Archives.

27. William Smith, ed., "Journal Kept in Quebec in 1775 by James Jeffery," *The Essex Institute Historical Collection*, number 50 (April 1914): 97-150. Cramahé arrived in Quebec with General Wolfe. Because he spoke fluent French and was a good administrator, he was invited to remain in the city as secretary to Governor Murray.

28. Writing in 1907, historian Justin Smith identified one of Arnold's Indian couriers as the informer. Smith wrote, "Arnold's Indian messenger had placed his letters from the Great Carrying-Place to Mercier and Schuyler in the hands of the British authorities, and they knew that a force was on the move against them." See Smith, *Our Struggle For the Fourteenth Colony*, 2: 9. Smith's simple explanation of how the British first learned about the Arnold Expedition has been perpetuated by later historians who, in my opinion, did not consider or underestimated the sophistication of the British in planting double agents, interrogating deserters and prisoners, and intercepting enemy dispatches.

29. The evidence against Hall consists of a letter that Arnold wrote to Lieutenant Steele in which he mentioned Hall by name. As background, Arnold dispatched Steele with 20 ax men and a surveyor on October 12, from the Great Carry, to clear the portages and take a survey of the country as far as Lake Magentic. Private John Hall was one of the men in Steele's party. On the following day, October 13, Arnold wrote Steele, telling him to have Hall

accompany the two Indians to Quebec. Hall was selected for this mission because he spoke French. The text of Arnold's October 13 message to Steele reads:

> Sir—I have sent the bearer and another Indian to Quebec with letters, and must have John Hall, as he speaks French, to go to Sartigan with them, and get all the intelligence he possibly can in regard to the number of troops there, the disposition of the Canadians, and advice from Gen. Schuyler. When he arrives at Sartigan he must employ some Frenchmen, that can be depended on, to go to Quebec with the Indians, to deliver their letter and get an answer; for which purpose I have sent twenty dollars for him to take. Desire him to caution the Indians not to let any one know of our march, but to sound the inhabitants and find out how they stand affected, and whether our coming would be agreeable to them. If he does not choose to go alone, you must send a man with him, and both must return to us at Chaudiere pond as soon as possible; taking particular notice of the river, whether our batteaux can pass down.

This letter is in "Arnold's Letter Book," Maine Historical Society. Also see Smith, *Arnold's March from Cambridge to Quebec*, 356.

30. Force, ed., *American Archives* (Fourth Series): 3:1418-1419.

31. Clark, ed., *Naval Documents of the American Revolution*, 2: 70. For the armament and crew of the *Hunter* see *ibid.*, 2: 743. Although the *Hunter* was a small warship, she could easily have sunk or scattered the unarmed ships that transported the Arnold Expedition from Newburyport to Fort Western and saved the British a lot of trouble.

32. The Royal Navy classified its frigates into various categories based on the number of cannons each carried. The *Lizard* was called a "Sixth Rate," the smallest type of frigate in use at the time.

33. Clark, ed., *Naval Documents of the American Revolution*, 2: 705.

34. W.W. Abott et al., eds., *Papers of Washington, Revolutionary War Series*, 2: 106-107; Miller, *Sea of Glory—The Continental Navy Fights for Independence* (New York: David KcKay Company, Inc., 1974), 66.

35. W.W. Abott et al., eds., *Papers of Washington, Revolutionary War Series*, 2: 106-107.

36. Miller, *Sea of Glory*, 66.

37. Hearn, *George Washington's Schooners*, 31-32. This book is recommended (pages 26-36) for anyone interested in the complete story of American efforts to capture the two British store ships bound for Quebec. St. John Island was renamed Prince Edward Island in 1798.

38. Clark, ed., *Naval Documents of the American Revolution*, 2:1,018. The Marines were a seaborne military police whose function included maintaining discipline aboard Royal Navy ships.

Note that the log refers to the "Marines" and not the Royal Marines. The name change took place in 1802, and any reference to the Royal Marines in the American Revolution is incorrect. At the time of the American Revolution, British Marines wore red regimental coats with white facings. Their facing color was changed to (royal) blue in 1802. Among the ways that British Marines could be distinguished from regular British troops was their distinctive uniform buttons, which bore the image of an anchor.

39. General Schuyler informed headquarters of Allen's severe treatment in a letter dated November 28, 1775. Angered by the news, Washington wrote his counterpart in the British army, Major General William Howe, whose headquarters were in the besieged city of Boston, complaining about Allen's rough handling. Washington's letter is dated December 18, 1775, and Howe responded a few days later. Washington wrote:

> We have just been informed of a Circumstance, which were it not so well Authenticated, I should scarcely think creditable; It is that Col. Allen who with his small party was defeated & taken prisoner near Montreal., has been treated without regard to decency, humanity, or the rules of War—That he has been thrown into Irons & Suffers all the hardships inflicted upon common Felons. I think it my duty Sir to demand & do expect from you, an ecclaircisment [sic] on this Subject; At the same time I flatter myself from the Character which Mr. Howe bears, as a man of Honour, Gentleman & Soldier, that my demand will meet with his approbation: I must take the liberty also of Informing you that I shall consider your silence as a confirmation of the truth of the report & further assuring you, that whatever Treatment Colonel Allen receives—whatever fate he undergoes— such exactly shall be the treatment & Fate of Brigadier Prescot, [General Richard Prescott, captured in Canada] now in our hands.
>
> Permit me to add Sir that we have all here the highest regard & reverence for your great and personal Qualities & Attainments, and that the Americans in general esteem it not as the least of their misfortunes, that the name of Howe—a name so dear to them [a reference to General Howe's older brother, Lord George Augustus, who was killed during the French and Indian War]—should appear at the head of the Catalogue of the Instruments, employed by a wicked ministry for their destruction.

With due respect, I have the honour to be Sir, Yr Most Obedt & Hble sert [servant]

Howe responded without once referring to Washington as a general. In his letter, Howe pointed out that Governor Carleton commanded in Canada:

> In answer to your letter of the 18th inst. I am to acquaint you that my command does not Extend to Canada, nor having received any Accounts wherein the name of Allen is mentioned, I cannot give you the Smallest Satisfaction upon the Subject of your letter; But trusting Major General Carleton's conduct will never incur censure upon any occasion, I am to conclude in the instance of your Enquiry that he has not forfeited his past pretensions to decency & humanity . . . that I find cause to resent a sentence in the conclusion of your letter big with Invective against my Superiors, and insulting to myself, which Should obstruct any further intercourse between us.

See W.W. Abbot et al., eds., *Papers of Washington, Revolutionary War Series*, 2: 575-576, 586.

Ethan Allen was transported in chains to England, where he arrived in late December 1775. The British, however, decided not to put Allen on trial and returned him to America. They shipped him home aboard a warship that sailed from England on January 8, 1776. After a circuitous voyage Allen arrived in British-held New York City in October 1776, where he remained until being released in May 1778.

40. Writing from Boston on December 3, 1775, Genera; William Howe wrote to the Earl of Dartmouth that Cramahé felt Quebec would fall to the rebels: "By a letter received last night from Lieutenant-Governour Cramahé . . . there is too much reason to fear that, by a general defection of the Canadians, the whole Province of Quebeck will fall into the hands of the Rebels." See Froce, ed., *American Archives* (Fourth Series): 4:170.

41. Lieutenant Governor Cramahé to Major General William Howe, November 8, 1775, in Kenneth G. Davies, ed., *Documents of the American Revolution, 1770-1783* 21 vols. (Shannon: Irish University Press, 1972- 1981), 11: 175.

42. Brown and Peckham, eds., *Journals of Henry Dearborn*, 54. Contrary to commonly held beliefs, Indians coveted money as much as whites, and they hired themselves out as scouts and auxiliary soldiers in exchange for payment in hard currency.

43. Shipton and Swain, eds., "William Humphrey's Journal" in *Rhode Islanders Record the Revolution*, 18.

44. Henry, *An Accurate and Interesting Account . . . In the Campaign Against Quebec*, 74-75.

45. W.W. Abbot et al., eds., *Papers of Washington, Revolutionary War Series*, 1: 462-463 footnotes.

46. *Ibid.*, 2: 42, 2: 44 footnote 10.

47. *Ibid.*, 1: 461-462.

48. *Ibid.*, 1: 459.

49. *Ibid.*, 1: 458.

50. Washington to Schuyler, October 4, 1775, Camp at Cambridge, in *Ibid.*, 2: 95-96. Washington included a copy of the September 13, 1775, report from scouts Dennis Getchell and Samuel Berry, who had traveled the expedition's intended route as far as the Dead River.

51. Arnold to Montgomery, November 8, 1775, from "St. Marie, 2 1-2 leagues from Point Levi," in "Arnold's Letter Book," Maine Historical Society.

52. Smith, *Our Struggle for the Fourteenth Colony*, 2: 21.

53. W.W. Abbot et al., eds., *Papers of Washington, Revolutionary War Series*, 1: 458.

54. Senter, *Journal of Dr. Isaac Senter*, 25.

55. Brown and Peckham, eds., *Journals of Henry Dearborn*, 54.

56. "Stocking Journal" in Roberts, ed., *March to Quebec*, 558.

57. Clark, ed., *Naval Documents of the American Revolution*, 2: 1,018.

58. Senter, *Journal of Dr. Isaac Senter*, 25.

59. Clark, ed., *Naval Documents of the American Revolution*, 2: 1,018. For a description of the *Charlotte* see *ibid.*, 2: 1,038.

60. Senter, *Journal of Dr. Isaac Senter*, 26.

61. Fred C. Würtele, ed., *Blockage of Quebec in 1775-1776 by the American Revolutionists* (Quebec, Literary and Historical Society of Quebec: 1906), 6.

62. Arnold mentioned Halstead in a letter to Congress dated January 24, 1776, "General Montgomery, on his arrival in this country, was pleased to appoint Mr. John Halstead Commissary; he is a gentleman, has been very active and zealous in our cause, is a merchant, and capable in his department, in which I beg to leave to recommend his being continued." See Roberts, ed., *March to Quebec*, 118.

63. Brown and Peckham, eds., *Revolutionary War Journals of Henry Dearborn*, 56. Dearborn was not with the army at this time. He was sick in bed, probably in a wayside tavern from November 6-28. His journal entries for the dates of his confinement are based on accurate information provided to him by other members of the expedition.

64. "Morrison Journal" in Roberts, ed., *March to Quebec*, 531.

65. For references to Arnold being compared to Hannibal, see Smith, *Our Struggle For the Fourteenth Colony*, 2: 3.

66. W.W. Abbot et al., eds., *Papers of Washington, Revolutionary War Series*, 2: 498.

67. Force, ed., *American Archives*, Fourth Series: 3, 1,420.

68. Clark, ed., *Naval Documents of The American Revolution*, 2: 944; Stone, ed., "Thayer Journal," 18; Cohen, ed., *The Journal of Capt. Thomas Ainslie*, 21-22.

69. Telescope is a nineteenth century word. This instrument was called a spy glass, glasses, or a glass at the time of the American Revolution. Early spy glasses were heavy with a narrow field of view. However, they were relatively light, short, and effective, especially at night, by the time of the Revolutionary War due in great measure to the invention of the achromatic lens by John Dollard in 1758. The type of spy glass used during the American Revolution was usually a three-inch-long round wooden tube with a single brass pull (extension) used to focus the instrument. Larger, heavier, and higher quality spy glasses were made at the time for use aboard ships. Spy glasses were also made for scientific applications during the eighteenth century. These glasses were usually made entirely of brass and mounted on a tripod.

70. The map *Plan de la ville de Quebec* was created and published in Paris in 1755 by George-Louis Le Rouge. There were numerous later maps of Quebec available, especially versions printed in England celebrating Britain's capture of the city from the French in 1759, but they tended to feature the positions of the opposing French and British forces during the decisive Battle of the Plains of Abraham (September 13, 1759) instead of the details of the city.

71. Clark, ed., *Naval Documents of the American Revolution*, 2: 964. In this letter Captain Hamilton referred to the *Magdalen* as a schooner, but this ship appears on a list titled "Return of Men For Defense of Quebec, November 16, 1775" as a sloop. As an experienced Royal Navy captain, Hamilton knew the difference between a sloop (one mast) and a schooner (a fore and aft rigged ship with at least two masts), and I trust his description of the *Magdalen* over any other source.

72. *Ibid.*, 1,038-1,039. Here is the complete *Return of Men For Defense of Quebec, November 16, 1775:*

	Officers	Privates
Royal Artillery	1	5

Recruits belonging to Royal Emigrant Regt.	14	186
Lizard Frigate Marines	2	35
Effective Seamen	19	114
Hunter sloop Effectives	8	60
Magdalen armed sloop	4	16
Charlotte armed Sloop	4	46
Maters, Mates, Carpenters & Seamen belonging to the transports & merchant ships that have been impressed		74
Artificers & Carpenters		80
British Militia (including Officers)		200
Canadian Militia		300
Royal Fusileers on board the *Fell & Providence*	3	60
Seamen belonging to said vessels	8	72
	63	1,248

Note that the above return states that the *Fusileers* (fusiliers) were on board the *Fell & Providence* on November 16. There are frequent references in British documents to the inclusion of a party of fusiliers at Quebec during the 1775-76 siege. See, for example, Edmund Burke, *An Impartial History of the War in America* (London: R. Faulder, 1780), 241. Their commander is identified as "Captain Owen" in Cohen, ed., *Journal of Capt. Thomas Ainslie*, 37.

The term fusilier comes from the word fusil, which means a short flintlock musket. Fusiliers were originally armed with these special weapons as part of their elite status in the British army. *An Universal Military Dictionary* identifies the fusilier regiments in the British army at the time of the American Revolution: "There are three [fusilier] regiments in the English service: the royal regiment of Scotch Fuziliers [sic], raised in 1678; the royal regiment of English Fuziliers, raised in 1685; and the royal regiment of Welsh Fuziliers, raised in 1688-1689." See Smith, *An Universal Military Dictionary*, 110.

The Royal Regiment of English Fusiliers was officially designated the 7th Regiment of Foot in 1751. However, it was sometimes identified as the 7th Royal Fusiliers as a kind of military shorthand. It was also referred to as the Royal Regiment of Fusiliers or the Royal Fusiliers. The regiment arrived at Quebec in July 1773 and was one of three British regiments stationed in Canada at the start of the American Revolution. The 7th (Royal Fusilier) regiment was divided by Governor Carleton between St. Johns, Chambly, and Quebec City. The bulk of the regiment was at the siege of St. Johns and eventually surrendered to General Montgomery's army. See Philip R.N. Katcher, *Encyclopedia of British, Provincial, and German Army Units 1775-1783* (Harrisburg, Pennsylvania: Stackpole Books, 1973), 31-32.

Sixty members of Royal Fusiliers were stationed at Quebec. They accompanied Colonel Maclean's Royal Highland Emigrant regiment in September to reinforce St. Johns but turned back when that fort surrendered to the Americans. It appears that these 60 British soldiers remained behind when Colonel Maclean made his dash by land to get back in Quebec. They apparently returned to Quebec on November 19 aboard the *Fell* with Carleton and aided in the defense of the city.

73. Hatch, *Thrust For Canada*, 37.

74. Martin, *Benedict Arnold Revolutionary Hero*, 144-145.

75. Arnold to Montgomery in Force, ed., *American Archives* (Fourth Series): 3:1635. Montgomery wrote Schuyler on November 3, 1775, "I have the pleasure to acquaint you the garrison surrendered last night. This morning we take possession. . . ." See *Ibid.*, 1392.

76. Arnold stated that his corps affected the crossing of the St. Lawrence between 9:00 p.m. and 4:00 a.m. See Arnold to Montgomery in Force, ed., *American Archives* (Fourth Series): 3:1684. The time of Arnold's departure is confusing; there is a copy of a letter he wrote to Montgomery dated November 14, 1775, from Point Levi in Roberts, ed., *March to Quebec*, 85. Since Arnold was in the first wave of boats to cross the river, it would have been impossible for him to have written a letter from Pointe de Lévy on November 14 and cross the St. Lawrence at 9:00 p.m. on the 13th. However, the same letter appears in Force, ed., *American Archives* (Fourth Series): 3:1635, dated "Point Levi, November 13, 1775." I believe that the date in Force is correct because the text of Arnold's letter includes the following line: "I have near forty canoes ready; and as the wind has moderated, I design crossing this evening." It is certain that the Arnold Expedition crossed the river on the night of November 13-14. There is no explanation why Roberts dated this letter November 14.

77. "Stocking Journal" in Roberts, ed., *March to Quebec*, 559.

78. Arnold to Washington, November 20, 1775, in W.W. Abbot et al., eds., *Papers of Washington, Revolutionary War Series*, 2: 403.

79. "Arnold Letters" in Roberts, ed., *March to Quebec*, 88.

80. Henry, *An Accurate and Interesting Account . . . In the Campaign Against Quebec*, 128.

81. "Fobes Journal" in Roberts, ed., *March to Quebec*, 587.

82. [Excerpts from] John Stake, "The case of Lieutenant John Strake of His Majesty's Navy, together with a Short Sketch of the Operations of the War in Canada, in which he was employed during the Years 1775, 1776 and 1777. . ." in Clark, ed., *Naval Documents of the American Revolution*, 2: 1,075.

83. Manuscript note of an interview between Aaron Burr and W.W. (probably William Willis, the recording secretary of the Maine Historical Society) in 1831 upon the occasion of the presentation of Arnold's letter book to the society by Aaron Burr. See "Arnold's Letter Book," Maine Historical Society.

84. Force, ed., *American Archives* (Fourth Series): 3:1724.

85. Major Henry Caldwell served under General Wolfe and settled in Quebec at the end of the French and Indian War. Caldwell commanded the British militia in the city. The mansion that Arnold occupied for his headquarters was not owned by Caldwell. He leased it from General James Murray, who was a former governor of Canada. The house was surrounded by several outbuildings and the entire estate was called "Sans Bruit."

86. Bray & Bushnell, eds., *Military Journal of Jeremiah Greenman*, 44 footnote 58.

87. Meigs, *Journal of the Expedition Against Quebec*, 22.

88. The sentry's name was George Merchant, a member of Morgan's Virginia rifle company. Merchant was part of the scouting party commanded by Lieutenant Archibald Steele that Arnold dispatched from Fort Western to explore the Dead River and find Natanis.

The British took a keen interest in Merchant, who was one of the first of the fearsome American riflemen to be captured. Young Merchant fit the profile; he was sent to Britain as a provincial curiosity. An English magazine mentioned his appearance in London: "The Rifleman who was brought here from Quebec. . .is a Virginian, above six feet high, stout and well-proportioned. . . . He can strike a mark with the greatest certainty, at two hundred yards distance. He has a heavy provincial pronunciation, but otherwise speaks good English. The account he gives, is, that the troops in general are such kind of men as himself, tall and well-proportioned." See Don Higginbotham, *Daniel Morgan*, 39.

89. Clark, ed., *Naval Documents of the American Revolution*, 2: 1,017.

90. "Journal of Major Matthias Ogden, 1775 In Arnold's Campaign Against Quebec." *Proceedings of the New Jersey Historical Society*, New Series Vol. XIII (1928): 29.

91. For details of this incident see "Arnold's Letters" in Roberts, ed., *March to Quebec*, 88; Arnold to Cramahé (letter dated Nov. 15, 1775) in *Ibid.*, 88-9. According to Arnold, the British fired a total of 15 cannon shots toward his corps, all of which fell short of their mark and bounced harmlessly on the ground.

92. Cohen, ed., *Journal of Capt. Thomas Ainslie*, 22.

93. For the comment about Maclean see Stedman, *The History of the Origin, Progress, and Termination of the American War*, 1: 134.

94. W.W. Abbot et al., eds., *Papers of Washington, Revolutionary War Series*, 2: 565 note.

95. Smith, *Our Struggle for the Fourteenth Colony*, 1: 450.

96. Hatch, *Thrust for Canada*, 61.

97. Some of Maclean's men must have reached Quebec by boat because the journal of the *Lizard* for November 12, 1775, states, "Arrived here a Shooner & a Sloop from above with part of Col. McChains Regiment." See Clark, ed., *Naval Documents of the American Revolution*, 2: 1,018.

The *Fell* is often referred to as a "snow," and is described as such in the literature of the 1775 American invasion of Canada. Snow is a correct term to describe a type of two-masted ship very similar in appearance to a brig (in the eighteenth century a brig was a two-masted ship "shipped rigged," meaning its sails were perpendicular to the masts). Calling a ship a snow probably derived from the French word *senau* or *senaut*, which means a barge. The *Fell* is also referred to as a brigantine (a brig with slightly different rigging). For example, in a letter written from Quebec at the end of November 1775, Carleton is described as arriving in the city aboard a brigantine (the *Fell*). See *An Account of the State of Quebeck* in Force, ed., *American Archives* (Fourth Series): 4:1723.

Some other contemporary sources identify the *Fell* as a schooner (a two-masted ship with sails rigged "fore and aft," meaning the sails were in line with the masts). However, this probably was a mistake made by landlubbers who called any two-masted ship a schooner or did not know the difference between a schooner and a brig (or brigantine or snow). For an excellent glossary of eighteenth century nautical terms see Jack Coggins, *Ships and Seamen of the American Revolution* (Promontory Press, 1969), 212-216.

The October 5, 1775, issue of the Quebec *Gazette* provides additional information about the *Fell*: "equipp'd with 16 nine-pounders [sixteen cannons which fired a nine pound cannon ball], besides Swivels [small cannons often mounted on the railing of a ship], etc,. And 100 true tars, on board of which Commodore Napier hoisted his flag. . . ." See Stanley, *Canada Invaded*, 82.

98. Arnold to Montgomery, November 8, 1775, from "St. Marie, 2 1-2 leagues from Point Levi," in "Arnold's Letter Book," Maine Historical Society.

99. For information about the number of men with Maclean when he arrived in Quebec see the letter written by Lieutenant John Starke from Quebec, dated November 20, which includes the line: "At this time, Lieut Col. Maclean who had crossed the country arrived in the Town with about 100 Men." See Clark, ed., *Naval Documents of the American Revolution*, 2: 1,075.

Apparently Fraser reached Quebec on November 5, 1775, with recruits for the Royal Highland Emigrants. The journal of the *HMS Hunter* recorded their arrival: "Anchored here a Schooner from Newfoundland and a Sloop from the Isle of St John [today's Prince Edward Island] both with recruits." See *Ibid.*, 2: 943. Additional information about these recruits appears in an historical journal article titled "When Newfoundland Helped to Save Canada," which describes most of the men who enlisted in Maclean's regiment as young Irishmen who had come to the Avalon peninsula section of Newfoundland to work in the "fishery [fishing business], but who were young, brave and foolish enough to try their hand at war." The article also explains most of these Irish recruits were artisans and carpenters who helped repair Quebec's crumbling defenses. See Robert Saunders, "When Newfoundland Helped to Save Canada," *Newfoundland Quarterly*, Vol. 49, No. 3 (1949): 19.

The fact that the Newfoundland recruits were used primarily as artificers helps explain the following:

> An Account of the State of Quebeck, Etc., At the End of November, 1775. . . . The expectations from Colonel Maclean are entirely vanished.He was deserted by his people at the River Sorel, and obliged to fly, with eighty men, to Quebeck, with great expedition. The Highlanders he enlisted were so few as not to be worth mentioning. There were about one hundred came from the Island of St. John's, [most of them were recruited in Newfoundland] trading to Quebeck, but who have not entered as soldiers; and from thence, on the expectation that they would enlist, I suppose the report arose of his having raised a Regiment of them. . . .

See Force, ed., *American Archives* (Fourth Series): 3:1725.

At the time, Newfoundland (and portions of modern Labrador) was classified by the British government as a fishing station rather than a colony.

100. An example of Maclean's influence on the military situation at Quebec appeared in the minutes of a British council of war held in the city on November

16, just a couple of days following his arrival in the city. Attending the meeting were Maclean, Cramahé, Captains Hamilton and McKenzie from the Royal Navy, Major Henry Caldwell, who commanded the British militia, and several other lower-ranking officers and government officials. With Maclean in charge, the council unanimously agreed "to defend the Town to the last extremity." See Clark, ed., *Naval Documents of the American Revolution*, 2: 1,038.

101. Smith, *Our Struggle for the Fourteenth Colony*, 2: 20.

102. Clark, ed., *Naval Documents of the American Revolution*, 2: 1,075.

103. Gordon, D.D., *The History of the Rise, Progress, and Establishment, of the Independence of the United States,* 2: 132. Here is a longer excerpt from his description in his history of the war of Enos' return to Cambridge and subsequent court-martial:

Let us attend to colonel Enos. His return to camp excited both astonishment and indignation. A court martial was ordered to sit upon him; when it appeared, that he had but three days provision, and was about one hundred miles from the English settlements. . . . It was the unanimous opinion of the court, that colonel Enos was under a necessity of returning; and he has been acquitted with honor. A number of officers of the best character are fully satisfied, and persuaded that his conduct deserves applause rather than censure. Had he not returned, his whole division must have been starved.

104. For the total number of men with Arnold see W.W. Abbot et al., eds., *Papers of Washington, Revolutionary War Series*, 2: 403. For the times of Arnold's departure from Ste. Foye and arrival at Point aux Trembles, as well as number of effectives, see Arnold to Montgomery, November 20, 1775, in Clark, ed., *Naval Documents of the American Revolution,* 2: 1,079.

105. Henry, *An Accurate and Interesting Account. . . . In the Campaign Against Quebec*, 94-95.

106. Manuscript letter, Aaron Burr to Timothy Edwards, November 22, 1775, from "Point aux Tremble," in "Burr Papers," New York Historical Society, reference CtFaiHi: 2876.

107. John Marshall, *Life of George Washington, Commander in Chief of the American Forces* 5 vols. (Philadelphia: C.P. Wayne, 1804-1807), 2: 309.

108. Thomas Walker, a Montreal merchant and American sympathizer, gave a sworn statement, dated April 24, 1776, at Philadelphia. Walker was arrested as an American agent by the British at Montreal and put on board one of the ships bound for Quebec. His affidavit includes information about the ships and military equipment captured at Sorel. Walker said that 135 Americans captured 11 enemy ships at Sorel. His information is interesting because all of the ships and hardware captured at Sorel was used during the American siege of Quebec:

The vessels given up were, viz: His Majesty's Brigantine Gaspee, commanded by Lieutenant Royal: Also . . . Captain Lisote, [commanding] a large schooner, two nine-pounders in the waist, besides quarter-deck guns and swivels, twenty-four seamen, each armed with a musket, bayonet, and broad-sword. Captain Bouchet, [commanding] another large schooner, armed like the other before mentioned, compliment twenty sailors, besides several other large schooners, fitted with swivels, &c. All the vessels towed after them a batteau, with one or more canoes or small boats, in order to make a descent, or escape by flight, as occasion should offer.

See Force, ed., *American Archives* (Fourth Series): 4:1178.

109. Schuyler to Washington, November 28, 1775, from Tyonderoga, in W.W. Abbot et al., eds., *Papers of Washington, Revolutionary War Series*, 2: 453.

110. Clark, ed., *Naval Documents of the American Revolution*, 2: 1,073. Some historians claim that Carleton arrived in Quebec with a detachment of Redcoats belonging to the 7th Regiment. Supporting this idea is the anonymously written *The History of the Civil War in America* (London, 1780), 130, which states: "on the 20th [November 1775] General Carleton got into Quebec, bringing with him a Captain and fifty men [most sources state 60 men] of the 7th regiment, who were on board the armed ship [the brig *Fell*] with him." This information is correct, as evidenced by the "Return of Men For Defense of Quebec, November 16, 1775" (this list appears in footnote 72 in this chapter), which lists 60 fusiliers onboard the *Fell*. While Carleton escaped the American trap at Sorel alone or with one or two of his aides in a small boat, he was later picked up by the *Fell*, which had the 60 British regulars on board. They were returning to Quebec following Colonel Maclean's failed attempt to raise the siege of St. Johns.

111. Shipton and Swain, ed., "Humphrey Journal" in *Rhode Islanders Record the Revolution*, 29. There is some controversy regarding the time and date of Montgomery's arrival. For example, Arnold wrote Washington that Montgomery arrived on December 3. See W.W. Abbot, et al., eds., *Papers of Washington, Revolutionary War Series*, 2: 495. After examining the various sources available to him at the time, Justin Smith concluded that Montgomery arrived at Point aux Trembles on the night of December 2. See Smith, *Our Struggle for the Fourteenth Colony*, 2: 577.

112. Henry, *An Accurate and Interesting Account . . . In the Campaign Against Quebec*, 98.

113. Shipton and Swain, ed., "William Humphrey Journal" in *Rhode Islanders Record the Revolution*, 29-30.

114. "Morison Journal" in Roberts, ed., *March to Quebec*, 534.

115. Henry Steele Commager and Richard B. Morris, *The Spirit of Seventy-Six* 2 vols. (Indianapolis and New York: The Bobbs-Merrill Company, Inc., 1958), 1: 203.

116. Sheldon, *General Richard Montgomery*, 128.

117. Washington's Instructions to Arnold, September 14, 1775, included the following: "In Case of an Union with General Schuyler, or if he should be in Canada upon your Arrival there, you are by no means to consider yourself upon a Separate & Independant Command but are to put yourself under him & follow his Directors. Upon this Occasion & all others I recommend most earnestly to avoid all Contention about Rank—In such a Cause every Post is honourable in which a Man can serve his Country." See W.W. Abbot et al., eds., *Papers of Washington, Revolutionary War Series*, 1: 458. Washington probably included this order based on Arnold's combative behavior toward Benjamin Hinman, who arrived at Fort Ticonderoga in June 1775 to replace him. For details of the dispute between Arnold and Hinman see *Ibid*, 1: 121 note 2.

118. Arnold to Washington, November 20, 1775, Point aux Trembles, in "Arnold's Letter Book," Maine Historical Society.

119. Arnold to Schuyler, November 27, 1775, Point Aux Trembles, "Arnold's Letters" in Roberts, ed., *March to Quebec*, 98-99.

120. For Montgomery's remark about Arnold see Shelton, *General Richard Montgomery*, 128. Arnold's appraisal of Montgomery can be found in Force, ed., *American Archives* (Fourth Series): 4:589.

121. Cohen, ed., *Journal of Capt. Thomas Ainslie*, 30.

122. In a report to Washington dated December 5, 1775, and captioned "Before Quebec," Arnold wrote, "Inclosed is a Return of my Detachment amounting to 675 Men. . . ." See W.W. Abbot et al., eds., *Papers of Washington, Revolutionary War Series*, 2: 495. The return mentioned in Arnold's letter is dated November 29, 1775, and is in *The George Washington Papers* at the Library of Congress. It shows a total strength of 675, including 59 sick men. The return does not include about 50 Indians who were recruited by Arnold following his arrival in Canada.

123. Arnold wrote Washington on December 5, 1775: "I continued at Pt. Aux Trembles until the 3rd instant, when to my great joy Gen. Montgomery joined us, with artillery and about 300 men. Yesterday [December 4] we arrived here and are making all possible preparations to attack the city. . . ." See "Arnold's Letters" in Roberts, ed., *March to Quebec*, 101. For weather on December 3 see Cohen, ed., *Journal of Capt. Thomas Ainslie*, 25.

124. The fact that Livingston joined Montgomery at Quebec is confirmed in a letter Montgomery wrote to General Schuyler on December 5 from Quebec. Montgomery wrote, "Colonel Livingston is on his way, with some part of his regiment of Canadians." See Commager and Morris, eds., *The Spirit of Seventy-Six*, 1: 202.

125. Force, ed., *American Archives* (Fourth Series): 4:309-310.

Chapter Nine

1. Codman, *Arnold's Expedition to Quebec*, 134.

2. All weather conditions in Quebec during December 1775 are from Cohen, ed., *Journal of Capt. Thomas Ainslie.*, 25-32.

3. *Ibid.*, 26.

4. For the rumor of Russian troops coming to help the Americans conquer Quebec see *Ibid.*, 25.

5. *Ibid.*

6. Henry, *An Interesting and Accurate Account . . . In the Campaign Against Quebec*, 88. The relevant passage in Henry's remembrance says that Arnold "was well known in Quebec. Formerly he had traded from this port to the West Indies, most particularly in the article of horses.—Hence he was despised by the principal people. The epithet of 'Horse-jockey,' was freely and universally bestowed upon him by the British." The earliest known reference to Arnold being called a "horse jockey" appeared in a letter that Governor Carleton wrote to The Earl of Darmouth on June 7, 1775. Referring to Arnold's raid on St. Johns, Carleton said, "Captain Hazen arrived express at Quebec and brought me an account that one Benedict Arnold, said to be a native of Connecticut and a horse-jockey, landed a considerable number of armed men at St John's. . . ." See K.G. Davies, ed *Documents of the American Revolution 1770-1783*, (Dubin: Irish University Press, 1975) vol. IX, 157. The Americans used this epithet to describe Arnold following his treason.

7. Richard M. Lederer Jr., *Colonial American English* (Essex, Connecticut: A Verbatim Book, 1985), 125.

8. *Extract of a Letter From a Gentleman in the Continental Service*, dated "Before Quebeck, December 16, 1775," in Force, ed., *American Archives* (Fourth Series): 4:290.

9. Artillery at the time of the American Revolution was either made of brass (actually bronze) or iron. Brass cannons were lighter in weight and less prone to burst than iron. However, iron cannons had a longer range than brass. Brass was also a more costly material than iron and required greater manufacturing skills to

forge into a cannon barrel. As a result the bulk of the cannons used during the American Revolution, especially those manufactured in America by the rebels, were made of iron. A 12-pound iron cannon weighed from 2,900 to 3,400 pounds and could be fired up to 1,800 yards. In comparison, a brass 12-pounder weighed from 1,200 to 1800 pounds with a maximum range of 1,400 yards. As a further comparison, a brass 32-pounder (the British had them at Quebec) could weigh up to 5,500 pounds and had an effective range of 1,900 yards. Note the 500-yard advantage in range between a brass 12-pounder and 32-pounder; 1,400 yards for the 12-pounder vs. 1,900 yards for the 32-pounder.

10. Montgomery to Robert R. Livingston, November 1775, Montreal, in Force, ed., *American Archives* (Fourth Series): 3:1638-1639.

11. *Ibid.*

12. Montgomery to Schuyler, December 18, 1775, in *Ibid.*, 4: 309-310.

13. Lieutenant Colonel Rudolphus Ritzema, second in command of the 1st New York regiment, wrote in his journal on November 28, "The six months for which the men of our Regiment were enlisted being nearly expired, agreeable to general orders they were enlisted anew to the 15th of April next." See T.W. Egly Jr., *History of the First New York Regiment* (Hampton, New Hampshire: Peter E. Randall, 1981), 12.

14. Montgomery to Robert R. Livingston, November 1775, Montreal, in Force, ed., *American Archives* (Fourth Series): 3:1638-1639.

15. *Ibid.*

16. Ainslie may have played a larger role in Quebec's defense than he is given credit for, as evidenced by a letter written by an officer in Montgomery's army who said, "Was it not for Carleton, Cramahe, Colonel Maclean. . .and Hanslic [Ainslie], Collector of the Customs, we should have been in Quebeck before now." See *Extract of a Letter From a Gentleman in the Continental Service*, December 16, 1775, "Before Quebeck," in Force, ed., *American Archives* (Fourth Series): 4:290.

17. Cohen, ed., *Journal of Capt. Thomas Ainslie*, 27.

18. *Ibid.*, 21.

19. *Ibid.*, 22-23.

20. Andrew Melvin, ed., *Journal of James Melvin*, 24.

21. Commager and Morris, eds., *The Spirit of Seventy-Six*, 203. For information about Antill, see Paul R. Reynolds, *Guy Carleton* (New York: William Morrow and Company, Inc., 1980), 78. For information about the duties of a military engineer, see Smith, *An Universal Military Dictionary*, 81-2.

22. William Nelson, *Edward Antill, A New York Merchant of the Seventeenth Century, and His Descendants* (Paterson, New Jersey: The Press Printing and Publishing Co., 1899), 19-20. Antill was later appointed a

lieutenant colonel and second in command of the 2nd Canadian regiment (also designated Congress' Own and commanded by Colonel Moses Hazen) and served in that capacity until he retired on May 1, 1782. He was taken prisoner during a raid on Staten Island, New York, on August 22, 1777, and exchanged on November 2, 1780. He died in 1789.

23. For the organization of Carleton's defenders see Stanley, *Canada Invaded*, 87. For the number of men in each of Carleton's brigades see Ward, *The War of the Revolution*, 1: 188.

24. "Journal of the Most Remarkable Occurrences in Quebec, From the 14th of November, 1775 to the 7th of May, 1776, By an Officer of the Garrison," *Collections of the New York Historical Society For the Year 1880* (New York: Printed for the Society, 1881), 178.

Sheldon Cohen attributes this diary to Jacob Danford, who was a civilian employee of the Board of Ordnance in Quebec. See Cohen, ed., *The Journal of Capt. Thomas Ainslie,* 13. However, subsequent research has produced a new and different diary kept by Danford. See John F. Roche, ed., "Quebec Under Seige, 1775-1776: The 'Memorandums' of Jacob Danford," *The Canadian Historical Review*, vol. L, no. 1 (March 1969): 68-81. Hereafter cited as Roche, ed., *Memorandums of Jacob Danford*.

Danford arrived in Quebec from England in 1766. In 1774 he became a civilian employee of the Board of Ordnance in Quebec and was in charge of the preparation, inspection, and distribution of ammunition for the artillery defending the city during the American siege. Because of his expert knowledge, his journal is cited in matters concerning artillery.

25. See French, *The First Year of the American Revolution*, 602.

26. Force, ed., *American Archives* (Fourth Series): 4:289.

27. Reynolds, *Guy Carleton*, 80. Carleton had established a policy of no negotiations with the rebels months before when he said, "I shall return no answer, nor enter into any Correspondance with Rebels, not thinking myself at liberty to treat otherwise those who are Traytors [sic.] to the King, without His Majesty's express Commands." See Smith, *Our Struggle For the Fourteenth Colony*, 2: 103.

28. Details of this story appear in a letter that Carleton wrote to General Howe dated January 12, 1776, from "Quebeck." Carleton said, "The 7th [December 7], a woman stole into town, with letters addressed to the principal merchants, advising them to an immediate submission, and promising a great indulgency in case of their compliance." See Force, ed., *American Archives* (Fourth Series): 4: 656. The quote from Montgomery's letter to the merchants of Quebec is from Shelton, *General Richard Montgomery*, 131.

29. Reynolds, *Guy Carleton*, 81.

30. Andrew Melvin, ed., *James Melvin's Journal*, 21. The British offer to American soldiers who deserted was signed by Maclean and read:

> Conditions to be given to such soldiers as shall engage in the Royal Highland Emigrants. They are to engage during the present troubles in North America only. Each soldier is to have 200 acres of land in any province in North America he may think proper, the king to pay the patent fees and surveyor-general., besides twenty years free of quit rent. Each married men gets fifty acres for his wife and fifty for each child on the same terms, and as a gratuity besides the above great terms, one guinea levy money.

31. *Extract of a Letter From the Gentlemen in the Continental Service*, dated "Before Quebeck, December 16, 1775," in Force, ed., *American Archives* (Fourth Series): 4:290.

32. Senter, *Journal of Dr. Isaac Senter*, 30-31; Heitman, *Historical Register of Officers of the Continental Army,* 606. According to Heitman, Wool, a New Yorker, was appointed a lieutenant in Lamb's Artillery Company on August 2, 1775. His subsequent military career included an appointment as a captain in the 2nd Continental Artillery in 1777. He resigned from the army three years later and died in 1794. The December 9, 1775, date for the opening of the mortar battery is from Shelton, *General Richard Montgomery*, 133.

33. Smith, *An Universal Military Dictionary*, 186.

34. Reynolds, *Guy Carleton*, 82.

35. Cohen, ed., *Journal of Capt. Thomas Ainslie*, 28.

36. Henry, *An Interesting and Accurate Account . . . In the Campaign Against Quebec*, 109.

37. Senter, *Journal of Dr. Isaac Senter*, 47.

38. Cohen, ed., *Journal of Capt. Thomas Ainslie*, 29.

39. *Ibid.*

40. Roche, ed, *The Memorandums of Jacob Danford*, 71.

41. *Extract of a Letter To a Gentlemen in New-York*, dated "Montreal, December 17, 1775," in Force, ed., *American Archives* (Fourth Series): 4:296.

42. "Fobes Journal" in Roberts, ed., *March to Quebec*, 589.

43. This episode appears in a report that Carleton wrote to General Howe in Boston. See Force, ed., *American Archives* (Fourth Series): 4:656.

44. Cohen, ed., *Journal of Capt. Thomas Ainslie*, 29.

45. Force, ed., *American Archives* (Fourth Series): 4:290.

46. Montgomery to Carleton, December 16, 1775, "Quebeck," in *Ibid.*, 289.

47. *Ibid.*

48. Montgomery to Wooster in *Ibid.*, 288-289.

49. Fred G. Würtele, ed., "Journal of the Siege From 1st Dec, 1775" [author unknown, believed to be a artillery officer] in *Blockade of Quebec in 1775-1776 by the American Revolutionists* (Port Washington, NY: Kennikat Press, 1970), 14-15. This diary was originally published in 1906 by the Literary and Historical Society of Quebec.

50. "Pierce Journal" in Roberts, ed., *March to Quebec*, 692.

51. Senter, *Journal of Dr. Isaac Senter*, 31.

52. "Haskell Diary" in Roberts, ed., *March to Quebec*, 483. The only other woman known to have accompanied the Arnold Expedition as far as Quebec was identified as the wife of Sergeant Grier of the Pennsylvania troops. Private Haskell mentioned her death in his diary entry for April 18, 1776: "a woman belonging to the Pennsylvania troops was killed to-day by accident—a soldier carelessly snapped his musket which proved to be loaded." See *Ibid.*, 495.

53. Montgomery to Wooster, December 16, 1775, "Head-Quarters before Quebec," in Force, ed., *American Archives* (Fourth Series): 4:288-289. Montgomery made it clear in this revealing communiqué that his initial plan was to feint an attack on the lower town while the real assault took place against the upper town. Montgomery said, "I propose the first strong northwester to make two attacks by night: one, with about a third of the troops, on the lower town, having first set fire to some houses, which will, in all probability, communicate their flames to the stockade lately erected on the rock [heights] near St. Roque [St. Roch—the suburb closest to the lower town]; the other upon Cape Diamond bastion, by escalade."

54. Montgomery to Schuyler, December 18, 1775, in *Ibid.*, 309-310.

55. "Stocking Journal" in Roberts, ed., *March to Quebec*, 561.

56. Würtele, ed., "Journal of the Siege From 1st Dec., 1775", 28. The quote reads, "All the Guns in the flanks were scaled & new load wt. grape & cannister shott." Although the use of canister shot is associated with the American Civil War, it existed at the time of the American Revolution. See Harold L. Peterson, *Round Shot and Rammers* (New York: Bonanza Books, 1969), 27.

57. Cohen, ed., *Journal of Capt. Thomas Ainslie*, 28.

58. Cohen, ed., *Ibid.*, 30-31.

59. Henry, *An Accurate and Interesting Account . . . In the Campaign Against Quebec*, 109.

60. Elizabeth A. Fenn, *Pox Americana, The Great Smallpox Epidemic of 1775-82* (New York: Hill and Wang, 2001), 63.

61. "Pierce Journal" in Roberts, ed., *March to Quebec*, 694. Surprisingly, Pierce did not mention smallpox in his list of maladies that, according to other diarists, was present in the American camp at the time.

62. Senter, *Journal of Dr. Isaac Senter*, 31.

63. "Haskell Diary" in Roberts, ed., *March to Quebec*, 482.

64. Bray & Bushnell, eds., *Military Journal of Jeremiah Greenman*, 23.

65. Smallpox is spread through direct contact with an infected person or through fairly prolonged close (within about six feet) contact. The disease also is spread through contact with infected bodily fluids or contaminated objects such as bedding or clothing.

Since smallpox has been eradicated (the last known case in the world was in 1977) there is little current information available about the disease. However, there was an outbreak of smallpox in October 1945 in a U.S. Army hospital in Nagoya, Japan, which showed the ease with which the disease could spread. Twenty-two American service personnel contracted the disease during this brief episode.

Army medical personnel present during the outbreak later reported that the disease began with a high fever that subsequently dropped, although never to normal, before spiking again. Although some patients had pustular lesions, those who died had confluent subcutaneous hemorrhages (from bleeding into the pustules) that rapidly involved the entire body, with a similar enanthema (eruption on a mucous membrane) involving the enanthema of the oral cavity, respiratory mucosa, and entire gastrointestinal tract. The pain was intense, and morphine relieved it only marginally. Commenting on the ease with which smallpox spread, the American doctors noted that every soldier who contracted smallpox had been in the hospital for some other medical problem two weeks prior to the onset of the disease. They recalled that a messenger who stopped in the hospital's laboratory for a cup of coffee returned two weeks later with smallpox. See Murray Dworetzky, M.D., "Smallpox, October 1945," *The New England Journal of Medicine*, Vol. 346, No. 17 (April 2002): 1,329.

66. Private Melvin mentioned in his journal the commandeering of the nunnery for use as a hospital: "We were quartered in a nunnery near the town, but it was wanted for a hospital." See Andrew A. Melvin, ed., *James Melvin's Journal*, 59.

67. See Louis C. Duncan, *Medical Men in the American Revolution* (New York: Augustus M. Kelley, 1970), map of Quebec opposite page 90 shows the location of the smallpox hospital.

68. "Pierce Journal" in Roberts, ed., *March to Quebec*, 698.

69. "Haskell Diary" in *Ibid.*, 485. Haskell's diary entry for December 28, 1775, reads, "All the houses in the neighborhood are full of our soldiers with the small-pox. It goes favorably with the most of them."

70. Cohen, ed., *Journal of Capt. Thomas Ainslie*, 27.

71. W.W. Abbot et al., eds., *Papers of Washington, Revolutionary War Series*, 3: 84, footnote.

72. "Pierce Journal" in Roberts, ed., *March to Quebec*, 699.

73. Rifleman Henry said that all officers in the army with the rank of captain and above were invited to this council. See Henry, *An Accurate and Interesting Account . . . In the Campaign Against Quebec*, 111.

74. The primary sources for information about this meeting are the "Pierce Journal" in Roberts, ed., *March to Quebec*, 699, and a letter from Montgomery to Schuyler, dated December 26, 1775, in Force, ed., *American Archives* (Fourth Series): 4:464-465. Some historians erroneously refer to this meeting as a briefing for Arnold's officers. See, for example, Stanley, *Canada Invaded*, 93, which says, "The original plan of attack was a simple one. It was discussed at a meeting of company officers at an operations group at Arnold's headquarters on December 23rd."

75. "Pierce Journal" in Roberts, ed., *March to Quebec*, 699.

76. French, *The First Year of the American Revolution*, 612.

77. Montgomery to Schuyler, December 26, 1775, in Force, ed., *American Archives* (Fourth Series): 4:464.

78. "Pierce Journal" in Roberts, ed., *March to Quebec*, 701.

79. Montgomery to Schulyer, December 5, 1775, at "Holland-House [Montgomery's Headquarters], near the Heights of Abraham" in Force, ed., *American Archives* (Fourth Series): 4:190.

80. *Ibid*. Meigs, who attended the meeting, said that the "matters. . .were happily settled." See Meigs, *Journal of the Expedition Against Quebec*, 32. However, Montgomery said that the problem with Arnold's three dispirited companies were not resolved at the meeting. Montgomery wrote, "This dangerous party threatens the ruin of our affairs. I shall, at any rate, be obliged to change my plan of attack, being too weak to put that in execution I had formerly determined on." See letter from Montgomery to Schuyler, December 26, 1775, "Head-Quarters before Quebec," in Force, ed., *American Archives* (Fourth Series): 4:464.

81. Senter, *Journal of Dr. Isaac Senter*, 32.

82. Brown and Peckham, eds. *Revolutionary War Journals of Henry Dearborn*, 65.

83. Bray & Bushnell, eds., *Military Journal of Jeremiah Greenman*, 23.

84. Cohen, ed., *Journal of Capt. Thomas Ainslie*, 32.

85. Henry, *An Accurate and Interesting Account . . . In the Campaign Against Quebec*, 100.

86. Cohen, ed., *Journal of Capt. Thomas Ainslie*, 33. There is an additional interesting reference to clothing for Arnold's corps in Ford, ed., *Journals of the Continental Congress*, 7: 81, which concerns the reimbursement of expenses to Captain Dearborn: "For a suit of clothes allowed him [Dearborn] by Gen.

Montgomery, and for his expenses from camp to this place in order to settle his accounts, 294 dollars (The value of the suit, 33-1/3 dollars) was deducted." While this interesting reference does not indicate the type of clothing that Montgomery gave to Dearborn (a uniform or civilian clothing?) it reflects the fact that officers had to pay for their own clothing and equipment.

87. Ward, *The War of the Revolution*, 1: 185, 451 footnote 19. Rifleman Henry said that he had "a fine white blanket coat," and "a bonnet rogue [red hat]" with a white lining during the siege of Quebec. He also remarked that his "gloves being good and well lined with fur." See Henry, *An Accurate and Interesting Account . . . In the Campaign Against Quebec*, 109.

88. See, for example, Henry, *An Accurate and Interesting Account . . . In the Campaign Against Quebec*, 111.

89. Trousers resemble modern pants. Overalls at the time were loose-fitting above the knee, tight-fitting below the knee, and spread out at the bottom to cover the shoes.

90. Charles Botta, *History of the War of the Independence of the United States of America* 2 vols. (New Haven: Nathan Whiting, 1836), 1:288. This popular early history of the Revolution went through many editions. The first American edition was published in 1820.

91. "Stocking Journal" in Roberts, ed., *March to Quebec*, 561.

92. Brown & Peckham, eds., *Revolutionary War Journals of Henry Dearborn*, 65.

93. "Morison Journal" in Roberts, ed., *March to Quebec*, 535.

94. "Stocking Journal" in *Ibid.*, 562.

95. W.W. Abbot et al., eds., *Papers of Washington, Revolutionary War Series*, 2: 403-404.

96. Stone, ed., "Thayer Journal," 27.

97. *Ibid.*

98. The phrase forlorn hope is derived from the Dutch *verloren hoop*, which means lost troop.

99. Cohen, ed., *Journal of Capt. Thomas Ainslie*, 31.

100. *Ibid.*, 32.

101. *Ibid*; Henry, *An Accurate and Interesting Account . . . In the Campaign Against Quebec*, 111.

102. Shelton, *General Richard Montgomery*, 139.

103. Henry, *An Accurate and Interesting Account . . . In the Campaign Against Quebec*, 112.

104. There are several creditable sources that state Captain Lamb was accompanied by only a part of his artillery company. One American officer, who survived the attack, identifying himself only as "A Solider," wrote an undated

but convincing account of the event in the New York *Gazette*. He stated: "About four o'clock in the morning, the detachment being assembled in St. Roque's [a reference to Arnold's segment of the attack, launched from the suburb of St. Roch] together with Captain Lamb, and part of his company of Artillery, with a field piece, mounted on a particular carriage, for the conveniency for carrying it through the snow." See Force, ed., *American Archives* (Fourth Series): 4:707. For the number of Canadians and Indians with Arnold see Shelton, *General Richard Montgomery*, 140. For the number of artillerymen accompanying Lamb in the attack see Isaac Q. Leake, *Memoir of the Life and Times of Gen. John Lamb* (Albany: Joel Munsell, 1850), 127.

105. "Pierce Journal" in Roberts, ed., *March to Quebec*, 692. Pierce said, "300 more Yorkers [troops belonging to the 1st New York regiment] and Canadians arrived this day from moreal [Montreal]." For Brown's command of 160 men see Martin, *Benedict Arnold, Revolutionary Hero*, 164.

106. Senter, *Journal of Dr. Isaac Senter*, 32-33. For details of Livingston's preparations for his attack on St. John's Gate see Force, ed., *American Archives* (Fourth Series): 4:482.

107. "Stocking Journal" in Roberts, ed., *March to Quebec*, 562.

108. Commager and Morris, eds., *The Spirit of Seventy-Six*, 1: 254.

109. John Ferling, *A Leap in the Dark*, 155.

110. There is no known reference to a street or path in colonial Quebec called Dog Lane. While this narrow shoreline path is described in detail in many of the journals, none of the diarists mention it by name. The name Dog Lane apparently was adopted by later historians.

111. Senter, *Journal of Dr. Isaac Senter*, 33; Cohen, ed., *Journal of Capt. Thomas Ainslie*, 38.

112. Senter, *Journal of Dr. Isaac Senter*, 33.

113. For the correct date of the American attack see Reynolds, *Carleton*, 83. This author comments on the confusion regarding the date of the American attack and confirms that it took place on the night of December 30-31. The date of the attack is confusing because some accounts, including those by John Joseph Henry and Abner Stocking, say it took place on the night of December 31-January 1. However, more credible sources—including Carleton, Arnold, and Ainslie—stated that it occurred during the night of December 30-31.

114. *Extract of a Letter From Canada, Dated February 9, 1776*, in Force, ed., *American Archives* (Fourth Series): 4:706-707. For information about the Portuguese coin called a johannes, which is a slang expression and so named because the coin had the portrait of John V on its face, see Lederer, *Colonial American English*, 110, 125.

115. Shelton, *General Richard Montgomery*, 141.

116. "Pierce Journal" in Roberts, ed., *March to Quebec*, 703.

117. Stanley, *Canada Invaded*, 95.

118. The location of Carleton's headquarters is mentioned in Billias, ed., *George Washington's Opponents*, 119.

119. Cohen, ed., *Journal of Capt. Thomas Ainslie*, 33-34.

120. The relative positions of the various companies and officers during the attack are from Stone, ed., *Thayer Journal*, 28.

121. Smith, *Our Struggle for the Fourteenth Colony*, 2: 131.

122. Roche, ed., *Memorandums of Jacob Danford*, 72.

123. Leake, *Life of John Lamb*, 130.

124. James Graham, *The Life of General Daniel Morgan, of the Virginia Line of the Army of the United States* (New York: Derby & Jackson, 1859), 96.

125. *Ibid.* This story is one of the most controversial aspects of the American attack on Quebec. The source is creditable: it is claimed to be included in a letter Morgan wrote after the war describing his participation in the conflict at the request of General Henry (Light Horse Harry) Lee who was writing a history of the Revolutionary War in the South. Lee's book, *Memoirs of the War in the Southern Department of the United States* 2 vols. (Philadelphia: Bradford and Inskeep, 1812), contains a biographical sketch of Morgan (vol. 1:388-391) that includes his participation in the Arnold Expedition and attack on Quebec. However, it does not give any details of the action at the second barricade. The assertion that Morgan reached the second barricade and found it abandoned first appears in James Graham's *The Life of Daniel Morgan*, published in 1859. Graham states (p.96) that his source for the story is "a short sketch written by himself [Morgan], of his early military career." I believe that Graham is referring to the above-mentioned letter Morgan wrote to Henry Lee.

A portion of the illusive Morgan letter to Lee appeared in "General Daniel Morgan, An Autobiography," *Historical Magazine*, vol. IX, No. 6, Second Series (June, 1871): 379-380. The pertinent text reads:

> [W]e arrived at the barrier-gate [second barricade], where I was ordered to wait for General Montgomery, and a fatal order it was, as it prevented me from taking the garrison, having already made half the town prisoners. The sally-port through the barrier was standing open; the guard left it; and the people came running, in seeming platoon [sic], and gave themselves up, in order to get out of the way of the confusion that was likely to ensue. I went up to the edge of the upper town, with an interpreter, to observe what was going on, as the firing had ceased. I found no person in arms at all. I returned and called a Council of War of what officers I had . . . Here I was

overruled by hard reasoning. . . . To these arguments I sacrificed my
own opinion and lost the town.

This story also appears in the modern literature of the Revolutionary War,
including Higginbotham's *Daniel Morgan* and Martin's *Benedict Arnold
Revolutionary Hero*. These excellent historians have accepted Morgan's letter as
accurate. I believe that Morgan's letter is genuine but, after an exhaustive study
of the Arnold Expedition, I feel that it was the boastful reminiscences of an old
veteran. First, there is no corroborating evidence to support Morgan's story. In
fact, the opposite is true. Jacob Danford said that the second barrier was
"vigorously defended" (see Roche, ed., *Memorandums of Jacob Danford*, 72).
Second, Morgan's letter includes several other statements that unquestionably
are incorrect and meant to inflate his participation in the campaign. For example,
Morgan boasted that after retreating with Arnold to Point aux Trembles, "I
marched back, with my three Companies, and renewed the siege." Morgan
further brags, "I kept up the siege, till the arrival of General Montgomery." This
story is absurd. Third, Morgan said that he assumed command following Arnold
being wounded: "I sent him [Arnold] off, with two of my men, and took his
place, for although there were three field officers present [Greene, Meigs, and
Bigelow], they would not take the command, alleging that I had seen service, and
they had not." While Captain Morgan probably had more combat experience
than the other officers on the scene, they were courageous men who were
unlikely to have relinquished overall command of the assault to Morgan.

126. The time of Montgomery's approach to the fortified house is from a
report by Colonel Campbell to General Wooster dated December 31, 1775, from
the "Holland-House," in Force, ed., *American Archives* (Fourth Series): 4:480.

127. Wandell and Minnigerode, *Aaron Burr*, 1: 54.

128. Stanely, *Canada Invaded*, 98.

129. French, *The First Year of the American Revolution*, 615.

130. Smith identified Barnsfare (he spelled the name as Barnsfair) as the
master of the brig *Fell*. See Smith, *Our Struggle for the Fourteenth Colony*, 2:
142. There are several important accounts praising the leadership and courage of
Barnsfair and Coffin. Captain Ainslie, for example, said about the action at
Fraser's house: "Much has been said in commendation of Mr. Coffin's cool
behaviour; his example at Pres de Ville had a noble effect on his follow soldiers,
they behav'd with the greatest spirit." See Cohen, ed., *Journal of Capt. Thomas
Ainslie*, 36.

131. Leake, *Memoir of the Life and Times of John Lamb*, 128; "Extract of a
Letter From Canada, Dated February 9, 1776," in Force, ed., *American Archives*
(Fourth Series): 4:706-707.

132. "Extract of a Letter From Canada, Dated February 9, 1776," in Force, ed., *American Archives* (Fourth Series): 4:706. Joseph Ware was a common soldier on the Arnold Expedition. He was captured in the attack on Quebec and subsequently wrote out a list of everyone taken. His list confirms that there were 13 men killed from the "York forces" (Montgomery's column). Ware also says that one of Montgomery's men was wounded and captured in the battle. See "Joseph Ware's Journal" in Roberts, ed., *March to Quebec*, 40.

Montgomery's civilian guide is identified as (Mr.) Desmarais in Codman, *Arnold's Expedition to Quebec*, 232. This guide was among those killed in the initial cannon blast and small arms fire from the blockhouse. Arnold's column was also accompanied by a guide but there is no known record of his (or her) name. While the Americans may have had information about the layout of the lower town, guides were important to help them find their way in the blizzard through Quebec's streets.

133. Manuscript notes of 1831 interview with Aaron Burr found in *Arnold's Letter Book*, Maine Historical Society.

134. Donald Campbell served as a lieutenant and quartermaster in the Royal American Regiment during the French and Indian War and was placed on half-pay (reserve status) at the end of that conflict. He was a patriot sympathizer with a long-standing grudge against the royal government of New York stemming a 1738 claim his father (Captain Lauchlin Campbell) made for 100,000 acres of land in the Lake Champlain Valley. Young Campbell gave up his half-pay in the British army in July 1775 to accept an appointment by the Continental Congress as deputy quartermaster general for the Northern army with the rank of colonel. Following his appointment, he wrote General Washington a flattering letter July 26, 1775, in which he asked the commander-in-chief for an appointment to brigadier general and quartermaster general of the Continental Army. See W.W. Abbot et al., eds., *Papers of Washington, Revolutionary War Series,* 1: 173-174. Washington appointed Thomas Mifflin to the post of quartermaster general, leaving Campbell to accompany Montgomery's army to Canada in the capacity of deputy quartermaster general for the Northern army. A detailed biography of Campbell, including his father's New York land claim, are in *Ibid.*, 1: 174-175 notes.

135. Leake, *Memoir of the Life and Times of John Lamb*, 128.

136. Randall, *Benedict Arnold, Patriot and Traitor*, 220.

137. Henry, who claimed to have walked the battlefield after the event took place, was one of the first to tell the story of the drunken sailor firing the fatal cannon shot that killed Montgomery. While Henry's account is one of the most important eye-witness records from the American Revolution, as previously noted, he actually dictated his war experiences to his daughter years later (1811)

from his deathbed. Since so many years had elapsed, the accuracy of Henry's narrative is questionable: It is virtually impossible for a single round of grapeshot to kill 13 men located at various locations and distances from the cannon. However, according to Henry:

> The hero Montgomery came. The drowsy or drunken guard did not hear the sawing of the posts of the first palisade. . . . The column [Montgomery's troops] entered with manly fortitude. [Then Montgomery cut through the second wooden fence.] Even now there had been but an imperfect discovery of the advancing of an enemy, and that only by the intoxicated guard. The guard fled; the general advanced a few paces. A drunken sailor returned to his gun, swearing he would not forsake it while undischarged. This fact is related from the testimony of the guard on the morning of our capture, some of those sailors being our guard. Applying the match, this single discharge deprived us of our excellent commander.

See Henry, *An Accurate and Interesting Account . . . In The Campaign Against Quebec*, 129-130. Modern historians have repeated Henry's story as historic fact. See, for example, Milton Lomak, *Aaron Burr, The Years From Princeton to Vice President*, 41.

Henry must have walked the ground where Montgomery was killed sometime late in the spring of 1776 while he was a British prisoner in Quebec, because he mentioned "that all danger from without had vanished [an American attack]." Henry then tells a lovely anecdote: "the government [Governor Carleton] had not only permitted the mutilated palisades [fence] to remain without renewing the enclosure, but the very sticks sawed by the hand of our commander still lay strewed about the spot." See Henry, *An Interesting and Accurate Account . . . In the Campaign Against Quebec*, 140.

The story of the drunken sailor firing the cannon that killed Montgomery was recently retold in Desjardin's *Through a Howling Wilderness*, 176-177. His source for the story is Francis Nichols, a lieutenant in Hendricks' Rifle Company. However, Nichols' unit was fighting at the other end of the lower town at the time, so he could not have witnessed this event. His account can only be based upon hearsay among the Americans, likely intended to discredit the bravery of the enemy.

138. Würtele, ed.,"Lt. Colonel Macleans Letter" in *Blockade of Quebec*, 103-104. Here are the highlights of Maclean's letter to John Coffin, which confirms the determination of the officers and men defending the blockhouse against Montgomery's attack:

Quebec, 28 July, 1776.

Sir. —As I am, in a few days, going to England with despatches [sic] from the Commander-in-Chief, I should be glad to know if I could be of any service to you. . . . To your resolution and watchfulness on the morning of Dec. 31st, 1775, in keeping the guard at the Pres-de-Ville under arms, waiting for the attack which you expected; the great coolness with which you allowed the rebels to approach; the spirit which your example kept up among the men, and the very critical instant in which you directed Capt. Barnsfare's fire against Montgomery and his troops—to those circumstances alone do I ascribe the repulsing the rebels from that important post where, with their leader, they lost all heart.

139. Stanley, *Canada Invaded*, 98.

140. Brown and Peckham, eds., *Revolutionary War Journals of Henry Dearborn*, 67.

141. Senter, *Journal of Dr. Isaac Senter*, 52.

142. Thomas Jones, *History of New York During the Revolutionary War* 2 vols. (New York: Printed for the New York Historical Society, 1879), 1: 310.

143. "Letter attributed to Major Henry Caldwell of the British Army to General James Murray" in Commager and Morris, ed., *The Spirit of Seventy-Six*, 1: 205.

144. W.H. Whiteley, "The British Navy and the Siege of Quebec, 1775-6," in *The Canadian Historical Review*, Vol. LXI, Number 1 (March 1980): 9.

145. Henry, *An Accurate and Interesting Account . . . In the Campaign Against Quebec*, 117-118.

146. Writing in 1788, historian William Gordon said that a half an hour elapsed from the time that the rebels overran the first barricade to their attack, led by Morgan, against the second barricade. See Gordon, *The History of the Rise, Progress and Establishment, of the Independence of the United States*, 2: 186.

147. Ward, *The War of the Revolution*, 1: 193. This story is probably true because Captain Ainslie wrote in his journal on December 31, 1775: "We had kill'd Capt. Anderson formerly a Lt in the Navy. . ..." See Cohen, ed., *Journal of Capt. Thomas Ainslie*, 38.

148. Isaac Q. Leake, Lamb's biographer, related a family tradition concerning the artilleryman's participation in the attack. The story is that Lamb received orders to abandon his cannon, which was stuck in the snow, and lead his artillerymen, armed with muskets, in the attack. Lamb was assaulting the second barrier when he spied an enemy gunner with a linstock (a pole with a burning piece of cord) about to fire off a cannon loaded with grapeshot. Captain Lamb

tried to fire his fusee (a carbine—a short musket favored by officers) twice but the gun did not fire because the gunpowder was wet: "and in the act of priming for the third effort, the cannon was discharged. A grape shot hit Lamb on the left cheek, near the eye, and carried away part of the bone; the force of the blow and the concussion of the shot, stunned him, and threw him senseless upon the snow. Some of his faithful fellows carried him into a cooper's shop [barrel maker] near at hand, and laid him upon a pile of shavings, still insensible." See Leake, *Memoir of the Life and Times of Gen. John Lamb*, 131. Lieutenant William Heth, who saw Lamb months later, confirmed the head wound: "The Enemy discharged a field piece with grape shot, one of which struck him below the left eye, taking away part of his cheek & cheek Bone—Just missing his Ear. . . ." See "The Diary of Lt. William Heth," *Winchester, Virginia Historical Society Annual Papers* vol. 1 (Winchester, Virginia, 1931), 50.

149. Cohen, ed., *Journal of Capt. Thomas Ainslie*, 37. Captain George Law, or Lawes, joined the British army in 1756 as a second lieutenant in the 61st Regiment of Foot. He saw considerable combat during the French and Indian War in the Caribbean and retired as a half-pay first lieutenant at the end of the war (1763). Laws immigrated to Canada sometime prior to the start of the American Revolution. He is sometimes incorrectly identified as an officer in the Royal Engineers and/or a captain in the Royal Highland Emigrants during Montgomery's attack. He was appointed a captain in the Emigrants in 1777 and participated with his new regiment in Burgoyne's 1777 campaign. See Horatio Rogers, ed., *A Journal Kept in Canada and Upon Burgoyne's Campaign in 1776 and 1777 by Lieut. James M. Hadden* (Albany, New York: Joel Munsell's Sons, 1884), 137.

150. Brown and Peckham, eds., *Revolutionary War Journals of Henry Dearborn*, 69. British Major Henry Caldwell had a similar experience during the fighting in Quebec's lower town. Caldwell said he got separated from his troops while reconnoitering in the vicinity of Lymeburner's wharf, which was under fire from the rebels positioned in the back rooms of one of the houses facing the wharf. While trying to locate the exact position of the enemy fire, a rebel called out to him in the storm, "Who is there." Caldwell replied, "A friend—who are you?" The answer came back, "Captain Morgan's company." Caldwell told them to have good heart for they would soon be in the town and immediately got behind a pile of nearby lumber from which he was able to make his escape. See Commager and Morris, eds., *The Spirit of Seventy-Six*, 1: 205-206.

151. Henry, *An Accurate and Interesting Account . . . In the Campaign Against Quebec*, 119; W.T.P. Short, ed., "Journal of the Principal Occurrences during the Siege of Quebec by the American Revolutionists under Generals Mont- gomery and Arnold in 1775-76" in Würtele, ed., *Blockade of Quebec*, 69.

This diary is attributed to Captain John Hamilton, commander of the *HMS Lizard*. It was originally published in London by Simpkin and Co. in 1824.

152. *Ibid.*, 75. Natanis was quickly released as part of Governor Carleton's efforts to get the Indians to help him.

153. Codman, *Arnold's Expedition to Quebec*, 243. A similar and earlier published account of Morgan's surrender appears in Graham, *The Life of General Daniel Morgan*, 103. My reference to the fighting ending at 8:00 a.m. is from Cohen, ed., *Journal of Capt. Thomas Ainslie*, 38. Ainslie said: "The whole affair was over by eight in the morning & all the Prisoners were securely lodged."

Daniel Morgan seems to be a favorite subject for Revolutionary War storytellers. In another tall tale, after being taken prisoner, the British tried to bribe Morgan to join them. The story appears in Alexander Garden, *Anecdotes of the Revolutionary War in America* (Charleston, South Carolina, 1822), 58. Here is the story about Morgan as it appears in Garden's book: "His bravery well known, and his activity justly appreciated, an attempt was made by an officer of rank in the British service to induce him, by the tender of wealth and promotion, to join the royal standard; but, with the true spirit of Republican virtue, he rejected the proposition, requesting the tempter—- 'Never again to insult him by an offer, which plainly implied that he thought him a villain.'"

154. Senter, *Journal of Dr. Isaac Senter*, 34.

155. *Ibid.*, 34-35.

156. Arnold to Wooster, December 31, 1775, from "General Hospital," in Force, ed., *American Archives* (Fourth Series): 4:481-482.

157. Dr. Senter mentioned this incident in his journal: "January 1, 1776. All in obscurity; no intelligence from the troops in the lower town. Some suggesting they were all prisoners, &c., while others imagined they were in possession of the lower town, and waiting for assistance to enter the upper town. While in this suspense, Mr. [Mathew] Duncan, a young gentleman volunteer, desired the Colonel [Arnold] would give him liberty to attempt passing into the lower town in quest of the little detachment; received orders, went, but no return." See Senter, *Journal of Dr. Isaac Senter*, 35.

Mathew Duncan was from Philadelphia, and following his capture and exchange at Quebec, he was appointed a captain in the 5th Pennsylvania Battalion (January 5, 1776). He was captured again when Fort Washington (an American fort on upper Manhattan Island) surrendered to the British on November 16, 1776. See Heitman, *Historical Register of Officers of the Continental Army*, 206-7.

Lieutenant William Heth provided some additional details of Duncan's capture in his diary:

Mr. Matthew Ducan [sic], a Young Gent Volunteer from Philadelphia who crossed St Charles River from Beaux Port to the Lower Town—At a Considerable distance from the Picketts [guards] he observ'd a man whom he believed to be Maj. Bigelow—& who upon Becoming convincd—Mr. Duncan it was the major & that we were in possession of the Lower Town—But upon his Advancing closer he saw his mistake—when too late as the Centinel presented [raised his musket] & ordered him to halt. Tho' he was made a prisoner so simply—it cannot be denyd but he shew'd himself a young Gent of Spirit & from he being a very sensible, sober steady young man—he will, I hope, be taken proper notice of.

See *Diary of Lieutenant William Heth*, 39.

158. Cohen, ed., *Journal of Capt. Thomas Ainslie*, 36. Writing to General Wooster on January 2, 1776, Arnold said that Meigs brought him the first accurate information concerning the fate of his Kennebec corps: "We have been in suspense, with regard to my detachment, until this afternoon, when Major Meigs was sent out, with a flag, for the officers' baggage, who, he says are all taken prisoners, except Captain Hendricks, Lieutenant Humphreys, of the Riflemen, and Lieutenant Cooper, who were killed in the action." See Roberts, ed., *March to Quebec,* 104.

Chapter Ten

1. Codman, *Arnold's Expedition to Quebec*, 247.
2. There are several references to Meigs' visit to the American camp, the most interesting being the journal of Lieutenant William Humphrey, who was captured during the battle. His entry for January 2, 1776, reads in part: "This day, the third of my imprisonment, Major Meigs was allowed by Genl. Carleton to go out and get in our baggage and to return on Friday [January 4]." See Shipton and Swain, ed., *Rhode Islanders Record the Revolution*, 35.
3. Cohen, ed., *Journal of Capt. Thomas Ainslie*, 37. Although Ainslie said that 426 were "taken," a careful reading of his diary entry shows that he used the term to include killed and captured rebels. This number included 40 men from Lamb's artillery company. Their commander, Captain Lamb, was among the prisoners. He was found badly wounded in a cooper's (barrel maker) shop on the Sault-au-Matelot. His fine clothing had been stripped from his body by looters

and he was barely alive. A British army surgeon managed to save his life, but Lamb lost his left eye and his face was permanently disfigured.

Ainslie's figure is close to two other creditable sources. One is the journal kept by Joseph Ware, a common soldier on the Arnold Expedition captured in the attack. Ware said that the Kennebec corps losses in the attack were 440 officers and enlisted men, including 35 killed and 33 wounded. He gives a separate figure for the York forces (Montgomery's column), which was 13 killed and one wounded. Ware puts the total American losses at 454. See Roberts, ed., *March to Quebec*, 40.

The other important source for American losses was Captain Dearborn's journal. He was also captured by the British and his lengthy journal entry for December 31, 1775, included: "Kill'd & wounded according to the best accounts I could obtain, Amounted to about one Hundred men, the number kill'd on the Spot, about 40." Dearborn also listed the names of 34 officers from the Arnold Expedition taken prisoner, to which he added: "The Number of Serg. [Sergeants] and Corpor. & Privates Taken, but not wounded, are about 300." Dearborn's total is 474. See Brown & Peckham, ed., *Revolutionary War Journals of Henry Dearborn*, 74-77. A detailed list of American officers captured at Quebec appears in Force, ed., *American Archives* (Fourth Series:): 4:708-709. This list is particularly interesting because it includes the names of all junior officers and volunteers who surrendered.

I believe that Private Ware's figure of 454 total American losses (killed or captured) in the attack on Quebec is the most accurate, based on his detailed list and the number of men involved in the assault.

4. Captain Jonas Hubbard (sometimes spelled Hurlbert) was from Worcester, Massachusetts. He was among the first militiamen to take up arms against the British and was appointed a captain in (Artemas) Ward's Massachusetts regiment shortly after the war began. See Heitman, *Historical Register of Officers of the Continental Army*, 305. According to Thayer's journal, Hubbard was wounded at the outset of the attack as Arnold's column was passing along what later historians called Dog Lane. See Thayer Journal, 28. His death is confirmed by Ebenezer Wild, whose diary entry for January 1776 included the following: "Captain Hubbard died with the wound he received in coming in." See Windsor, ed., *The Diary of Ebenezer Wild*, 10. On June 17, 1776, the Massachusetts General Assembly passed a resolve: "That Mary Hubbard be paid the wages of her late husband, Captain Jonas Hubbard, who went on the expedition against Quebec and after his arrival there, Died." See Roberts, ed., *March to Quebec*, 573.

5. Cohen, ed., *Journal of Capt. Thomas Ainslie*, 38.

6. Meigs Journal in Roberts, ed., *March to Quebec*, 193.

7. Force, ed., American Archives (Fourth Series): 4:589-590.

8. Henry, *An Accurate and Interesting Account...In the Campaign Against Quebec*, 114. Kenneth Roberts said that no one knows what subsequently happened to Smith and speculated that he died later in 1776 from smallpox. (See Roberts, ed., *March to Quebec*, 360-61 footnote). However, Francis Heitman, that tireless researcher into the lives of Continental army officers, gives a detailed biography of Smith's subsequent military career, and states that he retired from the army in February 1778 as a colonel and died in 1794. See Heitman, *Historical Register of Officers of the Continental Army*, 505-506. Another creditable source also acknowledges Smith's later military service, stating he resigned his commission in November 1776, returned to the army as a major of the 9th Pennsylvania Regiment the following January, and resigned again in February 1778. See W.W. Abbot et al., eds., *The Papers of George Washington, Revolutionary War Series*, 2: 43 footnote.

9. Burr worked for Arnold until the end of May 1776, when he left Canada on public business (probably carrying dispatches) and never returned. See Kline, ed., *Political Correspondence and Public Papers of Aaron Burr*, 2 vols. (Princeton, New Jersey: Princeton University Press, 1983), 1: lxii.

10. Smith, ed., *Letters of Delegates to Congress*, 3: 18. The complete reference to the Arnold Expedition in Hooper's letter reads, "We impatiently wait to know the fate of Quebec. Montgomery and Arnold are now before Quebec & if Courage and Perseverance can give success, I know of None who have better pretensions to it than these brave Officers. Arnold's Expedition has been marked with such scenes of misery, that it requires a stretch of faith to believe that human nature was equal to them. Subsisting upon dead dogs, devouring their Shoes & leather of their Cartouch [cartridge] Boxes are but part of that Catalogue of woe which attended the expedition. Heaven seems to have interposed in preserving almost miraculously what still remains of the brave little Army, & placing them in health & spirits to compleat the grand work of the subduction [sic] of Canada."

11. Ibid, 58. Howes was not the first person to compare Hannibal to Arnold. Writing to Samuel Adams on December 5, 1775, James Warren (president of the Massachusetts Provincial Congress) compared Arnold's achievement "with Hannibal's over the Alps." See Martin, *Benedict Arnold Revolutionary Hero*, 184.

12. Samuel Ward to Deborah Ward (his daughter), December 24, 1775, in Smith, ed., *Letters of Delegates to Congress*, 2: 518.

13. For information about Thomas' appointment see Ford, ed., *Journals of the Continental Congress*, IV: 186. Congress' resolution, dated March 6, 1776, read: "That Brigadier General Thomas be appointed to command the forces in

Canada...." On the same date Congress promoted him from a brigadier to a major general. Thomas replaced Montgomery while Schuyler, who remained too ill to leave his Albany mansion, continued as the senior major general and commanding officer of the Northern Department.

14. Codman, *Arnold's Expedition to Quebec*, 288.

15. Cohen, ed., *Journal of Capt. Thomas Ainslie*, 50-51.

16. Stocking Journal in Roberts, ed., *March to Quebec*, 567.

17. Henry, *An Accurate and Interesting Account...In the Campaign Against Quebec*, 160-161.

18. Ibid, 170.

19. Brown and Peckham, eds., *Revolutionary War Journals of Henry Dearborn*, 82.

20. Codman, *Arnold's Expedition to Quebec*, 301.

21. Parole was a system in use at the time that offered prisoners of war limited freedom on their word of honor that they would remain within a specified area as a non-combatant until such time as they were exchanged or otherwise absolved from their parole. Parole was usually reserved for officers who were considered gentlemen and whose word of honor could be trusted. General Schuyler paroled the British officers captured at St. Johns, Chambly and Sorel. Governor Carleton, however, did not return the compliment, because Quebec was under siege and he could not risk having paroled American officers roaming around the city or surrounding rebel held countryside.

Prisoner exchanges had to be negotiated informally between the Americans and the British during the Revolutionary War because the British government refused to recognize the legitimacy of the Continental Congress or its armed forces. The royal government's policy concerning exchanges was stated in February 1, 1776, instructions from Lord Germaine to General Howe. The British had captured several rebel naval officers who were being sent to Howe in Boston:

> It is hoped that the possession of these prisoners will enable you to procure the release of such of His Majesty's officers and loyal subjects as are in the disgraceful situation of being prisoners to the Rebels; for although it cannot be that you should enter into any treaty or agreement with Rebels for a regular cartel or exchange of prisoners, yet I doubt not by your own discretion will suggest to you the means of effecting such exchange, without the King's dignity and honour being committed, or His Majesty's name used in any negotiation for that purpose.

See Lord George Germaine to Major General Howe, dated Whitehall, February 1, 1776, in Force, ed., *American Archives* (Fourth Series): 4:903.

As a result of this policy, prisoner exchanges had to be negotiated on an informal basis according to the sentiment of the British commanding officer on the scene. Carleton was disinterested at first in negotiating prisoner exchanges with the Americans, whom he considered to be traitors.

22. See, for example, Mark Boatner, *Encyclopedia of the American Revolution* (New York: David McKay Company, Inc., 1976), 1205-1206: "As a volunteer in Thompson's Pa. Bn, 9 Sept.'75-March '76, he and Aaron Burr took part in Arnold's march to Quebec (An interesting collection of scoundrels, but their performance in this expedition was creditable)."

A recently published reference to Wilkinson being on the Arnold Expedition is Brendan Morrissey, *Quebec 1775* (Oxford, United Kingdom: Osprey Publishing Ltd., 2003), 56: "As villains of the Revolution, Wilkinson and Burr barely rank below Arnold (post-betrayal) and are remarkable only for their ability to survive some highly dubious acts. Yet strangely both showed considerable fortitude and bravery during Arnold's expedition and the attack on Quebec. Wilkinson was born in Maryland, studied medicine and joined Thompson's Pennsylvania rifle battalion at the outbreak of war. He befriends Burr the march through Maine and, after being promoted to captain, replaced Burr as Arnold's aide-de-camp."

23. W.W. Abbot et. al., eds., *Papers of Washington, Revolutionary War Series*, 6:389.

Bibliography

Manuscript Sources

Joseph Trumbull Papers, Connecticut Historical Society

Library and Archives Canada

Benedict Arnold's letter book and a journal of a tour from the St. Lawrence to the Kennebec (Montresor's journal), Maine Historical Society Collection

The Papers of Aaron Burr, New York Historical Society

The Emmet Collection, New York Public Library

Philip J. Schuyler Papers, New York Public Library

Reed Collection, Valley Forge National Historical Park

Published Primary Sources

Abbot, W.W., et al., eds. *The Papers of George Washington, Revolutionary War Series*. 12 vols. to date. Charlottesville, Virginia: University Press of Virginia, 1985–.

Baxter, James Phinney. *Documentary History of the State of Maine*. 2nd series, vol. 14. Portland: Lefavor-Tower Company, 1910.

Bray, Robert C. & Bushnell, Paul E. eds., *Diary of a Common Soldier in the American Revolution, 1775-1783—An Annotated Edition of the Military Journal of Jeremiah Greenman*. DeKalb, Illinois: Northern Illinois University Press, 1978.

Brown, Lloyd A. and Peckham, Howard H. eds., *Revolutionary War Journals of Henry Dearborn 1775-1783*. Chicago: The Caxton Club, 1939.

Chastellux, Marquis de. *Travels in North-America, In the Years 1780, 1781, and 1782*. 2 vols. London: Printed for G.G.J. and J. Robinson, 1787.

Clark, William Bell ed. *Naval Documents of the American Revolution*. 10 vols. to date. Washington, D.C.: U.S. Government Printing Office, 1964– .

Cohen, Sheldon S., ed. *Canada Preserved, The Journal of Captain Thomas Ainslie*. Canada: The Copp Clark Publishing Company, 1968.

Commager, Henry Steele and Morris, Richard B., eds. *The Spirit of Seventy-Six*. 2 vols., Indianapolis and New York: The Bobbs-Merritt Company, Inc.

Corner, George W. ed. *The Autobiography of Benjamin Rush*. Princeton, New Jersey: Princeton University Press, 1948.

Davies, K.G., ed. Documents of the American Revolution, 1770-1783 (Colonial Office series), 21 vols., Shannon, Irish University Press, 1972-1981.

Fitzpatrick, John C. ed. *The Writings of George Washington*, 39 vols. Washington, D.C.: Government Printing Office, 1934-44.

Ford, Worthington C., et. al., eds. *The Journals of the Continental Congress, 1774-1789*. 34 vols. Washington D.C.: Government Printing Office, 1904-37.

Force, Peter, ed. *American Archives: Fourth Series, A Documentary History of the English Colonies in North America, From the King's Message to Parliament, of March 7, 1774, to the Declaration of Independence of the United States*. 6 vols. Washington, D.C.: published by M. St. Clair Clarke and Peter Force, 1843 and *Fifth Series, A Documentary History of the Origin and Progress of the North American Colonies; of the Causes and Accomplishment[sic] of the American Revolution: and of The Constitution of the Government For the United States to The Final Ratification Thereof.* 3 vols. Washington, D.C.: published by M. St. Clair Clarke and Peter Force, 1848.

Foner, Eric, ed. *Thomas Paine Collected Writings*. New York: Literary Classics of the United States, Inc., 1995.

Greenwood, John. *A Young Patriot in the American Revolution*. Westvaco, 1981.

Henry, John Joseph. *An Accurate and Interesting Account of the Hardships and Sufferings of that Band of Heroes, Who Traversed the Wilderness in the Campaign Against Quebec in 1775*. Lancaster, Pennsylvania: William Greer, 1812.

Jefferys, Thomas. *The Natural and Civil History of the French Dominions in North and South America*. London: Printed for Thomas Jeffreys, 1760.

Kalm, Peter. *Travels Into North America; Containing Its Natural History, and A Circumstantial Account of its Plantations and Agriculture in General.* 2 vols. London: Printed for T. Lowndes, 1772.

Kline, Mary-Jo, ed. *Political Correspondence and Public Papers of Aaron Burr.* 2 vols. Princeton, New Jersey: Princeton University Press, 1983.

Lee, Charles, *The Lee Papers.* 4 vols. New York: New York Historical Society, 1871-1874.

Lesser, Charles H., ed. *The Sinews of Independence: Monthly Strength Reports of the Continental Army.* Chicago, University of Chicago Press, 1976.

Meigs, Maj. Return J. *Journal of the Expedition Against Quebec, Under Command of Col. Benedict Arnold.* New York: privately printed, 1864.

Melvin, Andrew A, ed. *The Journal of James Melvin Private Soldier in Arnold's Expedition Against Quebec In the Year 1775.* Portland, Maine: Hubbard W. Bryant, 1902.

Ogden, Matthias. "Journal of Major Matthias Ogden, 1775 In Arnold's Campaign Against Quebec." *Proceedings of the New Jersey Historical Society,* New Series Vol. XIII (1928): 17-30.

Officer of the Garrison (name unknown). "Journal of the Most Remarkable Occurrences in Quebec." *Collections of the New York Historical Society for the Year 1880.* New York: Printed for the Society, 1881.

Roberts, Kenneth. *March to Quebec, Journals of the Members of Arnold's Expedition Including the Lost Journal of John Pierce.* Garden City, New York: Doubleday & Company, Inc., 1940.

Rogers, Horatio, ed. *Journal Kept in Canada and Upon Burgoyne's Campaign in 1776 and 1777 by Lieut. James M. Hadden.* Albany, New York: Joel Munsell's Sons, 1884.

Scull, G.D. ed. "Journals of Capt. John Montresor 1757-1778," in *Collections of the New York Historical Society for the Year 1881.* New York: New York Historical Society, 1882.

Senter, Isaac, "The Journal of Isaac Senter, Physician and Surgeon to the Troops Detached From the American Army Encamped at Cambridge, Mass., on a Secret Expedition Against Quebec. . ." *Bulletin of the Historical Society of Pennsylvania,* Vol I, No.5 (1846).

Shipton, Nathaniel N. and Swain, David, eds. *Rhode Islanders Record the Revolution: The Journals of William Humphrey and Zuriel Waterman.* Providence: Rhode Island Publications Society, 1984.

Smith, Paul H., ed. *Letters of Delegates to Congress 1774-1789.* 26 vols. Washington, D.C.: United States Government Printing Office, 1976-2000.

Stedman, Charles. *The History of the Origin, Progress and Termination of the American War*. 2 vols. London: 1794.

Stone, Edwin Martin, ed. *The Invasion of Canada In 1775: Including the Journal of Captain Simeon Thayer, Describing the Perils and Sufferings of the Army Under Colonel Benedict Arnold....* Providence, Rhode Island: Knowles, Anthony & Co., Printers, 1867.

Showman, Richard K. *The Papers of General Nathanael Greene*. 12 vols. to date. Chapel Hill: The University of North Carolina Press, 1976–.

Tatum, Edward H. *The American Journal of Ambrose Serle*. San Marino, California: The Huntington Library, 1940.

Wilkinson, James. *Memoirs of My Own Time*. 3 vols. Philadelphia: Printed by Abraham Small, 1816.

Würtele, Fred C., ed. *Blockade of Quebec in 1775-1776 by the American Revolutionists*. Quebec: Literary and Historical Society of Quebec, 1906.

Winsor, Justin, ed. *Arnold's Expedition Against Quebec 1775-1776, The Diary of Ebenezer Wild With a List of Such Diaries*. Cambridge, Massachusetts: John Wilson and Son, 1886.

Secondary Sources

Adams, Hannah. *A Summary History of New-England From the First Settlement at Plymouth, to the Acceptance of the Federal Constitution. Comprehending a General Sketch of the American War*. Dedham, Massachusetts: H. Mann and J. H. Adams, 1799.

Alden, John Richard. *General Gage in America*. Baton Rouge: Louisiana State University Press, 1948.

———. *The American Revolution 1775-1783*. New York: Harper & Brothers, 1954.

Arnold, Isaac N. *The Life of Benedict Arnold*. Chicago: Jansen, McClurg & Company, 1880.

Babits, Lawrence E. *A Devil of a Whipping, The Battle of Cowpens*. Chapel Hill, The University of North Carolina Press, 1998.

Bellesiles, Michael A. *Revolutionary Outlaws, Ethan Allen and the Struggle for Independence on the Early American Frontier*. Charlottesville, University Press of Virginia, 1993.

Berg, Fred Anderson. *Encyclopedia of Continental Army Units*. Harrisburg, Pennsylvania, Stackpole Books, 1972.

Billias, George Athan, ed. *George Washington's Opponents, British Generals and Admirals in the American Revolution*. New York: William Morrow and Company, Inc., 1969.

Blanco, Richard L., ed. *The American Revolution 1775-1783*. 2 vols. New York: Garland Publishing, Inc., 1993.

Bland, Humphrey. *A Treatise of Military Discipline: In Which is Laid Down and Explained The Duty of the Officer and Solider, Through the Several Branches of the Service*. London: R. Baldwin, J. Richardson, T. Longman, S. Crowder & Co., 1762.

Buell, Miss Rowena. *The Memoirs of Rufus Putnam*. Boston and New York: Houghton, Mifflin and Company, 1903.

Burke, Edmund (attributed to). *An Impartial History of the War in American Between Great Britain and Her Colonies, From the Commencement to the end of the Year 1779*. London: R. Faulder, 1780.

Codman, John, II. *Arnold's Expedition to Quebec*. New York: The Macmillan Company, 1901.

Coffin, Robert P. Tristram. *Kennebec, Cradle of Americans*. New York: Farrar & Rinehart Incorporated, 1937.

Coggins, Jack. *Ships and Seamen of the American Revolution*. Promontory Press, 1969.

Dandridge, Danske. *Historic Shepherdstown*. Charlottesville, Virginia: The Michie Company, 1910.

Davis, Matthew. *Memoirs of Aaron Burr With Miscellaneous Selections From His Correspondence*. 2 vols. New York: Harper & Brothers, 1836 & 1837.

Desjardin, Thomas A. *Through a Howling Wilderness* (New York, St. Martin's Press, 2006).

Druckman, Nancy. *American Flags, Designs for a Young Nation*. New York: Harry N. Abrams, Inc, 2003.

Duncan, Louis C., *Medical Men in the American Revolution*. New York: Augustus M. Kelley, 1970.

Egly, T.W., Jr. *History of the First New York Regiment*. Hampton, New Hampshire: Peter E. Randall, 1981.

Ferling, John. *A Leap in the Dark*. Oxford and New York: Oxford University Press, 2003.

———. *The First of Men, A Life of George Washington*. Knoxville: The University of Tennessee Press, 1988.

Ferguson, E. James. *The Power of the Purse*. Chapel Hill: The University of North Carolina Press for The Institute of Early American History and Culture, 1961.

Fenn, Elizabeth A. *Pox Americana, The Great Smallpox Epidemic of 1775-82*. New York: Hill and Wang, 2001.

Fischer, David Hackett. *Washington's Crossing*. New York: Oxford University Press, 2004.

Freeman, Douglas Southall. *George Washington—A Biography*. 7 vols. New York: Charles Scribner's Sons, 1954-7.

French, Allen. *The Taking of Ticonderoga in 1775: the British Story*. Cambridge, Massachusetts: Harvard University Press, 1928.

——. *The First Year of the American Revolution*. Boston and New York: Houghton Mifflin Company, 1934.

Garraty John A. and Carnes, Mark C. gen. eds. *American National Biography*. 30 vols. New York and Oxford: Oxford University Press, 1999.

Gerlach, Don R. *Proud Patriot, Philip Schuyler and the War of Independence, 1775-1783*. Syracuse, New York: Syracuse University Press, 1987.

Gordon, William. *The History of the Rise, Progress, and Establishment, of the Independence of the United States of America: Including an Account of the Late War. . .* 4 vols. Privately printed. London, 1788.

Graham, James. *The Life of General Daniel Morgan, of the Virginia Line of the Army of the United States*. New York: Derby & Jackson, 1859.

Hatch, Robert McConnell. *Thrust For Canada, The American Attempt on Quebec in 1775-1776*. Boston: Houghton Mifflin Company, 1979.

Chester G. Hearn. *George Washington's Schooners-The First American Navy*. Annapolis, Maryland: Naval Institute Press, 1995.

Heitman, Francis B. *Historical Register of Officers of the Continental Army*. Washington, D.C.: The Rare Book Shop Publishing Company, Inc., 1914.

Higginbotham, Don. *Daniel Morgan Revolutionary Rifleman*. Chapel Hill: The University of North Carolina Press, 1961.

(Author Unknown). *The History of the Civil War in America*. Privately printed. London, 1780.

Humphreys, David. *An Essay on the Life of the Honorable Major-General Israel Putnam*. Hartford, Connecticut: Hudson and Goodwin, 1788.

Huston, James A. *Logistics of Liberty, American Services of Supply in the Revolutionary War and After*. Newark, Delaware: University of Delaware Press, 1991.

Jackson, John W. *The Pennsylvania Navy 1775-1781: The Defense of the Delaware*. New Brunswick, New Jersey: Rutgers University Press, 1974.

James, Captain W.M. *The British Navy in Adversity*. New York: Longmans, Green and Co. Ltd., 1926.

Katcher, Philip R.N., *Encyclopedia of British, Provincial, and German Army Units 1775-1783*. Harrisburg, Pennsylvania, 1973.

Leake, Isaac Q. *Memoirs of the Life and Times of General John Lamb*. Albany, New York: Joel Munsell, 1850.

Lederer, Richard M., Jr. *Colonial American English, Words and Phrases Found in Colonial Writing, now Archaic, Obscure, Obsolete, or Whose Meanings Have Changed*. Essex, Connecticut: A Verbatum Book, 1985.

Lomask, Milton. *Aaron Burr, The Years from Princeton to Vice President 1756-1805*. New York: Farrar-Straus-Giroux, 1979.

Lossing, Benson J. *The Pictorial Field-Book of the Revolution*. 2 vols. New York: Harper & Brothers, 1860.

Malone, Dumas, ed. *Dictionary of American Biography*. 20 vols. New York: Charles Scribner's Sons, 1932.

Marshall, John. *The Life of George Washington, Commander in Chief of the American Forces*. 5 vols. Philadelphia: C.P. Wayne, 1804-1807.

Martin, James Kirby. *Benedict Arnold Revolutionary Hero, An American Warrior Reconsidered*. New York: New York University Press, 1997.

Martyn, Charles. *The Life of Artemas Ward, The First Commander-in-Chief of the American Revolution*. New York: Artemas Ward, 1921.

Mayer, Holly A. *Belonging to the Army: Camp Followers and Community During the American Revolution*. Charleston: University of South Carolina Press, 1996.

Merwin, Henry Childs. *Aaron Burr*. Boston: Small, Maynard & Company, 1899.

Miller, Nathan. *Sea of Glory: The Continental Navy Fights for Independence*. New York: David McKay Company, Inc., 1974.

Murray, James A.H., et al., eds. *Oxford English Dictionary*. 20 vols. Oxford: Clarendon Press, 1989.

Neimeyer, Charles Patrick. *America Goes to War: A Social History of the Continental Army*. New York: New York University Press, 1996.

Neumann, George C. *Battle Weapons of the American Revolution*. Texarkana, Texas: Scurlock Publishing Co., Inc., 1998.

Oliver, Sandra L. *Saltwater Foodways: New Englanders and Their Food, at Sea and Ashore, in The Nineteenth Century*. Mystic, Ct.: Mystic Seaport Museum, Inc., 1995.

Parkman, Francis. *A Half Century of Conflict*. 2 vols. Boston: Little, Brown and Company, 1892.

——. *Count Frontenac and New France Under Louis XIV*. Boston: Little, Brown, and Company, 1896.

——. *Montcalm and Wolfe*. Boston: Little, Brown and Company, 1955 (reprint).

Parmet, Herbert S. and Hecht, Marie B. *Aaron Burr Portrait of an Ambitious Man*. New York: The Macmillan Company, 1967.

Peterson, Harold L. *Round Shot and Rammers*. New York: Bonanza Books, 1969.

——. *The Book of the Continental Soldier*. Harrisburg, Pennsylvania: The Stackpole Company, 1968.

Ramsay, David. *The History of the American Revolution*. 2 vols. Trenton, New Jersey: James J. Wilson, 1811 (a reprint of the original 1789 edition).

Reynolds, Paul R. *Guy Carleton, A Biography*. New York: William Morrow and Company, Inc., 1980.

Richardson, Edward W. *Standards and Colors of the American Revolution*. The University of Pennsylvania Press, 1982.

Rowe, William Hutchinson. *The Maritime History of Maine*. Gardiner, Maine: The Harpswell Press, 1989.

Royster, Charles. *A Revolutionary People at War, The Continental Army and American Character, 1775-1783*. Chapel Hill, North Carolina: The University of North Carolina Press, 1979.

Sellers, Charles Coleman. *Benedict Arnold: The Proud Warrior*. New York: Minton, Balch & Company, 1930.

Shelton, Hal. T. *General Richard Montgomery and the American Revolution*. New York: New York University Press, 1994.

Smith, Captain George. *An Universal Military Dictionary*. London: Printed for J. Millan, 1779.

Smith, Justin H. *Arnold's March From Cambridge to Quebec*. New York: G.P. Putnam's Sons, 1903.

——. *Our Struggle For the Fourteenth Colony, Canada and the American Revolution*. 2 vols. New York: G.P. Putnam's Sons, 1907.

Stanley, George F.G. *Canada Invaded 1775-1776*. Toronto: A.M. Hakkert Ltd., 1973.

Stevenson, Roger. *Military Instructions for Officers Detached in the Field*. Philadelphia: R. Aitken, 1775.

Ward, Christopher. *The War of the Revolution*. 2 vols. New York: The Macmillan Company, 1952.

Wallace, Willard. *Traitorous Hero, The Life and Fortunes of Benedict Arnold*. New York: Harper & Brothers, 1954.

Wandell, Samuel H. and Minnigerode, Meade. *Aaron Burr*. 2 vols. New York: G.P. Putnam's Sons, 1925

Warren, Mrs. Mercy Otis. *History of the Rise, Progress and Termination of the American Revolution*. 3 vols. Boston: Printed by Manning and Loring, for E. Larkin, 1805.

Weber, Ralph E., ed. *Masked Dispatches: Cryptograms and Cryptology in American History, 1775-1900*. National Security Agency, 1993.

Wood, Gordon S. *The American Revolution, A History*. New York: The Modern Library, 2002.

Wright, Robert K., Jr. *The Continental Army*. Washington, D.C.: Center of Military History, United States Army, 1989.

Monographs, Articles, Dissertations, and Exhibition Catalogs

Allen, William. "Account of Arnold's Expedition." Maine Historical Society Collections 1 (1831): 499-532.

Bell, Richard G. "The Court Martial of Roger Enos". *Connecticut Bar Journal*, Vol. 73, No. 6

Boylston, Arthur W., M.D. "Clinical Investigation of Smallpox in 1767." *The New England Journal of Medicine*, Vol. 346, No. 17 (April 25, 2002).

Crist, Robert Grant. *Captain William Hendricks and the March to Quebec* (1775). Carlisle, Pennsylvania: The Hamilton Library and Historical Association of Cumberland County, 1960.

Dworetzky, Murray, M.D. "Smallpox, October 1945." *The New England Journal of Medicine*, Vol. 346, No. 17 (April 25, 2002).

Gerlach, Don R. "Philip Schuyler And The Road to Glory A Question of Loyalty and Competence." *The New York Historical Society Quarterly*, Vol. XLIX, No. 4 (October 1965).

"Colonel Christopher Greene." *The Magazine of History*, Vol. XXIII, July 1916, No. 1.

Heth, William. "The Diary of William Heth." Winchester, *Virginia Historical Society Annual Papers,* Vol. 1 (1931): 27-118.

Huston, James A. "The Logistics of Arnold's March to Quebec." *Military Affairs*, Vol. 32, No. 3 (Dec., 1968): 110-124.

"Maine Indians in the Revolution." *Sprague's Journal of Maine History*, Vol. 6, No. 3 (Jan. 1919).

McAuliffe, Mary C. *Timothy Bigelow The Patriot of Worcester*. Master of Education thesis, The State Teachers College at Hyannis, Massachusetts, 1941. A copy of this thesis is at Bridgewater State College, Bridgewater, Massachusetts.

Nelson, William. *Edward Antill: A New York Merchant of the Seventeenth Century, and His Descendants*. Paterson, New Jersey: The Press Printing and Publishing Company, 1899.

Ogden, Matthias. "Journal of Major Matthias Ogden, 1775 in Arnold's Campaign Against Quebec." *Proceedings of the New Jersey Historical Society, New Series*, vol. XIII (1928).

Roch, John F., ed. "Quebec Under Seige, 1775-1776: The 'Memorandums' of Jacob Danford." *The Canadian Historical Review*, Vol. L, No.1 (March 1969).

Saunders, Robert. "When Newfoundland Helped to Save Canada," *Newfoundland Quarterly*, Vol. 49, No. 3, 1949.

Squier, Frank, ed. "Diary of Ephraim Squier," *Magazine of American History*, No. 2, part 2 (1878).

Whiteley, W.H. "The British Navy and the Siege of Quebec, 1775-76." *Canadian Historical Review*, Vol. 61, No. 1, March 1980.

Index